KANT'S THEORY OF KNOWLEDGE

KANT'S THEORY OF KNOWLEDGE

An Analytical Introduction

GEORGES DICKER

OXFORD

UNIVERSITY PRESS

2004

OXFORD

UNIVERSITY PRESS

Oxford   New York
Auckland   Bangkok   Buenos Aires   Cape Town   Chennai
Dar es Salaam   Delhi   Hong Kong   Istanbul   Karachi   Kolkata
Kuala Lumpur   Madrid   Melbourne   Mexico City   Mumbai   Nairobi
São Paulo   Shanghai   Singapore   Taipei   Tokyo   Toronto

Copyright © 2004 by Oxford University Press, Inc.

Published by Oxford University Press, Inc.
198 Madison Avenue, New York, New York 10016
www.oup.com

Oxford is a registered trademark of Oxford University Press

Library of Congress Cataloging-in-Publication Data
Dicker, Georges, 1942–
Kant's theory of knowledge : an analytical introduction / Georges Dicker.
p. cm.
Includes bibliographical references and index.
ISBN 0-19-515306-5; ISBN 0-19-515307-3 (pbk.)
1. Kant, Immanuel, 1724–1804. Kritik der reinen Vernunft.
2. Knowledge, Theory of.   3. Causation.
4. Reason.   I. Title.

B2779.D53   2004
121—dc22   2003061010

9 8 7 6 5 4 3 2 1

Printed in the United States of America
on acid-free paper

To Alvina

Preface

The parts of Kant's *Critique of Pure Reason* that present the constructive side of his theory of knowledge are the ones most commonly read by students and most intensely discussed by many Kant scholars. I refer especially to the Transcendental Aesthetic and the Transcendental Analytic, where Kant attempts to defend the possibility of human knowledge against the skeptical empiricism of David Hume without going back to the rationalism of a Leibniz, Descartes, or Spinoza. These sections of the *Critique* are also universally recognized to be among the most difficult of all philosophical writings, and students find them quite impenetrable if approached without the help of secondary sources. There are, of course, numerous scholarly works on the *Critique* that devote attention—indeed, often hundreds of pages—to these texts. All such works with which I am familiar are of extraordinarily high quality, in terms of both their philosophical merit and their depth of understanding of Kant's thought. As will be evident from this book, I have learned an enormous amount from several of these works, especially those of Robert Paul Wolff, Peter Strawson, Paul Guyer, Jonathan Bennett, James Van Cleve, and Henry Allison. These works, however, are in the main too difficult to be usable by all but graduate students and the most motivated and able undergraduates. There is also a number of books on the *Critique* written with student readers in mind. Some of these books are excellent, and it will be evident that I have benefited greatly from them as well, especially those of Justus Hartnack, T. E. Wilkerson, and W. H. Walsh. Yet there is not one of these books to which I would send a student and say: "Read this book alongside the *Critique*, and you will get a good understanding of what Kant was trying to show and of how he tried to show it." Rather, I would tell students to peruse these books in the way I myself have done: to look at each for insights into this or that part of what Kant says but not to expect a balanced analysis that both fits the text of the *Critique* and makes sense out of its complex arguments.

The aim of this book is to offer such an analysis for those crucial sections of the *Critique* where Kant presents the constructive side of his theory of knowledge.

This is an immodest aim and one that I could not hope to fulfill if I did not stand on the shoulders of giants. Drawing on their work, I shall try to show that the first half of the *Critique of Pure Reason* contains a sustained and challenging line of argument that is intended both to defend the possibility of common sense and scientific knowledge against a skeptical empiricism and to restrict human knowledge to the experienced or empirical world. I refer to the line of argument begun in the Transcendental Deduction of the Categories and continued in the Analogies of Experience. My analysis of this extended argument is offered primarily in chapters 4 and 5 on "the Central Argument of the Analytic," though its context is prepared in chapter 2 in the discussions of arguments about space and of Transcendental Idealism, and the argument is extended even further in the last section of chapter 7 on the Second Analogy. The analysis draws freely on and references the work of Wolff, Strawson, Guyer, and others, but it is intended to be as unified and student-friendly as possible, given the inherent difficulty of Kant's thought. I reconstruct the arguments in numbered steps and in such a way that their validity is obvious or can be verified by the simplest rules of sentential logic; my aim is to make Kant's ideas as accessible as possible without undue oversimplification.

In addition to the attempt to reconstruct what I call "the Central Argument of the Analytic," this book is intended to provide a balanced and reasonably detailed treatment of the main episodes in the first half of the *Critique* that relate less directly to the Central Argument, including the Metaphysical Deduction, the Schematism, the Axioms of Intuition, the Anticipations of Perception, the Third Analogy, and the Postulates of Empirical Thought. I also discuss in some depth two important sections, the First Analogy and the Refutation of Idealism, that go beyond and buttress the Central Argument, respectively.

Three unusual aspects of the book's organization call for some comment. First, in chapter 3, I deal with the Axioms of Intuition, Anticipations of Perception, and Postulates of Empirical Thought directly after introducing the forms of judgment and the categories with which Kant associates those principles. My reason for doing so is that although Kant himself discusses these principles after the Transcendental Deduction, they do not depend on it and are more naturally thought of in connection with the Metaphysical Deduction. This organizational strategy also allows me to go straight from the Transcendental Deduction to the Analogies, thereby making the unity of the Central Argument more evident. Second and perhaps more controversially, I discuss the second edition version of the Transcendental Deduction (the "B-Deduction") only after presenting in some depth the idea of the two time-orders that Kant does not expound until later, in the Analogies. I do so because, for reasons that can be given only in the course of the analysis itself, I believe that the B-Deduction adds little to the first-edition version of the Deduction unless it is interpreted in light of the doctrine of the Analogies. Third, I discuss the Schematism at the end of the book, in the appendix. Like some other commentators, I find the Schematism especially opaque, but I think it makes more sense when interpreted in light of what comes before and after it in the *Critique*. Each of these organizational points is signposted within the text, and readers who might initially wish to pursue only the most central line of argument are given suggestions on what sections can be passed over and returned to later. As another aid to student readers, I indicate at the start of the endnotes to each chapter what sections or sections of the *Critique* that chapter should be read with.

It is my hope that this book will be useful to undergraduate students who are reading Kant in courses on the history of modern philosophy and in more narrowly focused courses on Kant, to graduate students, and to those of my peers who are not Kant specialists but who have an interest in teaching and studying Kant. I also hope that some features of the book, such as the manner in which I show how the Transcendental Deduction dovetails with the Analogies, my interpretation of Transcendental Idealism, my analysis of the First Analogy, and my elaboration and defense of Guyer's reconstruction of the Refutation of Idealism, will be of interest to Kant scholars.

Acknowledgments and a Note on the Translation

I am deeply grateful to a number of colleagues, friends, and students for comments, criticisms, suggestions, and encouragement. Professor Kenneth G. Lucey read the entire manuscript and provided extremely valuable comments on every chapter, including both philosophical issues and matters of style and presentation. His detailed critique led me to make innumerable improvements and to rewrite much of chapter 8. It has made this book more solid and readable than it would otherwise have been. Professor Derk Pereboom generously provided very insightful, thoughtful, and knowing comments on the entire manuscript as well. His comments led me to correct several inaccuracies and to make significant improvements in the treatment of several crucial points. Professor James Van Cleve provided very helpful and probing comments on chapter 9, which led me to make several improvements. Professor Richard Mancuso of the physics department at SUNY Brockport kindly answered some physics questions bearing on chapter 8. The students in my Spring 2003 Kant course at SUNY Brockport, especially Melissa Birmingham, Andrew Leoni, and Chris Plochocki, made comments and wrote papers that led me to make some very significant improvements as well. Needless to say, I alone am responsible for whatever shortcomings remain.

My editor at Oxford University Press, Peter Ohlin, was unfailingly helpful with various matters that came up as I was working on the manuscript. I am also grateful to SUNY Brockport for course releases and for a sabbatical leave in Fall 2002 that made it possible for me to complete this work in a timely fashion, despite my teaching and administrative obligations. Last, but not least, I wish to express my gratitude to Alvina Greenberg, not only for her loving support and wise counsel, but also for expertly preparing beautiful camera-ready copies of the diagrams in this book.

Cambridge University Press kindly granted permission to quote passages from Paul Guyer, *Kant and the Claims of Knowledge*, copyright © Cambridge University Press 1987, reprinted with the permission of Cambridge University Press. Cambridge University Press also kindly granted permission to quote passages from

Jonathan Bennett, *Kant's Analytic*, copyright © Cambridge University Press 1966, reprinted with the permission of Cambridge University Press. Hackett Publishing Company kindly granted permission to quote passages from Justus Hartnack, *Kant's Theory of Knowledge*, copyright © Hackett Publishing Company, Inc. 2001, reprinted by permission of Hackett Publishing Company, Inc. All rights reserved. Peter Smith Publisher kindly granted permission to quote passages from Robert Paul Wolff, *Kant's Theory of Mental Activity*, Peter Smith Publisher, Inc., Gloucester, Mass., 1973. Thompson Publishing Services kindly granted permission to quote passages from Peter F. Strawson, *The Bounds of Sense: An Essay on Kant's* Critique of Pure Reason (London: Routledge, 1990). Chapter 7 is reprinted in part from my book, *Hume's Epistemology and Metaphysics: An Introduction* (London: Routledge, 1998), as is a short section of chapter 4. I thank Thompson Publishing Services for permission to reprint this material.

All quotations from Kant's *Critique of Pure Reason* are taken from *Immanuel Kant's Critique of Pure Reason*, trans. by Norman Kemp Smith (New York: St. Martin, 1965). A note is in order to explain my use of the venerable Kemp Smith translation rather than the more recent translations of Guyer-Wood or Pluhar. The main reason, aside from long habituation and familiarity, is that I prefer "knowledge" to "cognition" as a translation of *Erkenntnis*. For in the constructive part of the *Critique of Pure Reason* with which this book is primarily concerned, the success that Kant is interested in concerns knowledge that certain things (or propositions) are true (e.g., that there are objects which must be conceived as being other than the self, that every observable event has a cause, that all substances that can be known to coexist in space on the basis of nonsimultaneous perceptions causally interact, etc.), not mere "cognition" with respect to these things, whatever exactly that would be. Also, Kant presents his problem as that of showing that certain *judgments* or *principles* constitute knowledge; he seeks "synthetic *a priori*" knowledge, not just "synthetic *a priori*" cognition (whatever that would be). As for cases in which Kant uses *Erkenntnis* in the plural or for nonpropositional cases, Kemp Smith's "modes of knowledge" is not significantly inferior to "cognitions." Of course, there is also the passage where Kemp Smith has Kant speak of "false" knowledge (A 58/B 83), but it seems quite unnecessary to adopt an across-the-board translation of *Erkenntnis* as "cognition" in order to avoid an isolated oxymoron. Finally, I doubt that non–German-reading readers of this book who use the Guyer-Wood or the Pluhar translation will find the book any less useful than those who use Kemp Smith. I have, of course, used the standard A/B pagination—"A" for page references to the first German edition of the *Critique of Pure Reason*, "B" for page references to the second edition—which is found in the margins of the pages of the Kemp Smith, Guyer-Wood, and Pluhar translations.

Contents

KANT'S THEORY OF KNOWLEDGE

Introduction

1.1 Kant, Rationalism, and Empiricism

1.1.1 Kant as Synthesizer of Rationalism and Empiricism

Kant is sometimes introduced as the philosopher who synthesized rationalism and empiricism. Of course, this cannot mean that Kant simply adopted the central views of both the rationalists and the empiricists, for even within each of these schools of thought there are major disagreements. For example, among the rationalists, Descartes held that there are many purely thinking substances and one extended substance that makes up the entire physical world; Spinoza held that there is only one substance, which is both thinking and extended and may be called either "God" or "Nature"; and Leibniz held that there exist infinitely many nonextended substances called "monads" and that extension is merely an appearance; among the empiricists, Locke held that matter exists and we can know that it does, Berkeley held that matter does not exist, and Hume held that we cannot know whether matter exists or not though we cannot help believing that it does. Furthermore, there are fundamental disagreements between the two schools of thought. For example, the rationalists held that humans possess some ideas that are not derived from any experience, whereas the empiricists held that all of our ideas must be derived from experience. Thus, in order for the claim that Kant synthesized rationalism and empiricism to be coherent, it would have to mean that he selected certain doctrines of the rationalists and certain doctrines of the empiricists and put them together into his own philosophy.

But even this qualified version of the statement that Kant synthesized rationalism and empiricism is very inadequate, for Kant did not simply conjoin certain rationalist and empiricist views. Rather, he profoundly transformed those views themselves, in such a way that their meaning and implications were deeply altered. The result was a system of philosophy, called "the Critical Philosophy," which is very different from any simple merger of rationalist and empiricist views. In the final analysis, Kant's Critical Philosophy turns its back on both rationalism and empiricism. Nevertheless, it combines elements of both. It can truly be said of Kant's philosophy that it *rejects* both rationalism and empiricism yet *incorporates* elements of rationalist and empiricist thought. What, then, does Kant reject and what does he incorporate from each?

1.1.2 Kant's Relation to Rationalism

In spite of the differences between them, the rationalists all held that humans can have knowledge of a nonempirical reality—a realm of things that straightforwardly exist but yet cannot be perceived by the senses or accessed by introspection. They all maintained that we can have knowledge of certain entities, such as God, immortal souls, and substances underlying things' properties, that are not objects of any possible experience, that is, that can never be presented to us either in sense perception or in introspection. Kant rejects this claim. The main *destructive* aim of his *Critique of Pure Reason* is to show that there can be no human knowledge at all of any nonempirical reality. In this respect, Kant is as much of an empiricist as David Hume.

But although Kant holds that humans can have no knowledge about any nonempirical reality, he does not deny that the existence of such a reality is a legitimate topic of human concern. On the contrary, he believes that there are three specific topics of rationalist metaphysics that are legitimate, important, and even inevitable topics of human concern. These are God, human immortality, and human freedom. Kant's position with respect to these topics is, briefly, this: although we cannot *know* whether God exists, whether there is an immortal human soul, or whether humans have free will, we may *believe* in God, immortality, and freedom. Furthermore, for purposes of action and morality, we *ought* to believe in them despite the fact that there is no way we can know whether these beliefs are true. Kant's position, then, is that whereas we must admit that our *knowledge* extends only as far as the limits of experience, still there are reasons of an essentially moral sort for believing in God, immortality, and freedom. As he puts it in a famous sentence, "I have . . . found it necessary to deny *knowledge*, in order to make room for *faith*" (B xxx).

1.1.3 Kant's Relation to Empiricism

The fundamental principle of empiricism is that all of our ideas must come from experience, that is, from sense perception or the introspective awareness of our own states of mind. Kant does not accept this principle, for he sees the development of empiricism from Locke to Hume, and especially Hume's work, as showing that the principle leads to skepticism—to the impossibility, not only of rationalist metaphysics, but also of scientific knowledge and everyday, "commonsense" knowledge. Now the main *constructive* aim of the *Critique of Pure Reason* is to uphold the possibility of scientific and commonsense knowledge against Hume's skeptical empiricism.[1] To this end, Kant holds that there are certain special concepts that do not originate in experience but have what he calls "objective validity." Kant names these concepts "Pure Concepts" or "Pure Categories of the Understanding" (he gives a complete list, or "table," of these at A 80/B 106). The two most important pure concepts or categories are substance and causality.

The adjective "pure" expresses Kant's view that these special concepts are not in any way derived from experience. They are not, for example, copies of any sense impressions; nor do they come from experience in any other manner. To register this fact, Kant frequently also calls them "*a priori*" concepts. Yet, the pure concepts or categories do yield knowledge, provided that one extremely important condition is satisfied.

What is this condition? It is that the subject matter of the knowledge must fall within the range of possible experience. To put it in Kant's way, the pure concepts can yield knowledge only when they are *applied* to actual or possible experience. Thus Kant's position, summarized in figure 1–1, is that although the pure concepts are not derived from experience, they can contribute to our knowledge only when they are applied to experience. This means that the pure concepts can never yield any metaphysical knowledge, in the rationalist sense of "metaphysical." The pure concept of causality, for example, cannot be used to prove the existence of God because God is not a possible object of experience (sense perception or introspection), but a pure concept has its legitimate application only within the field of possible experience.

Why does Kant hold that the pure concepts or categories yield knowledge only when they are applied to actual or possible experience? He holds this view because of one of the fundamental principles of his philosophy, a principle that has to do with the nature of any thinking, judging, or asserting that contains or conveys knowledge. This is that such thinking requires two things: (a) concepts and (b) something to which the concepts are applied. To think, judge, or assert in a way that embodies or expresses knowledge is, for Kant, to apply a concept to something. The only exception to this principle is thinking that simply relates one concept to another, as in the judgments "roundness is a shape" or "red is a color." But thinking that embodies knowledge beyond knowledge of mere conceptual relations, or judgments that affirm something about how the world is, must conform to the principle. For example, if I think, judge, or assert, "this is a desk," this requires (a) that I possess the concept of a desk and (b) that there exist something to which I can apply my concept. Now I can apply a concept to something X only if X is in some manner presented or given to me. But things can only be presented

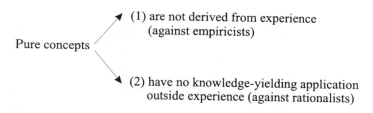

Pure concepts

(1) are not derived from experience
(against empiricists)

(2) have no knowledge-yielding application
outside experience (against rationalists)

FIGURE 1–1

or given to human beings in experience, that is, in sense perception (which Kant calls "outer sense") or introspection (which Kant calls "inner sense"). Kant sometimes suggests that there could be nonhuman knowers to whom things are presented in some way other than sense perception or introspection. But he maintains that at least for humans, awareness of things can consist only in their being perceived by the senses or accessed by introspection. Therefore, at least for humans, the knowledge-yielding application of concepts, which is the same thing as thinking or judging that expresses knowledge, is limited to actual or possible experience—to what can be given in what Kant calls "sensibility." This implies that we can have knowledge only of what falls within the range of possible experience.

I close this subsection with some terminological points. Kant frequently uses the term "intuition"; this is his most general word for the items to which concepts are applied. Thus intuitions include items presented in sense perception and introspection (including imagined items); they include everything that is presented or given to a conscious subject. This use of the term "intuition" is completely different from the use of that term in Descartes or in Locke, where intuition refers to the grasp of a logical or conceptual connection between ideas or concepts. Kant also uses the term "pure intuition." A pure intuition, for Kant, is a form that the items presented in sense perception and introspection must take. As we will see in Chapter 2, he argues that there are two such pure intuitions or (as he also calls them) "pure forms of sensible intuition," namely space and time (A 22/B 36).

1.2 Kant's Reduction of His Agenda to Its Simplest Form

1.2.1 Kant's Simplifying Question

As my remarks about Kant's relation to empiricism and to rationalism have shown, Kant has a twofold aim in the *Critique of Pure Reason*: (1) constructively, to defend the possibility of scientific and everyday ("commonsense") knowledge against Hume's skeptical empiricism, and (2) destructively, to show that traditional metaphysics is impossible. In the "Introduction" to the *Critique*, he tries to reduce this basic agenda to its simplest form: "How are *a priori* synthetic judgments possible?" As he puts it:

> Much is already gained if we can bring a number of investigations under the formula of a single problem. For we not only lighten our own task, by defining it accurately, but make it easier for others, who would test our results, to judge whether we have succeeded in what we set out to do. Now the proper problem of pure reason is . . . : How are *a priori* synthetic judgments possible? (B 19)

In the next chapter, I shall argue that there is reason to doubt that Kant's project can really be encapsulated in this famous question. In section 2.4, I shall introduce an alternative way, proposed by P. F. Strawson, of formulating Kant's basic question, and in 2.5, I shall adopt a modified version of Strawson's proposal. But to appreciate the advantages of such alternatives, it is necessary first to understand Kant's own way of conceiving and formulating his task. Therefore, throughout the present chapter and in the first three sections of the next chapter, I shall take Kant at his word and assume that his problem can be reduced to the question of how synthetic *a priori* judgments are possible. Our immediate task, then, is to see why Kant thinks that his problem can be reduced to this question.

To understand Kant's question, we need to see how he works up to it. He starts by making two important distinctions: (1) the *a priori/a posteriori* distinction; (2) the analytic/synthetic distinction. In the next two subsections, I explain these distinctions by presenting definitions of the terms "*a priori*," "*a posteriori*," "analytic," and "synthetic" and noting some ways in which Kant's own usage relates to these definitions. Then, I show how Kant uses the distinctions to focus the disagreement between rationalism and empiricism and to introduce his own Critical position.

1.2.2 A Priori *and* A Posteriori

The *a priori/a posteriori* distinction is essentially an epistemological one; it pertains to two different kinds of knowledge. According to the most common use of these terms, "*a priori*" means "known prior to experience," or better (since the priority in question is not a matter of coming earlier in time), "known independently of experience," whereas "*a posteriori*" means "known posterior to experience," or better (since the posteriority in question is not a matter of coming later in time), "known dependently on experience."[2] And indeed, Kant's own basic notion of *a priori* is 'independent of experience,' and his basic notion of *a posteriori* is 'dependent on experience.' As we shall see, these basic notions allow Kant to apply the terms "*a priori*" and "*a posteriori*" to a wide array of things, including knowledge, judgments, propositions, concepts, and intuitions. Today, however, philosophers often define these terms as they apply to propositions, and this is the way Kant himself uses the term "*a priori*" in his simplifying question, except that he applies it to "judgments" instead of "propositions." But as Stefan Körner suggests, we can think of a judgment simply as "a proposition asserted by somebody."[3] So we may, without distorting Kant's meaning, begin by defining the terms "*a priori*" and "*a posteriori*" as they apply to propositions or judgments.

Letting *p* stand for any judgment or proposition, we can define the term "*a priori*" as follows:

D1: *p* is *a priori* = *df* *p* can be known independently of experience.

For example, the statements "1 + 1 = 2" and "No one can be his or her own parent" are classified as *a priori* because they can be known to be true independently of experience: one need not make any observations or perform any experiments to know that these statements are true. Although an *a priori* proposition must be knowable independently of experience, it may *also* be known by experience. For example, although mathematical statements are *a priori*, many of them are complex and so known independently of experience (by abstract mathematical reasoning) only by mathematicians who can grasp their proofs, whereas other people may know them on the basis of experience—for example, by hearing of their truth from mathematicians or reading that they are true in mathematics books. Thus, "can be known independently of experience" does not mean "cannot be known by experience"; rather, it means roughly "can be known without experience." To see why this is still only roughly right, note that for a person to know even a simple *a priori* statement like "1 + 1 = 2" or "No one can be his or her own parent," some experience is required, namely, the experience needed to learn the meanings of terms—of "1," "+," "2," "parent," and so on. Thus, if "knowable independently of experience" meant "knowable without *any* experience whatsoever," then no statement would be *a priori* because a statement cannot be known to be true by a person unless that person understands the statement, but a person cannot understand a statement unless he or she understands its constituent terms, and those terms cannot be understood (at least by human beings) unless their meanings have been learned through various appropriate experiences. Therefore, a more accurate interpretation of the phrase "can be known independently of experience" in D1 is this: "can be known without experience, except for the experience required to learn the meanings of *p*'s constituent terms."

By contrast, there are many statements that cannot be known in this way. Consider for example the statement "Some people are over six feet tall." Even after one fully understands (the meanings of the terms in) this statement, one may be completely in the dark as to whether the statement is true or false: only experience can determine this. Such statements are classified as *a posteriori* or, synonymously, as "empirical" statements. "Snow is white" and "There are nine planets" are other examples of *a posteriori* or empirical statements. Thus the term "*a posteriori*" is also an epistemological one, which contrasts directly with "*a priori*." As applied again to propositions or judgments, it can be defined this way:

D2: *p* is *a posteriori* (empirical) = *df p* can be known only by experience.

The phrase "can be known only by experience" requires some clarification, for it does not mean, as one might think, "can be known just by experience" or "can be known by experience alone." At least some *a posteriori* statements require reasoning, as well as experience, in order to be known; for example, our knowledge of scientific laws rests not only on observations but also on complex inferences or extrapolations from those observations. More fundamentally, many philosophers would hold that no statement is knowable *just* by experience because of a point made by none other than Kant. This is the point, already mentioned, that thinking that embodies knowledge requires both concepts and something to which concepts are applied. This point implies that all knowledge requires conceptualization, which is a form of thought that philosophers often contrast with the raw data of experience. Thus, instead of meaning "can be known just by experience," the phrase "can be known only by experience" in D2 means this: "cannot be known without experience, other than or in addition to the experience needed to learn the meanings of *p*'s constituent terms."

As I have said, Kant's pivotal notion of the *a priori* as "independent of experience" makes it possible for him to apply the term "*a priori*" to a wide range of things, including not only judgments and propositions but also knowledge, concepts, and intuitions. The "independence" in question means something different as it applies to each of these things. As applied to judgments and propositions, it means that an *a priori* judgment or proposition can be *justified* without appealing to particular facts that are known by experience or observation. To see this more clearly, notice that when I said (in the second paragraph of this subsection) that

> the statements "1 + 1 = 2" and "No one can be his or her own parent" are classified as *a priori* because they can be known to be true independently of experience: one need not make any observations or perform any experiments to know that these statements are true

I could have said instead that

> the statements "1 + 1 = 2" and "No one can be his or her own parent" are classified as *a priori* because they can be *justifiably believed* to be true independently of experience: one need not make any observations or perform any experiments to be *justified in believing* that these statements are true.[4]

Likewise, as applied to knowledge—at least to "propositional" knowledge or "knowledge-that" (something is the case)—the independence lies again in the fact that *a priori* knowledge does not rest on experience in a *justificatory* sense of "rest on." As applied to concepts, however, the independence means that the concepts are not derived from experience. Finally, as applied to intuitions, it means that the intuitions in question (space and time, as Kant will show) are not obtained by sense perception or introspection. Much more will be said in later chapters about Kant's notion of *a priori* as it applies to concepts and to intuitions.

Kant also applies the terms "*a posteriori*" and "empirical" not just to judgments and propositions but also to knowledge, concepts, and intuitions. When he does so, his meaning contrasts directly with calling these items *a priori*. An *a posteriori* proposition or judgment is one that can be justified only by appealing to particular facts that are known by experience or observation. *A posteriori* knowledge rests on experience in a *justificatory* sense of "rest on." An *a posteriori* or empirical concept is one that is derived from experience, like the concept of a cat. An *a posteriori* or empirical intuition is one obtained by sense perception or introspection, like the sight of a cat or the feeling of peacefulness.

Kant offers us a criterion for identifying *a priori* knowledge, propositions, and judgments: necessity and strict universality (B 3–4). To see how this criterion is supposed to work, consider the proposition 'every even number is divisible by 2.' Its truth is necessary because there cannot be any counterexamples, and strictly universal because there not only *are not* but there *cannot be* any exceptions to it (B 4). Is this criterion redundant? Perhaps not because strict universality seems not to work for singular *a priori* propositions, like '9 is an odd number.' But this proposition is still necessarily true. So it seems that strict universality entails necessity, but not vice versa, and that necessity is the fundamental criterion.

Kant's adoption of necessity as the fundamental criterion of the *a priori* accords with his often-repeated and important claim that no proposition that rests on experience can be necessary. As he puts it:

> Experience tells us, indeed, what is, but not that it must necessarily be so, and not otherwise. (A 1)

> Experience teaches that a thing is so and so, but not that it cannot be otherwise. (B 3)

That a body is extended is a proposition that holds *a priori* and is not empirical. For, before appealing to experience, I have already in the concept of body all the conditions required for my judgment. I have only to extract from it, in accordance with the principle of contradiction, the required predicate, and in so doing can at the same time become conscious of the necessity of the judgment—and that is what experience could never have taught me. (B 11–12)[5]

Mathematical propositions . . . are always judgments *a priori*, not empirical; because they carry with them necessity, which cannot be derived from experience. (B 14–15)

Some contemporary philosophers, following Saul Kripke, would say that scientific statements about "natural kinds," like "water is H_2O," are *a posteriori* yet necessary.[6] This raises complex issues that I cannot explore here. Suffice it to say that a follower of Kant would not accept this view but would hold instead that the statement "water is H_2O" was once an empirical hypothesis that has now become a definition: that no substance that was not H_2O would count as being water, no matter how much like water it was, is a result of the way we use the term "water" rather than of some metaphysical necessity. This need not be taken to mean that "water is H_2O" was once contingent and then became necessary; it is compatible with saying that the statement is, if true, then necessarily true. For saying that it was once an empirical hypothesis need not mean that it was once true but contingent, but only that it was once not known to be true.

1.2.3 Analytic and Synthetic

Whereas the notions of *a priori* and *a posteriori* are epistemological ones having to do with the way in which a proposition can be known, the notions of analytic and synthetic are semantical ones, having to do with what makes a proposition true or false. To avoid misrepresenting the current philosophical landscape, I should first note that the analytic/synthetic distinction is by no means uncontroversial. Some contemporary philosophers, notably W. V. Quine, have questioned the tenability of the distinction; others defend it.[7] My purpose here, however, is to explain how the distinction enters into Kant's attempt to reduce his agenda to its simplest form. So, I shall not enter into the controversy concerning the tenability of the analytic/synthetic distinction, but I shall rather assume that the distinction is tenable and expound it as it is usually understood by those who accept it.

The basic definition of an analytic statement is this:

D3: *p* is analytic = *df p* is true solely in virtue of the meanings of its constituent terms.

An example is "all bachelors are unmarried eligible men."[8] Notice that although this statement is not couched in the form of a definition—it does not start with "a bachelor is . . ." or "the term 'bachelor' means . . ."—it is really a definition since "bachelor" just means "unmarried eligible man." This is why the statement is true solely in virtue of the meanings of its constituent terms. Definitions, then, are one type of analytic statement.

Another type of analytic statement consists of what we may call "conceptual truths." These are not definitions, but they are still true in virtue of meanings. An example is "something cannot be both round and square." Although not a definition of either "round" or "square," this statement is still true in virtue of those terms' meanings, or of the *concepts* 'round' and 'square,' for "round" is defined partly in terms of "having no angles," and "square" is defined in terms of "rectangular," which in turn is defined in terms of "having four angles."

The third and most fundamental type of analytic statement consists of statements that are true in virtue of their logical form. Two examples are "either it is raining or it is not raining" and "it is not both raining and not raining." To see why these two statements are true because of their logical forms, we can extract their respective forms, as follows:

either *p* or *not p*

not (*p* and *not p*)

It is obvious that any statement having one of these forms, no matter what specific sentence one substitutes for *p*, must be true. This is why the two statements about raining, as well as any other statements obtained by substituting a given statement for *p* in either form, can be said to be "true because of their logical form." You may ask: why are such statements analytic? The answer is that, like definitions and conceptual truths, they are true solely in virtue of the meanings of their constituent terms. Specifically, our sample statements are true in virtue of the meanings of the terms "either-or," "not," and "and"—terms that give the statements their logical form and that are called "logical connectives."

Some contemporary philosophers would define analyticity in a slightly different way from that given in D3. They would say that an analytic statement is one whose truth depends solely on logical laws and definitions. To illustrate, consider the statement "all bachelors are unmarried." Since "bachelor" is defined as "unmarried eligible man," substituting synonyms for synonyms in this statement yields the statement "all unmarried eligible men are unmarried." But this statement has the form "All ABC's are C's," or, in the symbolism of modern logic, the form "$(x)[(Fx . Gx . Hx) \supset Hx]$"—forms that express laws of logic.

There is an important relationship between analyticity and contradiction: the negation (denial) of an analytic statement is always a contradiction, and conversely the negation of a contradiction is always an analytic statement. Thus, for example, the negation of "all bachelors are unmarried eligible men" is "some bachelors are not unmarried eligible men." But since "bachelor" means "unmarried eligible man," the negated statement says that some unmarried eligible men are not unmarried eligible men, which is a contradiction (since it says that some men are both eligible and unmarried and not eligible and unmarried). Conversely, the negation of "some bachelors are not unmarried eligible men" is "all bachelors are unmarried eligible men," which is analytic. Similar considerations apply to the other examples I have given. Thus, for instance, the negation of "either *p* or *not p*" is "neither *p* nor *not p*," which means the same as "*not p* and (also) *not not p*," which means simply "*not p* and *p*," which is, of course, a contradiction. Conversely, the negation of "*not p* and *p*" is "*not (not p* and *p*)*," which is analytic.

The term that contrasts with "analytic" is the last of Kant's four terms, "synthetic." It can be defined this way:

D4: *p* is synthetic = *df p* is not true or false solely in virtue of the meanings of its constituent terms.

For example, the statements "all bachelors are taxpayers," "there are nine planets," and "every event has a cause" are each synthetic. None of these is true solely in virtue of its constituent terms, and each of them can be denied without embracing a contradiction. Notice how the first statement, "all bachelors are taxpayers," contrasts with "all bachelors are unmarried." Notice also that the third statement, "every event has a cause," could be turned into an analytic truth by substituting "effect" for "event." As David Hume remarked, "every event has a cause" is to "every effect has a cause" as "every man is married" is to "every husband is married."[9]

Kant's use of the terms "analytic" and "synthetic" differs in one important respect from the contemporary one just described: Kant restricts his attention to subject-predicate propositions. Thus, he introduces the analytic-synthetic distinction this way:

In all judgments in which the relation of a subject to the predicate is thought (I take into consideration affirmative judgments only, the subsequent application to negative judgments being easily made), this relation is possible in two different ways. Either the predicate B belongs to the subject A, as something which is (covertly) contained in this concept A; or B lies outside the concept A, although it does indeed stand in connection with it. In the one case I entitle the judgment analytic, in the other synthetic. (A 6/B 10–A 7/B 10)

As can be seen from this passage, Kant defines an analytic proposition (judgment) more narrowly than does D3, as a proposition whose predicate concept is contained in its subject concept; he restricts analyticity to subject-predicate propositions in which the predicate can be extracted from the subject by analysis. Bertrand Russell and other twentieth-century philosophers have rightly urged that certain other kinds of propositions should also be allowed to count as analytic. For example, if-then propositions whose truth turns purely on the meaning of terms, such as "If X is to the left of Y, then Y is to the right of X" or "If A is taller than B and B is taller than C, then A is taller than C," have just as good a title to be called "analytic" as does Kant's example, "All bodies are extended." In this connection, we might note that Kant does occasionally seem to concede that a non–subject-predicate proposition could be analytic, as in this passage:

The propositions, that if equals be added to equals the wholes [the sums] are equal, and that if equals be taken from equals the remainders are equal, are analytic propositions. (A 164/B 204)[10]

Kant makes an extremely important point about the difference between analytic and synthetic propositions: only synthetic propositions can be informative about nonlinguistic reality or can increase our knowledge of nonlinguistic reality; by contrast, analytic propositions serve only to explain our meanings or provide information only about linguistic reality.[11] Consider, for example, the proposition that *all bodies are extended* (have shape and size). This proposition would remain true even if there existed no bodies; it would remain true no matter what (nonlinguistic) reality was like. Therefore, it cannot possibly convey any information about (nonlinguistic) reality. All it does is indicate that "having a shape and size" is part of what we mean by "being a body"; that is why it can be said to provide information about *linguistic* reality—about the use of language. By contrast, consider the proposition that *all bodies have weight.* This proposition happens to be true, but if the laws of nature were different—if there were no such thing as gravity—it would be false. To put it more simply, the way the world is determines whether the proposition is true or false. Therefore, the proposition describes the world as being a certain way; it is genuinely informative about reality. Kant expresses the point this way:

> [Analytic judgments], as adding nothing through the predicate to the concept of the subject, but merely breaking it up into those constituent concepts that have all along been thought in it, although confusedly, can also be entitled explicative. [Synthetic judgments], on the other hand, add to the concept of the subject a predicate which has not been in any wise thought in it, and which no analysis could possibly extract from it; and they may therefore be entitled ampliative. If I say, for instance, 'All bodies are extended', this is an analytic judgment. For I do not require to go beyond the concept which I connect with 'body' in order to find extension bound up with it. To meet with this predicate, I have merely to analyze the concept. . . . The judgment is therefore analytic. But when I say, 'All bodies are heavy', the predicate is something quite different from anything that I think in the mere concept of body in general; and the addition of such a predicate therefore yields a synthetic judgment. (A 7/B 11)

> Through analytic judgments our knowledge is not in any way extended, and . . . the concept which I already have is merely set forth and made intelligible to me. (A 7–8)

> Analytic judgments are very important, and indeed necessary, but only for obtaining . . . clearness in the concepts. (A 10/B 14).

Here is another way to make the point that analytic propositions convey no information about nonlinguistic reality. Suppose that the universe were very simple—so simple that it could be described with just one proposition. Let that proposition be either *p* or else *not p.* Now if in fact the universe is as *p* says it is, then *p* is true and *not p* is false; whereas if in fact the universe is as *not p* says it is, then *p* is false and *not p* is true. But what of the analytic proposition that *either p or not p?* Well, clearly that proposition is true no matter what the universe is like: it is true whether *p* is true and *not p* is false or *p* is false and *not p* is true. The situation can be represented by means of a truth table, as shown in figure 1–2. As the truth-table shows, "*p* or *not p*" (symbolized as "*p* v ~*p*") remains true ("true" is represented as "T") whether we suppose that *p* is true and *not p* (symbolized as "~*p*") is false ("false" is represented as "F"), or that *p* is false and *not p* is true: it is true regardless of what our simple universe is like. So, unlike *p*, which describes the universe as being one way, and *not p*, which describes it as being another (opposite) way, *p* or *not p* does not describe it as being any way at all: it is wholly "neutral" and remains true "no matter what." This graphically illustrates the point that analytic propositions do not convey any information about nonlinguistic real-

p	$\sim p$	$p \vee \sim p$
T	F	T
F	T	T

FIGURE 1–2

ity. They can convey information only about linguistic reality—in this instance, about the meaning or correct use of "or" ("$\vee$") and "it is not the case that" ("$\sim$"). An example illustrates the same point: suppose a weather forecaster says: "tomorrow it will either rain or not rain." Then she has not done her job; she has told us nothing about what tomorrow's weather will be like.

1.2.4 *Kant's Classification of Knowable Propositions*

The key to seeing how Kant attempts to use his four terms in order to reduce his agenda to its simplest form is to note that these terms can be used to classify all possible knowable propositions. As a preliminary point, notice that since one cannot know a false proposition—since "S knows that p" entails that p is true—we can limit this classification to true propositions.[12] We could avoid this limitation by construing "knowable" to mean not just "knowably true" but also "knowably true or knowably false" and by stipulating that "analytic" applies to any proposition that is either true or false solely in virtue of meanings, that is, to what are sometimes called "analytically false," as well as to "analytically true," propositions. But there is no advantage to be gained by these maneuvers, so we shall confine the classification to true propositions.

Now, no true proposition can be neither analytic nor synthetic: it must be one or the other—either true solely in virtue of meanings or true not solely in virtue of meanings. Furthermore, no knowable proposition can be neither *a priori* nor *a posteriori*: every such proposition must be knowable independently of experience (i.e., knowable without experience except for the experiences required to learn the meanings of its constituent terms) or else knowable only by experience (i.e., not knowable without experience other than just the experiences required to learn the meanings of its constituent terms). Thus, every knowable proposition must be either analytic or synthetic and either *a priori* or *a posteriori*. Furthermore, it is clear that no proposition can be both analytic and synthetic or both *a priori* and *a posteriori*. Thus, simply by the permutations allowed by Kant's four terms, there are just four possible classes of knowable propositions: (1) analytic *a priori*, (2) synthetic *a priori*, (3) analytic *a posteriori*, and (4) synthetic *a posteriori*. We can represent these four classes diagrammatically, as shown in figure 1–3.

To see how Kant arrives at his simplifying question (about the possibility of synthetic *a priori* judgments), observe how this classification can be used to focus the issue between rationalism and empiricism—that is, to express both the points

Analytic   Synthetic

	Analytic	Synthetic
A priori	1	2
A posteriori	3	4

FIGURE 1–3

of agreement and the point of disagreement between the two schools. Rationalists and empiricists agree on three points.

1. Both would affirm that there are instances of class 1 and 4. They would agree, for example, that at least definitions and the principles of logic are analytic *a priori* and that perceptual judgments and the laws of physics are synthetic *a posteriori*.[13]

2. Rationalists and empiricists would agree that there are no instances of class 3, and thus that all analytic propositions are *a priori*. This is so because if a proposition is analytic—if it is true solely in virtue of the meanings of its constituent terms—then surely experience is not required to determine its truth: that can be known just by understanding what the proposition says. Kant himself makes this point clearly:

> It would be absurd to found an analytic judgment on experience. Since, in framing the judgment, I must not go outside my concept, there is no need to appeal to the testimony of experience in its support. (A 7/B 11)

3. Rationalists and empiricists agree that although instances of class 1 are important, they are not informative about nonlinguistic reality. Kant himself also makes this point quite clearly:

> Analytic judgments are very important, and indeed necessary, but only for obtaining that clearness in concepts which is requisite for [what] will lead to a genuinely new addition to all previous knowledge. (A 10/B 14)

The fundamental reason for this point—that analytic statements remain true no matter what nonlinguistic reality is like—has already been explained.

What, then, is the disagreement between rationalists and empiricists? This: rationalists affirm, whereas empiricists deny, that there are instances of class 2. Thus, as Kant's famous question suggests, the disagreement between rationalism and empiricism, at least as theories of knowledge, can be reduced to the issue of whether there are synthetic *a priori* propositions.

The reason that rationalists must affirm that there are synthetic *a priori* propositions is the following. They hold that there are knowable propositions about nonlinguistic *and nonempirical* reality—about such entities as God, immortal souls, or unperceivable substances underlying things' observable properties. These propositions cannot be analytic *a priori* because then they would convey no information about nonlinguistic reality. They cannot be synthetic *a posteriori* because then they could be known only by experience. They cannot be analytic *a posteriori* because there are no such propositions. So they must be synthetic *a priori*.[14]

The reason that empiricists deny that there are synthetic *a priori* propositions is this: such a proposition would be both informative about nonlinguistic reality and knowable just by thinking. But empiricists are convinced that any proposition that conveys information about nonlinguistic reality must be based on experience. They find it utterly mysterious, even incredible, that a proposition could be both informative about nonlinguistic reality and yet knowable independently of experience (except for the experience needed to learn the meanings of terms) or just by pure thinking. So, they hold that the only propositions that can be known *a priori* are analytic ones that convey no information about nonlinguistic reality.

It is important to be clear about exactly what empiricism means by denying that there are synthetic *a priori* propositions. This denial does not mean, as is sometimes thought, that there are no propositions that are synthetic but nonempirical (i.e., synthetic but not *a posteriori*). Rather, it means that any such proposition would be *unknowable*. In other words, the empiricists' denial that there are synthetic *a priori* propositions does not mean that no proposition is both synthetic and not knowable by experience, but rather that no proposition is both synthetic and knowable independently of experience. Thus, empiricism, as here understood, implies that any proposition that was synthetic but not knowable by experience, while still a genuine proposition, would not be knowable independently of experience either, and so would be utterly unknowable. Some twentieth-century empiricists, namely, the logical positivists of the 1930s and 1940s, went even further; they proposed the "verifiability criterion of meaning," according to which every meaningful sentence must express either an analytic proposition or a proposition that is verifiable or testable by some empirical procedure. They held, accordingly, that no genuine proposition can be both synthetic and nonempirical. Sentences that seem to express such propositions, they held, are actually meaningless: they may be grammatically well-formed strings of words, but like the sentence "green emotions dance chemically," they do not express any proposition. Logical positivism is now defunct, however, for a variety of reasons, one of them being that the verifiability criterion is itself neither analytic nor testable by some empirical procedure, and so implies its own meaninglessness. It is important to note, therefore, that the weaker doctrine that any synthetic proposition which is not knowable by experience is unknowable is, if correct, strong enough to ruin the hopes of rationalist metaphysicians.[15]

Against the background of Kant's focusing of the issue between rationalism and empiricism, we can finally sketch his own position, as well as see why he tries to encapsulate his task in the question "How are *a priori* synthetic judgments possible?" Kant maintains, with rationalism and against empiricism, that there are synthetic *a priori* propositions. But he also imposes a restriction on them that rationalists would reject and that reflects the empiricist element of his position: even though these propositions are not based on experience, *they must apply or refer only to objects of possible experience.* To get a better grasp of what Kant is claiming, and of why he finds it necessary to ask how synthetic *a priori* propositions are possible, let *p* be any proposition that he holds to be synthetic *a priori*. By saying that *p* is synthetic *a priori*, he is saying that

(a) *p* cannot be known just by understanding the meanings of its constituent terms, yet

(b) *p* can be known independently of experience.

But how is this possible? How can a proposition be known to be true independently of experience, or just by pure thinking, unless its truth depends solely on the meanings of its constituent terms? How can one possibly deny the empiricists' basic conviction that no proposition that is genuinely informative about the world can be known independently of experience, but that any such proposition must instead rest on experience of the world? Kant believes that his main constructive task in the *Critique* can be reduced to answering this question, and that his main destructive task can be reduced to showing that the question cannot be answered if the proposition in question refers to nonempirical reality.

1.3 The Plan of the Critical Philosophy and the Structure of the *Critique*

1.3.1 The Overall Structure of the Critique of Pure Reason

We have seen that one of Kant's fundamental principles is that thinking or judging that carries or conveys knowledge requires two things: (a) concepts and (b) things to which the concepts are applied. Kant's term for the particular items to which concepts are applied is, as we noted, "intuition(s)." So his fundamental principle about thinking can be expressed in Kant's own terminology by saying that when a person thinks or judges in a way that expresses knowledge, the person applies a concept to an intuition, or by saying that such thinking or judging requires both concepts and intuitions. Kant expresses this principle in a famous dictum "Thoughts without content are empty, intuitions without concepts are blind" (A 51/B 75). The principle holds for all thinking or judging that conveys knowledge except that which is concerned only with the relations between two or more concepts. But such conceptual relations yield only analytic propositions: "It is evident that from mere concepts only analytic knowledge, not synthetic knowledge, is to be obtained" (A 47/B 64–65). It is the first sort of thinking, expressed in synthetic propositions, that Kant intends to focus upon in the *Critique of Pure Reason*.

To fully investigate such thinking, it seems that Kant would have to survey (a) concepts, (b) intuitions, and (c) the various ways in which concepts apply to intuitions—an impossibly large undertaking if one is talking about all concepts and all intuitions. But Kant's project is not nearly so large as that. He is not especially interested, for example, in cases like one where I apply the concept 'desk' to a desk.[16] The reason he is not especially interested in such cases is that the judgment "This is a desk" is merely empirical or *a posteriori*. Nor is Kant especially interested in cases such as the one in which I judge that all metals are good conductors of heat. For the main generic difference between this case and the desk case is that, instead of applying a concept to just a single item, I now apply the concept 'good conductor of heat' to very many items, most of which are for me items of possible experience rather than actual experience. But the metal case is still only an empirical or *a posteriori* judgment since it is based on experience. In other words, in the desk case we have an *a posteriori* proposition of the form "this is an A," whereas in the metal case we have an *a posteriori* proposition of the form "all A's are B's." Both propositions are synthetic, but both are also *a posteriori*. Since Kant is interested especially in cases where applying a concept is supposed to yield a synthetic *a priori* proposition, our two examples, as well as many other different sorts of examples that could be mentioned, are of no special interest to him.

Kant is interested, then, in cases where applying concepts to intuitions is supposed to yield synthetic *a priori* knowledge, that is, knowledge expressible in propositions that are strictly universal or at least necessary, and at the same time informative about non-linguistic reality, rather than only about the relations between concepts or meanings. Such knowledge, as we have said, cannot possibly be based on experience, which can show us how things are but never how they must be. Kant's position, as we have also seen, is that such knowledge can result from the application of a pure concept—one that is not derived from experience.

It might seem, then, that we are now ready to go straight to a study of the nature and use of the pure concepts or categories. But if we did this, we would be skipping over what Kant regards as an important question. If there are certain pure concepts whose application yields synthetic *a priori* knowledge, might there not also be certain intuitions whose nature is such that they provide synthetic *a priori* knowledge when concepts are applied to them? Might there not be certain pure intuitions, as well as pure concepts? Kant's view is that there are indeed certain pure intuitions and that in order to investigate synthetic *a priori* knowledge we must study both the pure concepts and the pure intuitions. Now, in doing this, one could start either from the side of the pure concepts or from the side of the pure intuitions. For historical and strategic reasons that will become evident as we proceed, Kant begins with the pure intuitions rather than the pure concepts. This order of proceeding is reflected in the one-page table of contents that he provided for the first edition of the *Critique* (A xxiii–xxiv). (Kant himself provided no table of contents for the second edition, but his editors and translators have provided one, which lists the many subdivisions of the main parts of the work.) By looking at this page, one can see what the general structure of the *Critique* is. Here are Kant's chief headings, followed by brief descriptions of what is to be found under each of them.

INTRODUCTION

Here Kant formulates the *a priori*/*a posteriori* and the analytic/synthetic distinctions and attempts to reduce his problem to its simplest form.

I. TRANSCENDENTAL DOCTRINE OF THE ELEMENTS

The "Elements" are simply the pure intuitions and the pure concepts or categories. The pure intuitions are treated in Part I, entitled "Transcendental Aesthetic"; the pure concepts in Part II, entitled "Transcendental Logic."

The Transcendental Aesthetic is subdivided into a section on space and a section on time because there will turn out to be just two pure intuitions, and these are space and time.

The Transcendental Logic is subdivided into two major sections: the Transcendental Analytic and the Transcendental Dialectic. In the Analytic, Kant discusses the application of the pure concepts or categories within the field of experience; he discusses the categories, so to speak, on "good behavior." In the Dialectic, he discusses the attempt to apply the pure concepts outside the field of experience; he discusses the categories on "bad behavior." Let me elaborate a little on what Kant tries to show in each of these sections.

The burden of the Analytic is to show that the pure concepts can be legitimately applied to the world we experience. This is the part of the *Critique* that has been the most studied and discussed by philosophers in recent years, for it is here that Kant tries to show that we can have secure knowledge of the natural world, despite the skeptical thrust of Humean empiricism. The Analytic, then, is the main constructive part of the *Critique*. The arguments of the Analytic are deep, very difficult, and completely new and ground-breaking in relation to the history of philosophy before Kant. The greater part of this book will be devoted to analyzing and appraising those arguments.

In the Dialectic, Kant criticizes systematically any attempt to apply the categories outside the field of experience. His general argument is that whenever one attempts to do this, one is led into error, contradiction, and paradox. The Dialectic, then, is the destructive part of the *Critique*. The primary target is the ambition of rationalism to provide knowledge about nonempirical reality. Its most important parts, which are listed in the longer table of contents supplied by Kant's editors, are the Paralogisms of Pure Reason, the Antinomy of Pure Reason, and the Ideal of Pure Reason. In the Paralogisms, Kant argues that, contrary to Descartes, we can have no knowledge of a substantial self or soul. In the Antinomy, he tries to show that the attempt to demonstrate truths about nonempirical reality leads to four pairs of "antinomies"—four cases in which we can "prove," by equally cogent arguments, both a "thesis" and its contradictory "antithesis": (1) that the world both has and does not have a beginning in time and limits in space; (2) that every composite thing is composed of ultimate, indivisible parts and also that every composite thing is infinitely divisible; (3) that not everything in the world is determined by causal laws, allowing for freedom, and also that everything in the world is determined by causal laws, so that there is no freedom; (4) that the world contains or was caused by a necessary being and also that there is no necessary being. In the Ideal of Pure Reason, Kant identifies and seeks to refute the three main metaphysical arguments for the existence of God: the Ontological Proof, which tries to prove that God exists merely from the concept of God as an absolutely unsurpassable being; the Cosmological Proof, which tries to prove that the world requires God as its cause or ultimate explanation; and the Physicotheological Proof (now better known as the Teleological Argument or Argument from Design), which tries to show that the means-ends structuring of the world requires God as a designer or "Divine Architect." In the Dialectic, Kant is also anxious to prepare the ground for his view that although we can have no knowledge of non-empirical reality, we are entitled and indeed obligated to believe in or "postulate" God, immortality, and human freedom. This view is essential to Kant's moral philosophy and is richly developed in his other works, notably the *Critique of Practical Reason.*

II. TRANSCENDENTAL DOCTRINE OF METHOD

In this section, which is much shorter and less often studied than the Transcendental Doctrine of the Elements, Kant does several different things. He discusses the difference between the synthetic *a priori* knowledge obtained in mathematics and in philosophy; he provides a strong defense of freedom of communication and open-mindedness in metaphysical discussions; he contrasts the role of hypotheses in science and in philosophy and reflects on his own "transcendental" style of philosophical argument; he contrasts theoretical with practical (moral) philosophy, and philosophy with other types of knowledge; and he compares his own critical philosophy with other approaches, such as dogmatism, empiricism and skepticism.

1.3.2 How the Major Sections of the Critique
Relate to Kant's Simplifying Question

Now that we have a general idea of what Kant tries to accomplish in each of the major sections of the *Critique*, let us relate Kant's aims in each section to his question about synthetic *a priori* judgments. We have seen that in the Introduction to the *Critique*, Kant claims that the whole problem of the Critical Philosophy can be encapsulated in the question "How are synthetic *a priori* judgments possible?" I have already said that there is reason to doubt that Kant's problem really can be reduced to this question, but throughout the present chapter my policy is to take Kant at his word and assume that his project can be reduced to answering it. So let us ask how this question relates to the tasks that Kant sets for himself in the Aesthetic, Analytic, and Dialectic.

Let's start by looking at the question itself. It has at least two possible meanings, depending on whether one stresses the word "how" or the word "possible":

(a) Assuming that synthetic *a priori* judgments are possible, what is the explanation of the fact that they are possible?

(b) Are synthetic *a priori* judgments really possible, and if so what is the proof that they are possible?

The crucial difference between these two interpretations is that question (a) assumes that synthetic *a priori* judgments are possible, whereas question (b) does not assume this. Question (a) takes it as an unquestioned fact or datum that synthetic *a priori* judgments are perfectly legitimate; all it asks for is an explanation of this fact. It is the question with the stress on the word "how." It is analogous to the question "How is it possible for airplanes to fly?" asked by a person who knows perfectly well that they can fly. All the person wants is an explanation of this fact, in terms of physical laws, the plane's structure, and so on. Question (b), on the other hand, does not take it as an unquestioned fact that synthetic *a priori* judgments are legitimate. On the contrary, it asks for a proof of this fact, if indeed it is a fact. The implication is that if no such proof can be given, then we must admit that synthetic *a priori* judgments are not or at least may not be possible.

Here one might object that if a satisfactory *explanation* can be given of how synthetic *a priori* judgments are possible, then this also *proves* that they are possible, so that questions (a) and (b) are not really distinct. But even if a satisfactory explanation of *p* usually amounts to a proof that *p*, I do not think that this is the case here, for the following reason. An explanation has two main components: the proposition(s) to be explained, called the *explanandum*, and the proposition(s) that provide the explanation, called the *explanans*. Usually, the *explanans* consist of propositions that not only imply the truth of the *explanandum* but also are themselves well established, as are, for example, the laws of physics involved in an explanation of how airplanes can fly. But when Kant asks question (a), he places only one constraint on the *explanans*, namely, that it must imply the truth of the *explanandum*, in this case, that it must imply that synthetic *a priori* judgments are possible.[17] He does not require that there be any independent support or evidence for the truth of the *explanans* itself. Accordingly, his explanation of how synthetic *a priori* judgments are possible, proceeding as it does from principles that are designed to imply their possibility but have no other, independent basis, cannot be regarded as a proof that they are possible. This point should become clearer when we look at the specific episodes where Kant addresses question (a).

Having distinguished two meanings of Kant's question, I wish to suggest, at the risk of some oversimplification, that in the Aesthetic, Kant takes his question in sense (a), whereas in the Analytic and the Dialectic, he takes it in sense (b). In the Aesthetic, Kant provides an explanation, in terms of the pure intuitions (especially space), of how we succeed in making certain synthetic *a priori* judgments. In the Analytic, on the other hand, he advances a proof, or rather a series of related proofs, that certain *a priori* synthetic judgments are possible. Finally, in the Dialectic, he argues that certain synthetic *a priori* judgments are not possible or legitimate.

The explanation for these different ways of proceeding is that the judgments that Kant is concerned with in the Aesthetic, Analytic, and Dialectic concern different areas of knowledge. In the Aesthetic, Kant is concerned with the propositions of mathematics, especially of geometry, which he takes to be obviously synthetic *a priori*. In the Analytic, he is concerned with what he regards as the basic synthetic *a priori* principles underlying all our knowledge of the natural world, especially physics. In the Dialectic, he is concerned with the claims of transcendent metaphysics. This is reflected in the fourfold way in which Kant himself interprets his simplifying question in the Introduction to the *Critique*:

> In the solution of the above problem [i.e., the problem of how synthetic *a priori* judgments are possible], we are at the same time deciding as to the possibility of the employment of pure reason in establishing and developing all those sciences which contain a theoretical *a priori* knowledge of objects, and have therefore to answer the questions:
>
> How is pure mathematics possible?
>
> How is pure science of nature possible?
>
> . . .
>
> How is metaphysics, as natural disposition, possible?
>
> . . .
>
> How is metaphysics, as science, possible? (B 20)

The first two questions are addressed, respectively, in the Aesthetic and the Analytic, the last two in the Dialectic.

My discussion so far implies that Kant had different views about what needed to be shown concerning mathematics, natural science, and metaphysics. We must now look at the reasons for his different attitudes toward mathematics, on the one hand, and science and metaphysics, on the other hand. To bring these reasons out, let us compare a proposition of Euclidean geometry with the principle that every event must have a cause—a principle that will underlie either only natural science or both science and metaphysics, depending on whether it applies only to the empirical world or to a nonempirical reality as well. Let us compare what Kant evidently took to be his task with respect to each of these propositions.

Consider first a proposition of geometry, for instance, Kant's own example that "the straight line between two points is the shortest." In the first place, Kant was certain that such a proposition is *a priori* because its truth is necessary and strictly universal: there is and can be no exception to it; of this Kant was sure. (The strict universality of the proposition is more obvious when it is stated as an explicit generalization: "Given any two points, the shortest line between them is a straight line.") Hence it cannot be an *a posteriori* proposition whose truth rests on experience; it must be an *a priori* proposition whose truth is independent of experience. But in the second place, Kant was certain that the proposition is synthetic, not analytic. To understand why he was confident of this, consider the brief passage where he discusses the proposition:

> Just as little is any fundamental proposition of pure geometry analytic. That the straight line between two points is the shortest, is a synthetic proposition. For my concept of straight contains nothing of quantity, but only of quality. The concept of the shortest is wholly an addition, and cannot be derived through any process of analysis, from the concept of the straight line. Intuition, therefore, must here be called in: only by its aid is the synthesis possible. (B 16)

Kant is evidently saying something like the following. It is no part of the concept of a straight line that it is also the shortest distance between two points, for mere reflection on the *qualitative* notion of a straight line fails to reveal any connection with the *quantitative* notion of being the shortest line between two points. Therefore, the proposition is not analytic. So it must be synthetic. But its necessity and strict universality shows that it is also *a priori*. Therefore, it is both synthetic and *a priori*. Kant regards this little piece of reasoning as totally sufficient to show that his example (and all other geometrical propositions) is synthetic *a priori*. Whether he is right need not concern us for the time being. For now, I only want to call attention to the fact that Kant takes the synthetic *a priori* character of geometry as virtually an unquestionable datum, requiring only a very simple argument to establish it. But he does admit that this datum calls for an explanation, for, if it is not reflection on such concepts as 'straight line' and 'shortest line' and 'point' that reveals the necessity and strict universality of geometrical propositions, then, Kant wants to know, what does reveal it? His answer, which will be given in the Aesthetic, is hinted at in the final sentence in the passage: "Intuition, therefore, must be called in; only by its aid is the synthesis possible." We will consider what this means in the next chapter. The point I want to establish now is that Kant takes the synthetic *a priori* nature of geometry not as something to be proved but as something to be explained. Thus he regards question (a) as the only important question to be raised about the mathematical propositions that he is concerned with in the Aesthetic.

But now, what about the propositions that Kant will consider in the Logic, such as the causal principle (the principle that every event must have a cause)? Would it have been satisfactory for Kant to begin by assuming that this principle is a necessarily and universally true synthetic *a priori* proposition, and then merely to ask for an explanation of how we can know its truth? Kant's early writings, and particularly his inaugural dissertation of 1770, show that for a period of time, he did indeed regard this as a satisfactory way of formulating his problem. Indeed, during this "Pre-Critical" period (as it is called) in the development of his thought, Kant even assumed that causality and the other pure concepts could be applied outside the field of possible experience so as to yield *a priori* knowledge of a nonempirical reality, which he called "the intelligible world." Kant was then under the influence of the German rationalist Christian Wolff, who was himself a follower of Leibniz. Wolff specialized in composing systematic textbook versions of Leibniz's philosophy, which was presented in this form to German students, including the young Kant. Once he had digested these books, Kant freely engaged in the metaphysical disputes of the day, concerning the ultimate nature of the universe as supposedly known by pure intellect unassisted by any sense experience. In one important respect, it is true, Kant's position already differed from that of Wolff. This was in his theory of space and time, which is essentially the same in Kant's dissertation of 1770 and in the *Critique*, which appeared eleven years later. Already in the dissertation, Kant argues that space and time are pure intuitions. This, as will be seen in the following chapter, is essentially the doctrine of the Transcendental Aesthetic. But apart from this important exception, Kant was during his Pre-Critical period a thoroughgoing rationalist. The problem as he saw it was not to prove that the pure concepts of cause and substance apply to nonempirical reality but only to explain how they do so. As for the question of whether they apply to the natural world described by the sciences, Kant did not even see this as a problem.

Some time after the publication of his Dissertation, however, Kant's development took a new turn. First, he began to wonder how pure concepts can possibly relate to a nonempirical reality or intelligible world. After all, these concepts spring directly from the mind; they are not caused by, nor do they cause, the nonempirical reality. How then, being so to speak completely divorced from that reality, can they yield any knowledge of it?[18] Second, he began to appreciate the force of Hume's attack on rationalist views concerning the principle of causality. Kant himself describes the effect that Hume's arguments had on him in a famous statement in the *Prolegomena to Any Future Metaphysics:* "I openly confess my recollection of David Hume was the very thing which many years ago interrupted my dogmatic slumber and gave my investigation in the field of speculative philosophy a quite new direction."[19]

Why should Hume's arguments have "awoken Kant from his dogmatic slumber?" Let us note just one point about Hume's arguments concerning the causal principle: that those arguments do not merely show that the causal principle cannot be applied to a nonempirical reality. They go much deeper than that, for they are intended to show that even if we restrict ourselves to events in the natural or empirical world, we cannot know *a priori* that all such events must have causes. All we can say is that all the events that we have so far observed have had causes, from which we may infer inductively that probably all events in the natural world have causes. In other words, we cannot say that the causal principle is necessary and strictly universal; rather, for Hume it is only an empirical generalization. Now, Kant regards this result as totally unacceptable, for it threatens not only rationalist metaphysics but also physical science as Kant conceives it. Kant believed that the Newtonian physics that he knew rests on the principle that every event must have a cause. So he saw Hume's critique of that principle as undermining not only rationalist metaphysics but also physics. So in the constructive part of the *Critique,* he tries to show that the principle can be reinstated as an *a priori* truth, as long as its application is restricted to possible experience. In this way, he seeks to safeguard the certainty of physics, without legitimizing traditional metaphysics.[20]

Let us conclude this introduction by relating what has been said to some useful terminology. In the Transcendental Aesthetic, we should expect what Kant scholars call a "regressive" argument. This is an argument that starts by assuming that certain synthetic *a priori* judgments are possible, and it proceeds to give an explanation of this fact. A regressive argument, then, provides an answer to the question about synthetic *a priori* judgments, taken only in sense (a): "Assuming that synthetic *a priori* judgments are possible, what is the explanation of the fact that they are possible?" The judgments that Kant will assume to be synthetic *a priori* are those of mathematics and especially geometry, and the general explanation of their synthetic *a priori* status will be that space and time are pure intuitions. In the Analytic, on the other hand, we should expect what Kant scholars calls a "progressive" argument. This is an argument that proves the possibility of certain synthetic *a priori* judgments by deducing it from basic premises that even a skeptic must acknowledge. Such an argument, if valid, provides an affirmative answer to the question about synthetic *a priori* judgments, taken in sense (b): "Are synthetic *a priori* judgments really possible, and if so what is the proof that they are possible?"

Kant has his own set of terms for the regressive and progressive forms of argument. He calls the regressive form the "analytical method," and the progressive form the "synthetical" method. This use of the terms has nothing to do with the analytic/synthetic distinction. It figures prominently in the early sections of the *Prolegomena to Any Future Metaphysics*. There Kant points out that whereas (most of) the *Critique of Pure Reason* proceeds synthetically, the *Prolegomena* proceeds analytically. This is an important difference between the *Critique* and the *Prolegomena*, and it accounts for the much greater importance and bulk of the *Critique*. For throughout the *Prolegomena* Kant simply assumes that mathematics, as well as the causal principle, are synthetic *a priori* and proceeds to ask what makes them possible. In the *Critique*, on the other hand, Kant does this only in the Aesthetic, where he is concerned with mathematical knowledge.

Having said this, I must warn the reader that in the *Critique*, Kant does not always keep the two methods of exposition distinct; instead, he frequently runs them together, which often gives his arguments an air of vicious circularity. There is a very stark example of this in the Introduction. Just after raising the questions "How is pure mathematics possible?" and "How is pure science of Nature possible?" Kant goes on to say:

> Since these sciences actually exist, it is quite possible to ask how they are possible; for that they must be possible is proved by the fact that they exist. (B 20–21)

This makes it sound as though Kant is simply going to assume that we have *a priori* knowledge of the synthetic principles underlying natural science, for instance, the causal principle. But if Kant made this assumption, then he would be assuming the very thing that Hume denied and would thus be begging the question. There are many passages in the Analytic where Kant does in fact argue in this regressive manner. As I shall try to show, however, the Analytic also contains a progressive argument, which does not assume, but attempts to prove, the possibility of the synthetic *a priori* principles that Kant regards as basic to our knowledge of nature.[21]

Geometry, Space, and Transcendental Idealism

2.1 The Nature of Space and the Argument from Geometry

We have seen that Kant gives only a very brief argument for his view that the propositions of geometry are synthetic *a priori*. This is the argument, given in the *Critique's* Introduction, that although geometrical propositions are necessary and strictly universal, they cannot be known by mere reflection on concepts. Kant's example, you will recall, is the proposition that *the straight line between two points is the shortest.* Kant argues that this proposition is *a priori* because it is necessarily true and there can be no exception to its truth (it is "necessary and strictly universal"), and that it is synthetic because its truth cannot be determined just by analyzing the concepts "straight line" and "shortest distance between two points." Therefore, the proposition is both synthetic and *a priori.* Kant regards this simple argument as decisive, which is why I said that he takes the synthetic *a priori* status of geometry as virtually an unquestionable datum.

On the other hand, Kant does think that this datum calls for an explanation, for it affirms that one can know that a proposition is necessarily true, in spite of the fact that its truth does not follow from the meanings of its constituent terms. But if its truth does not follow from the meanings of its constituent terms, then what does its truth depend on? We cannot of course reply that it depends upon facts known by experience, for experience could show us only that up to now a straight line has always been the shortest distance between two points; it cannot show us that this must be so. Thus the truth of the proposition depends neither upon meanings nor upon empirical facts. What then does it depend upon? This question must be answered if we are to understand how the synthetic *a priori* status of geometry is possible.

Kant's answer is hinted at, as we have seen, by his statement that "intuition must be called in; only by its aid is the synthesis possible." What does this hint mean, and how does Kant follow up on it in the Transcendental Aesthetic?

First, let us recall that "intuition" for Kant always refers to something presented or given to a knower, whether in sensory awareness or imagination. Thus, when Kant says that "intuition must be called in," he evidently means that the truth of a geometrical proposition depends on something that can be presented or given to a knower. He is evidently saying that in order to grasp a geometrical truth, one must perform a kind of experiment in imagination or physically: one must construct something in imagination, with pencil and paper, or in some similar manner. As Kant puts it, you must "give yourself an object in intuition" (A 47–48/ B 65). To revert to the example of how I know that the shortest line between two points must be a straight line, the construction I must generate or the intuition I must give myself is as follows. I imagine or actually draw two points and several different lines connecting them, including a straight line, as shown in figure 2–1. Having done this, I see at once that the straight line between the two points is the shortest one. But that is not all that I see. I see not only that the straight line *is* the shortest one but also that it *must* be, and that there could not be any exception to this truth. I thus know that the proposition *the straight line between two points is the shortest one* (or that *given any two points, the shortest line between them is a straight line*) is a necessary and strictly universal truth, yet one not based on conceptual relations or meanings. In other words, I have an item of synthetic *a priori* knowledge.

However, this explanation is so far incomplete, for it does not yet explain what it is about the intuition that I have given myself that renders it necessary that the straight line between two points is the shortest one. In other words, we have yet to identify or isolate the factor in the experiment that accounts for the necessity and strict universality of the proposition that the straight line between two points is the shortest one. What is this factor?

Kant's answer is that it is the nature of space. It is because of the nature or structure of space that a straight line not only is but also must be the shortest distance between two points. More generally, it is the nature or structure of space that accounts for the necessity and strict universality of all geometrical propositions. Furthermore, geometry is the science of space, in that geometrical principles describe the nature or structure of space.

This answer plunged Kant into the middle of one of the most heated controversies of eighteenth-century philosophy and science. This controversy concerned

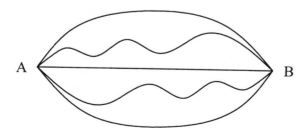

FIGURE 2–1

the true, metaphysical nature of space; it was a controversy over the question "What is space?" Since Kant was now committed to the thesis that it is the nature of space that explains the synthetic *a priori* status of geometry, he could not avoid this question. There were two parties to the controversy: the followers of Newton and the followers of Leibniz. Kant worked out his own position by reflecting on the opposed positions of these two thinkers.

According to Newton, space is *both real and absolute.* Space for Newton is real in that it exists independently of any mind (except possibly God's mind: Newton refers to space as "God's sensorium"). It is absolute in that it also exists independently of any objects in space, so that space—empty space—would still exist even if there were absolutely nothing in it. So for Newton, space is a kind of absolute container of all the things in it. Newton's reason for holding this view is that he was convinced that it was the only view compatible with his laws of motion, that is, the only tenable view, scientifically speaking, no matter what its metaphysical implications might be.

According to Leibniz, on the other hand, space is *both ideal and relative.* This view is bound up with Leibniz's metaphysics, according to which all existence is made up of simple substances called monads. Since the monads are absolutely simple and indivisible, they are not spatial: they have no shapes, sizes, or volumes, only perceptions. And since all existence is made up of these nonspatial entities, space cannot be something real, as Newton claims. Instead, space is ideal: it is merely something that appears in the perceptions of the monads, rather than something that really exists. For Leibniz, this does not mean that space is totally unreal, for even an appearance has some degree of reality, just as a rainbow has some degree of reality, to use Leibniz's own analogy. Leibniz calls space a "well-founded phenomenon," meaning that although it is merely an appearance, it has a foundation in the (perceptions of) the nonspatial monads, somewhat as the colored bands in a rainbow have their foundation in transparent droplets of water. Furthermore, for Leibniz space is also relative, rather than absolute, as for Newton. This means that for Leibniz space is nothing but a set of relations between the things that are said to be in space. For example, the space in a room is nothing over and above a set of relations between the various pieces of furniture and other objects said to be in the room. Thus if space were totally empty, then it would not make sense to talk of there being places in space; nor indeed would it make sense to talk of there being such a thing as space at all.

Kant's position on space, which he first put forward in his Inaugural Dissertation of 1770 and which remained essentially unchanged in the *Critique*, is a kind of compromise between Newton's and Leibniz's positions—an attempt to extract what Kant sees as the element of truth in each position and to combine it with the element of truth in the other. But the importance of Kant's position goes beyond the fact that it provided an alternative to the Newtonian and the Leibnizian views. For Kant, it also served as the stimulus or springboard for the famous "Copernican Revolution in Philosophy" that he announces in the Preface to the second edition of the *Critique*, and which I shall describe in the next section.

Kant's position on space (and on time too; he treats these in the same way) is as follows: space is *ideal and absolute.* Thus Newton is wrong in holding space to be real but right in holding it to be absolute, and Leibniz is wrong in holding space to be relative but right in holding it to be ideal. Let us look first at Kant's reasons for this view and then at its implications.

Kant's argument against Newton's view goes this way:

> Those who maintain the absolute reality of space and time . . . have to admit two eternal and infinite self-subsistent non-entities (space and time), which are there [i.e., which exist] (yet without there being anything real) only in order to contain in themselves all that is real. (A 39/B 56)

This seems like a weak argument. Kant seems to be saying that anyone who maintains that space is real must maintain also, and self-contradictorily, that (a) it is unreal ["there (yet without there being anything real")], and must hold as well that (b) it contains in itself things that are real. No doubt this would be an absurd position, but why should a Newtonian grant point (a), that space is unreal? Newton's view is just the opposite. So this "argument" seems to be little more than a dogmatic denial of Newton's view. Kant is evidently saying that the notion of an eternal, infinite, and self-subsistent space (and time) is absurd—a metaphysical monstrosity—but he has not shown that it is. As we shall see shortly, however, he has another reason, one closely related to his "Copernican Revolution in Philosophy," for rejecting the idea that space is real.

Kant's argument against Leibniz's view that space is relative is stated immediately after his rejection of Newton's view. It goes this way:

> If they . . . regard space . . . as relations of appearances, alongside . . . one another—relations abstracted from experience, and in this isolation confusedly represented—they are obliged to deny that *a priori* mathematical doctrines have any validity in respect of real things (for instance, in space), or at least to deny their apodeictic certainty. For such certainty is not to be found in the *a posteriori*. (A 39–40/B 56–57)

Kant is arguing that if space is just certain relations between things [whether we call these "appearances," as Kant here does (for reasons to be considered later), is irrelevant to the argument], then we must deny the synthetic *a priori* status of geometry. For remember that according to Kant, the propositions of geometry describe the structure of space. So if space is just certain relations between things said to be in space, then what the propositions of geometry describe is just those relations. But those relations can be known only *a posteriori*, on the basis of experience. For example, that a particular table is to the left of a particular desk is a fact that can be known only by experience, and the same holds for the spatial relations between any objects. Therefore, if space were just those relations, then the propositions of geometry would depend on facts known by experience and so could not have the necessity, strict universality, and certainty that they in fact possess. Kant concludes, therefore, that although Leibniz is right in thinking that space is ideal, he is wrong in thinking that it is relative. Space is ideal and absolute.

Let us now develop more fully what Kant means by saying that space is ideal; this is important if we are to grasp why Kant believes that his theory about the nature of space explains the synthetic *a priori* status of geometry. We may start by quoting a passage where Kant himself states what the nature of space must be in order for it to explain the synthetic *a priori* status of geometry. The passage is the core of what Kant calls the "Transcendental Exposition of the Concept of Space," and he introduces it by telling us what he means by such an exposition:

> I understand by a transcendental exposition the explanation of a concept, as a principle from which the possibility of . . . *a priori* synthetic knowledge can be understood. For this purpose it is required (1) that such knowledge does really flow from the given concept, and (2) that this knowledge is possible only on the assumption of a given mode of explaining the concept. (B 40)

The passage goes this way (I have used ellipses to bring out only the basic line of argument, but the reader is urged to compare the quoted material with Kant's text):

> Geometry is a science which determines the properties of space synthetically, and yet *a priori*. What then, must be our representation of space, in order that such knowledge of it may be possible? It must in its origin be an intuition. . . . Further, this intuition must be *a priori*, that is, it must be found in us prior to any perception of an object. . . . How, then, can there exist . . . an . . . intuition which precedes the objects themselves? . . . Manifestly, not otherwise than in so far as the intuition has its seat in the subject only, as the formal character of the subject. . . . Our explanation is thus the only explanation that makes intelligible the *possibility* of geometry, as a body of *a priori* synthetic knowledge. (B 41)

A little later, Kant goes on to say that

> Space does not represent any determination that attaches to the objects themselves, and which remains even when abstraction has been made of all the subjective conditions of intuition. . . . It is the subjective condition of sensibility, under which alone outer intuition is possible for us. . . . It is, therefore, solely from the human standpoint that we can speak of space. . . . If we depart from the subjective condition under which alone we can have outer intuition, namely, liability to be affected by objects, the representation of space stands for nothing whatsoever. (A 26/B 42)

These two quotations reveal that when Kant asserts that space is ideal, he means something much stronger than that space is something that appears rather than something fully real. Kant gives Leibniz's theory a new twist that radically transforms its significance. For Kant, to say that space is ideal (or "transcendentally ideal," as his complete expression goes) means that it is *a permanent, built-in feature of the human knower, as opposed to something that exists independently of the knower.* An analogy invented by one of Kant's foremost twentieth-century English commentators, H. J. Paton, should help to introduce Kant's view.[1] Suppose that a man has a pair of blue-tinted glasses permanently and irremovably affixed to his head. On the one hand, it is obvious that the man does not create or even alter the things he sees through the glasses. On the other hand, it is obvious that he can never see anything except as blue. But finally, just to the extent that the way he sees things (i.e., as blue) is determined by the glasses rather than by the object seen, it is necessary for him to see them that way, and he can know in advance of experience that he will always see things as blue. Kant's doctrine of the ideality of space is that just as the man in the analogy has a permanently fixed pair of blue glasses that makes everything he sees appear blue, so humans are equipped with a cognitive faculty, which Kant calls "sensibility," that makes everything that we perceive appear spatial. To put the point a bit more carefully, since Kant does not think that introspectible items like emotions or thoughts are spatial, human sensibility makes everything that we perceive as being *other* than our own subjective states of mind appear spatial. Kant expresses this view in several different ways, for example, by saying that space is a "subjective condition of intuition," a "form of sensibility," a "pure form of intuition," and the "form of outer sense."

Kant believes that only this view can account for the fact that the propositions of geometry are necessarily true. (I think that this belief is his chief reason for rejecting the Newtonian view of space as something that exists independently of human knowers). Thus, Kant's reasoning in the "Transcendental Exposition of the Concept of Space," in the next-to-last quotation above, can be summarized in the following "Argument from Geometry":

(1) The propositions of geometry are synthetic *a priori*.
(2) This is possible only if space is a subjective condition of intuition.

∴ Space is a subjective condition of intuition.

This is the regressive argument I alluded to earlier, in which Kant starts from the synthetic *a priori* status of geometry as a datum and seeks to offer an explanation of it. The argument is essentially one from the *necessary* character of geometrical propositions to the *subjective* character of what those propositions describe. This link between the necessary and the subjective is the nerve of the argument, and the argument stands or falls depending on the legitimacy of such a link.

2.2 The Doctrine of Transcendental Idealism

Legitimate or not, the connection that Kant makes between necessity and subjectivity is the heart of a central doctrine of the *Critique*, the doctrine known as Transcendental Idealism. This doctrine was probably suggested to Kant by his argument from geometry, and in turning to it now, we are trying to reproduce the progression of his own thought.

The best way to become acquainted with Transcendental Idealism is to read a famous passage from the Preface to the second edition of the *Critique*:

> Hitherto it has been assumed that all our knowledge must conform to objects. But all attempts to extend our knowledge of objects by establishing something in regard to them *a priori*, by means of concepts, have, on this assumption ended in failure. We must therefore make trial whether we may not have more success in the tasks of metaphysics, if we suppose that objects must conform to our knowledge. This would agree better with what is desired, namely, that it should be possible to have knowledge of objects *a priori*, determining something in regard to them prior to their being given. We should then be proceeding precisely on the lines of Copernicus' primary hypothesis. Failing of satisfactory progress in explaining the movements of the heavenly bodies on the supposition that they all revolved round the spectator, he tried whether he might not have better success

if he made the spectator to revolve and the stars to remain at rest. A similar experiment can be tried in metaphysics, as regards the *intuition* of objects. If intuition must conform to the constitution of the objects, I do not see how we could know anything of the latter *a priori*; but if the object (as object of the senses) must conform to the constitution of our faculty of intuition, I have no difficulty in conceiving such a possibility. (B xvi–xvii)

In this passage Kant announces what he called the "Copernican Revolution in Philosophy," whose basic idea is as follows. All previous philosophy has assumed that in knowing, it is the nature of the thing known that determines the content of our knowledge. It has never occurred to any philosopher to question this assumption. But on this assumption, it is impossible to understand how we can have synthetic *a priori* knowledge about the thing known, for things are presented to human knowers in experience, which can never yield any knowledge of necessity. Suppose, then, that we stand the traditional assumption on its head. Instead of assuming that it is the object known that dictates the content of knowledge to the knowing subject, suppose that the knowing subject contributes to the object as known certain of its structural features. This will not mean that the knower creates or even alters things as they are in themselves. Nor will it mean that knowers need be aware of the fact that they are contributing to the content of knowledge. But it will mean that in knowing, humans unconsciously and inevitably, because of their own, built-in nature, impose on the object as known certain of its basic structural features. It will also mean that we can never know things as they are in themselves, apart from our own special contribution to the content of knowledge. But finally, Kant believes that just to the extent that this knowledge is determined by the knowing subject rather than the object known, it will be necessary, *a priori* knowledge.

We have already seen that one of the structural features that Kant holds to be imposed by our minds on objects is none other than their spatiality. But this is not all: Kant treats *time* in a strictly parallel manner. For Kant, time, no less than space, is a built-in feature of the human knower, a "pure form of intuition" or an "*a priori* intuition." That Kant treats time in the same way as space is evident from passages like these:

> Time is not something which exists of itself, or which inheres in things as an objective determination, and it does not, therefore, remain when abstraction is made of all subjective conditions of its intuition. . . . [T]ime is nothing but the subjective condition under which alone intuition can take place in us. (A 33/B 49)

> Time is therefore a purely subjective condition of our (human) intuition . . . and in itself, apart from the subject, is nothing. (A 35/B 51)

> Time and space, taken together, are the pure forms of all sensible intuition . . . if the subject, or even only the subjective condition of the senses in general, be removed, the whole constitution and all the relations of objects in space and time, nay space and time themselves, would vanish. (A39/B 56–A 42/B 59)

> [T]he conditions of space and time [are] conditions which are originally inherent in the subject. (A 43/B 60)

It is . . . indubitably certain, that space and time, as the necessary conditions of all outer and inner experience, are merely subjective conditions of all our intuition. (A 48–49/B 66)

In one respect, however, time is an even more fundamental form of intuition than space, for, Kant holds, only objects of *outer* intuition or "outer sense"—that is, objects perceived as being distinct from oneself and from conscious states of oneself—have to be spatial. By contrast, *all* objects of intuition, whether they are distinct from the self and its conscious states or merely conscious states of the self, like mental images or thoughts or emotions, must be given to us in time. Since even such purely introspectible items must be experienced in time, time is properly the form of inner intuition or, as Kant also calls it, "inner sense." But since all experienced items—whether "inner" or "outer"—must be in time, Kant declares:

> Time is the formal *a priori* condition of all appearances whatsoever. Space, as the form of all outer intuition, is so far limited; it serves as the *a priori* condition only of outer appearances. But since all representations, whether they have for their objects outer things or not, belong, in themselves, as determinations of the mind, to our inner state; and since this inner state stands under the formal condition of inner intuition, and so belongs to time, time is an *a priori* condition of all appearance whatsoever. (A 34/B 50)

The upshot is that all of our intuitions must be presented to us in a spatiotemporal framework—that everything we encounter in intuition must be in time and that everything we encounter as an object distinct from ourselves and our own conscious states must also be in space.

But this is still not all there is to Kant's Copernican Revolution in Philosophy; the human knower's built-in features include even more than the pure forms of intuition or pure forms of sensibility. To see what more they include, consider the next few sentences of the passage from the *Critique's* second-edition Preface, quoted above, where Kant is announcing his Copernican Revolution:

> Since I cannot rest in these intuitions if they are to become known, but must relate them as representations to something as their object, and determine this latter through them, either I must assume that the *concepts*, by means of which I obtain this determination, conform to the object, or else I assume that the objects, or what is the same thing, that the *experience* in which alone, as given objects, they can be known, conform to the concepts. In the former case, I am again in the same perplexity as to how I can know anything *a priori* in regard to the objects. In the latter case the outlook is more hopeful. For experience is itself a species of knowledge which involves understanding; and understanding has rules which I must presuppose as being in me prior to objects being given to me, and therefore as being *a priori*. They find expression in *a priori* concepts to which all objects of experience necessarily conform, and with which they must agree. (B xvii–xviii)

What Kant has just said is that the knower's built-in features include the pure concepts or categories of the understanding, as well as the forms of intuition, for knowledge requires both intuitions and concepts; as Kant puts it: "I cannot rest in these intuitions if they are to become known." But again, concepts can yield synthetic *a priori* knowledge only if they are imposed upon experience rather than being abstracted from experience. Kant's position, then, is that both the forms of intuition and the pure concepts of the understanding are permanent, built-in features of human knowers. From this it follows that (1) all intuitions must be given to us in a spatiotemporal framework, that is, at least in time or else in both time and space, and that (2) all intuitions must be conceptualizable in certain basic ways, such as substance and cause. Furthermore, it also follows that we can never know what things are like apart from the ways in which they appear to us in sensibility's forms of intuition and are conceptualized by the understanding's categories. We can never know what Kant calls "things-in-themselves" or "noumena," as opposed to appearances or phenomena. Yet the things in themselves are needed if one is to avoid saying, as Kant certainly wishes to avoid saying, that we just create reality.

If there is any one doctrine that Kant seems to have been most fond and proud of, and which he insists upon most strongly in the *Critique*, it is this doctrine of Transcendental Idealism. Perhaps it is not hard to see why Kant was so wedded to this doctrine: it seemed to provide a way of establishing both the constructive and the destructive tasks of the *Critique*. On the one hand, it implies that we can have *a priori* knowledge of the experienced world, for that world must conform to our forms of intuition and pure concepts. It must, in brief, be a system of substances causally interacting in space and time. Thus, Humean skepticism is answered. But on the other hand, we can have no knowledge of a nonempirical, transcendent reality; since we cannot know things apart from the ways they appear to us in sensibility and are conceptualized by our understanding. Thus rationalist metaphysics, or dogmatic metaphysics as Kant calls it, is definitively shown to be impossible.

However, these two goals are achieved at a huge cost. The natural world that we know is identified with appearance, and the nonempirical realm that we do not know is identified with reality. As P. F. Strawson puts it:

> The doctrine is not just that we can have no knowledge of a supersensible [nonempirical] reality, but that reality *is* supersensible and that we can have no knowledge of it [emphasis added].[2]

In a word, we can know appearances but not reality. Later, we shall ask whether it is possible to interpret Kant's doctrine of Transcendental Idealism in a way that avoids this paradoxical consequence.

Kant himself, however, seems to have welcomed the consequence, for it harmonized well with the moral and religious interests that are in the background of his arguments in the *Critique of Pure Reason* and come to the fore in his other works. It allowed Kant to draw firmly the line between the sphere of knowledge and that of "faith," and to add that whereas knowledge is confined to appearances, faith may attach itself to reality.

2.3 The Argument from Geometry and Other Arguments Regarding Space

In the preceding two sections, I expounded Kant's argument from geometry and the doctrine of Transcendental Idealism to which it led him. In this section, I want to examine critically the argument from geometry, as well as to examine some additional arguments that Kant gives in the Transcendental Aesthetic to support his view that space is an *a priori* form of intuition.

2.3.1 Two Criticisms of the Argument from Geometry

The argument from geometry, you will recall, goes this way:

(1) The propositions of geometry are synthetic *a priori*.
(2) This is possible only if space is a subjective condition of intuition.

∴ Space is a subjective condition of intuition.

In defense of premise (1), Kant uses this example: "the straight line between two points is the shortest." It can be argued, however, that this example fails to show that geometrical propositions are synthetic *a priori*,[3] for there are basically two ways of defining "straight line." For certain purposes, the term can be defined like this:

D1: L is a straight line = *df* there is no line with the same endpoints as L that is shorter than L.

For certain other purposes, the term can be defined this way:

D2: L is a straight line = *df* L is the path taken by a light ray (through a medium of uniform refraction index); or L is the path along which a stretched cord lies when its tension is stretched without limit.

On D1, the proposition that *the straight line between two points is the shortest* is analytic *a priori*, for on D1, we may substitute the following expression for the term "straight line" in that proposition: "line, such that there is no line having the same endpoints as it has that is shorter than it is." But when we make this substitution into our proposition, the result is this: "The line, such that there is no line having the same endpoints as it has that is shorter than it is, is the shortest line between two points," which is an analytic statement. On D2, on the other hand, the proposition that *the straight line between two points is the shortest* is synthetic *a posteriori*, for on D2, we may replace the term "straight line" in this proposition with the expression "path taken by a light ray (through a medium of uniform refraction index)" or the expression "path along which along which a stretched cord lies when its tension is stretched without limit." But when we make these substitutions into the proposition, the result is either "The path taken by a light ray (through a medium of uniform refraction index) is the shortest distance between two points" or "The path along which a stretched cord lies when its tension is stretched without limit is the shortest distance between two points," both of which are synthetic *a posteriori*. It is not an *a priori* truth, but rather an empirical discovery, that a light ray traveling from point A to point B through a medium of kind K takes the shortest route from A to B; likewise, it is not an *a priori* truth, but an empirical discovery, that a cord that is pulled forcefully from opposite directions traverses the shortest distance between the two points from which the pulling originates. The upshot is that on D1, the proposition that *the straight line between two points is the shortest* is analytic *a priori*, whereas on D2, it is synthetic *a posteriori*. So whichever definition of "straight line" is used, this proposition is, contra Kant, not synthetic *a priori*. Rather, it is either analytic *a priori* or synthetic *a posteriori*, just as an empiricist opponent of Kant would claim. Therefore, assuming that other geometrical propositions are susceptible to a similar analysis, premise (1) of the argument from geometry seems to be false.

Premise (2) is also open to a damaging objection. The key idea of premise (2), as I have said, is the link between subjectivity and necessity: the subjective nature of space is supposed to explain the necessity of geometrical truths. But, the objection goes, how can the necessary truth of a proposition be explained by a *contingent fact* about the human mind? Kant's view implies that if the nature of the human mind changed—if the ways humans structure their experience changed—then the propositions in question would become *false*. How, then, can they be *necessarily* true?

2.3.2 Other Arguments Regarding Space

In a section called "Metaphysical Exposition of this Concept" (i.e., the concept of space), Kant presents four arguments to support his view that space is an *a priori* intuition.[4] Although Kant gives these arguments just before the "Transcendental Exposition of Space" that contains the Argument from Geometry, in this subsection I shall inquire whether they can support the conclusion that this argument fails to establish. I shall argue that they cannot do so, though they do make a number of other important points.

Before looking at Kant's arguments, we should be sure that we understand the distinction that they all presuppose, between an intuition and a concept. "Intuition," as we have already seen, is Kant's most general term for the items to which concepts can be applied. Intuitions are essentially singular: one and the same intuition cannot occur twice, though two intuitions could be exactly alike except for their spatial or temporal positions. For example, two different sightings of a dog could be exactly alike except for occurring at different times or in different places, but even if they were exactly alike, they would be two numerically distinct dog sightings, not just one dog sighting. By contrast, a concept is essentially general, in the sense that one and the same concept can have many instances. For example, the concept 'dog' has all dogs as its instances, and even if there were no dogs, it would remain possible for there to be dogs to serve as instances of the concept. This point can also be put by saying that the terms "class concept" and "general concept" (the latter of which Kant uses in this section) are redundant: it is the nature of a concept to designate a class or to apply generally. It might be objected that a concept like 'round square' cannot have any instances. But even if we grant the questionable claim that there is such a concept as 'round square,' it remains true that if it could have any instances at all, it could have more than one.

According to Kant, concepts and intuitions can each be either empirical or *a priori* ("pure"). An empirical concept is one that is derived from sensory experience or introspective awareness, like the concepts 'dog' or 'joy,' respectively; a pure concept is one that is not derived from such experience, like the concepts 'substance' and 'cause' (about which much more will be said later). An empirical intuition is one that is obtained in sensory experience or introspection, like the sight of a dog or the feeling of joy. A pure intuition is one that, although not obtained in sensory or perceptual experience, necessarily characterizes or "belongs" to some or to all empirical intuitions, like time space and time, respectively. Kant, as we will see more fully later, denies that space and time can themselves be perceived, but he holds that objects of sensory experience must be spatial and temporal and that introspected items must be temporal.

The purpose of the four arguments Kant gives in the "Metaphysical Exposition" of the concept of space is to show, cumulatively, that space is (a) *a priori* not empirical, (b) an intuition, not a concept, so that it can only be an *a priori* intuition.

The first argument goes this way:

> Space is not an empirical concept which has been derived from outer experiences. For in order that certain sensations be referred to something outside me (that is, to something in another region of space from that in which I find myself), and similarly in order that I may be able to represent them as outside and along-side one another, and accordingly not only as different but in different places, the representation of space must be presupposed. The representation of space cannot, therefore, be empirically obtained from the relations of outer appearance. On the contrary, this outer experience is itself possible . . . only through that representation. (A 23/B 38)

An initial question about how to interpret this argument is this: why does Kant state its conclusion as "space is not an empirical *concept*," when his view is that space is not a concept *at all*, but rather an intuition? I suggest that this is simply misleading language, for what Kant is here really arguing is that the *concept of space is* not an empirical concept; this argument is not about space per se but about the concept of space. (Of course, there can be a concept *of* space even if space is not itself a concept, just as there can be a concept of a dog even though a dog is not itself a concept.) The argument nevertheless bears on the nature of space itself (of what Kant here calls "the representation of space") because showing that the concept of space is not an empirical concept shows that *if* space is an intuition, then it must be a pure intuition since an empirical intuition could answer only to an empirical concept.

A second, more difficult question of interpretation arises from the second (and key) sentence of the passage. It might well appear that this sentence says only these two things:

- In order to perceive anything as existing spatially outside myself, I must perceive it as being in space.
- In order to perceive anything as existing spatially alongside or separate from other things, I must perceive it as being in space.

But these are truistic or tautologous claims, from which nothing of interest follows. Some recent commentators, however, have taken Kant to be making a much more interesting and important pair of claims:

- In order to perceive anything as existing distinct from myself, I must perceive it as being *spatially* outside myself.
- In order to perceive anything as being distinct from another thing(s), I must perceive the things as being *spatially* separate, or in different places.

Thus, focusing on the first members of these two pairs of claims, Henry Allison says:

> The . . . claim is that the representation of space must be presupposed if I am to refer my sensations to something "outside me" (*ausser mir*). . . . Since 'ausser' is normally a spatial term, the claim that space must be presupposed in order to refer my representations (sensations) to something ausser mir might appear to be a mere tautology. . . . This way of construing the argument, however, is misleading. The crucial point is that by 'outer sense' is meant a sense through which one can become perceptually aware of objects as distinct from the self and its states. . . . Consequently, Kant's claim that the representation of space functions as the condition by means of which we can become aware of things as ausser uns is [not] tautological . . . it is at least conceivable that some other "sensible beings" might possess this awareness under other conditions. . . . The gist of the . . . claim is, therefore, that the representation of space is the condition or presupposition of human awareness, but not of any conceivable awareness of objects as distinct from the self and its states. . . . What the argument claims is that the representation of space functions within human experience as a means or vehicle for the representation of objects as distinct from the self. . . . [5]

Allison's point is that Kant should not be taken as saying, tautologously, that in order to perceive anything as existing spatially outside myself, I must think of it as being in space. Rather, he should be taken as saying, much more significantly, that in order to perceive anything as existing distinct from myself, or as being *other* than myself, I must think of it as existing *spatially outside* myself. In the same vein, but focusing on both members of Kant's pair of claims, Paul Guyer says:

> [Kant's] argument sounds tautologous—objects cannot be represented in space unless they are represented in space—but comparison with the version of the argument in [Kant's] inaugural dissertation suggests that what Kant means is that objects cannot be represented as *distinct* from each other or the self *at all* except by being represented as having *diverse* spatial locations. [6]

Whether this is in fact what Kant meant to say might be disputed; after all, Kant does explicitly paraphrase "outside me" (*ausser mir*) as "in another region of space than that in which I find myself." [7] Furthermore, his language in his inaugural dissertation is only slightly less committal on the point:

> For I may only conceive of something as placed outside me by representing it as in a place which is different from the place in which I am myself; and I may only conceive of things outside one another by locating them in different places in space. [8]

For the Allison-Guyer interpretation to be correct, the words "placed outside me" must be taken in a nonspatial sense to mean simply "other than me" or "distinct from me," and the words "outside one another" must likewise be taken to mean merely "different from each other"—readings that might be questioned. Still, the Allison-Guyer reading makes what Kant is saying interesting rather than trivial, as well as essential for the development of crucial arguments that he advances later in the *Critique*, so I shall adopt it.

Reading Kant's passage in this way, we can extract from it the following argument for his conclusion that the concept of space is not an empirical concept:

(1) If the concept of space is an empirical concept derived by abstracting it from the perception of things distinct from oneself or separate from each other, then it must be possible to perceive things as distinct from oneself and separate from each other without already having the concept of space.

(2) In order to perceive anything as being distinct from oneself or separate from other things, one must perceive it as being spatially outside the self or spatially separate from other things.

(3) In order to perceive anything as being spatially outside the self or spatially separate from other things, one must already have the concept of space.

(4) In order to perceive anything as being distinct from oneself or separate from other things, one must already have the concept of space [from (2) and (3)].

(5) It is not the case that one can perceive things as distinct from oneself and separate from each other without already having the concept of space [from (4)].

(6) The concept of space is not an empirical concept derived by abstracting it from the perception of things distinct from oneself or separate from each other [from (1) and (5)].

This argument may well succeed in showing that the concept of space is a very fundamental one that we "bring" to experience rather than abstract from experience. But does it entail that space is a subjective condition of intuition that we contribute to objects or impose on them, or that it is a built-in feature of our own minds analogous to Paton's blue spectacles? The answer seems to be no, for even if the concept of space cannot be abstracted from experience, it does not follow that space isn't a feature of reality that exists independently of human minds. To be sure, one possible explanation of our having a concept of space that is not abstracted from experience would be that space is nothing but a subjective form of intuition. But that is not the only possible explanation, for it could also be that our nonempirical concept of space happens to correspond to a feature of reality. (Analogously, it has sometimes been pointed out that even if the man with blue spectacles must see everything as blue, reality itself might also be blue; this is called "the problem of the neglected alternative.") There might, for example, be a good evolutionary explanation of why human beings are hardwired to have the concept of space. Kant's only way of ruling out such alternative explanations of our having this concept would be to say that they do not account for the necessity and universality of geometrical truths, that is, to revert to his argument from geometry. But then the present argument gives no independent support for Kant's position.

Kant's second argument goes like this:

> Space is a necessary *a priori* representation, which underlies all outer intuitions. We can never represent to ourselves the absence of space, though we can quite well think it as empty of objects. It must therefore be regarded as the condition of the possibility of appearances, and not as a determination dependent upon them. (A 24/B 39)

This argument is very sparse; it seems to be nothing more than this:

(1) We can never represent to ourselves the absence of space.
(2) We can think of space as empty of objects.

∴ (3) Space is "a condition of the possibility of appearances, not a determination dependent upon them."

This argument gestures toward the fundamental importance or pervasiveness of space in human experience, but beyond that it is difficult to see how it lends any support to Kant's position. Peter Strawson expresses the difficulty very clearly:

> The ... argument turns on the assertions that *(a)* "we can never represent to ourselves the absence of space" though *(b)* "we can quite well think it as empty of objects." This suggests a kind of thought-experiment which we are invited to undertake. But ... it is far from clear what the experiment is or what its results imply. We can, say, close our eyes and imagine a featureless blackness; or say to ourselves the words "limitless empty space" and seem to be meaning something. Does this verify *(b)*? And, if so, what is shown thereby? Is it held that we could not do such things unless the spatial relatedness of items of which we are aware of as so related were entirely due to our cognitive constitution? This seems too large a step. What about *(a)*? Perhaps it means that we cannot really make intelligible to ourselves the conception of a wholly non-spatial experience. Perhaps we cannot indeed. But, if so, the point has still to be argued; and, if successfully argued, would only show that space was an *a priori* feature of experience in the sense of the austere interpretation [i.e., in the sense that "we cannot really make intelligible to ourselves the conception of" an experience that lacks this feature, in this case, the feature of spatiality] rather than in that of the transcendental idealist interpretation, of "*a priori*". To derive a transcendental idealist conclusion, we should need a further argument to show that no feature of experience could be *a priori* in the first sense without being *a priori* in the second.[9]

Kant's third argument is this:

> Space is not a discursive or, as we say, a general concept of relations of things in general, but a pure intuition. For, in the first place, we can represent to ourselves only one space; and if we speak of diverse spaces, we mean thereby only parts of one and the same unique space. Secondly, these parts cannot precede the one all-embracing space, as being, as it were, constituents out of which it can be composed; on the contrary, they can be thought only as *in* it. Space is essentially one; the manifold in it, and therefore the general concept of spaces, depends

solely on [the introduction of] limitations. Hence it follows that an *a priori*, and not an empirical, intuition underlies all concepts of space. (A 24–25/B 39)

The purpose of this argument, it would seem, is to support Kant's view that space itself is not a concept but rather a (pure) intuition. The argument can be reconstructed this way:

> (1) If space were a general concept, then it would be possible for it to have many instances.

This premise is unassailable: as we have seen, it is the nature of a (class or general) concept that it can have many instances. If someone thinks that 'round square' is a counterexample (despite what was said about this example above), then we can stipulate that (1) applies only to self-consistent concepts. The next and key premise is this:

> (2) Different spaces are parts of one unique space, not different instances of the concept of space.

This premise seems to be true: the space occupied by Yankee Stadium, for example, is not an instance of the concept of space as Yankee Stadium is an instance of the concept 'stadium'; rather, that space is a part of one all-embracing space. The next premise is this:

> (3) If (2) is true, then it is not possible for the concept of space to have many instances.

The thought behind this premise is that if different spaces are parts of space rather than instances of the concept of space, then the only possible candidates for being plural instances of the concept of space are disqualified; for what could these instances possibly be, if not parts of space? It seems, then, that the only instance of the concept of space is the totality of space itself. But from (2) and (3), this follows:

> (4) It is not possible for the concept of space to have many instances.

Furthermore, this follows from (1) and (4):

> (5) Space is not a general concept.

To arrive at Kant's conclusion, one further premise is needed:

> (6) If space is not a general concept, then it is a pure intuition.

It is clear enough, given Kant's dichotomy of concept and intuition, that if space is not a concept, then it is an intuition. But as previously indicated, the first argument of Kant's "Metaphysical Exposition" (the first argument discussed in the present subsection) has already shown that if space is an intuition, then it cannot be an empirical intuition; for then the concept of space would be an empirical concept—which that argument showed is not the case. Thus, premise (6) appears to be correct. But from that premise, together with (5), there follows Kant's conclusion:

(7)   Space is a pure intuition.

This seems to be a good argument, turning on some interesting conceptual points. But does it support the view that space is a *subjective* condition of intuition? The answer seems again to be: clearly not.

Kant's fourth argument is this:

> Space is represented as an infinite *given* magnitude. Now every concept must be thought of as a representation which is contained in an infinite number of possible representations (as their common character), and which therefore contains these *under* itself; but no concept . . . can be thought of as something containing an infinite number of representations *within* itself. It is in this latter way, however, that space is thought; for all the parts of space coexist *ad infinitum*. Consequently, the original representation of space is an *a priori* intuition, not a concept. (B 40)

The purpose of this argument is the same as that of the previous one: to show that space is an intuition and not a concept. Again, this argument takes it as already established that if space is an intuition, then it is a pure or *a priori* intuition rather than an empirical one. The argument can be formulated this way:

(1)   If X is a concept, then X subsumes an infinite number of possible instances but X does not contain an infinite number of components.
(2)   Space does not subsume an infinite number of possible instances but does contain an infinite number of components.
(3)   Space is not a concept [from (1) and (2)].
(4)   If space is not a concept, then space is an intuition.
(5)   If space is an intuition, then space is an *a priori* intuition.
(6)   Space is an *a priori* intuition, not a concept [from (3), (4), and (5)].

The thought behind premise (1), I suggest, is that whereas any general or class concept can potentially have an infinite number of instances (e.g., there could be an infinite number of stars, or things answering to the concept of a star), no concept had by humans can be infinitely rich, or have an infinitely rich content, simply by virtue of the limitations of human minds. The thought behind premise (2) is that whereas space itself does contain an infinite number of parts, not even the concept of space has an infinite number of instances (indeed, as already suggested, that concept has only one instance, the totality of space). Again, this argument appears to be quite plausible. But again, it seems quite incapable of showing that space is in any sense subjective, or that it is a feature of our minds.

We have now examined each of the arguments that Kant gives in the Transcendental Aesthetic to support his views about space. We have seen that only one of these arguments—the Argument from Geometry that he gives under the rubric "Transcendental Exposition of Space"—even bears on his view that space is a *subjective* condition of intuition, or as I have put it, a built-in feature of the human knower, analogous to Paton's blue spectacles. I have tried to show that this argument is unsuccessful. So at this point, it appears that Kant's case for his famous doctrine of Transcendental Idealism, inasmuch as it rests on and is inspired by the Argument from Geometry, is unsuccessful. In the section of the Transcendental Aesthetic devoted to time, Kant tries to support his doctrine by arguing that time no less than space is a subjective condition of intuition. But the arguments that he gives are close counterparts of, and subject to essentially the same criticisms as, the ones he gives for space. So I will assume that Kant's Transcendental Aesthetic has not made the case for Transcendental Idealism. Furthermore, as I argue in the next section, Transcendental Idealism is subject to certain grave difficulties of its own.

2.4 Some Criticisms of Transcendental Idealism

The cornerstone of Kant's doctrine of Transcendental Idealism is the distinction between appearances and things-in-themselves. Appearances, which Kant also calls phenomena, comprise the entire world of things in space and time; things-in-themselves, which Kant also calls noumena, are things existing totally apart from human knowers and their forms of intuition. This view is subject to some major difficulties, involving chiefly the notion of a thing-in-itself.

There are two standard interpretations of this notion. According to the *two-world view*, which is favored by most of Kant's earlier commentators, things-in-themselves are a completely different set of entities than appearances or phenomena.[10] The key difference between these two sets of entities is that appearances are, but things-in-themselves are not, in space or in time since space and time are merely forms of human intuition, to which only appearances conform. According to the *one-world view*, which is favored by a number of recent Kant scholars, things-in-themselves are not a different set of entities than appearances.[11] The difference is rather one of "point of view": we must distinguish between things as they appear to us and things as they are in themselves. The very same things that appear to us as spatial and temporal, as they are in themselves, are neither in space nor in time.

Whichever of the two views we take, Kant's doctrine is very puzzling. Can we really make sense of the notion of a thing that is neither in space nor in time? It would have to be something such that such questions as "where is it?"; "how far away is it?"; "for how long has it existed?"; "when did it come to be?"; "when will it cease to be?" simply lack any answers. Nor could we intelligibly suppose that such things ever change since change is incomprehensible if it is not in time. Admittedly, there may be certain kinds of entities, which we can call "abstract entities," that cannot meaningfully be said to exist in space or to have a beginning or an end of existence in time. Consider, for example, any number, say, the number 7. It makes no sense at all to suppose that it exists somewhere in space or that it began to exist at some point in time or will cease to exist at some point in time. Likewise, at least according to philosophers who follow in Plato's footsteps, universals like whiteness or goodness are abstract entities that do not exist in space and time. But not all philosophers would agree that numbers really exist (some would say that they are reducible to sets of pairs, sets of triplets, etc.), and not all philosophers would agree that universals exist (some would say that they are reducible to sets of ordinary things that resemble each other). Furthermore, it would certainly be a strange view to hold that apart from appearances, *only* numbers and other abstract entities exist, and there is no indication that Kant held such a view.

Nor is there any indication that he held things-in-themselves to be abstract entities; on the contrary, he seems to have thought of them as standing in some quasi-causal relation to appearances, which would be incomprehensible if they were abstract entities. Furthermore, at times he applies the distinction between appearances and things-in-themselves to the self, thus distinguishing between the self as it is in itself (the "noumenal self") and the self as it appears (the "empirical self"). But he cannot have thought that the noumenal self is an abstract entity like a number or a universal, if only because he thinks of it as somehow an originator of human actions and bearing moral responsibility for them.

Kant's doctrine is also susceptible to some serious internal problems. He frequently says that things-in-themselves are utterly unknowable (see, for example, A 30/B 45, A 42–43/B 59–60). Yet, the very view that there are things-in-themselves involves making claims about them, such as the claims that (1) they exist, (2) they are not in space, and (3) they are not in time. As James Van Cleve points out, this does not mean that Kant is caught in a flat contradiction:

> [The difficulty] is sometimes presented as though Kant falls into an outright contradiction—he says that there can be no knowledge of things in themselves, then proceeds to make an impressive number of claims about them. If this is indeed what Kant does, he is open to reproach but not to a charge of contradiction. What he is guilty of is rather pragmatic paradox, the sort that is involved in any assertion of the form 'p, but I do not know that p'. Such an assertion is self-enfeebling . . . but not self-refuting.[12]

Van Cleve is right: Kant's position is not self-contradictory. Thus, what another commentator describes as "the ancient objection that Kant is inconsistent in positively asserting both that things in themselves *are not* spatial or temporal but also that we can *know nothing at all* about things in themselves" is mistaken, at least if "inconsistent" means *logically* or *formally* inconsistent.[13] However, a critic of Kant can respond by saying that the objection that Kant's position is "self-enfeebling"— that it involves saying that "there exist nonspatial things-in-themselves that are not in space and time, but I do not know that things in themselves exist or whether they are in space or in time"—remains untouched, and that it seems embarrassingly weighty.

Another difficulty stems from the fact that Kant holds that things-in-themselves in some fashion ground or account for appearances. But what does this mean? It would most naturally be taken to mean that things-in-themselves are the *causes* of appearances. But the notion of a cause operating outside of time and space (and having its effects in space and time) is quite unintelligible. Furthermore, to say that things-in-themselves ground appearances is to make yet another very significant claim about things-in-themselves, while admitting that this claim cannot be known to be true.

In the face of such difficulties, some of Kant's successors proposed to retain his theory that space, time, and the categories are built-in features of the human subject that contribute structural features to objects as we know them, but to give up his theory that there are things-in-themselves that exist totally apart from human knowers. But the price of giving up the thing-in-itself while retaining the Transcendental Idealist view that the mind contributes structural features to the objects of knowledge is that one must hold that the mind literally creates the world—one must espouse Absolute Idealism. This is a view that Kant himself would have rejected (though his philosophy inspired it).

Another, very different possible reaction to the problems generated by the thing-in-itself is to adopt a purely "analytic" interpretation of Kant. On this approach, which is defended by P. F. Strawson in his highly influential book, *The Bounds of Sense: An Essay on Kant's* Critique of Pure Reason, Kant is seen as asking the following question: "What can we know about the structure of any experience that we can make intelligible to ourselves?" He is then seen as answering, in the Transcendental Aesthetic, that (1) such experience must be temporal, and as proposing (though not yet proving) that some of it must be spatial, and as proving, in the Analytic, that (2) such experience must be conceived as being of spatially located objects existing independently of our perceptions of them and obeying causal laws. However, the analytic interpretation rejects any attempt to establish these results by reference to built-in features of the human knower or the human mind; Kant's entire "transcendental psychology," as Strawson calls it, is to be shunned.

An important advantage of Strawson's approach is that it reduces the dependence of Kant's position on the legitimacy of the synthetic *a priori*. I indicated earlier that there is reason to doubt that Kant's project can really be reduced to his question about the possibility of synthetic *a priori* judgments. We now know what this reason is: it is highly questionable that Kant's chief example of synthetic *a priori* propositions, namely, the truths of geometry, really are synthetic *a priori*. Suppose that they are instead analytic. In that case, some of them, such as Kant's own example that *the straight line between two points is the shortest*, are obviously or elementarily analytic, in the sense that simple reflection on the meaning of their terms reveals their analyticity. (Thus, as we saw, the analyticity of Kant's example becomes manifest when one sees that "straight line" just means "line, such that there is no shorter line with the same endpoints.") On the other hand, other geometrical truths will be unobviously analytic, in the sense that although their analyticity cannot be seen by simple reflection on the meaning of their terms, they follow logically from truths that are obviously analytic. Now suppose that it turns out that some of the propositions describing the structure of any experience that we can make intelligible to ourselves are unobviously analytic—that complex argument from obviously analytic premises shows that nothing that we would call "experience" could lack the structure described by those propositions. In other words, suppose that propositions of the form *experience has structural feature F* turn out to be unobviously analytic—that complex arguments turning on simple conceptual facts show that nothing could count as experience unless it had structural feature *F*. Although, as we have seen, analytic truths are in an important sense uninformative—they remain true no matter what the world is like—analytic truths of this kind would be interesting and instructive. To show that nothing we would call "experience" could lack certain structural features would be a significant discovery and would constitute an important increase in our knowledge. This point can be brought out indirectly by considering an analogy with the ontological argument for the existence of God. In Anselm's version of that argument, God is first defined as the greatest conceivable being or, in Anselm's words, "the being than which a greater cannot be conceived." Anselm then argues that this being must really exist, for otherwise it would not be the greatest conceivable being since it would have been still greater if it had existed. One way to criticize this argument is to say that it only shows that nothing that lacked existence could count as the greatest conceivable being but fails to show that anything does count as the greatest conceivable being—that is, that God really exists. Now suppose that Kant can show that propositions of the form *experience has structural feature F* are unobviously analytic, so that nothing that would count as experience could lack structural feature *F*. Would it be a good objection to reply that this fails to show that anything counts as experience? Clearly not, for we know that experience occurs. Thus showing that propositions of the form *experience has structural feature F* are unobviously analytic, I suggest, would answer to Kant's constructive aims just as well as would establishing that such propositions are synthetic *a priori*.[14]

Although I think that Kant can do without the synthetic *a priori*, I believe that Strawson's purely analytic interpretation of Kant deprives some of Kant's most important arguments (especially ones in the Transcendental Analytic) of their force. The main problem for Strawson's approach, as I see it, is that even if his reconstructions of Kant's arguments are sound, they show only that we must *conceive our experience as* being of spatially located objects existing independently of our perceptions of them and obeying causal laws. It is then open to a critic to respond that for all this shows, it may be that the world is totally different from the way we must conceive it: even if argument can show that we must *conceive* our experience as being of an objective and causally ordered world, there may in fact *be* no objects located outside our minds and no causal relations. To block this criticism, I believe that some version of Kant's Transcendental Idealism must be invoked.

2.5 A "Weak" Interpretation of Transcendental Idealism

In line with my objection to Strawson's purely analytic interpretation of the *Critique*, I shall now propose what I call the "weak" interpretation of Transcendental Idealism (hereafter abbreviated as "weak TI"). To introduce weak TI, let me first try to formulate, in much the same spirit as Strawson, the basic question that Kant is asking in the constructive portion of the *Critique*. I suggest that he is asking this question: what can we know about what human experience must be like, without prejudging or even addressing the question of whether that experience conforms to things as they are quite apart from our experience—indeed without even addressing the question of whether things as they are in themselves are the same or other than things as we experience them? Given Kant's dichotomy of intuition and concept, this question breaks down into two questions:

1. What can we know about how anything must be *perceived* by us, without addressing or making any judgment on the question whether this is the same or different from the way things are apart from the way we perceive them?

2. What can we know about how we must *think* that things are, or conceptualize them, without addressing or making any judgment on the
question of whether the way we conceptualize things conforms to
things as they may be apart from such conceptualization—indeed,
without addressing or making any judgment on the question of
whether things as they are in themselves are the same as or other than
things as we conceptualize them?

These questions open up, so to speak, a kind of logical space in which we can
talk about human experience without worrying whether it conforms to things as
they may be in themselves, apart from our ways of experiencing them. If the result
of talking within this space is that we can establish some truths about how we
must perceive and think of things, then the question of whether things as they are
in themselves, apart from the ways in which we must perceive and think of them,
are the same or other than things as we must perceive and think of them, becomes
as moot as it is unanswerable.

Weak TI attempts to answer our two "what-can-we-know" questions. Its fundamental thesis is that *there are* ways in which we humans must perceive and think
of things, and that we can neither know nor have any conception of what things
might be like apart from our ways of perceiving and conceptualizing them. More
fully, weak TI consists of the following three theses:

(1) We must perceive all things in time and all things distinct from ourselves and our own mental states as being in space.
(2) We must think of some of the things we perceive as being distinct
from ourselves and of every event we perceive as having a cause.
(3) We can have no knowledge about, nor even any conception of, what
things are like apart from the ways in which we must perceive and
think of them; nor can we intelligibly suppose that things might be
different from the ways we must perceive and conceptualize them.

Kant defends (1) largely in the Aesthetic and (2) in the Analytic. Thesis (3) is the
one that blocks the objection that there might for all we can know be a radical
split between the world as we must perceive and conceive it and the world as it
really is in itself.[15] In that sense, it may be called an "idealistic" thesis, and its
inclusion is the reason why I call the set of theses "weak Transcendental *Idealism*."
But if that label seems misleading, I could dispense with it: my concern is not
with the name; it is, rather, to show that these theses are at least part of what Kant
is holding and that they are plausible on their own terms. In defense of the attribu-
tion to Kant of thesis (1), I would point to several passages in the Aesthetic that
were discussed in sections 2.2 and 2.3.2 (notably, though not exclusively, A 34/B
50–51 and A 23/B 38). Thesis (2), we will see, is argued for in the Analytic. As
for the "idealistic" thesis (3), I believe that it is at least part of what Kant is saying
in such passages as this:

What objects may be in themselves, and apart from all this receptivity of our
sensibility, remains completely unknown to us. We know nothing but our mode
of perceiving them—a mode which is peculiar to us, and not necessarily shared

> in by every being, though, certainly, by every human being. With this alone have
> we any concern. (A 42/B 59)

What Kant is saying here can just as well be put by saying that what objects are like apart from the ways we must perceive (and by extension, conceive) them, or the ways in which we must experience them, is unknown to us, and moreover cannot sensibly be of any concern to us. That, at any rate, seems to me to be the defensible element in Kant's view that we can have no knowledge of things as they are in themselves. As I see it, this means that we must be totally agnostic on the question of what things are like apart from the ways in which we must perceive and conceive them; we cannot even know whether they are like or unlike things as we must perceive or conceive them. So, for example, we cannot know that things-in-themselves are *not* in space or in time or that they *are* in space or in time. I would not claim that this interpretation is easily reconcilable with *everything* Kant says; there are episodes in the Transcendental Dialectic, for example, that may well require interpreting Kant as affirming that things-in-themselves are nonspatial and nontemporal and that the entire space-time world of appearances exists only in our minds. But I would claim, and will try to show in the chapters to follow, that my way of reading Kant maximizes the philosophical interest and plausibility of the constructive part of his thought about human knowledge. Furthermore, my reading preserves the advantage of Strawson's approach mentioned above, of reducing the reliance of Kant's constructive program on the synthetic *a priori*. It leaves open the possibility that at least some of Kant's constructive claims may be true not because they are synthetic *a priori*, but rather, as Jonathan Bennett puts it, "because of certain very complex and unobvious conceptual facts."[16] It also leaves open the possibility that some of these claims may be true because their truth is, in a sense to be explained in the next chapter, a necessary condition of the possibility of experience. Whether and to what extent these possibilities are realized will be considered in subsequent chapters.

Categories and Principles of the Understanding

3.1 The Structure of the Transcendental Analytic

In the Transcendental Analytic, Kant tries to prove that the categories have what he calls "objective validity." For Kant, to say that a category has objective validity means that a certain principle associated with the category has a special status. Officially, this status is that the principle is synthetic *a priori*. As I have already indicated, however, there is reason to think that at least some of the principles that Kant takes to be synthetic *a priori* are instead unobviously analytic, and so I shall assume that if Kant shows that a principle associated with one of his categories is unobviously analytic, that too shows that the category is objectively valid.[1] But there is still another special status, which Kant argues that some of the principles associated with his categories possess, and the possession of which confers objective validity on the corresponding category: he argues that the truth of these principles is a necessary condition of our having the kind of experience we unquestionably have. For example, when Kant says that the category of causality has objective validity, he means that the truth of the causal principle—the principle that every event must have a cause—is a necessary condition of our having the kind of experience we unquestionably have. As we will see in 5.5, there is some question of whether principles of this kind are synthetic *a priori* or even unobviously analytic, though in 5.6.2 a case will be made for holding that they are at least unobviously analytic. But as I shall also argue, even if these principles are neither synthetic *a priori* nor unobviously analytic, showing that they are necessary conditions of the kind of experience we unquestionably have—that, as Kant sometimes puts it, they make such experience possible—is a powerful way to justify or "prove" them. So I shall assume that showing that a principle has this special status is also a way of showing that the corresponding category is objectively valid.

The fact that the objective validity of a category amounts to a certain principle having a special status accounts for the organization of the Analytic into two books, the "Analytic of Concepts" and the "Analytic of Principles." In the Analytic of

Concepts, Kant introduces the categories and gives a very important argument, commonly called the "Transcendental Deduction of the Categories," which contains the first and most basic part of his argument for the objective validity of the categories but does not by itself suffice to show that any specific category is objectively valid.[2] In the Analytic of Principles, he completes this argument by showing that certain specific categories are objectively valid, that is, by proving that the specific principles associated with those categories have the kind of status just described. For brevity's sake, I shall often describe this undertaking simply as "proving" those principles.

Since Kant holds that there are twelve categories, it would seem that proving the objective validity of the categories should require proving twelve different principles. In fact, however, Kant offers proofs for only five principles because he organizes his twelve categories into four groups of three each—three categories of *quantity*, three categories of *quality*, three categories of *relation*, and three categories of *modality*—but he seeks to prove three distinct principles only for the categories of relation, which are *substance*, *cause*, and *reciprocity*. He calls these three principles the "Analogies of Experience"; the First Analogy corresponds to the category of substance, the Second Analogy to the category of cause, and the Third Analogy to the category of reciprocity. For the categories of quantity and quality, Kant seeks to establish only one principle for each of these two groups of three. He calls these two principles the "Axioms of Intuition" and the "Anticipations of Perception"; the Axioms of Intuition correspond to the three categories of quantity, the Anticipations of Perception to the three categories of quality. As for the three categories of modality, there is a principle associated with each of the three in that group, but those three principles, which Kant calls the "Postulates of Empirical Thought," are merely definitions, and Kant accordingly offers no proofs but only an "explanation" of each of them.

Within this complicated structure, there is one line of argument, which I shall call "The Central Argument of the Analytic," that stands out as the most important. This is the line of argument by which Kant tries to prove the objective validity of the categories of substance and cause, and thus to show against Hume's skeptical empiricism that we must conceptualize our experience as being of substances causally interacting in space and time. The argument begins with the Transcendental Deduction, given in Chapter Two of the Analytic of Concepts, entitled "The Deduction of the Pure Concepts of Understanding," and continues in the First and Second Analogies of Experience, given in the long Chapter Two of the Analytic of Principles, entitled "System of all Principles of Pure Understanding." It is preceded by the opening chapter of the Analytic of Concepts (and of the whole Analytic), entitled "The clue to the Discovery of all Pure Concepts of the Understanding," and it is interrupted by Chapter One of the Analytic of Principles, entitled "The Schematism of the Pure Concepts of Understanding," and by the first several sections of the long second chapter of the Analytic of Principles. Before reaching the Analogies, that chapter includes two introductory sections ("The Highest Principle of all Analytic Judgments" and "The Highest Principle of all Synthetic Judgments"), as well as the Axioms of Intuition and the Anticipations of Perception; after the Analogies, it includes the Postulates of Empirical

Thought, between the second and third of which Kant inserts a short but important section called "Refutation of Idealism."

The material that precedes, the material that interrupts, and the material that follows the Central Argument of the Analytic, is less important (with the exception of the Refutation of Idealism) than the Transcendental Deduction and the first two Analogies of Experience that contain this central line of argument. Nevertheless, it contains some very interesting ideas, and it is important for getting a grasp of the Transcendental Analytic as a whole. In the present chapter, accordingly, I propose to discuss this material by analyzing the first chapter of the Analytic of Concepts (which is also the opening chapter of the Transcendental Analytic), as well as certain sections of the Analytic of Principles that do not depend on the Central Argument of the Analytic (notably the Axioms of Intuition, Anticipations of Perception, and Postulates of Empirical Thought). In the chapters following this one, I shall focus squarely on the Central Argument of the Analytic. However, if you want to go straight to that argument, then this book is written in such a way that the rest of the present chapter can be skipped now and returned to later.

3.2 Discovering the Categories: Forms of Judgment as the Guiding Clue

As suggested by its title, "The Clue to the Discovery of all Pure Concepts of the Understanding," the first chapter of the Analytic seeks to *discover* what pure concepts or categories there are. This task of discovering the categories contrasts sharply with the task of *justifying* the categories (i.e., proving the principles associated with them), which Kant does not begin until the Transcendental Deduction in the following chapter. So it is important to bear in mind that Kant's sole purpose in the first chapter of the Analytic is to find out what categories humans actually employ; he is not yet concerned to show that their employment is legitimate or leads to any knowledge. The chapter is commonly called "The Metaphysical Deduction" because of this remark, which Kant makes later:

> In the *metaphysical deduction* the a priori origin of the categories has been proved through their complete agreement with the general logical functions of thought. (B 159)

Kant's label, "metaphysical deduction," has stuck.

Kant's remark also alludes to the fundamental idea of the metaphysical deduction, which is that the categories can be discovered by examining the basic logical forms of *judgment* (what Kant here calls "the general logical functions of thought"). This idea rests on the point that concepts are used primarily within propositions or, in Kant's favored idiom, to make judgments. As he puts it, "Now the only use the understanding can make of these concepts is to judge by means of them" (A 68/B 93). Consider for example the concept 'horse.' When is that concept used—when, so to speak, does it come to life? The answer is when someone makes a judgment or statement about horses, such as "all horses are herbivorous" or "some horses are thoroughbreds." Following up on this clue, Kant thinks that in order to discover the pure concepts, he need only survey or inventory the basic logical *forms* of judgments or propositions. His idea is this: a judgment or proposition has both a content and a logical form; for example, the judgment that all horses are herbivorous has the concepts 'horse' and 'herbivorous' as its content—it can sensibly be said to "contain" these concepts. But this proposition also has something that remains when we abstract from that content, namely, its logical form, which we can express as "All A's are B's." This remainder, Kant thinks, also consists of a concept, namely, the concept of unity, because, as we shall see more fully later, the judgment "all A's are B's" gathers into *one* class all the things that are A's.[3] Now the concepts that constitute the content of the proposition that all horses are herbivorous are empirical; they are derived from experience. But what about the concept that makes for this judgment's logical form? That concept, Kant thinks, is not derived from experience; it is a "pure" or *a priori* concept. Generalizing from this example, one can grasp Kant's idea that by studying the various possible logical forms of judgments, we can *discover* what pure concepts there are. As he puts it:

> In this manner there arise precisely the same number of pure concepts of the understanding which apply *a priori* to objects of intuition in general, as . . . there have found to be logical functions in all possible judgments. For these functions specify the understanding completely, and yield an exhaustive inventory of its powers. (A 79/B 105)

In a helpful discussion of the metaphysical deduction, Justus Hartnack explains Kant's idea in another way:

> If the understanding is the faculty of making judgments by means of concepts, then it seems clear that we can discover the fundamental concepts of the understanding, which Kant calls categories, by an examination of the form of the judgments themselves. To make a judgment is an activity of the understanding employing concepts, and the logical structure or form of the judgment must therefore be an expression of that category, or those categories, which are used.[4]

Notice that Hartnack works into his explanation Kant's view that judging is an activity of the faculty of mind that he calls "the understanding," which he contrasts with the faculty of mind by which humans are acted upon in sense perception, which he calls "sensibility." This brings into the picture an aspect of Kant's position that one encounters throughout the *Critique*—namely, his dichotomy of the human mind's capacities into an active faculty, the understanding, that forms concepts, makes judgments, and contains the pure concepts, and a relatively passive faculty, sensibility, whose affectation results in intuitions, and which also contains the pure forms of intuition, space, and time, to which those intuitions must conform. Knowledge is then seen as the product of those two faculties working together. The dichotomy of understanding and sensibility is the psychological counterpart of Kant's seminal distinction between concepts and intuitions. Kant's belief that, in discovering the pure concepts, he is also discovering the structure of the faculty of understanding leads him to make statements such as this:

> By 'analytic of concepts' I do not understand their analysis, or the procedure usual in philosophical investigations, that of dissecting the content of such concepts as may present themselves and so of rendering them more distinct, but the hitherto

rarely attempted *dissection of the faculty of the understanding* itself, in order to investigate the possibility of concepts *a priori* by looking for them in the understanding alone as their birthplace, and by analyzing the pure use of this faculty. (A 65–66/B 90)

This passage makes it sound as if Kant intends to give an account of the pure concepts only as capacities or processes of mind, rather than as having a certain content or meaning; but in fact he will do both (and tends not to distinguish the two), and I will continue to emphasize the latter rather than the former.

3.2.1 *Kant's Table of Judgments*

Let us proceed, then, to Kant's classification of the basic logical forms of judgment, exhibited by him in the "Table of Judgments" that he presents in A 70/B 95 and reproduced as figure 3–1. As this table of judgments shows, Kant assigns

I

Quantity of Judgments

Universal

Particular

Singular

II		III
Quality		*Relation*
Affirmative		Categorical
Negative		Hypothetical
Infinite		Disjunctive

IV

Modality

Problematic

Assertoric

Apodeictic

FIGURE 3–1

to every judgment four different characteristics: a quantity, a quality, a relation, and a modality, and each of these characteristics can be instantiated in one of three different ways: the quantity of a judgment can be universal, particular, or singular; the quality of a judgment can be affirmative, negative, or infinite; the relation of a judgment can be categorical, hypothetical, or disjunctive; the modality of a judgment can be problematic, assertoric, or apodictic.[5] Kant maintains that every judgment must, with respect to its logical form, be one of the three instantiations of each of the four characteristics; for example, the form of the judgment "all politician are liars" is universal, affirmative, categorical, and assertoric, and the form of the judgment "George Bush, Jr., is not a Democrat" is singular, negative, categorical, and assertoric. Let us look more closely at each of the characteristics and their instantiations.

The first two characteristics, quantity and quality, are based, except for a couple of modifications, on the classical logic of Aristotle. Aristotle offered the classification of propositions shown in figure 3–2. Let us turn first to the quantity of a judgment. Suppose, for example, that I make a judgment about philosophers. Then, Aristotle thought, it can be about all philosophers (e.g., "all philosophers are humans"), in which case it is universal, or it can be about some philosophers (e.g., "some philosophers are women"), in which case it is particular. Kant would point out that it can also be about a particular philosopher, say, Socrates, as in the judgment "Socrates is wise." Aristotle and the classical logicians who followed in his footsteps treated such a singular judgment as a special case of the universal, that is, as saying that all members of the one-member class, Socrates, are wise or that "All 'Socrateses' are wise." They did so for the sake of convenience because in determining what logical inferences can be drawn from a proposition of the form "All S is P" (or "All S's are P"), it makes no difference whether the class of S's contains many members or only one member. Kant approves of this simplification in the context of studying only logical relationships between different forms of propositions, but he thinks that in studying judgments with a view to determining what pure concepts they involve, a singular judgment, since it relates to a universal one "as unity relates to infinity," deserves its own special place in the classification of judgments. This is why, under the rubric of quantity, he adds the singular to Aristotle's classifications of universal and particular.

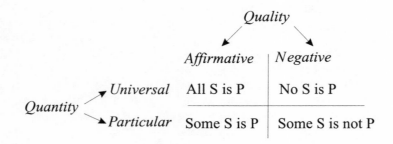

FIGURE 3–2

Next, let us consider the quality of a judgment. Suppose that I make a judgment about Socrates. Then, Aristotle thought, it can affirm something about Socrates (e.g., "Socrates is mortal"), in which case it is affirmative; or it can deny something about Socrates (e.g., "Socrates is not jealous"), in which case it is negative. (Notice that these two judgments also happen to be singular ones; this begins to illustrate Kant's point that any judgment must be an instantiation of *each* of the four characteristics.) Kant, however, again modifies Aristotle's scheme by adding a third instantiation of "quality," that is, the infinite, to cover cases of "the logical affirmation made in a judgment by means of a merely negative predicate" (A 72/ B 97). Kant's example of an infinite judgment is "the soul is non-mortal." Kant notes that the logical form of such a judgment is an affirmation—the judgment says that something *is* such-and-such—but argues that it should nevertheless be distinguished from an affirmative judgment. The reason appears to be that whereas an affirmative judgment, say, "the soul is a living thing," merely places its subject in the limited class of living things, the infinite one, "the soul is nonmortal" places its subject in the unlimited class of nonmortal things (a class that includes not only immortal things but also undying, inanimate things, like rocks and stars, since a thing can only be said to be mortal if it was alive at some time, and whatever is not mortal is of course nonmortal).[6] Kant also notes that the infinite judgment serves to "limit" the "infinite sphere of the possible," not, of course, by making it smaller, but rather because it confines the soul to that (infinite) part of it that contains as its members all nonmortal or undying things, and excludes the soul from that part of it whose domain is mortal things. He also notes that more things than just the mortal ones could be excluded from the infinite class of nonmortal or undying things without thereby enriching the concept of the soul. For example, if I were to consider the class of all nonmortal things except for rocks, I would now be "limiting" the infinite class of nonmortal things by considering only the infinite part of it that contains no rocks (but does contain souls). But I would not thereby have enriched my conception of the soul.

In addition to quantity and quality, Kant holds that every judgment must have what he calls a relation. He identifies three relations: categorical, hypothetical, and disjunctive. In a categorical judgment, the relation is between subject and predicate. For example, if I say, "Socrates is wise," then the essential point about this judgment is that it ascribes the predicate "wise" to the person referred to in the subject as "Socrates." The logical structure of the judgment is a subject-predicate relation. In a hypothetical judgment, there is a relation between ground and consequence. As Hartnack puts it:

> In the judgment, "If there is lightning, then there will be thunder," what is stated
> is that in case there is lightning, the lightning will be the reason for the subsequent thunder, i.e. the thunder will be a consequence of the fact that there is
> lightning.[7]

Notice that there is a major difference between the subject-predicate relation asserted by a categorical judgment and the ground-consequence relation asserted by a hypothetical judgment: the subject-predicate relation links two terms or concepts and occurs within a single judgment, whereas the ground-consequence relation holds between two complete judgments. As Kant puts it: "In the [categorical] judgment only two concepts are considered to be in relation to each other, in the [hypothetical] judgment, two judgments" (A 73/B 98). Notice also that a hypothetical judgment does not assert that its antecedent (if-clause) is true and also does not assert that its consequent (then-clause) is true; rather, it asserts only that *if* its antecedent is true, *then* its consequent is true. As Kant puts it: "Whether both of these propositions in themselves are true remains unsettled here. It is only the implication that is thought by means of [a hypothetical] judgment" (A 73/B 98–99).

A disjunctive judgment also asserts a relation between two (or more) complete judgments. Kant defines the disjunctive form of judgment as follows:

> [T]he disjunctive judgment contains a relation of two or more propositions to each other, a relation not, however, of logical sequence [as in the hypothetical judgment], but of logical opposition, in so far as the sphere of the one [judgment] excludes the sphere of the other, and yet at the same time of community, in so far as the propositions taken together occupy the whole sphere of the knowledge in question. (A 74/B 99)

Hartnack expounds what Kant is saying with admirable clarity:

> [A] disjunctive judgment states that two or more judgments exclude each other, that one and only one of them is true, and that all the judgments that comprise the disjunction exhaust the possibilities. If I say, "He is either a carpenter or a mason or a police officer," I have (according to Kant's use of disjunction) asserted that . . . if . . . he is a carpenter, then . . . he is neither a mason nor a police officer. [Furthermore,] in saying that he is either a carpenter or a mason or a police officer I am therewith excluding all other possibilities. He cannot, for example, be a farmer. In other words, what is affirmed is that he is one of the three things. If I know that he is neither a mason nor a police officer, I thereby also know that he is a carpenter.[8]

Hartnack adds the following important clarification:

> The disjunctive judgment says that either the statement p or the statement q is true. It is generally recognized that such a judgment can be understood in two ways. It can be understood in the [so-called inclusive] sense that we are saying that [at least one of the statements is true and] perhaps they are both true ("On his bookshelf you will only find books by Kant or by Hume"); or it can be understood to mean . . . that either p is true or q is true, but that they are not both true ("The meetings are led either by the chairman or the vice-chairman"). It is in this last sense (the so-called exclusive meaning) that Kant here takes the disjunctive judgment. In other words, if p is true (the meetings are led by the chairman) then it has to follow that q is false (the meetings are not led by the vice-chairman). And if q is true (the meetings are led by the vice-chairman) then it has to follow that p is false (the meetings are not led by the chairman).[9]

The fourth formal characteristic of judgments, modality, differs from the other three in that its three instantiations—the problematic, the assertoric, and the apodictic—do not affect the content of a judgment; in other words, regardless of whether a specific judgment is problematic, assertoric, or apodictic, its factual content remains the same because the modality of a judgment concerns only the attitude or stance taken toward the (content) of a judgment, rather than the nature of a judgment's content. Consider, for example, the judgment that "Hillary Rodham Clinton will run for the presidency of the United States." One can use that judgment to express merely a possibility—to say that maybe Hillary will run—in which case it is what Kant calls a "problematic" judgment. Or one can use it to express the belief that she will run—to say that it is true that she will run—in which case it is what Kant calls an "assertoric" judgment. Or, finally, one could use it to express the belief that it is necessary that she will run—that necessarily, she will run—in which case Kant calls it an "apodictic" judgment. Notice, then, that the content of the judgment—Hillary will run for U.S. president—remains exactly the same whether the judgment is put forward problematically, assertorically, or apodictically; what varies is only the attitude taken toward the judgment, or the way in which the judgment is put forward or considered. In the field of modal logic (the branch of logic dealing with possibility and necessity), this point is recognized as follows: a given judgment, p, is prefaced by the operator "possibly" (written as a diamond) if the judgment is problematic, p is prefaced by the operator "necessarily" (written as a square) if the judgment is apodictic, and p is not prefaced by either of these operators if the judgment is assertoric.[10] Kant says that in a hypothetical judgment such as "if it rains, then the ground is wet," each of the two component judgments (the antecedent "it rains" and the consequent "the ground is wet") is only problematic; only the implication or relation expressed by the judgment as a whole is assertoric; likewise, in a disjunctive judgment such as "either he is a mason or he is a policeman or he is a carpenter," each of the component disjuncts ("he is a mason," "he is a policeman," "he is a carpenter") is only problematic; only the disjunction as a whole is assertoric.[11]

Having now surveyed the four formal characteristics of judgments and their instantiations, we have completed the exposition of Kant's Table of Judgments. Before looking at how he derives from it his Table of Categories, however, we should pause for some critical discussion of the Table of Judgments itself.

3.2.2 Criticisms of the Table of Judgments

It is now generally recognized that Kant's table has several weaknesses, stemming from his assumption that the logic of his day, which was based primarily on the logic of Aristotle, contained the final and eternal truth about logic. In a notorious remark, he says:

> That logic has already, from the earliest times, proceeded upon this sure path [of a science] is evidenced by fact that since Aristotle it has not required to retrace a single step. . . . It is remarkable also that to the present day this logic has not been able to advance a single step, and is thus to all appearance a closed and completed body of doctrine. (B viii)

In fact, however, logic since Kant's time has developed explosively. As a result of the work done by philosophers such as Gottlob Frege, Bertrand Russell, and Alfred North Whitehead in the early twentieth century, logic has become immeasurably more powerful than it was when Kant assembled his Table of Judgments. Here are three illustrations of this point.[12]

(1) There is no treatment in Aristotle's logic, and no place in Kant's Table of Judgments, for existential judgments such as "The president of the United States exists"; such judgments are not reducible to subject-predicate ones, and there is no place for them under the heading of Relation.

(2) Consider the judgments

    (a) Kant was German

and

    (b) The man who wrote the *Critique of Pure Reason* was German.

For Kant, (a) and (b) have exactly the same logical form: they are both singular judgments. But in modern symbolic logic, their structure is seen as very different: (a) is analyzed as containing a constant referring to Kant, usually represented by a lowercase letter, say "a," and a predicate designating the property of being German, usually represented by a capital letter, say "G." The whole sentence is symbolized as "Ga," which is read as "a is G."[13] But (b) is analyzed as a complex existential judgment that contains two quantifiers and two variables and that says: "There exists an x such that x wrote the *Critique of Pure Reason* and for any y, if y wrote the *Critique of Pure Reason*, then y is identical with x, and x is German."[14] This, in turn, is taken to be equivalent to a statement that contains a "definite description" as its subject, read as "The x such that x wrote the *Critique of Pure Reason* is German."[15]

(3) As a final illustration, consider the valid argument

    All cats are animals
    ―――――――――――――――――
    ∴ All heads of cats are heads of animals.

In classical, Aristotelian logic, there is no way to show that this argument is valid. Its form would have to be represented as

    All A's are B's
    ―――――――――――――
    ∴ All C's are D's

which is plainly invalid. But in modern logic, the form of the argument can be rendered in a way that is demonstrably valid (using the rules of modern logic) and that goes like this:

    For any x, if x is a cat, then x is an animal.
    ――――――――――――――――――――――――――――――
    ∴ For any x, if there exists a y such that y is a cat and x is the head of y, then there exists a y such that y is an animal and x is the head of y.[16]

In addition to the fact that the development of logic after Kant undermines his view that his table of judgments represents the absolute and final truth of the matter about the most basic logical forms of all judgments, there is a certain arbitrariness about his table of judgments. Under the rubric of "Relation" he includes, as we have seen, only the categorical, hypothetical, and disjunctive forms. But why not also include other forms, such as the conjunctive ("and") form? As some commentators have said, it seems that Kant knew in advance what categories he wanted to include in his system and adjusted his table of judgments to fit those categories, rather than using that table as his sole "clue" to the discovery of the categories.

Be that as it may, it is important to note that the weaknesses in Kant's table of judgments do not in themselves deeply compromise Kant's position. For remember that the entire purpose of the metaphysical deduction is only to *discover* what categories there are. In the central argument of the Analytic that starts in the transcendental deduction and continues in the "Principles" chapter, on the other hand, Kant tries to prove that his categories are objectively valid. Furthermore, to anticipate a little the nature of his arguments, in the case of the two most important categories, namely, substance and cause, he tries to do this by means of an argument that shows that those categories are *necessary conditions of experience*, meaning by this that human experience would not even be possible unless these categories were objectively valid, that is, unless the principles associated with them were true. An argument of this type—one that shows that the kind of experience we unquestionably have would be impossible unless a certain principle were true—is now called (no doubt due to Kant's label) a "transcendental argument." This is a powerful kind of argument because it shows that anyone who admits that he or she has the kind of experience we unquestionably have is logically committed to the truth of the principle in question. As we shall see, Kant does not offer transcendental arguments for the principles associated with his other categories, such as the Axioms of Intuition and the Anticipations of Perception. Rather, he supports those principles by more direct argumentation intended to show that they are synthetic *a priori* (or at least unobviously analytic) truths about experience— that they must apply, in Strawson's words, to any experience that we can "make intelligible to ourselves."[17] Now if Kant can really prove by these various arguments that the principles associated with his categories have the special status of being necessary conditions of experience, or of being synthetic *a priori* or unobviously analytic truths about experience, then he does not need the metaphysical deduction at all: that section of the *Critique* becomes superfluous. For then he will have shown that certain specific categories are objectively valid, but in doing this he will, of course, have also shown *what* these specific categories are. So it will hardly matter if his initial way of "discovering" them by surveying forms of judgment is flawed. Thus the weaknesses of Kant's Table of Judgments do not impugn his basic line of argument.[18]

3.3 From Judgments to Categories and from Some Categories to Some Principles

We may now turn to this question: what specific categories does Kant think can be derived from the different forms of judgment? Following Kant's own order of presentation, I shall successively discuss the derivations of the categories of quantity, quality, relation, and modality from the quantity, quality, relation, and modality of judgments, respectively. In another respect, however, I shall depart from Kant's order of presentation. Kant presents the principles associated with each of the categories only after the transcendental deduction, as if they all depended on that crucial argument. In fact, however, only the principles associated with the categories of relation, namely, the Analogies of Experience, depend on the transcendental deduction.[19] The principles associated with the categories of quantity (the Axioms of Intuition), quality (the Anticipations of Perception), and modality (the Postulates of Empirical Thought), despite their placement in the *Critique* after the transcendental deduction, do not depend on the transcendental deduction, and insofar as Kant argues for those principles, he does so in "Proofs" offered within the sections named after them. Accordingly, I shall discuss these principles and Kant's proofs of them in this chapter, directly after introducing the specific categories associated with them. On the other hand, I shall not discuss the Analogies of Experience until chapters 5–8, after presenting the transcendental deduction in chapter 4. This organizational strategy has the double advantage of enabling us to discuss the categories of quantity, quality, modality, and their associated principles together rather than separated by very different material, as well as to present the central argument of the Analytic as a continuous one rather than one whose earlier stage (the transcendental deduction) is separated from its later stage (the Analogies) by largely unrelated material. It also has the effect of making the present chapter the longest one in this book, but the chapter is divided into relatively brief subsections. Remember also that it is still possible at this point to skip the rest of this chapter and come back to it later if you wish (though if you have read this far, then it would be best not to skip section 3.3.3).

3.3.1 Categories of Quantity and Axioms of Intuition

The three instantiations of the quantity of judgments are, as we have seen, the universal, the particular, and the singular. According to the tables of judgments and of categories given at A 70/B 95 and A 80/B 106, respectively, the category derived from the universal form "All S is P" is *unity*. Hartnack offers an ingenious explanation of how this derivation would work:

> If I make the judgment that all cats are gray or, in general terms, that all S is P, I have created a unity, a unity that does not exist as a matter of course, does not exist of itself, does not exist empirically, but has been brought about by an act of the understanding, i.e., by the use of a concept. I have conceptually grasped all S (whatever S may stand for) as a unity. This I can do, Kant believes, only by using the category (the pure concept of the understanding) *unity*. Without this category it would not be possible to make a judgment about all of the infinitely many S's treated as a single concept, a single class, namely the class of all S.[20]

Next, in judging that "Some S is P," I neither place all S's into one class, creating a unity, nor is my judgment only about a single S. The concept needed to designate S's without targeting either all S's or any single S is the concept of *plurality*. To look at the point differently, you may recall from an elementary logic course that the particular judgment "Some S is P" is taken to mean "at least one S is P," where "at least one" allows that the judgment may apply to more than one S but to fewer than all the S's that there are. But in capturing this, so to speak, "intermediate" quantity, we are using the concept Kant calls "plurality." Finally, the category derived from the singular form of judgment is *totality*. Here is Hartnack's explanation of this point:

> I can express [a singular] judgment either by using the form, "This S is P," or by giving a name to this S, for example 'John,' thereby getting the judgment, "John is P." What I make the judgment about is not simply a part of this S or of John, but is the whole considered as a unity; it is about all that pertains to this S or to John. [For example, if I make the judgment "John is tall," then my judgment is about John as a whole, not just about his neck or his nose.] The category is, therefore, according to Kant, *totality*.[21]

We can summarize Kant's derivation of the categories of quantity from forms of judgment by means of figure 3–3. Here we should note a minor difficulty. Despite Hartnack's ingenious explanation of how unity is extracted from the universal and totality from the singular forms of judgment, it makes more sense to extract totality from the universal and unity from the singular forms of judgment (thus switching the places of "Unity" and "Totality" in the figure). Thus, Henry Allison writes:

> A minor problem is raised by Kant's correlations of the universal judgment with the category of unity and the singular judgment with the category of totality. It seems obvious that these correlations should be reversed.[22]

One of Kant's most careful commentators, H. J. Paton, takes the same view:

> The order in which the categories are given in A 80 = B 106 suggests that the category of totality is derived from the singular judgment. Although the same parallelism holds in [Kant's] *Prolegomena* . . . I believe this is a slip. . . . It is only natural to derive unity from the singular judgment.[23]

Paton goes on to explain the "slip" as follows. Kant makes the somewhat bemusing remark that "the third category in each class always arises from the combination of the second category with the first" (B·110).[24] But then, it does seem that totality rather than unity must be listed as the third category of quantity because "totality is plurality considered as unity."[25] (It would indeed be odd to say that unity was

Types of Judgment	Forms	Categories
Universal	All S is P; No S is P	Unity
Particular	Some S is P; Some S is not P	Plurality
Singular	X (X = a uniquely referring expression) is P; X is not P	Totality

FIGURE 3–3

totality considered as plurality.) On the other hand, in listing the forms of judgment, "Kant follows the traditional order (universal, particular, singular)."[26] Thus we have the resulting mismatch between the judgment forms and categories of quantity. If Kant had listed the forms of judgment in the opposite order—singular, particular, universal—then these forms would have better matched the categories as he lists them—Unity, Plurality, Totality—and the sense of his remark about obtaining the third category from the first two would be preserved as well. I shall not attempt to determine whether Hartnack is right to take Kant's presentation in the *Critique* at face value or whether Paton is right to regard it as harboring a careless error. In favor of Hartnack's view, it should be noted that "Kant's own papers . . . reveal that he tinkered endlessly with the lists of Judgments and Categories before hitting on the principle of four sets of three."[27] It is a little difficult to accept, then, that Kant allowed a careless error to survive in the canonical published version of these lists. On Paton's side, there is the evident naturalness of associating the universal form of judgment with totality and the singular form with unity, as well as Kant's remark about how the third category is supposed to result from the first two. There is also this remark of Kant's, not mentioned by Paton: "if . . . we compare a singular with a universal judgment . . . in respect of quantity, the singular stands to the universal as unity to infinity" (A 71/B 96). This explicitly connects the singular judgment form with unity, not with totality. But it is not crucial that we determine which reading conforms to Kant's real intentions because, as we have already noted, Kant associates all three categories of quantity with only a single principle, to which we may now turn our attention.

The principle of the Axioms of Intuition, as stated in the first edition, says: "All appearances are, in their intuition, extensive magnitudes" (A 162). Kant's definition of an extensive magnitude is this: "I entitle a magnitude extensive when the representation of the parts makes possible and therefore necessarily precedes, the representation of the whole" (A 162/B 203). This definition implies (a) that (to borrow Jonathan Bennett's words) "an extensive magnitude is one that something has by virtue of having *parts*," and that (b) those parts are in some sense prior to the whole.[28] I will discuss an issue raised by (b) shortly, but first let us ask: why does Kant think that all appearances that we intuit have extensive magnitude (or, as he puts it, "are extensive magnitudes")? The reason comes out when he glosses the "proof" of the principle like this: "As the [element of] pure intuition in all appearance is either space or time, every appearance is as intuition an extensive magnitude" (A 163/B 203). The missing premise of this proof is clearly that space and time are extensive magnitudes, for once that premise is supplied, the result is a straightforward proof of the principle (I slightly reword the principle to make the argument more obviously valid):

> Space and time are extensive magnitudes [premise of Kant's "Proof" of the principle of the Axioms of Intuition].
> All intuited appearances are in space and time [premise established in the Aesthetic].
>
> ---
>
> ∴ All intuited appearances are extensive magnitudes [principle of the Axioms of Intuition].

Why does Kant give the plural name "Axioms of Intuition" to this single principle? Paul Guyer offers the following explanation of this nomenclature:

> The principle of the axioms of intuition is not itself intended to be an axiom, let alone more than one; it is intended to be the principle which licenses the empirical *use* of the genuine axioms of intuition more properly so called, which are none other than the axioms of the relevant portion of mathematics itself.[29]

In other words, Kant sees the principle of the axioms as one that is assumed or presupposed whenever the axioms of mathematics are applied to the empirical world. This principle, then, is part of Kant's philosophy of mathematics, and despite its placement in the Analytic, it does not contribute to the central Argument of the Analytic but instead complements the Aesthetic by showing that pure mathematics (e.g., geometry) can be applied to empirical objects to yield, Kant thinks, synthetic *a priori* knowledge about them:

> This transcendental principle of the mathematics of appearances greatly enlarges our *a priori* knowledge. For it alone can make pure mathematics, in its complete precision, applicable to objects of experience. . . . Empirical intuition is possible only by means of the pure intuition of space and time. What geometry asserts of pure intuition is therefore undeniably valid of empirical intuition. (A 165/B 206)

To understand Kant's position better, let us consider an example. Suppose that there is an empirical object, say, a sail, which has the shape of a right triangle. The Pythagorean theorem tells us that the square on the hypotenuse of a right triangle is equal to the sum of the squares on its two other sides. By virtue of this theorem, if we know the length of the sail's bottom edge and of the edge along the mast, then we can calculate the length of the sail's longest edge. For example, if we know that the bottom edge is 6 feet long and the edge along the mast is 8 feet long, then we can calculate that the longest edge is 10 feet long because the square of the bottom edge, 36, plus the square of the edge along the mast, 64, is 100, and the square root of 100 is 10. But what makes it possible to apply the purely geometrical proposition that the square on the hypotenuse is equal to the sum of the squares on the two other sides in this kind of way—with what Kant calls "complete precision"—to obtain exact information about the dimensions of the sail? In other words, what makes it possible to "transfer" the purely geometrical truth expressed by Pythagoras's theorem (which according to Kant is descriptive of the structure of space itself) to the sail in order to obtain specific and useful information about its dimensions? Well, there is the fact that the sail is a spatial object—that it is *in* space. From this fact, it already follows that any noneliminable features of the portion of space occupied by the sail must be features of the sail. In other words, any feature F of the portion of space S occupied by the sail such that a portion of space that lacked F could not be identical with S—such as S's shape and size—must also be a feature of the sail. This much could already have been concluded from the Aesthetic. But there is more. To apply the Pythagorean theorem in this way to the sail, its edges, as well as the geometrical lines that they trace, must, of course, be measurable. But how is that possible? It is possible only if the lines traced by the sail's edges are divisible into smaller segments that can be equated with some unit of measurement that can be successively applied to them. In other words, this application of the Pythagorean theorem is possible only if lines—both the purely geometrical ones of which the theorem is true and the physical ones made by the sail's edges—are extensive magnitudes: they must both be "wholes" composed of parts that "necessarily precede" them, in the sense that the lines could not exist unless the smaller segments existed, though the smaller segments could exist even if the lines did not. As this example illustrates, the principle that all intuited appearances are extensive magnitudes makes possible the application of mathematics to the empirical world by making possible nothing less than mathematical measurement.

Commentators have raised a number of objections to Kant's discussion of the Axioms of Intuition. The most common objection is that Kant's definition of an extensive magnitude directly contradicts what he says about space in the Aesthetic.[30] There he said:

> These parts [of space] cannot precede the one all-embracing space, as being, as it were, constituents out of which it can be composed; on the contrary, they can be thought only as *in* it. (A 25/B 39)

If one compares the definition of extensive magnitude quoted earlier ("I entitle a magnitude extensive when the representation of the parts makes possible and therefore necessarily precedes, the representation of the whole.") with this passage, they seem to contradict each other: how can the parts "make possible and therefore necessarily precede the whole", and yet *not* "precede [the whole or be] constituents out of which it can be composed"? In Kant's defense, it may be replied that the contradiction is only apparent and can be resolved as follows. From an ontological point of view—one on which we try to say what space *is*—it is true that space is not composed of parts. We cannot disassemble space into parts as we can do to a bookcase, nor can we assemble it out of preexisting parts. Thus Kant can rightly say that "space is essentially one; the manifold in it [i.e., the many portions of space], and therefore the general concept of spaces, depends solely on [the introduction of] limitations" (A 25/B 39). By contrast, objects in space, like bookcases and houses, are composed of parts, such as planks, nails, and bricks. Even a rock is composed of parts, namely, its molecules and atoms. But from an epistemological point of view—one on which we try to know the dimensions of any spatial extent—space must have parts because we cannot measure any spatial extent unless we use some unit of measurement, which must be repeatedly applied in order to yield a measurement, and such measuring presupposes that space is divisible into equal portions that correspond to the unit of measurement.[31] Here the parts are prior to the whole, not in the sense that they can exist without the whole, but in the sense that no dimension can be assigned to the whole (or to any portion thereof) unless we have first determined what part of the whole corresponds to our unit of measurement. Thus from the ontological point of view taken in the Aesthetic, the whole of space is prior to its parts, but from the epistemological point of view taken in the Axioms of Intuition, the parts of space are prior to the whole.

Kant's discussion of the Axioms has also been criticized for saying that we can only think of a spatial object by successively thinking of its parts—for example, that we can only think of a line by constructing it successively in thought, just as we can only draw a line on paper with a pencil by starting at a point and running the pencil successively and continuously over contiguous portions of the paper. As Kant puts it:

> I cannot represent to myself a line, however small, without drawing it in thought, that is, generating from a point all its parts one after another. Only in this way can the intuition be obtained. (A 162–163/B 203)

Some commentators have claimed that this is wrong because we can instantaneously picture a line or line segment to ourselves. This criticism seems right. Kant may here have been misled by his view that our experience is essentially temporal—that our conscious states occur in temporal succession. Although this is one of Kant's most important ideas, he seems to misconstrue its implications here, for it does not follow from it that a line or spatial expanse cannot be intuited in its entirety at a single moment. As Jonathan Bennett says:

> A flash of sheet-lightning has extensive magnitude, not because time is needed for the whole sheet to be spread out, or for us to 'represent it' to ourselves, but just because it is spatially extended. Spatial extension stands on its own feet; it is not a special case of temporal extension.[32]

Finally, Kant is frequently criticized for what may appear to be the quite arbitrary association of the axioms of intuition with the categories of quantity. Recall that under the heading of quantity, Kant has three categories: Unity, Plurality, and Totality. Thus one is naturally led to expect three corresponding principles—three "axioms of intuition"—but all Kant actually gives, as we have seen, is one "principle of" the axioms of intuition. He mentions no specific axioms, and he even says that "as regards magnitude (*quantitas*), that is, as regards the answer given to the question, 'What is the magnitude of a thing?' there are no axioms in the strict meaning of the term" (A 164/B 204). The only clue to the meaning of the categories of quantity that Kant provided prior to stating the principle of the axioms was the Table of Judgments from which they were derived. Unity was officially derived from the universal judgment form, Plurality from the particular judgment form, Totality from the singular judgment form. This leads one to expect that the categories of quantity will have something to do with logical quantifiers like "all" and "some" and with singular referring expressions like proper names. But in fact the solitary principle that Kant gives seems to have nothing to do with these. Instead, it pertains to such questions as "How large is X?" or "How long did Y last?"[33] It ensures that such questions, when asked of spatiotemporal objects, always have an answer, that is, that such things always have extensive magnitudes in virtue of which mathematics can be applied to them. This may be correct, but it seems wholly unrelated to Kant's Table of Judgments and to the categories he derives from it.[34] Some commentators would say that this is just one example of a place in the *Critique* where Kant's *architectonic*—his highly systematic and orderly scheme of organization—breaks down and reveals its artificiality.

However, there is a possible answer that Kant could give to this criticism. In the short but difficult chapter of the *Critique* that Kant inserted at the beginning of Book II of the Analytic, entitled "The Schematism of the Pure Concepts of

Understanding," he argues that the categories, as pure concepts derived strictly from forms of judgment, are too abstract to relate directly to experience.[35] For the categories to relate to experience, they must each have a "schema" or be "schematized." Roughly speaking, a category's schema is an interpretation of the category that makes its application to experience easier to grasp. Since Kant holds that all experience is temporal, he argues that a category's schema is always a temporal feature or "determination of time" (A 138/B 177). Thus, for example, the schema for the category of substance is "permanence of the real in time," and the schema for the category of cause is succession in time according to a rule. Kant applies this theory to the categories of quality, in a way that, he might claim, makes the relation of those categories to the principle of the axioms less arbitrary. The categories of quantity, as we have seen, are invoked by the universal (e.g., "All S is P"), particular (e.g., "Some S is P"), and singular (e.g., "This S is P") forms of judgment; they are invoked when what modern logic calls "quantification" is used in a judgment. But how can abstract logical notions like "all" and "some" be applied to experience? Only, it would seem, if items of experience can be both individuated (identified and distinguished from each other) and counted. If we could not individuate and count items of experience, then the Kantian notions of unity ("allness"), particularity ("someness"), and singularity ("thisness") would be mere abstractions that could never get a foothold in our experience. But how can we individuate and count items of experience? Only, it would seem, in terms of their locations in space and time: what makes it possible for us to differentiate between, say, two otherwise identical coins is that they exist in different places or at different times. This, in turn, requires that space and time be divisible into "parts," that is, units of extension and units of time; it requires that they be "extensive magnitudes" in precisely Kant's sense. This requirement also brings us very near to what Kant calls the schema of magnitude, which he says is "*number*, a representation which comprises the successive addition of homogeneous units" (A 142/B 182). One problematic feature of this way of linking the categories of quantity to the axioms of intuition is Kant's insistence that number is a determination of time. Kant seems to think that just because counting is a process that takes place successively, numerical notions are essentially temporal. That is highly disputable, for surely arithmetical truths like $2 + 2 = 4$ would hold even if there were no such thing as time.[36] But the idea that abstract logical quantifiers like "all" and "some" can be applied to experience only if time and space are divisible into units—only if they are extensive magnitudes—seems quite plausible quite apart from the idea that number is itself a temporal notion.

Does Kant succeed in proving the objective validity of the categories of quantity, that is, in showing that the principle of the axioms has the special status of being (a) synthetic *a priori*, or (b) unobviously analytic, or (c) a necessary condition of human experience? As previously noted, he does not offer a transcendental argument for this principle, that is, one that shows its truth to be a necessary condition of the kind of experience we unquestionably have. Rather, the "proof" of the principle that he gives is the one discussed above, which went as follows:

Space and time are extensive magnitudes.
All intuited appearances are in space or (inclusive "or") in time.

∴ All intuited appearances are extensive magnitudes.[37]

Kant would presumably say that both premises of this argument are synthetic *a priori*, in which case the conclusion must also be synthetic *a priori*—which would mean that Kant certainly has succeeded. But if (both of) the premises are analytic rather than synthetic—a matter that I shall not try to resolve—then the conclusion is analytic, though it seems not to be obviously analytic. It seems not unreasonable to conclude, then, that Kant succeeds in proving the objective validity of the categories of quantity since he shows that their associated principle fits at least option (a) or option (b) above.

3.3.2 Categories of Quality and Anticipations of Perception

The three instantiations of the quality of judgments are, as we have seen, the affirmative, the negative, and the infinite. Here it seems that the transition from the form of judgment to the corresponding category is so obvious as to be almost trivial. It is difficult to improve on Hartnack's treatment, which begins this way:

In an affirmative judgment we assert that something *is* something or other; for example, that S is P. In other words, we assert that this S with its property P is a reality. In a negative judgment it is maintained, on the other hand, that something is *not* something or other, for example, that S is not P. In other words, what is denied is that this S with its property P is a reality. The categories corresponding to affirmative and negative judgments are therefore respectively *reality* and *negation*.[38]

As for the infinite judgment, "S is non-P," it asserts that S belongs in the infinite class of everything that is non-P, but it also limits the complementary class, P, by excluding S from it. So the category corresponding to infinite judgments is *limitation*. We may summarize these derivations by figure 3–4.

Kant's architectonic for the categories of quality is a mirror image of the one he uses for the categories of quantity; again, he offers only a single principle with a plural name: the "Anticipations of Perception." The principle of the anticipa-

Types of Judgment	Examples	Categories
Affirmative	Socrates is mortal	Reality
Negative	Socrates is not mortal	Negation
Infinite	Socrates is nonmortal	Limitation

FIGURE 3–4

tions, as stated in the first edition, says that "in all appearances sensation, and the *real* which corresponds to it in the object (*realitas phenomenon*), has an *intensive magnitude*, that is, a degree" (A 167).

What does this principle mean? We can begin to understand it by contrasting it with the principle of the axioms. The latter told us that all appearances, since they are in space or in time, have extensive magnitude: one can ask and answer questions about how long they last or how large they are. The principle of the anticipations points to another very general feature of appearances: they are more or less intense. For example, a sound not only lasts for a certain time but also has a certain loudness or softness (measurable in decibels); a patch of color not only has a certain size but is more or less saturated. The degree of loudness of the sound and the saturation of the color patch are intensive magnitudes. The terms "magnitude" and "degree" reveal that just as in the Axioms of Intuition, Kant is here concerned with a quantitative notion rather than with a logical one. The principle of the Anticipations, then, provides additional support for Kant's view that mathematics can be applied to empirical objects, for intensive magnitudes, like extensive magnitudes, can be measured, and the results can be mathematically expressed and manipulated.

Unlike extensive magnitudes, however, intensive magnitudes are not composed of parts. Kant says that the apprehension of intensive magnitude takes place in an instant and therefore does not require "a successive synthesis proceeding from parts to the whole representation" (A 167–168/B 209–210). This way of distinguishing intensive from extensive magnitude seems again to involve the questionable assumption that the extensive magnitude of an object—say, the length of a line—cannot be perceived instantaneously. But Kant's point that an intensive magnitude or degree is not a part of any whole is independent of that assumption. Paul Guyer illustrates this key difference between extensive and intensive magnitude as follows:

> For example, 5 feet of plank are literally part of my 8-foot bookshelf, even if I would have to use a saw to introduce a physical limit between those 5 feet and the remaining 3; but 60 degrees of heat are not literally *part* of today's temperature of 90 degrees: there is no way in which I could separate them from the remaining 30 degrees. Rather, they represent the temperature of a cooler day, with which today is being compared by means of a numerical ratio.[39]

This account of intensive magnitude is rough and preliminary, however, because in stating the principle of the anticipations, Kant does not ascribe intensive magnitude to "appearances" as such but rather to *sensation* and "the *real* which corresponds to [sensation] in the object." So his principle is part and parcel of a view of sense perception; it is really a conjunction asserting that (a) the sensations we obtain in sense perception must always have a degree or intensive magnitude, and (b) the corresponding qualities of "real" objects that these sensations are of must likewise always have a degree or intensive magnitude. Kant also puts point (b) this way:

> Corresponding to this intensity of sensation, an *intensive magnitude*, that is, a degree of influence on the sense (i.e. on the special sense involved), must be

ascribed to all objects of perception, in so far as the perception contains sensation. (B 208)

Here the reference to the object's "degree of *influence* on the sense (i.e. on the special sense involved)" unmistakably reveals that Kant is committed to a *causal* claim about perception. More precisely, it shows that Kant holds:

(1) What is causally responsible for the degree or intensity of the sensation obtained in perception is the degree or intensive magnitude of the (quality of the) perceived object that causes the sensation.

Furthermore, (1) obviously entails a claim about the object of perception, namely:

(2) Not only the sensation, but also *that in the object which is responsible for the sensation* (what Kant calls "the *real* which corresponds to [sensation] in the object," and what I just called "the quality of the object that causes the sensation") has a degree or intensive magnitude.

Each of these two claims calls for comment.

The basic assumption behind point (1) is that the characteristic sensation obtained upon perceiving a certain object is caused by that object. To make this assumption is to hold what philosophers today call a "causal theory of perception." The fundamental claim of such a theory is that an object of perception is always a cause of the sensation or sensory experience had when perceiving it. Philosophers who subscribe to the causal theory hold that it is an analytic truth about sense perception that the object perceived must be a cause of the sensation, sense impression, or perceptual experience had when perceiving that object; so, for example, if I see a pen, then the pen must be one of the causes of my present visual experience.[40]

Is a causal theory of perception compatible with Kant's Transcendental Idealism? On the weak interpretation of Transcendental Idealism proposed in the previous chapter (weak TI), there is no problem about the compatibility of such a theory with Kant's position. There is no incompatibility in holding, on the one hand, that we must perceive all objects in time and all objects distinct from ourselves as being in space; that we must conceptualize some of the things we are aware of as being distinct from ourselves and our own mental states; that we must conceive all observable events as having causes; and that we can have no knowledge about, nor even any conception of, what things are like apart from the ways in which we must perceive and think of them *and*, on the other hand, that the objects we perceive must be (conceived as being) causes of our perceptions of them. To put it more simply, it is perfectly consistent to hold that we must perceive and conceive the world as a spatiotemporal system of causally related things and that those things, when we perceive them, cause our perceptual experiences of them.

On the other hand, when one tries to combine the doctrine of the Anticipations of Perception with stronger versions of Transcendental Idealism (strong TI), which assert that there are nontemporal and nonspatial things-in-themselves, major difficulties arise. Consider first the "one-world" version of strong TI, on which things-in-themselves are not in space or in time but appear to us as spatial and temporal. Kant sometimes expresses himself in ways that suggest such a view and that make it sound fairly innocuous, as when he refers to "the absurd [view] that there can be appearance without anything that appears" (B xxvi–xxvii). This invites us to think of perception as always involving a thing that appears in some way to a perceiver. The thing's ways of appearing can be thought of as being effects of the thing when it stimulates someone's sense receptors. They can also be thought of as being relational properties of the thing because a thing cannot appear in any way at all unless it appears that way *to* a perceiver, and a relational property is precisely one that a thing has by virtue of standing in some relation to another thing (like the property of being a brother or of being north of).[41] But when this kind of view is combined with strong TI, then one must say that whereas the effects (things as they appear, or things' ways of appearing) are in space and time, the causes (things as they are in themselves) are not, which makes little if any sense. One may also be led to say that whereas some of a thing's relational properties (its ways of appearing) are instantiated in space and time, the thing that has these properties is not in space or time, which is surely absurd.

Consider next the "two-world" version of strong TI, on which nontemporal and nonspatial things-in-themselves are a separate set of entities from spatiotemporal appearances. This version of TI is associated with what Kant commentators call the "double-affection theory." According to this theory, what happens in perception is this: the thing-in-itself affects the noumenal self (the self as it is in itself, rather than as it appears to itself), as a result of which this noumenal self generates appearances. These appearances are themselves the ordinary, empirical objects that people say they see, touch, hear, smell, and taste. Furthermore, these empirical objects in turn affect the empirical self (the self as we ordinarily think of it), thereby causing it to have sensations or perceptual experiences. Since these sensations are caused by empirical objects that are nothing but appearances, they are "appearances of appearances," as Kant himself calls them in his *Opus postumum*.[42] On this theory, then, the production of sensations by the empirical self when it is affected by empirical objects is a process that occurs entirely in space and time and can be studied by empirical psychology, whereas the affection of the noumenal self by the thing-in-itself occurs outside space and time and remains shrouded in mystery. If we try to avoid this mystery by dropping the thing-in-itself from the theory, leaving in its place only the empirical object, which is a mere "appearance," then we are led to absolute idealism (as well as to what Kant himself, as we saw, calls "the absurd conclusion that there can be appearance without anything that appears"). So we have to accept either an unintelligible affection of the noumenal self by the thing-in-itself or absolute idealism. This unhappy situation is encapsulated in an epigram, loosely attributed to Kant's contemporary critic, F. H. Jacobi (1743–1819): "Without the thing in itself, I could not enter the Kantian philosophy; with it, I could not remain."[43] The upshot is that strong TI, whether we interpret it along the lines of the "one-world" view or the "two-world" view, cannot accommodate the causal aspect of perception embedded in Kant's principle of the Anticipations without running into absurdities. It is a distinct advantage of weak TI, then, that it can incorporate this aspect of perception without paradoxical results.

I turn next to the second point embedded in Kant's doctrine of the Anticipations, namely, that not only the sensation, but also *that in the object which is responsible for the sensation* (what he calls "the *real* which corresponds to [sensation] in the object") has a degree or intensive magnitude. This claim is reminiscent of things that one can find in contemporary philosophy of perception. For example, in his classic 1957 work, *Perceiving*, R. M. Chisholm gives this definition of what it is to see an object:

> "S sees X" means that, as a consequence of *x* being a proper *visual* stimulus of S, S senses in a way that is functionally dependent upon the stimulus energy produced in S by *x*.[44]

Chisholm's definition of seeing says that the way in which one senses in perception depends on an amount of energy attributable to the object; this is quite similar to Kant's claim that the intensity of a sensation corresponds to an intensity found in its cause. Still, there are important differences between Kant and Chisholm. One difference is that Kant has in mind a specific way, grounded in the physics of his day, in which the object possesses "intensity," for Kant is here invoking a scientific theory of matter that he favored, the dynamical theory. Paul Guyer describes the core of this theory as follows:

> The occupation of any determinate extent of space is not due to the presence in that region of a number of determinate atoms but is rather due to the balance in that region between the intensity of the attractive and repulsive forces there centered. . . . [So] we might conjecture that Kant held that at the most fundamental level of physical theory extensive magnitude really reduced to intensive magnitude, even if the opposite seems to be the case at some more superficial level. [For example,] whereas . . . in optics the intensity of illumination might seem to depend on the number of illuminated objects and their distance from a light source, in more basic physical theory such measurements would themselves depend on the intensity of attractive and repulsive forces that have no parts.[45]

But there is another difference, more important for our purposes, between Chisholm and Kant. Chisholm is trying only to *define* seeing; if the concepts he invokes are scientifically flawed, the result will only be that his definition is inapplicable to actual cases of seeing and in that sense incorrect. By contrast, Kant's principle of the Anticipations makes the substantive, synthetic claim that the intensive magnitude of a sensation corresponds to and is caused by the intensive magnitude of the (quality of the) matter that causes that sensation. But such a claim can only be known empirically; it is synthetic *a posteriori*. It cannot, therefore, be an *a priori* claim licensed by the categories of quality nor a truth reporting how we must conceive our experience. The only part of it that can plausibly be said to have that status is the claim that any sensation and certain sensible qualities must have some degree of intensity.[46] But the claim that the intensity of a sensation correlates with or depends upon the intensity of a sensible quality, or indeed of anything (such as attractive and repulsive forces) in matter, is an empirical hypothesis that cannot be derived from Kant's philosophical principles.

Does the principle of the Anticipations relate in any understandable way to the three categories of quality—reality, negation, and limitation? Perhaps we can say at least this. Think of a very intense sensation (and its correlate in the object) as being "very real"—as having a high degree of reality. Think of a less intense sensation (and its correlate in the object) as having a lesser, limited degree of reality. Finally, think of the total absence of any sensation as a lack of any reality. Then it seems that we have given some empirical meaning to the pure concepts of reality, limitation, and negation, respectively.[47] What remains very difficult to see is how these concepts, so interpreted, relate to the judgment forms from which Kant claims to extract them. Why, for example, should the affirmative judgment that S is P relate to a more intense sensation or quality than the infinite judgment that S is non-P or, for that matter, the negative judgment that S is not P? Kant's discussion of the categories of quality in the Schematism chapter (A 143/B 182– 183) does not help to answer these questions.

Does Kant succeed in establishing the objective validity of the categories of quality? It seems that the answer has to be a mixed verdict. On the one hand, the proposition that every sensation, as well as the proposition that certain sensible qualities (e.g., colors, sounds, smells, temperatures) that we take these sensations to be "of," must have a degree or intensive magnitude, certainly seems to be an *a priori* truth. Taking our clue from Kant's label, "Anticipations of Perception," we can *anticipate* with certainty, in advance of experience, that all sensations we experience and certain qualities we might encounter will have some intensive magnitude, though of course only experience can show what specific one they will have. Whether this truth is synthetic *a priori*, unobviously analytic, or perhaps even obviously analytic (once our attention is called to it) is a matter I shall not try to decide. On the other hand, as I have already suggested, the proposition that whenever a sensation having a certain intensive magnitude happens to be caused by an object that we perceive, that object must have a quality whose intensive magnitude corresponds to that of the sensation, is an empirical hypothesis. It seems not unreasonable to conclude, then, that Kant establishes as *a priori* that sensations, as well as certain sensible qualities, have intensive magnitude but not that there is a causal relation between these magnitudes. Furthermore, insofar as Kant seems inclined to treat the intensive magnitude of sensations as *evidence* for objects' qualities' having intensive magnitude, and thus for his preferred theory about the nature of matter, his view is again really only an empirical hypothesis.

3.3.3 *Categories of Relation*

Let us now turn to Kant's derivation of the important categories of relation from the three instantiations of the relation of judgments: categorical, hypothetical, and disjunctive. Here, as previously mentioned, we will consider only how Kant derives the categories from the judgment forms, leaving the discussion of the corresponding principles for later chapters.

Kant claims that from the categorical form, one can derive the category of Inherence and Subsistence (*substantia et accidens*), which we may call simply "substance." Now as Jonathan Bennett points out, "it is just not true that the only task of categorical judgments is to attribute properties to substances."[48] For example, the judgment "red is a color" says that the property *red* is included within the more general property *color*; it does not attribute the property *color* to any substance. However, Kant could reply that the judgment that red is a color is analytic and that his claim holds for synthetic categorical judgments. Thus, for example, the judgment "my car is red" attributes the property *red* to my car, and even if the judgment is reformulated as "red is the color of my car," thus making "red" its grammatical subject, it still entails "my car is red."

Does this really show that synthetic categorical judgments must employ the concept of substance? Before we can answer this question, we need to determine *what* concept of substance is at issue, for the term "substance," as it is used in philosophy, has a long history and a number of different meanings. Most basically, a substance is a bearer of properties; it is that which has or bears various properties but cannot itself be "had" or borne by anything else. This definition of substance goes back to Aristotle, and Kant himself offers it when he refers to "substance, meaning something which can exist as subject but never as predicate" (B 149; see also A 147/B 186 and B 289). James Van Cleve points out that "here, of course, the terms 'subject' and 'predicate' mark an ontological distinction between kinds of entity, not a grammatical distinction between types of linguistic item."[49]

The notion of a bearer of properties, however, has itself been interpreted in two main ways:

(1) It sometimes means simply what would ordinarily be called "a thing," like my car or an apple. It is certainly true that such things are bearers of properties, and it does not seem that they can in the relevant sense be borne or "had" by other things (though of course they can be "had" in other senses, such as being legally owned).

(2) In philosophy, the notion of a bearer of properties is often taken in a more theoretically loaded sense. It is taken to mean not simply a thing but rather a *component of a thing* that is distinct, not only from each of the thing's properties, but also from *all* of its properties taken collectively. On this interpretation, which I will call "the substance theory," one must not equate "thing" with "substance," for the substance theory is really a particular theory about what a thing is. The theory is best understood by contrasting it with a rival theory, commonly called the "bundle theory." According to the bundle theory, a thing is nothing but a collection of coexisting properties. By contrast, the substance theory says that a thing is composed not just of its various properties but also of a substance (often also called a "substrate" or "*substratum*") distinct from all those properties, to which the properties all belong. This substance, just because it is distinct from all properties, must itself be featureless; it must also be in principle unperceivable because anything that we can perceive would have to be a property or set of properties. John Locke, who is often interpreted as holding such a theory, called substance a "something-I-know-not-what" that underlies or supports a thing's properties. Many contemporary philosophers, under the influence of Hume and later empiricists, would reject substance taken in this sense because they

find the notion of an undifferentiated and in principle unperceivable substance unintelligible.

Which of these two concepts of substance does Kant think can be derived from the categorical form of judgment? The section of the *Critique* where Kant focuses on substance, the First Analogy, is one of the most difficult in the work, and it is hard to say exactly what notion of substance Kant means to defend there. But it seems clear enough that he rejects the bundle theory, for throughout the section, Kant emphasizes that substance is permanent, that it is what remains the same while only its properties or "accidents" change. This way of speaking inevitably suggests the main argument for the substance theory, the argument from change. According to this ancient argument, we can only make sense of the notion of a thing T changing from state A to state B, as opposed to T's ceasing to exist and something else beginning to exist in its place, if we accept that T is composed of something distinct from any of its states—something that continues to exist even if all of its states change.[50] Kant's language throughout the First Analogy strongly suggests that, whatever else he wants to say about substance, his view is a variant of this traditional one. Thus, for example, he writes:

> I find that in all ages, not only philosophers, but even the common understanding, have recognized this permanence as a substratum of all changes in appearances, and always assume it to be indubitable. The only difference in this matter between the common understanding and the philosopher is that the latter expresses himself more definitely, asserting that throughout all the changes in the world *substance* remains, and only the *accidents* change. (A 184/B 227)

In light, then, of Kant's apparent commitment to some variant of the substance theory, let us see whether the category of substance, taken in this sense, can be derived from the categorical form of judgment.

Justus Hartnack argues that it can:

> By a categorical judgment Kant means a judgment of the form, "S is P." As an example let us take the judgment, "This table is yellow." Here a distinction is made between the thing (the substance) and one of its properties, namely the property 'yellow.' . . . That we cannot identify the thing with its properties in the way Hume tried to do, is already apparent in the fact that the concept 'property,' in order not to lose all meaning, must be a property of something. And that we cannot do without the concept 'property' stems, Kant believes, from the categorical subject-predicate judgment. For in this judgment we attribute to a subject (a substance) a property; we ascribe a predicate to a subject.[51]

The argument that Hartnack presents here can be put this way:

(1) We make categorical (subject-predicate) judgments.
(2) Therefore, we cannot do without the concept 'property' [from (1)].
(3) The concept 'property' requires that of something of which it is a property—i.e., a substance.
(4) Therefore, we have the concept of substance [from (2) and (3)].

Here it would be more accurate to state step (3) as "The concept 'property' requires that of something of which its object (i.e., the property which is the object or denotation of the concept 'property') is a property." But be that as it may, the argument is inconclusive, at least if it is supposed to show, as the reference to Hume's position implies, that the bundle theory is wrong.[52] For why could one not identify a thing with all of its properties and say that what it is for a property to be "of" a thing is simply for it to be a member of the bundle of properties that constitutes the thing? This proposal seems not at all ruled out by the key third step of the argument.

To see better why the fact that a property must be a property *of* something does not rule out the bundle theory, we can use an illustration given by J. L. Mackie:

> Philosophers have often toyed with a logico-linguistic argument which seems to introduce such a substratum. We say that the thing here, the cat, *has* each of the properties. . . . So it seems that the thing itself must be distinct from each of its properties, and therefore from all its properties together: it must be something other than the properties, something in which they all inhere, and to which they all belong; and it is by belonging to this one underlying something that they are all held together and go to make one complete thing.[53]

The "logico-linguistic argument" that Mackie is describing can be put like this:

This cat *has* each of its properties (e.g., its furriness, blackness, agility, etc.).

∴ This cat is distinct from all of its properties (it is at best only *partially* composed of them).

If this argument were valid, that would support the idea that the concept of substance can be derived from the categorical form of judgment because the premise, being just another way of saying that this cat *is* black, furry, agile, and so on, is a categorical judgment. Furthermore, the argument may seem to be valid because it seems to have the same form as this valid argument:

John *has* a car, a house, a dog, and so on.

∴ John is distinct from his car, house, dog, and so on.

However, as Mackie says:

> The logico-linguistic argument for a substratum is not cogent. . . . While we can speak of a thing as distinct from each of its properties, including this one, so that we can say that the thing *has* this or that property, it does not follow that we must regard the thing as being distinct from all its . . . properties at once. If our ordinary style of speaking did commit us to this conclusion, we could only say, so much the worse for our ordinary style of speaking: there is no need to let it be authoritative in leading to so unacceptable a result. But in any case our ordinary style of speaking does not so commit us.[54]

To show that "our ordinary style of speaking" or, more to the point here, our categorical form of judgment does not commit us to the substance theory, Mackie argues as follows. It may be granted that

(1) This cat has property P

entails

(2) P belongs to a thing which is distinct from each of its properties including P.

However, (2) does not mean that

(3) P belongs to a thing which is distinct from *all* its properties.

Rather, it means either:

(4) $P \& P_1 \& P_2 \& \ldots P_n$ has P as a member (where $P \& P_1 \& P_2 \& P_n$ are properties referred to by "this cat")

or

(4a) $P_1 \& P_2 \& \ldots P_n$ coexist with P (where $P_1 \& P_2 \& \ldots P_n$ are properties referred to by "this cat").[55]

The "logico-linguistic argument," then, is a weak one, and this seems to confirm the point that the fact that we make categorical judgments does not commit us to the substance theory.

An ardent defender of the substance theory, however, might reply that

[a proponent of the substance theory] need not be interpreted as contending, absurdly, that a thing's "substratum" is a featureless "something" which exists independently of all that thing's qualities [properties]. . . . All he means is that the idea of "substratum" [or substance] is that aspect of our idea of a thing which remains when we *abstract* from the latter all our ideas of its particular qualities: in short, it is our idea of a thing's being a *bearer* of its qualities, considered in abstraction from any particular qualities it bears.[56]

Although this seems reasonable enough, it does not appear to be a version of the substance theory. For to say that we can abstract from our idea of a thing the ideas of all its qualities, to form the highly abstract idea of a bearer of all those qualities, is not to say that a bearer of qualities, as it exists in the world, is anything more than what we ordinarily mean by a thing—a thing which, moreover, could consist simply of a collection of coexisting qualities. Thus, the position suggested here is compatible with the bundle theory.

I conclude from these reflections that the only notion of substance that is derivable from the categorical form of judgment is the weaker one, on which a "substance" is simply what we would ordinarily call "a thing"—a thing which, furthermore, may be merely a bundle of properties. As I shall argue later, this also appears to be the only notion of substance whose objective validity can be established by the central argument of the analytic (despite the fact that the First Analogy defends a stronger notion of substance).

We may now turn to Kant's attempt to derive the category of causality from the hypothetical form of judgment. Here there is an obvious objection: not all hypothetical judgments involve the causal relation; for example, the judgment that *if the Empire State Building is taller than the Eiffel Tower and the Eiffel tower is taller than the leaning tower of Pisa, then the Empire State Building is taller than the leaning tower of Pisa* is a hypothetical judgment, but it does not use the concept of causality (we do not ordinarily suppose that the height of the Empire State Building and of the Eiffel tower have any effect on the height of the leaning tower of Pisa; i.e., that there is a causal connection here). Likewise, the judgment *if Kant was a philosopher and Einstein was a physicist, then Kant was a philosopher* is hypothetical, but it does not use the concept of causality. Obviously, one could multiply such examples.

Kant could plausibly reply, however, that when a hypothetical judgment is *synthetic*, then it does employ the concept of causality. Hartnack gives an example that neatly illustrates the point:

> Consider the example, "If it is raining, then the street is wet." This judgment does not imply that either of the two included judgments (namely the judgments [1] it is raining and [2] the street is wet) is true; what is being said is, rather, that the truth of the one judgment must be considered as the basis of the truth of the other. The [synthetic] hypothetical judgment cannot be made (its thought cannot be expressed) except by means of the concept *causality* (or *dependence*). Without this concept we would never be able to think, to comprehend, or to understand anything other than temporal succession.[57]

Hartnack points out that Kant's own example, "If there is a perfect justice, then the obstinately wicked are punished," has "the shortcoming that it is virtually (not to say entirely) a tautology"; evidently he also thinks, then, that Kant's derivation of the category of causality from hypothetical judgments can work only in the case of synthetic judgments of that form.[58]

The last category of relation, which Kant calls "community," is supposed to be derivable from the disjunctive form of judgment. To understand why Kant thinks so, one needs to bear in mind two points: (1) by "community," Kant means causal reciprocity; the principle associated with this category says that "all substances, insofar as they co-exist, stand in thoroughgoing community, that is, in mutual interaction" (A 211/B 256); (2) he takes disjunction, as explained above, in the "exclusive" sense, on which "*p or q*" means that at least one of the two statements is true but they are not both true. Kant thinks this means that the truth of *p* causally depends on the truth of *q* and vice versa; for if *p* is true then *q* must be false and if *p* is false then *q* must be true, and if *q* is true then *p* must be false and if *q* is false then *p* must be true—*p* and *q* must have opposite truth-values and are in that sense mutually dependent on each other.

Unfortunately, however, this attempt to derive the category of community seems fatally flawed. Paul Guyer notes:

> As is often pointed out, Kant's connection of the real relation of reciprocal influence with the logical notion of exclusive disjunction is the most tenuous piece of his metaphysical deduction of the categories.[59]

Why is this so? First, it can be objected that not every exclusive "or" statement employs the concept of causality (or, *a fortiori*, of mutual causation). For example, the statement that *either X is moving or X is not moving* is a straightforward application of the logical law of excluded middle that makes no use of causal notions. As before, one might try to defend Kant by suggesting that his claim is plausible for *synthetic* judgments. For example, the truth of the statement that *either X is moving in a straight line or X is moving in a circle* seems to involve causality, for we presume that there is some causal explanation of why X is moving in one of these two ways rather than, say, in a zigzag fashion. This point, however, certainly does not show that the events reported by X *is moving in a straight line* and X *is moving in a circle* are causally interdependent, if only because these events, far from producing each other, mutually exclude each other. Indeed, this example points to a crucial disanalogy, noted by Henry Allison, between exclusive disjunction and reciprocal causation:

> In the case of a disjunctive judgment, which Kant understands only in the sense of an exclusive disjunction, the assertion of one element entails the negation of the others, while in the case of the pure concept, the assertion of one element entails the assertion of the others. The only positive result that follows from [Kant's] . . . analysis is that both the disjunctive form and the pure concept involve the thought of a coordination of elements, which is contrasted with the thought of subordination that is involved in the hypothetical form and the pure concept of causality. This provides sufficient justification for distinguishing the pure concept of community from that of causality, but not for deriving it from the disjunctive form of judgment.[60]

Allison's criticism, I believe, ruins Kant's attempt to derive the category of community from the disjunctive judgment form. Insofar as this category can be derived from any form of judgment, the appropriate form is the biconditional, "if and only if" form rather than the disjunctive form, since "*p* if and only if *q*" is logically equivalent to "if *p* then *q* and if *q* then *p*." Thus, at least on the assumption that the category of causality can be plausibly derived from the hypothetical or conditional form of judgment in which the assertion of one element implies the assertion of the other, the category of mutual or reciprocal causation can be derived from the biconditional form in which the assertion of one element implies the assertion of the other and vice versa.

3.3.4 *Categories of Modality and Postulates of Empirical Thought*

Let us turn, finally, to Kant's derivation of the categories of modality from the problematic, assertoric, and apodictic forms of judgment. Here the transition from the forms of judgment to the categories is, as with the categories of quality, so obvious as to seem almost trivial: of course, the problematic judgment, "possibly *p*," uses the concept of *possibility*, and the apodictic judgment, "necessarily *p*," uses the concept of *necessity*. As for the assertoric judgment, *p*, it asserts the actuality or *existence* of the state of things reported by *p*. What is not trivial, however, is the way in which Kant goes on to interpret the concepts of possibility, existence, and necessity when he sets out their corresponding principles, the "Postulates of Empirical Thought." I have already noted that whereas the Axioms, Anticipations, and Analogies are principles that are supposed to possess a special status (of being synthetic *a priori* propositions, or unobvious analytic truths about the structure of experience, or necessary conditions of experience), the three Postulates are really only definitions. Kant himself says that, "the principles of modality are nothing but explanations of the concepts of possibility, actuality, and necessity, in their empirical employment" (A 219/B 266). Furthermore, as the phrase "in their empirical employment" suggests, the Postulates are not definitions of *logical* possibility or *logical* necessity; rather, they concern what some philosophers call "real" possibility and necessity. Accordingly, they contrast markedly with the logicometaphysical notions of possibility and necessity that are common in contemporary philosophy and that were first proposed by Leibniz, according to which "necessary" means "true in all possible worlds" and "possible" means "true in some possible world." By contrast, Kant's Postulates of Empirical Thought attempt to spell out what is meant by saying that some object or occurrence within the natural world we experience is possible, real, or necessary. Moreover, they attempt to do this against the background of what Kant thinks he has established by the time he gets to the Postulates, namely, that our experience is of objects in space and time governed by causal laws. We have of course not yet seen most of his case for this—it is developed in the central argument of the Analytic—but we can nevertheless understand Kant's definitions before we turn to that argument.

For Kant, to say that something is possible is not to say only that it is logically possible or free of contradiction: this is a necessary condition but not a sufficient one. Rather, to say that something is possible means that it conforms to the conditions of both intuition and thought; as Kant states it in the First Postulate: "That which agrees with the formal conditions of experience, that is, with the conditions of intuition and of concepts, is *possible*" (A 218/B 265). For example, according to Kant it is not self-contradictory to speak of a closed geometrical figure bounded by only two straight lines (since he thinks the truths of geometry are synthetic). But such a figure is nevertheless an impossibility because it does not satisfy the conditions determined by space as an *a priori* form of intuition—it does not accord with the nature of space as set out in the Transcendental Aesthetic.[61]

To say for Kant that something is actual, or that it exists, means that either it is actually sensed or observed or that it is caused by something that is sensed. Kant says, in the Second Postulate: "That which is bound up with the material conditions of experience, that is, with sensation, is *actual*" (A 218/B 265). His own explanation of this claim is very lucid:

> The postulate bearing on the knowledge of things as *actual* does not, indeed, demand immediate *perception* (and, therefore, sensation of which we are conscious) of the object whose existence is to be known. What we do, however, require is the connection of the object with some actual perception, in accordance with the analogies of experience, which define all real connection in an experience in general. . . . Our knowledge of the existence of things reaches, then, only so far as perception and its advance according to empirical laws can extend. If we do not start from experience, or do not proceed in accordance with laws of the empirical connection of appearances, our guessing or enquiring into the existence of anything will only be an idle pretense. (A 225–226/B 272–274)

Here Kant's claim that we cannot know the existence of anything unless we either perceive it or infer its existence from what we perceive carries the same empiricist message and echoes remarkably the following passage from David Hume:

> Though our conclusions from experience carry us beyond our memory and senses, and assure us of matters of fact, which happened in the most distant places and most remote ages; yet some fact must always be present to the senses or memory, from which we may first proceed in drawing these conclusions. . . . If we proceed not upon some fact, present to the memory or senses, our reasonings would be merely hypothetical; and however the particular links might be connected with each other, the whole chain of inferences would have nothing to support it, nor could we ever, by its means, arrive at the knowledge of any real existence.[62]

Finally, to say for Kant that something is necessary is not to say that it is logically necessary or that its opposite is self-contradictory. Rather, it is to say that it is governed by causal laws, or could have been predicted by using causal laws. This is the Third Postulate, which Kant states this way: "That which in its connection with the actual is determined in accordance with the universal conditions of experience, is (that is, exists as) *necessary*" (A 218/B 266). Kant uses the phrase "universal conditions of experience" instead of "causal laws" because he thinks he has shown in the Second Analogy that it is a necessary condition of experience that *everything* that happens in nature is governed by causal laws.

It is an implication of Kant's position, then, that everything that falls under the Second Postulate also falls under the Third Postulate—that everything that is actual, or exists in nature, is necessary, so that the actual and the necessary are coextensive. Consequently, as Hartnack points out, "the difference between the actual and the necessary is [merely] epistemological—it is a distinction with respect to our knowledge of the existing thing."[63] For example, if today I observe termites in my house, then I can judge, applying the category of existence and in conformity with the Second Postulate, that it is an established fact that there are termites in my house. But if I go on to learn the relevant laws of insect development and behavior and the relevant facts about the construction of my house, then I will see why it had to be the case that there are termites there and I can judge, applying the category of necessity and in conformity with the Third Postulate, that this is necessary.

Furthermore, Kant goes so far as to claim that whatever is possible is actual, so that the realm of the possible and the actual are coextensive. This doctrine, however, does not follow from Kant's definition of possibility in the First Postulate. There he defined the possible as "that which agrees with the formal conditions of experience, that is, with the conditions of intuition and of concepts." It follows that nothing that would violate the formal conditions of experience—such as a nontemporal event, a nonspatial object of perception distinct from oneself, a spatial object with no extensive magnitude, a sensation with no intensive magnitude, or an uncaused event—is possible. But it does not follow that everything that would satisfy the formal conditions of experience is actual. Furthermore, the doctrine that whatever is possible is actual is very strange. On the standard treatment of modalities, whatever is necessary is actual and whatever is actual is possible, so that whatever is necessary is possible. But we have just seen that for Kant, whatever is actual is necessary. If we combine this with the doctrine that whatever is possible is actual, we get the result that whatever is possible is necessary—which is very counterintuitive. It seems quite possible, for example, that I have exactly 3002 hairs on my head, but this seems nowise necessary and may well be false.

Why, then, does Kant hold this strange view? He gives two arguments for it. First, he argues:

> To enquire whether the field of possibility is larger than the field which contains all actuality . . . [is] tantamount to the enquiry whether things as appearances one and all belong to the sum and context of a single experience, of which every given perception is a part, a part which therefore cannot be connected with any other [series of] appearances, or whether my perceptions can belong, in their general connection, to more than one possible experience. (A 230/B 282–283)

Kant seems to be arguing here that if some things were possible but not actual, then those things could not even potentially enter into the same series of appearances as actual things. Given that the natural world that we can know is for Kant the (total) series of appearances—that is, the world of things as we must perceive and conceive them—this is tantamount to saying that if some things were possible but not actual, then those things could not even be potential occupants of the same natural world as actual ones. R. P. Wolff captures this line of thought:

> Kant argues that the realm of real possibility is no larger than that of actuality. . . . For the actual contains all that was, or is, or will be, and nothing more could ever conform to the conditions of experience. Otherwise there would be more than one nature, and more than one unity of [experience].[64]

But why should we agree with Kant that no unactualized, merely possible things could have belonged to the same world as do its actual occupants—that there would be, so to speak, no room left in the world for these things? Kant seems to be assuming what A. O. Lovejoy called the "principle of plenitude"—the principle that whatever is possible must sometime be actualized, so that the actual world (or at least its complete history) contains the maximum number of things that can exist in that world. But although this principle was arguably integral to the metaphysics of Leibniz and other thinkers whose views Kant favored during his "precritical" period, it does not appear to be one that can be defended on Kantian principles. It does not appear to be a basic truth about the structure of experience or one that could be shown to be a necessary condition of experience. It appears, rather, to be a holdover from the kind of metaphysics that Kant's *Critique of Pure Reason* seeks to discredit.

Kant's second argument for the doctrine that whatever is possible is actual is this:

> It does indeed seem as if we were justified in extending the number of possible things beyond that of the actual, on the ground that something must be added to the possible to constitute the actual. But this [alleged] process of adding to the possible I refuse to allow. For that which would have to be added to the possible, over and above the possible, would be impossible. (A 231/B 284)

This argument can be put as follows:

(1) If the possible does not coincide with the actual, then the actual must result from adding something to the possible.
(2) The only thing that can be added to the possible is the impossible.
(3) The impossible cannot be added to anything.

∴ The possible coincides with the actual.

Even if we allow the naive way in which this argument treats "the possible" and "the impossible"—as if these were things like flour and sugar that might be added to each other to make a cake—the argument commits a fallacy of equivocation. For in premise (2), "that can be added to" means "that is different from" or "that contrasts with" or even "that is a complement of." But in premise (3), "cannot be added to" means "cannot also be true" or "cannot also obtain" or "cannot also exist." It seems, then, that Kant gives no good reason for his doctrine that whatever is possible is actual.

Putting this strange doctrine aside, then, what message are we to take from Kant's Postulates? W. H. Walsh suggests that "the sting of this doctrine [the doctrine of the Postulates] is in its tail: it is Kant's claim to be able to rule possibilities out which is the most striking part of his theory."[65] We have already seen how Kant would use his doctrine to rule out the possibility of such things as a closed geometrical figure composed of only two straight lines. More generally, he would use it to rule out the possibility of anything that does not conform to our forms of intuition and to the principles associated with the categories of quantity, quality, and relation. But Kant goes further than this:

> A special ultimate mental power of *intuitively* anticipating the future (and not merely inferring it), or . . . a power of standing in community of thought with other men, however distant they may be . . . are concepts the possibility of which is altogether groundless, as they cannot be based on experience and its known laws; and without such confirmation they are arbitrary combinations of thoughts, which, although indeed free from contradiction, can make no claim to objective reality, and none, therefore, as to the possibility of an object such as we here profess to think. (A 222–223/B 270)

Here Kant tells us that whereas such things as precognition and mental telepathy are logically possible, they are not possible in the more interesting sense of being compatible with the known laws of nature. Today, philosophers make this point by saying that such things are logically possible but not physically possible, and Kant should be credited for making this now commonplace distinction. As Walsh notes: "Kant has proved so persuasive on the topic of real necessity as to appear now to have had little of importance to say about it."[66] On the other hand, it should also be noted that what Kant says about precognition, mental telepathy, and the like does not really follow from the doctrine of the Postulates as he states it, for that doctrine rules out only the possibility of things that do not conform to "the formal conditions of experience." It does not rule out the possibility of things that violate the known laws of nature—laws that can be known only empirically. To obtain this result, Kant would have to stipulate that the impossible includes not only what violates the formal conditions of experience but also what violates the laws of nature. Such a stipulation might seem to commit one, once again, to the objectionable view that whatever is possible is actual, but it does not really do that. For to say that nothing can violate the laws of nature is not to say that whatever conforms to those laws must obtain. It would violate the laws of nature to suppose that an egg can be dropped from twenty feet up and not break, but this does not mean that any egg has been dropped from twenty feet up and broken.

4

The Central Argument of the Analytic (I)
The Transcendental Deduction

4.1 Introduction

The chapter of Kant's *Critique of Pure Reason* entitled "The Deduction of the Pure Concepts of Understanding," usually called the "Transcendental Deduction of the Categories," is generally acknowledged to be the heart of the constructive part of the *Critique*. Yet, it is one of the most difficult and obscurely written chapters of the work; indeed, it is one of the most difficult of all philosophical texts. H. J. Paton compared reading it to crossing the Great Arabian Desert by foot; James Van Cleve writes that "it is more aptly compared to a tropical jungle."[1] My aim in this chapter is to give a reconstruction of the Transcendental Deduction, one that also treats it as the first stage of an extended argument that continues in the section called "The Analogies of Experience" and that can plausibly be regarded as the central argument of the Transcendental Analytic.[2]

4.2 The Problem of the Deduction

What is Kant's purpose in the Transcendental Deduction of the categories? When we look at the introductory Section I (A 84/B 116–A 95/B 129), we find that Kant is setting out to prove the objective validity of the categories. According to his official formulation of his task, this means that he is seeking to prove that the categories yield synthetic *a priori* knowledge. Knowledge of what? Not of things as they are in themselves, independently of the ways we must perceive and conceive them, but rather of things as we perceive and conceive them or, in Kant's idiom, of things as they appear to us. But some of that knowledge is merely empirical; it is based on how we are affected in sensibility. Rather, the categories are supposed to yield the *a priori* component of our knowledge of things as they appear or, still more accurately, one part of that component. For another part of the *a priori* component of our knowledge derives from the pure forms of intuition, space and time, which dictate that things must appear to us in a spatiotemporal framework (or more accurately, as we have seen, that all things must appear to us in time and that anything perceived as being distinct from the self and its states must appear to us in space). What the categories are supposed to yield in addition to this is that all the things we experience must be conceptualizable in terms of the categories. To put the point differently, just as the forms of intuition are supposed to yield *a priori* knowledge about the basic structure of human experience— that is, that it must be spatiotemporal—so the categories are supposed to yield further *a priori* knowledge about the basic structure of experience.[3]

Kant's official formulation of the task of the Transcendental Deduction, however, is misleading in two important ways. First, as we have seen, the equation of the objective validity of a category with its yielding synthetic *a priori* knowledge is too simple: to say that a category is objectively valid is to say that the principle associated with it has the special status of being synthetic *a priori*, or unobviously analytic, or a necessary condition of the kind of experience we unquestionably have. As we shall see, the third of these special statuses is the one that is most relevant to the Transcendental Deduction. Second, as we have also seen, insofar as Kant argues for the objective validity of the categories of quantity, quality, and modality, his arguments do not depend on the Transcendental Deduction since they occur in their entirety within the corresponding sections of the "Principles" chapter of the Analytic (the Axioms of Intuition, Anticipations of Perception, and Postulates of Empirical Thought). Thus the real purpose of the Transcendental Deduction is to serve as the first stage of an argument, completed only in the Analogies of Experience, that is meant to establish the objective validity of the categories of relation. But even this description is not quite right, for as we shall see, Kant does not really link the Transcendental Deduction to his third category of relation, the category of causal reciprocity or, as he calls it, "Community." Rather, the Transcendental Deduction is the first stage of an argument that is supposed to establish the objective validity of only the first two categories of relation, substance and cause. This argument as a whole, which I call "the central argument of the Analytic," is supposed to prove that all the things we experience must be conceptualizable in terms of the categories of substance and cause. In other words, it is supposed to show that experience must be conceptualizable as being of substances whose changes are governed by causal laws. Furthermore, it is supposed to prove this thesis by showing that its truth is a necessary condition of the kind of experience we unquestionably have, that is, by showing that if we have the kind of experience we unquestionably do, then we must conceptualize our experience as being of substances whose changes are governed by causal laws.

To appreciate the significance of this thesis, let us consider what Kant is up against. Consider what David Hume would say, or at any rate is committed to saying, about the most general features of experience:

(1) Items of experience are subjective.
(2) Items of experience are unconnected.

By (1), I mean that Hume, when all is said and done, is committed to the proposition that all we ever perceive is our own fleeting, private mental states—our own "impressions." We never perceive objective, publicly observable states of affairs; each of us is confined to a subjective, private realm. The only way out of this realm is by a chancy causal inference to physical objects as causes of our impressions—an inference that Hume himself rejects as worthless. Of course, this subjectivist strand in modern philosophy originated before Hume, notably in Descartes. The meaning of point (2) is that experience consists of a succession of items that are unconnected to each other. The full force of this point is brought out in Hume's rejection of any objective necessary connection between a cause and its effect. To be sure, Hume does think that our experience is ordered by certain associative psychological principles, such as the principle that if we repeatedly perceive A's followed by B's, then we come to expect a B upon perceiving an A; the principle that if we have noticed a resemblance between A and B, then perceiving or thinking of A leads us to think of B; and the principle that if we have noticed that A is spatially contiguous to B, then a mention of A leads us to think of B—principles that he calls "cause and effect," "resemblance," and "contiguity," respectively.[4] But for Hume, the absence of any perceived necessary connection between different items of experience means that it is perfectly conceivable, and so quite possible, that whatever order our experience exhibits should break down completely, that experience should become completely chaotic, and consequently that all these associative principles would cease to have any foothold and could operate no more. For Hume, then, experience is essentially a flux of *subjective* and *unconnected* items.

In the Transcendental Deduction (and its sequel in the Analogies of Experience), Kant argues that this Humean view of experience is false because it lacks certain basic structural features without which the kind of experience we unquestionably have would be impossible. These features are the ones embodied in the pure concepts or categories:

> The Transcendental Deduction of all *a priori* concepts has thus a principle according to which the whole inquiry must be directed, namely, that they must be regarded as *a priori* conditions of the possibility of experience, whether of the intuition which is to be met with in it or of the thought. (A 94/B 126)

This would be clearer if it spoke not of "a principle according to which the whole inquiry must be directed" but rather of "a principle *toward which* the whole inquiry must be directed."[5] For Kant is here announcing what is to be a key *conclusion* of the argument, namely, that the pure concepts are among the conditions that make experience possible (the other "conditions" being the forms of intuition, space and time). Now, although Kant speaks here and throughout the Transcendental Deduction of "all *a priori* concepts," his argument will really be directed at the pure concepts of substance and cause. But to prove that the concept of substance applies to experience is to disprove point (1) of the Humean view of experience—that items of experience are subjective.[6] Furthermore, to prove that the concept of cause applies to experience is to disprove point (2) of the Humean view—that items of experience are unconnected. Accordingly, Kant's Transcendental Deduction is an attempt to break out of both the subjectivism and the unconnectedness of the Humean view of experience, and to defeat as well the skepticism associated with that view. As such, it is one of the most ambitious arguments in modern philosophy.

Before turning to Kant's argument, however, we need to say more about the way in which it is supposed to disprove each of the two points in the Humean view. To begin with point (2), it is important to realize that Kant *agrees* with Hume that we do not perceive any necessary connections between distinct events or objects. So when he denies point (2), he is not asserting that necessary connections between items of experience are given in intuition. Rather, he is saying this: the kind of experience we unquestionably have would be impossible if our experience did not conform to certain laws or did not exhibit certain kinds of order. He is saying that given certain unquestionable features of our experience, this experience must also be fundamentally lawlike. He is denying Hume's view that our experience could conceivably become so disorderly that principles of association could no longer get a foothold.

Kant's position with respect to point (1) is more difficult to interpret, for in discussing the Transcendental Deduction, one must not forget Kant's so-called Copernican Revolution in Philosophy—his doctrine of transcendental idealism. Now, one proposition of this doctrine is that in intuition we are not presented with things as they are in themselves but only with things as they appear to us. There are reminders of this doctrine throughout the *Critique*. But does not the doctrine entail that items of experience *are* subjective, like Hume's "impressions" or Berkeley's "sensations or ideas"? The answer depends, of course, on how Kant's doctrine of transcendental idealism is interpreted. It will be recalled that I am construing this doctrine in a "weak" sense, as asserting three theses:

(1) We must perceive all things in time and all things distinct from ourselves and our own mental states as being in space.

(2) We must think of some of the things we perceive as being distinct from ourselves and of every event we perceive as having a cause.

(3) We can have no knowledge about, nor even any conception of, what things are like apart from the ways in which we must perceive and think of them; nor can we intelligibly suppose that things might be different from the ways we must perceive and conceptualize them.

Now, on this construal of Kant's doctrine, the doctrine does not entail that items of experience are subjective, for the doctrine says that we must conceptualize (some of) the things we perceive as being objects distinct from ourselves and in space and that we cannot know what things are like apart from the ways in which we must conceptualize them. But to say that (a) we *must* conceptualize some things as objects (or as "objective"), but (b) those things are really subjective, is precisely to say that we can know what things are like apart from the ways in which we must conceptualize them (i.e., they are then "subjective"), which contradicts part (3) of the doctrine. Notice, furthermore, that on this construal of Transcendental Idealism, the purpose of the Transcendental Deduction (and its sequel in the Analogies) is to establish part (2) of the doctrine.

4.3 Two Meanings of "Experience"

The purpose of the Transcendental Deduction, Kant says, is to show that the categories are *a priori* conditions of the possibility of experience. As I have said, the argument is really directed only at the categories of substance and cause, but for simplicity's sake I shall henceforth follow Kant's usage and speak of these simply as "the categories." The argument, then, is supposed to establish the conditional proposition that

If experience is possible, then the categories have objective validity.

For ease of reference, let us call this if-then proposition "the Deduction Principle." The core of the Transcendental Deduction is an argument for the Deduction Principle. We are invited to complete the argument by supplying the additional premise that

Experience is possible

and drawing the conclusion:

The categories have objective validity.

Before looking at Kant's case for the Deduction Principle, we need to understand what the term "experience" means in the principle. Kant uses this term with at least two different meanings. Sometimes, he uses it as a synonym for empirical knowledge. For example, in the very first paragraph of the Introduction to the *Critique*, he speaks of "that knowledge of objects which is entitled experience" (B 1). In another place he says that the categories "serve only for the possibility of *empirical knowledge*; and such knowledge is what we entitle experience" (B 147); elsewhere he says flatly that "empirical knowledge is experience" (B 166) and also that "experience is an empirical knowledge, that is, a knowledge which determines an object through perceptions" (B 218). But at other times, Kant uses "experience" as a synonym for "consciousness" or "awareness." For example, again in the first paragraph of the Introduction, he says that "all our knowledge begins with experience" and that "we have no knowledge antecedent to experience, and with experience all our knowledge begins" (B 1). Here, then, experience is not knowledge itself but rather something with which knowledge begins. What is that something? The natural answer is "consciousness," and Kant's explanation of the point suggests the same answer:

> There can be no doubt that all our knowledge begins with experience. For how could our faculty of knowledge be awakened into action did not objects affecting our senses partly of themselves produce representations, partly arouse the activity of our understanding to compare these representations, and, by combining or separating them, work up the raw material of the sensible impressions into that knowledge of objects which is entitled experience? (B 1)

Elsewhere, Kant says that "only by means of these fundamental concepts [i.e., the categories] can appearances belong to knowledge *or even to our consciousness*, and so to ourselves" (A 125; my emphasis). This appears to be a formulation of the

Deduction Principle, saying that consciousness (of "appearances") is possible only by means of the categories, that is, only if the categories are objectively valid.

So "experience" may mean empirical knowledge, or it may mean mere consciousness.[7] Whether it means the former or the latter has important implications for the significance of the Transcendental Deduction. Suppose that "experience" means "empirical knowledge." Then we must be sure to build into the meaning of "empirical knowledge" what Kant himself builds into it. Now, what Kant means by empirical knowledge, as is abundantly clear from the *Critique* as a whole, is knowledge of an objective world regulated by causal laws. But if this is what Kant means by "experience," then the Deduction Principle loses much of its philosophical interest, for it then states that if empirical knowledge in this full-blooded sense is possible, then the basic concepts that must apply for it to be possible, such as substance and causality, have objective validity. But this means that the additional premise needed to complete the argument—that experience is possible—begs the question against Hume because the premise now means that empirical knowledge in the full-blooded sense is possible. But this is precisely what Hume would question, for if the items we experience are subjective and unconnected "impressions," then, as Hume showed, it is very doubtful that we can have such knowledge.

In spite of this, there are historians of philosophy and Kant commentators who interpret "experience" in the Deduction Principle to mean "empirical knowledge," and it must be admitted that there is textual support for such an interpretation in the *Critique*.[8] It needs to be emphasized, however, that if one reads Kant in this manner, then one cannot regard him as a thinker who tried to answer Hume's skepticism. Rather, one must see Kant as only bringing to light certain fundamental presuppositions of commonsense and scientific knowledge, without making any attempt to defend these presuppositions against skepticism. In other words, one would have to view Kant as arguing regressively in the Analytic, just as he does in the Aesthetic. One would have to see him as first assuming the existence of commonsense and scientific knowledge and then trying to discover the pure concepts that make this knowledge possible, just as he assumed the existence of geometrical knowledge and then sought to discover the pure form of intuition that makes it possible.

Suppose, on the other hand, that "experience" in the Deduction Principle means "consciousness." Then that principle is a very powerful one, for it asserts that if consciousness or awareness is possible, then all experience must be structured in accordance with the laws and principles prescribed by the categories. Furthermore, since not even the most radical skeptic would deny that he is conscious, the premise that "experience is possible" now begs no questions, and the conclusion drawn from it and the Deduction Principle is compelling: one can deduce the objective validity of the categories from the mere fact of consciousness. At least one contemporary Kant scholar, Robert Paul Wolff, has argued for interpreting Kant in just this way.[9] The basic question that Wolff's interpretation raises is whether the notion of consciousness is rich enough to yield the objective validity of the categories as a deductive consequence.

To summarize: if the term "experience" in the Deduction Principle means "empirical knowledge," then it has such a rich meaning that the premise that "experience is possible" begs the question. On the other hand, if this term means mere consciousness, then it has such a narrow meaning that the question becomes whether the Deduction Principle can be established. This is a question that we shall investigate in what follows.

4.4 A Preliminary Sketch of the Deduction

To establish the Deduction Principle, Kant must produce a chain of reasoning that will link the possibility of experience (suitably interpreted) with the objective validity of the categories. Since the principle to be proved is an if-then proposition, we may naturally expect an argument with two or more if-then statements as premises. In other words, we may expect one or more inferences having the form "Hypothetical Syllogism." So, a simple, preliminary sketch of the Deduction will look like this:

(I) If experience is possible, then p.
(II) If p, then the categories have objective validity.

∴ (III) If experience is possible, then the categories have objective validity.

Thus, the question becomes this: is there any linking or "middle" proposition which is both a *necessary condition* of experience and a *sufficient condition* for the objective validity of the categories?

To answer this question, we must first settle the meaning of "experience"; otherwise we will not know what it is that we are seeking a necessary condition of. We saw in the previous section the implications that follow from choosing each of two different possible meanings for "experience" that are suggested by the text of the *Critique*. If we select "empirical knowledge," then the Deduction Principle unpacks the presuppositions of such knowledge but cannot show that those presuppositions are justified. If we select "consciousness" (with Wolff), then the Deduction Principle becomes a powerful one indeed since even Hume admits that he is conscious. Accordingly, let us select "consciousness," so as to investigate whether the Transcendental Deduction can really serve as a refutation of the Humean view of experience and the skepticism to which that view leads.

Thus our question becomes this: what are the necessary conditions of consciousness? Before tackling this question, one must say something about what consciousness is. Let me therefore make two points about the nature of consciousness:

(1) As philosophers who discuss intentionality like to say, consciousness is "consciousness of." It makes little or no sense, at least when focusing on the kind of consciousness that humans typically have, to say that someone is conscious but that there is nothing of which she is conscious. This does not mean, however, that the object of consciousness must always be a physical thing: it can be an imaginary entity like a unicorn or an illusory one like Hamlet's dagger.

(2) Consciousness is not only consciousness *of* something, but of *many* things. One might object that this is not an essential feature of consciousness because one can conceive of consciousness of a single, monotonous, unchanging object that lasts as long as the period of consciousness itself. I believe that because of views about the temporality of consciousness that we shall discuss later, Kant would say that even in such a case there is consciousness of many things, rather than just one thing, and that this is a necessary feature of consciousness. But for the moment, we need not worry about whether the manyness of the objects of consciousness is a necessary or a contingent feature of consciousness. To follow Kant, we need only admit that it is *true* that human consciousness, or consciousness of the kind we actually have, is not merely consciousness of something but of many things, of a variety of things.

Kant has a term for "consciousness of many things": the term "the manifold." Frequently, he adds the words "of representations" and talks about "the manifold of representations." The term "representation" is Kant's most general term for the contents of consciousness. It covers both intuitions and conceptual contents, whether these be *a priori* or empirical. One must make out what Kant means by it from the context. When the context is "manifold of representations," the expression means "consciousness of a multiplicity of sense impressions" or "consciousness of a multiplicity of appearances." But regardless of the context, the force of the term "representation" is to bring out Kant's view that what we are conscious of is things as they must be perceived and conceptualized by us, not "things-in-themselves," or things as they are apart from the ways in which we must perceive and conceptualize them.

The question now becomes this: if consciousness of a manifold of representations is possible, then what must be the case? In other words, what are the necessary conditions of (the possibility of) experience, understood as consciousness of a multiplicity or variety of representations?

In answer to this question, we need to bring in a key idea of Kant's Transcendental Deduction: that if consciousness of a manifold of representations is possible, then those representations must be contained in *one* self-same consciousness. The basic idea here is that if each representation were contained in a different consciousness, then there would be no consciousness of a manifold or manyness. Suppose that there is consciousness of a manifold of representations A, B, C, D, E, and so on. Then a necessary condition of this is that A, B, C, D, E, and so on must be contained in one identical consciousness. Otherwise, if A is contained in one consciousness, B in another consciousness, C in yet another consciousness, and so on, then there will be a consciousness of A, a separate consciousness of B, a separate consciousness of C, and so on, but there will be no consciousness of the manifold A, B, C, D, E, and so on.

Kant expresses this principle in a variety of different ways, and he has a variety of names for it, including "transcendental apperception" (A 107), "transcendental unity of apperception" (A 108), "unity of consciousness (A 108)," "unity of apperception" (A 118), "original apperception" (A 122), "pure apperception" (A 123), "original synthetic unity of apperception" (B 131), "necessary unity of apperception" (B 135), "synthetic unity of consciousness" (B 138), and others.[10] At B 135 he says that "the principle of apperception is the highest principle in the whole sphere of human knowledge." R. P. Wolff calls Kant's principle "the unity of consciousness" and treats it as the first premise of the Transcendental Deduction. His explanation of it is very helpful:

> What is the characteristic to which Kant is trying to call our attention? Light may be thrown on the problem if we make use of a trick first suggested by Brentano. Imagine, then, that we have written a six-word sentence on two different pieces of paper. We tear up the first piece so that each scrap contains just one word. (Suppose, for example, that the sentence is "The unicorn is a mythical beast.") The other piece we leave intact. Then we line up six people on one side of the room, each with a scrap of the first piece, and opposite them we stand a seventh person, to whom we give the whole sentence written on the untorn paper. Each member of the group of six reads the word which he has been given. Jones reads "The," Brown reads "unicorn," and so on. Smith, the seventh man, reads "The unicorn is a mythical beast." Now, every word of the sentence is contained in the consciousness of some member or other of the group of six. Similarly, every word of the sentence is contained in Smith's consciousness. But the two cases are absolutely different, for while in the former it is true that the separate parts of the sentence are contained in *some* consciousness, they are not contained in the *same* consciousness, and hence there is no *unity of consciousness* of them, as there is in the case of Smith. William James puts the point in the following way:
>
> > Take a sentence of a dozen words, and take twelve men and tell to each one word. Then stand the men in a row or jam them in a bunch, and let each man think of his word as intently as he will; nowhere will there be a consciousness of the whole sentence.
>
> The fact is that one consciousness of twelve words is not the same as twelve consciousnesses of one word each.[11]

Having introduced the notion of unity of consciousness, I can now fill out my preliminary sketch of the Transcendental Deduction as follows:

(I) If experience (= consciousness of a manifold of representations) is possible, then unity of consciousness is possible.

(II) If unity of consciousness is possible, then the categories have objective validity.

∴ (III) If experience is possible, then the categories have objective validity.

By considering this sketch, we can make out two main ideas of the Transcendental Deduction. The first idea is that consciousness of a multiplicity of items requires that these be contained in one self-same consciousness. This is the unity of consciousness principle that has just been presented. The second idea is that this unity of consciousness would be impossible in a Humean experience. For, as we have said, the categories—specifically, the categories of substance and cause—are concepts that can apply to experience only if items of experience have the objectivity and connectedness denied by the Humean view. Thus, premise (II) of the preliminary sketch really says that unity of consciousness is possible only in an objective, ordered world. This claim is the *most* basic idea of the Transcendental Deduction; whether and how it can be established, then, is the key question about the Deduction.

4.5 The Patchwork Theory of the Deduction

Now that we have a preliminary sketch of the Deduction, it would seem that we are ready to ask this question: what other premises does the Deduction contain? (In particular, by what premises does Kant justify premise II of the preliminary sketch?) Are these premises true? And are all the inferences in the argument valid?

Unfortunately, however, such a straightforward approach is not possible, for Kant does not present the Transcendental Deduction as a smooth, consecutive argument so that one can pick out premises and conclusions and proceed to evaluate the argument. Instead, he presents his material three times over, with significant differences of both content and mode of presentation. The first presentation is in Section 2 of the Deduction chapter of the first edition (A 95–A 114), immediately following the introductory Section 1. This section, usually called "the subjective deduction," is one of the most important and difficult passages in the *Critique*. It is important because it bristles with new ideas on every page, and difficult not only because it abounds in technical terms but also because it seems to lack any organization or unifying idea. The second presentation is in section 3 of the Deduction chapter of the first edition (A 115–A 130). In this passage, usually called "the objective deduction," Kant attempts, with limited success, to present the material of the subjective deduction in a clearer, more organized way, and he introduces some complications and draws some significant implications from the argument. The subjective and objective deductions together are called "the A-Deduction," because they constitute the Transcendental Deduction as Kant presents it in the first edition of the *Critique*. The third presentation, called "the B-Deduction," is the Transcendental Deduction as restated in the second edition of the *Critique* (B 151–B 169). Kant, then, rewrote the entire Transcendental Deduction for the second edition, no doubt because of the obscurity and incoherence of the first-edition version. In this rewritten version, the argument is more coherently presented, with premises and conclusions flowing in reasonably smooth succession. However, although the B-Deduction makes more sense as a formal structure than the A-Deduction, it remains largely opaque because some of its premises seem quite arbitrary, especially if they are not read against the background of ideas presented only in the A-Deduction (and even, I shall argue, in the Analogies of Experience).

Perhaps the main obstacle to grasping the Deduction as a single, coherent argument is the incoherence of the first-edition version, especially the subjective deduction, where many of Kant's deepest insights are nonetheless contained. The subjective deduction is indeed so incoherent in its organization that it is the subject of a special theory about how it was composed, called the "patchwork theory."

I shall now briefly explain this theory because I want to adopt a modified version of it in analyzing Kant's argument as presented in the first edition.

When Kant wrote the *Critique of Pure Reason*, he was already fifty-seven years old, and he still had the rest of his "critical philosophy" to expound, which he did in several later works, notably the *Critique of Practical Reason* and the *Critique of Judgment*. So he composed the first *Critique* (as the *Critique of Pure Reason* is often called) in an extremely short time—a period of four or five months. However, he had been meditating on and making notes for the work for some twelve years. The patchwork theory is that Kant did not actually compose the entire text of the *Critique* in those few months. Rather, he stitched together various passages that he had written at widely different times during his twelve years of reflection, and he wrote only a few new passages. This theory is supposed to account for the many inconsistencies in the *Critique* and for the presence of ideas that Kant was in the very process of rejecting, such as the application of the categories to things-in-themselves, which he seems to espouse in the first subsection (#13) of the introductory Section I of the Deduction chapter (A 85/B 117, A 88/B 120). The patchwork theory was devised by two major German commentators, Hans Vaihinger and Erich Adickes, in works that appeared in 1881–1882 and in 1929, respectively.[12] It was adopted by one of Kant's foremost English commentators and translators, Norman Kemp Smith, in 1923.[13] The theory was worked out in the greatest detail for the first-edition Deduction, of which individual passages and even sentences were dated. These passages, it was held, represent different strata of Kant's thought at different periods of his development, and this is why they are frequently inconsistent.

The patchwork theory was severely criticized in the 1930s by another of Kant's early twentieth-century English commentators, H. J. Paton.[14] Paton argued that Adickes and Vaihinger had grotesquely exaggerated the inconsistencies in Kant's work and that their method for dating passages was based on fancy rather than sound historical method.

I shall not explore this controversy. Rather, following Robert Paul Wolff in *Kant's Theory of Mental Activity*, I shall adopt a modified version of the patchwork theory. Wolff rejects as unfruitful the attempt to date passages chronologically. But he retains the idea that the Deduction, especially the subjective deduction, should be treated in stages. In other words, Wolff does not regard Kant's exposition in the subjective deduction as one argument presented in a disorganized way. Rather, he regards it as a series of arguments, each one seeking to remedy deficiencies of the previous one. This leads him to divide the subjective deduction into four different stages, whose order does not at all correspond to Kant's own order of exposition.

I do not find as many different stages in the argument as Wolff does, nor do I agree with his claim that an idea found in the later stages (synthesis) completely replaces a central idea of the earlier stages. Rather, I think that in the first edition of the *Critique* there are basically two different versions of the Deduction, and that the second version is a prolongation rather than a complete replacement for the first. Furthermore—and here I agree with Wolff (and many other Kant commentators)—I believe that the argument has yet a further prolongation in the

Analogies of Experience, where the objective validity of the individual categories of substance and cause is finally established.[15] In the next two sections, I present the first-edition version of the Deduction, or the "A-Deduction," by analyzing what I call the "first version" and the "second version" of the A-Deduction, respectively. Despite my differences from Wolff, my reconstruction of the entire A-Deduction is strongly influenced by his account. I shall defer detailed discussion of the B-Deduction until the next chapter because I think that despite its placement in Kant's text before the Analogies of Experience, it is best understood in light of ideas that Kant does not introduce until the Analogies.

4.6 The First Version of the Deduction

As I have said, the most fundamental idea of the Deduction is that unity of consciousness is possible only in an objective, ordered world — one in which the categories of substance and cause have objective validity.[16] To begin to see how this very strong claim can be defended, suppose that we ask: what unifies, or holds together in a single consciousness, a manifold of representations? This question is not easy to answer, for there are several possible answers that must be eliminated.

First, it will not do to answer that a manifold of representations can be unified by introspectively spotting some relation that the representations all have to the self or conscious subject. This is because of David Hume's famous point that we do not and cannot introspect the conscious subject. In his *A Treatise of Human Nature*, Hume argues that if one tries to spot oneself in introspection, one simply does not find it. All one finds, instead, is a constantly shifting vista of sensory impressions, feelings, sensations, and thoughts. One does not find, in addition to these, some single item that one could identify as one's own self. As Hume puts it:

> For my part, when I enter most intimately into what I call *myself*, I always stumble on some particular perception or other, of heat or cold, light or shade, love or hatred, pain or pleasure. I never can catch *myself* at any time without a perception, and can never observe anything but the perception. . . . If any one, upon serious and unprejudic'd reflexion, thinks he has a different notion of *himself*, I must confess I can reason no longer with him.[17]

Furthermore, Hume argues that it is not even *possible* to find oneself in introspection because "self or person is not any one impression, but that to which our several impressions and ideas are supposed to have a reference."[18] What Hume is saying can be put this way: to try to spot oneself by introspection is to try to introspect the very subject of consciousness — the subject that is conscious *of* all the objects that one is aware of. But this is like trying to see the point *from which* one sees everything. The attempt is bound to fail, for that point cannot be seen; it is the one point that can never be in one's visual field. Thus, not only does one *in fact* not spot oneself in introspection, but also one *could not* do so. Kant agrees with Hume's denial that the self can be found in introspection; he puts the point this way:

> Consciousness of self according to the determinations of our state in inner per-
> ception is merely empirical, and always changing. No fixed and abiding self can
> present itself in this flux of inner appearances. (A 107)

It follows that we cannot introspect the self *in relation* to representations since to
be introspectively aware of a relation between X and Y we must surely be aware
of both X and Y.[19]

Here it might be objected that the lack of an introspectible self does not
mean that representations cannot be unified by being related to a self—namely, a
nonintrospectible self. If Kant were seeking the conditions that enable us to *know*
that unity of consciousness obtains, then the lack of an introspectible self would
matter. But, the objection goes, Kant is only seeking the conditions that make
unity of consciousness obtain, not those that enable us to know that it obtains.
And the relation of representations to a nonintrospectible self could be all that is
needed for unity of consciousness to obtain.

Kant could make the following reply to this objection. Consider a set of representations A, B, C, D, E . . . that is not contained in one consciousness, that lacks
unity of consciousness. Then the objection suggests that it could acquire unity of
consciousness by the representations' being related to something of which there is
no consciousness—something that is completely unavailable to consciousness. But
this is impossible. It would be like trying to unify a view of one end of the Golden
Gate Bridge to a view of its other end, in order to get a view of the entire bridge,
by relating each separate view of the bridge's ends to something unperceivable.
Just as the two views of the bridge can only be unified into one view by each
being related to something that is itself viewable, so a set of representations can
only be unified in one consciousness by reference to something of which we can
be conscious, something that is at least available to consciousness. Perhaps this is
part of Kant's meaning when he says that "it must be possible for the 'I think' to
accompany all my representations" (B 131).

A second way in which a manifold of representations cannot be unified is by
spotting some necessary connections between the representations themselves, for,
as Hume also showed, we never observe any necessary connections between different representations. As Wolff says:

> Kant agrees completely with Hume's insistence that there is nothing in the repre-
> sentations themselves linking them together. The sight of the top of the desk does
> not compel me to conclude that it feels hard; its shape does not entail its weight.
> (If such connections existed, the propositions asserting them would be analytic.)[20]

Third, a manifold of representations cannot be unified by relations of association between them because, as Wolff shows, mere association is not sufficient for
unity of consciousness.[21] Suppose that John's and Mary's experiences have the
following unusual relationship: whenever John smells bacon, Mary imagines eggs;
and whenever Mary imagines eggs, John smells bacon. Then Mary's and John's
experiences of smelling bacon and imagining eggs stand in a relation of association—one leads to the other and vice versa—but they do not belong to one and
the same consciousness. For it is not the case that when John smells bacon, *he*
imagines eggs, or that when Mary imagines eggs, *she* smells bacon. To put it

differently, the bacon-smelling and egg-imagining experiences are not in the same mind.[22]

Finally, we cannot say that the representations in a manifold are unified in one consciousness because they are all in the head.[23] Even waiving objections to talking about heads in the context of trying to meet skeptical challenges to the applicability of concepts of physical objects, as well as possible objections to talk of representations being "in the head," this condition would not be sufficient: the representations might be in different parts of the brain that did not communicate with each other.

If the representations in a manifold cannot be unified in any of the above four ways—by standing in an introspectible relation to the self, by exhibiting necessary connections between each other, by association, or by being all in the head—then what does unify them? As preparation for presenting what he takes to be Kant's answer to this crucial question, Wolff offers us a clue, which he calls "the double nature of representations." A representation can be regarded in two different ways: (a) as a mental state or psychological episode in someone's psychic history or (b) as referring to something or having a meaning. Wolff quotes a passage by A. S. Pringle-Pattison that gives a clear account of this distinction:

> It is important to remember . . . the distinction signalized by Descartes between an idea as a mental state, a psychical occurrence, and the same idea functioning in knowledge and conveying a certain meaning. The former he called the [formal reality] of an idea, and in this respect all ideas stand upon the same footing. . . . The treatment of ideas so regarded belongs to psychology. But ideas exist not only as facts in the mental history of this or that individual; they also have . . . a 'content' or meaning; they signify something other than themselves. We regard them, in Descartes's words, 'as images, of which one represents one thing and another a different thing', and this is [an] important aspect of ideas for us. He calls it their [objective reality]. So regarded, ideas are the subject matter of epistemology or theory of knowledge.[24]

Wolff then points out that if we regard representations only in the first way—as psychological episodes in someone's conscious history—then, given the elimination of the four possible explanations of unity of consciousness discussed above, there is no way to explain what unifies or holds together the representations in a manifold of representations; that is, "it would seem that if we consider representations to be merely objects in consciousness, then we will never find an explanation for this . . . unity." However, suppose that we regard representations in the second way—as representing something or being "of" something. Then, Wolff says, such an explanation becomes available:

> But suppose we . . . recall that the contents of consciousness have a double nature: they are representations as well as objects of consciousness. Now we see that there is a way in which the contents of consciousness can establish necessary relations with one another. This is possible only if they are referred, *qua* [as] representations, to an object which serves as the ground of their unity.[25]

Kant's answer to the question of what unifies representations (following Wolff's interpretation), then, is this: the representations are unified by *referring to an ob-*

ject, by being *of* an object. As Kant himself puts it: "an *object* is that in the concept of which the manifold of a given intuition is *united*" (B 137). To grasp this key idea, let us first notice an easier but related point: that a set of representations can refer to an object only if they are all contained in one consciousness. Suppose, for example, that there is a representation of the back of a chair, a representation of the seat of a chair, and four representations of legs of a chair. For this set of representations to constitute a representation *of a chair,* they must be contained in one and the same consciousness. If the representations of the back of a chair, of the seat of a chair, and of each of the four legs of a chair were each contained in a different consciousness or were each presented to a different conscious subject, then this set of representations would not be a representation of a chair; it would not amount to consciousness of a chair. Now, Kant's point is a more difficult and less obvious one. It is the *converse* of the claim just made; to wit, that unless the representations referred to a chair, they would not all be contained in one and the same consciousness. In other words, it is the case not only that reference to an object requires unity of consciousness but also, conversely, that unity of consciousness requires reference to an object. For, as we have seen, unity of consciousness cannot arise from the fact that representations are related to an introspectible self, that there are necessary connections between the representations themselves, that the representations are related by association, or that they are all in the head. In light of the elimination of these four possibilities then, what does unify a manifold of representations? The answer given by Kant is that representations are unified by referring to an object—by being representations *of* an object. To see this better, notice that being related to an object is certainly one way to unify a manifold of representations: the object serves, so to speak, as an anchor for them. Kant's idea is that, in light of the elimination of the other possibilities mentioned, this is the *only* way to unify a manifold of representations in one consciousness.[26]

The idea that a manifold of representations can be unified in one consciousness only by referring to an object is the key idea of Wolff's "Stage I," and I believe that this idea must be retained even in the final version of Kant's argument (at least when the argument is built on the A-Deduction).[27] Before continuing the exposition of Kant's argument, therefore, let us pause to consider some possible objections to this crucial idea.

One possible objection is this. Imagine a very simple manifold—say, a visual field containing just one red circle and one green circle. Then to unify this manifold, wouldn't it be sufficient to make some judgment about the two circles, say, that the green circle is above the red circle or that the red circle is to the left of the green one? Why need these representations refer to an object in order for them to be contained in one consciousness?[28] (Of course, the colored circles in this scenario must not to be thought of as *physical* circles "out there" in space; for if they were, then the scenario would not be one in which representations are unified without referring to objects. Rather, the circles should be thought of as purely phenomenal objects—"objects" that could exist even in a hallucination, in a dream, or as after-images. Likewise, the "space" in which they reside is to be thought of as purely "phenomenal space": the kind of space that characterizes even a mental picture.)

In response to this objection, I think it must be granted that such a simple manifold could be unified in the manner described. But human experience is much more complex—indeed, exponentially more complex—than this simple model of a pair of colored circles. Not only is our visual experience extremely rich (as the saying goes, "a picture is worth a thousand words"), but also we continually obtain a multitude of tactile and auditory experiences, as well as olfactory and gustatory experiences. How are all these unified into one consciousness? One should not assume, on some quasi-mathematical model, that just because an array of a few colored circles could be unified by making judgments about their relative position in one's visual field, the same principle of unity can be extended to much more complex manifolds, for we are here talking about unity of *consciousness*, and (human) consciousness is limited in the degree of complexity that it can manage. For example, although one can multiply indefinitely the number of judgments that could in principle be made about the relative positions of colored circles just by adding more colored circles, the number of judgments that could in principle be made would soon outstrip the number of judgments that could actually be made together by any human mind. Kant's claim is that given the complexity of the manifold of representations in actual human experience, the only way to unify the manifold is by its representations referring to objects. I say "objects" here rather than "an object" because I think Kant's basic point is that unity of consciousness can be secured only if representations refer to what might be called an "objective scene" or an "objective situation"—one that can contain (and typically does contain) more than one object.

Here it might be countered that a manifold of representations is typically much simpler than the above account suggests. For example, if I am in my study and I look around, my manifold reduces to the sight of just a few items. This rebuttal, however, virtually answers itself, for what are these few items? Surely, they are physical *objects*. The underlying point here is that the same manifold can be described both in ways that make it sound very complex and in ways that make it sound much simpler. I can describe what I see when I look around my study in terms of hundreds of patches of color and their relations and contrasts or in terms of a few walls, some rows of books on a bookcase, and so forth. But notice that the simpler my description becomes, the more obvious it becomes that it has to be couched in terms of physical objects. So, the proffered rebuttal actually supports Kant's idea that a manifold needs to be unified by reference to objects.

A second possible objection is that Kant (and Wolff) is simply wrong to think that relation to an object is required to unify a manifold of representations because mere *copresence* of the representations to one consciousness is sufficient to explain such unity. Kant could reply that this objection just begs the question, for "copresence" is here merely another term for "unity of consciousness"—the very notion he is trying to explain. Further, copresence may seem to provide the needed explanation only because we can think schematically of a set of items that are all related to the same self by the relation of awareness. However, once we realize that we cannot spot any such self in introspection, we can see that copresence offers no explanation of the difference between a set of representations each of which exists in a different consciousness and a set of representations all of which are contained in one and the same consciousness. Rather, it is only a label for the latter phenomenon, which is the very one that we are trying to understand.

This reply may not be fully convincing. Consider the following remark, by James Van Cleve:

> How plausible is [Kant's] contention that relation to an object and unity of apperception go together? To my mind, it is not plausible at all. Could not *any* collection of representations, no matter how chaotic or phantasmagorical, have unity of apperception just in virtue of being cognized together?[29]

I assume that Van Cleve is using the term "unity of apperception" to mean the same as "unity of consciousness," and the expression "being cognized together" to mean the same as "being copresent." In that case, his underlying point is that copresence is simply a primitive, unanalyzable notion; it does not need to be accounted for in terms of anything else.

This is not an easy claim to counter, but I suggest that Kant could counter it as follows. For the claim that a collection of representations $R1, R2, \ldots, Rn$ is unified in one consciousness to make sense, we must be able to distinguish between two different scenarios: (1) the case where $R1, R2, \ldots, Rn$ are unified in one consciousness and (2) a case where $R1, R2, \ldots, Rn$ each occur in a different consciousness. Try, then, the following thought-experiment. First, imagine the case where $R1, R2, \ldots, Rn$ are all "cognized together."[30] Second, imagine a case where $R1, R2, \ldots, Rn$ are each cognized separately or occur in a different consciousness. In doing the former, do not imagine that $R1, R2, \ldots, Rn$ are related to a single introspectible self or conscious subject; and in doing the latter, do not imagine that $R1, R2, \ldots, Rn$ are each related to a different introspectible conscious subject. Also, do not suppose in either case that $R1, R2, \ldots, Rn$ are related to an object; instead, suppose that they are mere representations. Then is there any difference between what you imagined in the first case and what you imagined in the second case? When I try this experiment, I can find no difference between the two cases. So if I remain within the constraints of the experiment—that the only experienceable items involved are the representations themselves and that these relate neither to an introspectible self nor to an object—then I find that I cannot distinguish scenario (1) from scenario (2) and, therefore, cannot make sense of the claim that $R1, R2, \ldots, Rn$ are unified in one consciousness. But if I now suppose that $R1, R2, \ldots, Rn$ all relate to an object—that they together amount to the cognition of an object—then that supposition immediately serves to unify those representations in one consciousness. This thought-experiment supports Kant's contention that unity of consciousness and relation to an object go together.

A third possible objection is this: at best, Kant has shown that in order to unify a manifold of representations, one must have *concepts* of objects, but it does not follow that these concepts must be *instantiated*.[31] This is a simple but trenchant objection, which serves as an excellent acid test of Kant's position. In reply to the objection, two points may be made. First, the representations to be unified are not, or in any case are not only, conceptual contents or abstract ideas. Rather, they are particular items obtained in sensory experience—what Kant variously calls "empirical intuitions," "appearances," and "sensible appearances." Second, when Kant says that these must be referred to an object, this claim is equivalent to saying that they must be conceptualized as being of objects. Remember that in accordance with the "weak" interpretation of Transcendental Idealism, the whole purpose of Kant's argument is only to show that we must conceptualize our experience in a certain way, that is, as being of objects. When this point is combined with the thesis that we cannot know what things are like apart from the ways we must conceptualize them, nor indeed intelligibly suppose that things might really be different from the ways we must conceptualize them as being, we have as strong an answer to skepticism as Kant's Transcendental Deduction can provide.

A fourth possible objection was first raised by the American philosopher C. I. Lewis in a classic work entitled *Mind and the World Order*. Lewis asked: "Did the sage of Königsberg have no dreams?"[32] The point of this ironical question is that Kant's contention that representations can be unified only by referring to objects would have the absurd consequence that there can be no such things as dreams or hallucinatory experience. For this contention means, as Van Cleve puts it, that "there is no stretch of conscious experience that is not object-related experience."[33] In other words, if a manifold of representations can be unified only by the representations' referring to an object, then it seems that there can be no "object-less" experience, that is, no experience in which it only *seems* that one is perceiving objects although one is in fact not perceiving anything, as happens in a dream or a hallucination.

The proper Kantian reply to this objection, I believe, is that even in a dream or hallucination, our representations do "refer to objects" in the relevant sense of "refer," for they at least *seem* to be of objects. The things we dream of and hallucinate are unreal, but they are "objects" in a sufficiently weighty sense to confer unity on some manifolds of representations.

This reply, however, obviously leads to a crucial question: if the conditions necessary to unify a manifold of representations can be met even in a dream or hallucination, then how can the Transcendental Deduction possibly disprove point (1) of the Humean view of experience, namely, that items of experience are subjective? Or to pose a slightly different question, how can the Deduction possibly lead to a refutation of the external-world skepticism associated with the Humean view? How can it possibly show that unity of consciousness is possible only in an objective world? I believe that Kant can answer these questions but that his answer is best understood in the light of an idea that he introduces only in the Analogies of Experience. Thus, having noted the questions, I shall postpone discussing how Kant could answer them until we come to the Analogies in the following chapter.

Assuming, at least for the sake of the argument, that unity of consciousness does require that representations refer to an object, the next question is this: what does it mean to say that representations refer to an object or that they are "of" an object? Kant's answer to this question is based on a fundamental assumption, namely, that in answering the question, all that we may legitimately appeal to is the representations themselves. Kant puts it this way:

> At this point we must make clear to ourselves what we mean by the expression 'an object of representations'. We have stated above that appearances are ... nothing but sensible representations, which, as such and in themselves, must not be taken as objects capable of existing outside our power of representation. What, then, is to be understood when we speak of an object corresponding to, and consequently also distinct, from our knowledge? It is easily seen that this object must be thought only as something in general = x, since outside our knowledge we have nothing which we could set over against this knowledge as corresponding to it. (A 104)

> [I]t is clear that ... we have to deal only with the manifold of our representations ... and that x (the object) which corresponds to them is nothing to us—being, as it is, something that has to be distinct from all our representations.... (A 105)

> Appearances are the sole objects which can be given to us immediately.... But these appearances are not things in themselves; they are only representations, which ... have their object—an object which cannot itself be intuited by us, and which may, therefore, be named the non-empirical, that is, transcendental object = x. (A 108–109)

Kant's language in these passages is very difficult. But perhaps his main point can be paraphrased this way: in answering the question of what it means for representations to refer to an object, or to be "of" an object, the only resources that we may draw upon are things as we must experience them (i.e., our "representations" of things). We may not draw on any alleged knowledge of what things are like apart from our ways of experiencing them, that is, of what things are like in themselves; for we cannot know what things are like apart from our ways of experiencing them, or whether things as we must experience them are the same or other than things as they are in themselves. In other words, we must keep in mind the doctrine of Transcendental Idealism, understood in the "weak" sense that I have proposed.

Now, there is a classical answer to the question of what it means for representations to refer to an object. This answer, which we may call the "correspondence theory" or the "copy theory," is that our representations are copies of objects that are not themselves representations. This theory is illustrated by figure 4–1. Versions of this theory can be found in several of the great philosophers of the modern period, including Descartes and Locke. Kant, however, rejects the theory, for to

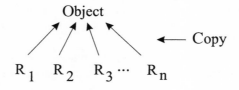

FIGURE 4–1

hold such a theory is precisely to violate the fundamental assumption noted above: it is to answer the question of what it means for representations to refer to an object on the basis of how things are supposed to be quite apart from the ways in which we must perceive and think of them—an enterprise that Kant thinks is bound to fail and that, indeed, he finds quite unintelligible. For the theory assumes that (a) things have ways of being that are totally independent of the ways we must perceive and think of them, and (b) our representations refer to things by copying or "mirroring" those ways of being.

What, then, is Kant's own answer to the question of "what we mean by the expression 'an object of representations'"? Let him speak for himself:

> [W]e find that our thought of the relation of all knowledge to its object carries with it an element of necessity; the object is viewed as that which prevents our modes of knowledge from being haphazard or arbitrary, and which determines them *a priori* in some definite fashion. For in so far as they are to relate to an object, they must necessarily agree with one another, that is, must possess that unity which constitutes the concept of an object. (A 104–105)

> If we enquire what new character *relation to an object* confers upon our representations, what dignity they thereby acquire, we find that it results only in subjecting the representations to a rule, and so in necessitating us to connect them in some one specific manner; and conversely, that only in so far as our representations are necessitated in a certain order as regard their time-relations do they acquire objective meaning. (A 197/B 242–243)[34]

Kant's answer to the question of what it means for representations to refer to an object, then, is that they refer to an object by being related *to each other* in a nonarbitrary or rule-governed way, in accordance with the *concept* of the object. Kant's view is illustrated in figure 4–2. For example, a representation of the back of a chair, a representation of the seat of a chair, and four representations of legs of a chair, can constitute a representation of a chair only by being organized in a certain "chairlike" way, by being related to each other in ways dictated by the concept of a chair.[35]

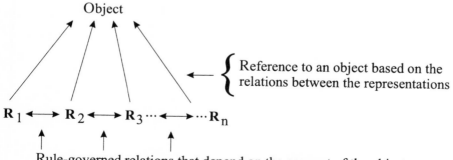

FIGURE 4–2

Let us summarize the two key ideas that we, following Wolff, have found in Kant's attempt to link unity of consciousness with the objectivity and connectedness that is lacking in the Humean view of experience:

(a) A manifold of representations can be unified in one consciousness only if the representations refer to an object.
(b) Representations can refer to an object only by being related to each other in a nonarbitrary, rule-governed way.

Putting (a) and (b) together—that is, deducing the obvious conclusion from them—we obtain

(c) A manifold of representations can be unified in one consciousness only if the representations are related to each other in a nonarbitrary, rule-governed way.

We can now incorporate these ideas into our preliminary sketch of the Deduction to obtain the first version of the Deduction. The preliminary sketch, you will recall, was this:

(I) If experience (= consciousness of a manifold of representations) is possible, then unity of consciousness is possible.
(II) If unity of consciousness is possible, then the categories have objective validity.

∴ (III) If experience is possible, then the categories have objective validity.

To construct the first version of the Deduction, we need only retain (I); replace (II) with (a), (b), and (c); and add a premise relating (c) to the categories. For the sake of expository smoothness, we will also renumber these statements, using only Arabic numbers, and substitute "only ifs" for (the logically equivalent) "if-thens" found in (I), (II), and (III). The result is this:

First Version of the Deduction, Incorporating the Key Ideas of Wolff's "Stage I"
(1) Experience is possible only if unity of consciousness is possible, that is, only if a manifold of representations can be unified in one consciousness.
(2) A manifold of representations can be unified in one consciousness only if those representations refer to an object.
(3) Representations can refer to an object only by being related to each other in a nonarbitrary, rule-governed way.
(4) A manifold of representations can be unified in one consciousness only if those representations are related to each other in a nonarbitrary, rule-governed way [from (2) and (3)].
(5) Representations are related to each other in a nonarbitrary, rule-governed way only if the categories have objective validity.
(6) Experience is possible only if the categories have objective validity [from (1), (4), and (5)].

Clearly, this argument can only be an incomplete, first version of the Deduction because, in step (5), the categories are brought in arbitrarily. Even if it were granted that "representations are related to each other in a nonarbitrary, rule-governed way," what does this have to do with any of Kant's categories, notably those of substance and cause? To begin to answer this question, we need to enrich the argument. This will be done in two further stages: one introducing Kant's idea of synthesis and leading to what we will call the second version of the Deduction, and a final stage, drawing on ideas not found in the Deduction chapter itself but only in the later section entitled "Analogies of Experience."

4.7 The Second Version of the Deduction

In the second version of the Deduction, two elements are introduced into the argument: (1) the temporality of consciousness and (2) the theory of synthesis. The temporality of consciousness was, of course, already introduced in the Transcendental Aesthetic, where Kant argued that all of our representations must occur in time:

> Time is the formal condition of all appearances whatsoever . . . since all representations, whether they have for their objects outer things or not, belong, in themselves, as determinations of the mind, to our inner state; and since this inner state stands under the formal condition of inner intuition, and so belongs to time, time is the *a priori* condition of all appearance whatsoever. . . . Just as I can say *a priori* that all outer appearances are in space . . . I can also say . . . that all appearances whatsoever, that is, all the objects of the senses, are in time, and necessarily stand in time-relations. (A 34/B 50–51)

Early in the Deduction chapter, Kant issues a strong reminder of this point, which will turn out to be crucial to his overall argument:

> Whatever the origin of our representations, whether they are due to the influence of outer things, or are produced through inner causes, whether they arise *a priori*, or being appearances have an empirical origin, they must all, as modifications of the mind, belong to inner sense. All our knowledge is thus finally subject to time, the formal condition of inner sense. In it they must all be ordered, connected, and brought into relation. This is [an] observation which, throughout what follows, must be borne in mind as being quite fundamental. (A 98–99)

This "temporality thesis," as P. F. Strawson calls it, is not one for which Kant offers any arguments. Instead, as Strawson says, Kant treats the temporality thesis as "an unquestionable datum to which we cannot comprehend the possibility of any alternative."[36] On this point, I agree with Kant (as does Strawson, who adds the words "and as such we may be content to regard it," immediately after the remark just quoted). It seems to me that the notion of a nontemporal consciousness or experience is unintelligible. As Strawson puts it, "To abstract altogether from the idea of time, of temporal sequence, while preserving that of experience . . . we may admit at once to be a task beyond our powers."[37]

The temporality thesis allows us to understand the implications of the unity of consciousness principle better than we could before the reintroduction of the idea of time. For that principle, which we concisely expressed as saying that experience is possible only if unity of consciousness is possible, now means that consciousness of a manifold of *successive* representations is possible only if those representations are contained in one *enduring* consciousness. This can be illustrated by an example given by Charles Arthur Campbell. Suppose that I hear a succession of strokes of a church bell: clearly this requires that each successive stroke be given to one and the same enduring consciousness. Otherwise, there would be no consciousness of the strokes *as a succession,* or as *coming one after another.* Instead, each stroke would belong in isolation to a different world of experience. Awareness of a succession of items is possible only if the successive items are given to a consciousness that retains its identity throughout the succession.[38]

Here is another way of looking at this matter. Suppose that in Campbell's scenario of hearing strokes of a church bell, I were to forget each stroke before hearing the next one. By the time I hear the second stroke, I have forgotten the first; by the time I hear the third stroke, I have forgotten the second, as well as the first, and so on. Then, according to Kant, two things would follow. First, there would be no consciousness of the strokes of the bell *as* a succession. If I forget the first stroke before hearing the second one, then I cannot be aware of the second stroke as being the *successor* of the first, that is, as being *second;* and if I forget the second stroke before hearing the third, then I cannot be aware of the third as the successor of the second, that is, as being third; and so on. In other words, consciousness of a succession of items *as* a succession requires that the earlier items be retained in consciousness. Second, if I forget each stroke before hearing the next one, then the strokes of the bell do not belong to one, enduring consciousness. For if each stroke is totally forgotten before the next one is heard, then what basis is there for saying that they were ever contained in a single consciousness? No basis at all, Kant would say. Furthermore, if such constantly renewed "forgetfulness" were a general feature of my consciousness, then there would be no basis for saying that "I" was a single conscious self at all. Instead, Kant says, "I would have as many-colored and diverse a self as I have representations . . . " (B 134). Kant's point is that unity of consciousness through time requires memory. Imagine a person who suffers not only from amnesia but also from perpetually renewed amnesia. Such a person, Kant holds, would have no unity of consciousness.

The point that unity of consciousness through time requires memory leads directly to a prominent feature of the Deduction that we have not yet discussed, namely, Kant's theory of synthesis. Kant is not content to speak in general terms of remembering earlier members of a succession of representations. His theory of synthesis is an attempt to analyze in detail the process by which past representations are remembered and the unity of consciousness through time made possible.

Kant distinguishes among three syntheses: the synthesis of apprehension in intuition, the synthesis of reproduction in imagination, and the synthesis of recognition in a concept. These are probably best thought of not as three different processes but as three aspects of one process. In any case, as we shall see, Kant's descriptions of each of them tend to spill over into the others.

Kant describes the synthesis of apprehension in intuition as follows:

> In order that unity of intuition may arise out of [the] manifold . . . it must first be run through, and held together. This act I name the *synthesis of apprehension,* because it is directed immediately upon intuition, which does indeed offer a manifold, but a manifold which can never be represented as a manifold, and as contained *in a single representation,* save in virtue of such a synthesis. (A 99)

This synthesis seems to involve two things: (a) the manifold is "run through," and (b) it is "held together." By the manifold's being "run through," I understand Kant to mean simply that representations are obtained or received in succession. In other words, (a) seems to be virtually identical with sense perception, as suggested by the words "apprehension in intuition." As for the manifold's being "held together," I believe that Kant is here already talking about the synthesis of reproduction, to which we may therefore turn now.

The synthesis of reproduction in imagination consists in reproducing the previous members of a succession of representations. Only then can they be remembered and the unity of consciousness through time thereby made possible. Kant's view is evidently that remembering a past representation consists in calling another one just like it to mind, or imagining a replica of it. The past representation is then said to be "reproduced in imagination." Kant describes this process as follows:

> [E]xperience as such necessarily presupposes the reproducibility of appearances. When I seek to draw a line in thought, or to think of the time from one noon to another, or even to represent to myself some particular number, obviously the various manifold representations that are involved must be apprehended by me in thought one after the other. But if I were always to drop out of thought the preceding representations (the first parts of the line, the antecedent parts of the time period, or the units in the order represented), and did not reproduce them while advancing to those that follow, a complete representation would never be obtained: none of the above-mentioned thoughts, not even the purest and most elementary representations of space and time, could arise. (A 101–102)

From this description, it seems clear that the way in which the manifold is "held together" is by being reproduced; indeed, in the next sentence Kant says that "the synthesis of apprehension is thus inseparably bound up with the synthesis of reproduction." Wolff describes the synthesis of reproduction this way:

> Now, if I kept forgetting the last representation of the manifold every time I came to a new one in the temporal order, I would not be thinking them together in one consciousness. There would be merely a succession of unitary and disjoint apprehensions, not a unity. If I look at a tree, then forget it and look at another, then forget it also and look at a third, and so on, I can not in any meaningful sense be said to have seen the forest. What I must do, therefore, as I proceed from one moment to the next, is to reproduce the representation which has just been apprehended, carrying it along in memory while I apprehend the next. In looking at a forest, I must say to myself, "There is a birch; and there is an elm, plus the birch which I remember, etc." The result of this repeated recollecting—or synthesis of reproduction in imagination, as Kant calls it—is the apprehension in one consciousness of a variety of representations which were originally disjoint. By carrying them forward, the mind has made it possible to think them as a unity.[39]

The synthesis of recognition in a concept is the most difficult of the three, as well as the most crucial one for Wolff's overall interpretation of the Deduction. Kant begins with the point that in order to remember a previous representation, it is not enough merely to reproduce it. One must also be aware that the reproduced representation, the replica, is qualitatively the same as the original, that is, that it *is* a replica. As Kant says:

> If we were not conscious that what we think is the same as what we thought a moment before, all reproduction in the series of representations would be useless. For it would in its present state be a new representation which would not in any way belong to the act whereby it was gradually generated. The manifold of the representation would never, therefore, form a whole, since it would lack that unity which only consciousness can impart to it. (A 103)

Wolff puts the point this way:

> But this [reproduction of past representations] is not yet enough. I must apprehend the succession by reproducing it, but I must also be aware that what I have just reproduced is identical with what I apprehended a moment ago.[40]

I take this point to be clear enough: in order to hear the third stroke of the bell *as* the third, for example, I must not merely reproduce the first and second strokes but also be aware that what I am reproducing is the first and second strokes.

However, according to Wolff, this requirement that reproduced representations be recognized as replicas of earlier ones is not all that Kant packs into the synthesis of recognition in a concept. The further claim that Wolff attributes to Kant is that the representations must be reproduced *according to a rule*. Certainly, there are several passages in Kant's text that support Wolff's interpretation, for example, this one:

> This [synthetic unity in the manifold of intuition] is impossible if the intuition cannot be generated in accordance with a rule by means of such a function of synthesis as makes the reproduction of the manifold a priori necessary, and renders possible a concept in which it is united. . . . But a concept is always, as regards its form, something universal which serves as a rule. The concept of body, for instance, serves as a rule in our knowledge of outer appearances. But it can be a rule for intuitions only in so far as it represents in any given appearances the necessary reproduction of the manifold, and thereby the synthetic unity in our consciousness of them. The concept of body, in the perception of something outside us, necessitates the representation of extension, and therewith representations of impenetrability, shape, etc. (A 105–106)

Here Kant can be interpreted as saying that unity of consciousness requires not only that representations be reproduced and recognized but also that they be reproduced according to a rule, which then makes it possible to apply to them a concept, such as the concept of body. If the representations were reproduced in a random, arbitrary way, then they would not answer to any such concept. This is the way in which Wolff understands Kant, as can be seen from this passage in Wolff:

> In general, when I apprehend a succession of representations by reproducing them in imagination, I must become conscious of two things: first, that the pres-

ent representations exactly resemble those which they reproduce, and second, that the representations before my mind belong to one set or group, and hence are unified. . . . What is it to be aware of a group of representations . . . "as a unity"? . . . The answer lies in the analysis of *rules*. The mind's activity in reproducing the successive intuitions of a manifold is not random, but regulated. It proceeds in accordance with a rule which determines the mind to act thus and in no other way. When I count . . . twelve stones, I do not recall any past representations which please my fancy. I am bound by the rules of counting to label the first stone "one." I must then recall that "one" while labeling the second, and must recall it as "one," not as "three" or "fifteen." I must continue on, obeying the rules, until I have reached "twelve." I then recall the previous eleven steps, and I am aware at that point that those recollected steps were performed *in accordance with the rule*. This is what [is meant by saying] that the steps [have] to be remembered as a series of *connected* acts. They are connected by being successive stages of a single rule-directed activity. The whole process, which enables me to know that there are twelve stones, is governed by a rule—in this case, the rule of counting. To conceive of "twelve" is actually to be conscious of the rule by which the mind has reproduced the succession of representations. As Kant says, "a concept is always, as regards its form, something universal which serves as a rule" [A 106]. To be exact, it is the rule for the reproduction in imagination of a manifold of intuition.[41]

Accordingly, when Wolff presents the later, "improved" versions of the Deduction, the idea that unity of consciousness requires rule-governed reproduction of the manifold becomes crucial. Indeed, it becomes so important that it *replaces* the key idea of his "Stage I" (and of our first version of the Deduction), which was that unity of consciousness requires that representations be referred to an object. Thus, while Wolff's first and second versions of the Deduction both include the premise

> The only way to unify a diversity of mental contents is by referring them *qua* representations to an object as the ground of their unity,

the third and subsequent versions drop this premise completely, and replace it with the premise

> The only way to introduce synthetic unity into a manifold of contents of consciousness is by reproducing it in imagination according to a rule.[42]

It is just here, however, that I must part company with Wolff. For it seems to me that whereas he shows clearly enough that the reproduction of past representations, as well as the recognition of the replicas as being the same as the original, is a necessary condition of unity of consciousness through time, he does not show that the representations must also be reproduced according to a rule.[43] Of course, *if* I am counting stones, then I must follow the rules of counting. But this does not show that in order to have a unified consciousness through time, I must count stones *or perform any other rule-directed mental activity*. It is also true that if I do count stones and apply the concept 'twelve' to my representations, or if I apply any other concept to a set of representations, then there is a sense in which I have "unified" those representations: I have subsumed them under one concept. But this point does not show that this kind of "synthetic unity," as Wolff calls it, is a necessary condition of unity of consciousness through time. Why would it not be sufficient to reproduce the representations in some random or arbitrary sequence?

To answer this question, I believe that one must revert to the idea that Wolff drops from his third and subsequent versions of the Deduction, namely, the idea that the only way to unify a manifold of representations is to refer them to an object.[44] Furthermore, one must also retain the idea that representations refer to an object by being related to each other in a nonarbitrary, rule-governed way. For these two ideas *already* show that unity of consciousness requires that representations be related to each other in a nonarbitrary, rule-governed way.[45] What follows when this result of the first version of the Deduction is combined with the point that representations are apprehended in temporal succession, so that the previous representations would always be dropping out of consciousness unless they were reproduced? It then follows that the only way the relations between the previous representations and the reproduced ones (the replicas) can be rule-governed is by the latter's being reproduced in a rule-governed order, or according to a rule. For if they were not reproduced in a rule-governed way—if they were reproduced in an arbitrary or random order—then obviously the relations between them and the previous representations would not be rule-governed.

My proposal, then, is that Kant's theory of synthesis should not be seen as *replacing* the points about the dependence of unity of consciousness on reference to an object and the analysis of reference to an object in terms of relations between representations found in Wolff's "Stage I" of the Deduction. Instead, the theory of synthesis must be *added* to those ideas, because of the temporality of consciousness, in order to continue the development of the Deduction. The result of developing the argument in this way is the following version of the Transcendental Deduction:

Second Version of the Deduction, Incorporating the Temporality
of Consciousness and the Theory of Synthesis
(1) Experience is possible only if unity of consciousness is possible, that is, only if a manifold of representations can be unified in one consciousness.
(2) A manifold of representations can be unified in one consciousness only if those representations refer to an object.
(3) Representations can refer to an object only by being related to each other in a nonarbitrary, rule-governed way.
(4) A manifold of representations can be unified in one consciousness only if those representations are related to each other in a nonarbitrary, rule-governed way [from (2) & (3)].
(5) Representations are apprehended in temporal succession.
(6) If (4) and (5), then unity of consciousness is possible only if representations are synthesized, that is, reproduced in imagination according to a rule.
(7) Unity of consciousness is possible only if representations are reproduced in imagination according to a rule [from (4), (5), and (6)].

(8) Representations can be reproduced in imagination according to a rule only if the categories are objectively valid.

(9) Experience is possible only if the categories are objectively valid [from (1), (7), and (8)].

A key premise of this argument is, of course, (6), which says that if a manifold of representations can be unified in one consciousness only by those representations being related to each other in a nonarbitrary, rule-governed way, and if representations are apprehended in temporal succession, then unity of consciousness is possible only if representations are not merely reproduced but also reproduced according to a rule (otherwise they would not be related to each other in a *rule-governed* way).

As we shall see, this second version of the Deduction incorporates an idea — rule-governed reproduction of successively apprehended representations — which is essential to a proof of the objective validity of the categories. But it is obvious that as it stands, the second version suffers from an insufficiency similar to the first version: the categories are still brought in arbitrarily, for why should one accept step (8) — the idea that rule-governed reproduction of representations implies the objective validity of the categories? Clearly, some further argumentation is needed to answer this question. This argumentation is not to be found in the Transcendental Deduction of the Categories itself. Rather, Kant only provides it in the "Analogies of Experience," where he first tries to give a "deduction" of specific categories, notably substance and cause.

The Central Argument
of the Analytic (II)

*The Analogies of Experience, the Two
Time-Orders, and the B-Deduction*

5.1 The Subjective Time-Order and the Objective Time-Order

In the Analogies of Experience, Kant introduces the key idea in the post-Deduction stage of the overall argument of the Transcendental Analytic: the idea of the subjective and the objective time-orders. The subjective time-order is the order in which representations are apprehended. To use an example that Kant gives in the Second Analogy, suppose you are looking at a house. You might see first the front of the house, then a side of the house, then the back of the house, and finally the other side of the house; this would happen if you were walking around the house. In this case, you would apprehend representations of the house successively in the order front, side, back, and other side of the house. This order of representations, which is dependent on your own position and movements, is the subjective time-order. By contrast, the objective time-order is *the order in which we conceive or judge the objects of our representations to exist.* In the case of the house, for example, you conceive or judge that the front, sides, and back of the house exist simultaneously or coexist in time, unlike the representations of those parts of the house, which exist successively.

The idea of the two time-orders is most forcefully presented in the Second Analogy, but it makes its first appearance in the introductory section on the Principle of the Analogies and also appears in the First Analogy. Here is the first passage:

> In experience, however, perceptions come together only in accidental order, so that no necessity determining their connection is or can be revealed in the perceptions themselves. For apprehension is only a placing together of the manifold of empirical intuition; and we can find in it no representation of any necessity which determines the appearances thus combined to have connected existence in space and time. But since experience is a knowledge of objects through perceptions, the relation [involved] in the existence of the manifold has to be represented in experience, not as it comes to be constructed in time, but as it exists objectively in time. (A 177/B 219)

Here the phrase "as it comes to be constructed in time" refers to the subjective time-order, and the phrase "as it exists objectively in time" refers to the objective time-order. As Wolff points out, Kemp Smith's translation of *zusammenstellen* as "constructed" is very unfortunate because it "gives an impression of active re-arrangement which is just the opposite of that intended by Kant." Wolff suggests that a better translation of the last clause would be one that "almost entirely avoids the implication of activity," namely,

> . . . the relation [involved] in the existence of the perceptions has to be repre-sented in experience not as they (the perceptions) come to be juxtaposed in time, but as it exists objectively in time.[1]

Wolff's remark here is well taken: it is crucial to understand that the subjective time-order is simply the order in which we happen to obtain or apprehend repre-sentations in sense perception; only the objective time-order involves an active rearrangement of those representations. Wolff's explanation of A 177/B 219 is also worth quoting:

> Now the only sort of relation which all representations bear to one another is time-relation, for time is the form of all consciousness. Given the double nature of representations, there are two possible time-orders in which they can be ar-ranged. The first is their time order as mere contents of consciousness, their subjective time-order. It is to this which Kant refers by the phrase "as it [the manifold of perceptions] comes to be placed together in time." The second possi-ble time-order of the contents of consciousness is their order *qua* representations, which is to say, the order in objective time of the states or events of which they are representations. This order may be quite different from the first, for events or states of which we become aware successively may in the object be contempora-neous. Kant later gives the example of the sides of a house, which are perceived one after the other, but objectively co-exist. The phrase, "but as it [the manifold] exists objectively in time," quite obviously refers to this second order.[2]

The second passage in the *Critique* that alludes to the two time-orders is this one, from the First Analogy:

> Our *apprehension* of the manifold of appearances is always successive, and is therefore always changing. Through it alone we can never determine whether this manifold, as object of experience, is coexistent or in sequence. (A 182/B 225)

Here Kant briefly touches on a key epistemological point that he will develop much more fully in the Second Analogy (and that will play a vital role in his attempt to prove there the objective validity of the category of causality), namely, that since the subjective time-order of representations is always successive, we cannot know merely from the fact that our representations occur successively whether they are representations of successive or coexistent objective states of af-fairs. To use Kant's other famous example from the Second Analogy, we cannot know, merely from the fact that our representations of a ship moving downstream occur successively, that we are observing a ship successively occupying different positions since our representations would also occur successively if we were observ-ing the coexisting sides of a house.

Kant's idea of two time-orders is fundamentally important for two reasons. First, it gives meaning, in a completely general and extremely powerful way, to the notion of objectivity. Second, it is a pivotal notion in the overall argument of the Transcendental Analytic, inasmuch as it is both a consequence of the Transcendental Deduction and the basic premise of the Analogies of Experience. In the next two sections, I shall address these two points in turn.

5.2 The Two Time-Orders, Objectivity, and Spatiality

The relation between the two time-orders and objectivity has been emphasized especially by P. F. Strawson in his influential book on the *Critique, The Bounds of Sense*. I shall start, then, by quoting a passage from Strawson, following which I shall explain the matter in my own fashion.

> For the world to be conceived as objective, it must be possible to distinguish between the order of perceptions occurring in one experiential route through it and the order and relations which the objective constituents of the world independently possess. That order and those relations cannot be determined by reference to the pure spatio-temporal framework itself, which is not a possible object of perception. Somehow or other, therefore, that objective order must be represented in the concepts we apply to, or under which we bring, the contents of our perceptions themselves. . . . The problem of the Analogies is to show how that order is, and must be, represented. . . . But Kant does not in fact pose the problem in this form. Throughout the Analogies the problem is represented solely as that of determining objective *time* relations. That this involves determining objective relations not merely in a temporal, but in a *spatio*-temporal order, is not something assumed by the argument, but something that, in a manner, emerges from it. . . . I have just said that Kant represents his problem in the Analogies as that of ascertaining the necessary conditions of determining objective time-relations. Nowhere, I think, is Kant's generalizing genius more clearly shown than in his reduction of this problem to this form. It is perhaps evident enough, given the arguments of the Transcendental Deduction, that the problem is to discover what is necessary to make a temporal succession of experiences (or perceptions) perceptions *of* an objective reality, a reality of which other temporal series of perceptions are also possible. But it was a great insight to perceive that this problem can be reduced to that of discovering the necessary conditions of distinguishing two sets of relations: (1) the time-relations between the objects which the perceptions are to be taken as perceptions of; (2) the time-relations between the members of the (subjective) series of perceptions themselves. If there were no way of making this distinction, then no meaning would attach to the distinction between objects of perception and perceptions of objects; and all the attendant notions would collapse too: the notion of a subjective or experiential route through an objective world . . . and hence the very notion of experience itself. If, on the other hand, the distinction can be made, then any necessary conditions of making it are necessary conditions of the possibility of experience.[3]

In this passage, Strawson asserts that the two time-orders are themselves a consequence of the Transcendental Deduction as he conceives it. The reconstruction of the Deduction that I have offered is very different from Strawson's, but as will be shown in the next section, it also leads to the two time-orders. For the moment, however, I want to focus on the fundamental relationship between the two time-orders and objectivity that Strawson so elegantly sets out.

To grasp this relationship better, we need to understand two points. First, as has already been said, the order in which we apprehend representations is merely a fact about how we happen to perceive things. It pertains to the perceiver and depends on such facts as the perceiver's bodily posture, movements, and position in space. That is why it can be called the "subjective" time-order. Second—and this is a new point—if representations can be said to possess a time-order (or time-relations) different from the (successive) order in which they are apprehended, then that will ipso facto provide a meaning for the claim that they are *of* items whose existence is not conceived solely as their being perceived—items that, unlike an after-image or a pain, are conceived as existing independently of being perceived and in that sense as being "objective," or qualifying as "objects." For consider the question: what can it mean to say that *a representation* has a different place in time than the time at which it is apprehended? For such a claim to make any sense at all, it can only mean that the representation has an object that it represents as existing at some time other than the time at which the representation is apprehended, or that the representation represents its object as existing at some time other than the time at which the representation itself occurs. Wolff's talk about the "double nature of representations" is helpful here. He suggests, you will recall, that a representation has two aspects: on the one hand, a representation is simply a "mental event"—an episode in someone's psychic history; considered in that light, it exists when and only when it is "had" or apprehended by a conscious being, and it is typically preceded and followed by other representations along with which it composes the subjective time-order. On the other hand, a representation refers to something that it represents as existing (or at least as being able to exist) at times other than itself—some object O that it represents as coexisting with, and being preceded and followed by, other things along with which O makes up the objective time-order. Only in this sense—that is, by being *of* something that is conceived as existing at a different time than the apprehension of the representation—can a representation be sensibly said to have a different place in time than the time at which it is apprehended. But this also means that the representation must be of an object whose existence is not conceived solely as its being perceived (whose *esse* is not conceived merely as *percipi*, as Berkeley would have put it). For things whose existence is conceived solely as their being perceived cannot possibly be conceived as having different positions in time than the perceptions themselves since that would entail that the very things that are conceived as existing only when being perceived are also conceived as existing at times when they are not being perceived, which is contradictory.

To put the point more briefly: the only way that our perceptions can be said to possess a time-order (or time-relations) different from the (successive) order in which they arise in consciousness is by being perceptions of things that are conceived or represented as possessing different time-relations than our perceptions of them.[4] But if the things we perceive must be conceived or represented as possessing different time-relations than our perceptions of them, then they must be conceived as being other than or different from our perceptions of them. For example, if the parts of a house must be conceived as existing simultaneously while our perceptions of them exist successively, then the parts of the house must be conceived as being different from our perceptions of them.

Furthermore, if the things we perceive must be conceived as being other than or different from our perceptions of them, then it seems that they must also be conceived as being able to exist independently of the self—as being other than the self and its conscious states. For surely the things we perceive are not conceived as being identical with the self, if only because the self is not perceived. Furthermore, the things we perceive are not conceived as being identical with any conscious states of the self other than the perceptions of those same things, because those other states of the self, even when they are also perceptions, are not perceptions of the "right" things. For example, it is not the case that a house that I see is conceived as being identical with the state of seeing an elephant, much less with the state of smelling a rose or tasting chocolate or feeling a pain. But if the things we perceive are not conceived as being identical with perceptions of them, or with the self, or with any conscious states of the self other than the perceptions of those same things, then the only alternative remaining is they must be conceived as being (totally) other than the self.

However, as we saw in section 2.3.2, Kant can be taken as having shown in the Transcendental Aesthetic that to perceive things as being other than the self— that is, to conceive the things we perceive as being other than the self—is to conceive them as being *spatially outside* the self. There Kant wrote that

> in order that certain sensations be referred to something outside me (that is, to something in another region of space than that in which I find myself) . . . the representation of space must be presupposed. (A 23/B38)

As we saw in 2.3.2, it is possible to interpret this claim in two different ways. It can be taken to express the tautology

> In order to perceive anything as existing spatially outside myself, I must perceive it as being in space.

Alternatively, it can be taken to express the much more interesting claim

> In order to perceive anything as existing distinct from myself, I must perceive it as being *spatially outside* myself.

Let us take Kant's claim, as I proposed earlier, in the second way. Then the connections Kant makes between the two time-orders, objectivity, and spatiality bear out what Strawson admiringly says in the passage I quoted above:

> The problem of the Analogies is to show how ["the order and relation which the objective constituents of the world independently possess"] is, and must be, represented. . . . But Kant does not in fact pose the problem in this form. Throughout the Analogies the problem is represented solely as that of determining objective *time* relations. That this involves determining objective relations not merely in a temporal, but in a *spatio*-temporal order, is not something assumed by the argument, but something that, in a manner, emerges from it. . . . I have just said that Kant represents his problem in the Analogies as that of ascertaining

the necessary conditions of determining objective time-relations. Nowhere, I think, is Kant's generalizing genius more clearly shown than in his reduction of this problem to this form.

Strawson offers us an illuminating way to grasp the conceptual connections between Kant's two time-orders, objectivity, and spatiality. He equates the idea that there is both a subjective time-order, which is just the successive order of our representations (perceptions), and an objective time order, which is the time-relations of the objects of our representations (perceptions), with the idea of "one experiential or subjective route through an objective world," that is, of an experiential route through a world through which other experiential routes are also possible. But this latter idea cannot be understood *only* in terms of a temporal succession of representations: it also requires a persisting framework that can only be conceived as a *spatial* one (or, Strawson says, a quasi-spatial one). But since this spatial framework itself cannot be perceived, it can enter into our experience only in the form of persisting or enduring *objects* in space.

To see better why the idea of one experiential route through an objective world cannot be understood only in terms of a temporal sequence of representations, consider what Strawson says:

> The idea of a mere temporal sequence of representations, of the from "Now A, now B, now C," etc., does not by itself contain the seeds of this idea. If and only if we enlarge the form to "*Here* now A," etc., and dwell on the implications of this addition, do we find the seeds of this idea. For the addition of "here" to "now" is completely otiose unless it carries with it the possibility of such contrasts as "somewhere else now" and "here again later on"; i.e. unless it carries with it the implications of a wider enduring spatial (or quasi-spatial) framework through which *one* experiential route is possible just because different experiential routes are possible.[5]

The key point here is that a temporal sequence of representations

Now A, now B, now C

does not contain even the seeds of the idea of one experiential route through an objective world (of one experiential route among other possible experiential routes through that world), unless we enrich it to

Here now A, etc.

But the addition of "here" to "now" means nothing unless it implies the possibility of such contrasts as

Somewhere else now

and

Here again later.

To see better why the notion of an experiential route through an enduring spatial framework requires experience of spatial *objects*, consider how Strawson continues the passage just quoted:

Therefore, since the "pure" framework itself is not a possible object of perception, the fundamental condition of the possibility [of the objective time-order] is the awareness of enduring objects in space (or, at least, some analogue of space which we can make intelligible to ourselves only *as* an analogue of space).[6]

Here Strawson draws on a point that Kant makes several times in the Analogies of Experience, namely, that "time cannot itself be perceived" (B 219, B 225, A 183/ B 226, B 233, B 257), and extends it to space as well. If this is so, then time (and space) can enter into our experience only if there are what we might call "perceptual stand-ins" for them, namely, enduring objects located in space.

Of course, it is tempting to ask, assuming that the existence of the objective time-order can be validly deduced from the Transcendental Deduction (an assumption to be examined in the next section), does this mean that there exist objects that *really* have time-relations other than those of our representations, as opposed merely to being *conceived or represented as* having such time-relations? Does it mean that there are things that really conform to the way we must think of them? But this question—if my "weak" interpretation of Kant's Transcendental Idealism is on the right track—is precisely the question Kant thinks we should not ask and cannot answer. For it amounts to asking, "What is reality like apart from the ways in which we must perceive and conceptualize things?" which is precisely the question that Kant holds we cannot answer. Reality could be just like the way in which we perceive and conceptualize things, or it could be different from it—we can't know this, and it does not matter.

This reference to Kant's Transcendental Idealism allows us to deal with the objection to Kant's argument that I postponed discussing in the previous chapter. The objection, it will be recalled, was that if the conditions required to unify a manifold of representations can be met even in a dream or a hallucination, then Kant's argument cannot refute point (1) of the Humean view of experience, that items of experience are subjective, nor the skepticism associated with that view. In reply to this, note first that the introduction of the two time-orders in the Analogies introduces objectivity in a stronger sense than could be explicitly found in the Transcendental Deduction. For, as we have seen, to say that our representations have a time-order distinct from the order of apprehension is to say that they are of items that are conceived as existing at times when they are not being perceived. The objector, however, need not be satisfied with this reply, for he can counter that, even in a dream, there is room for Kant's distinction between the two time-orders. For example, if I have a dream in which I seem to see a house, then even in this dream I conceive the parts of the house as existing simultaneously while my dream-perceptions of them exist successively. So, the objection continues, the introduction of the two time-orders does not close the gap left open by the Transcendental Deduction.

Kant could reply as follows. Although it is true that during the dream or hallucination, I conceive the objects of my representations as having a time-order distinct from the order of those representations, once I awaken from the dream or emerge from the hallucination, I no longer conceive the objects of those representations as having had such a distinct time-order. Instead, I now conceive them as having had the very same time-order as my representations of them. It may be tempting to retort that Kant has no right to assume that one can tell that one has awoken from a dream or emerged from a hallucination because as far as anything in his argument can show, all of one's representations might be dream perceptions or hallucinations. But this overlooks the "weak" form of Transcendental Idealism that underlies Kant's whole position. According to Kant, we cannot know nor even conceive of what things are like apart from the ways in which we must perceive and conceptualize them, nor can we intelligibly suppose that things might be different from the ways in which we must perceive and conceptualize them. So if his argument shows that we must conceive the objects of at least some of our representations as having different time-relations than our representations of them, then we cannot intelligibly suppose that all our perceptions are dreams or hallucinations. It is true that in some cases, the course of our experience is such that we only temporarily conceive the objects of our perceptions as having a time-order distinct from that of the perceptions. A certain break in the course of our experience, or the nonfulfillment of certain expectations about its course, leads us to judge that we were only dreaming or hallucinating. Even in such cases, once we classify the experiences as having been dreams or hallucinations, we integrate them into an overall "story"—really a history—of the self as an object in the world. But in other cases, the course of our experience continues smoothly on, our expectations about its course are for the most part fulfilled, and we therefore continue to conceive the objects of our representations as having had a time-order distinct from those representations. In these cases, we classify our experiences as having been genuine perceptions of physical objects. To suggest that, even in these cases, our representations may really be only dreams or hallucinations is to suppose that we can intelligibly suppose that things are different from the ways in which we must conceptualize them—a supposition that Kant rejects. It would seem, then, that Kant is in a position both to hold against skeptics that some but not all of our experiences could be dreams or hallucinations and to make use of ordinary, common-sense experiential criteria for distinguishing such experiences from "veridical" ones.

5.3 The Two Time-Orders and the Transcendental Deduction

Not only is Kant's notion of subjective and objective time-orders a powerful insight into the nature of objectivity, but is it also the pivotal notion in the overall argument of the Transcendental Analytic. For it is both a consequence of the Transcendental Deduction and the basic premise of the Analogies of Experience, where the objective validity of the categories of substance and cause is finally proved. As illustrated in figure 5-1, it is the stepping-stone, so to speak, between these two major episodes.

In this section, then, we shall consider how the two time-orders are supposed to follow from the Deduction and how they can lead to the justification of the categories of substance and cause. The second version of the Deduction, as you may recall, was as follows:

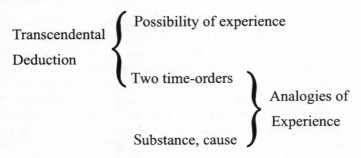

FIGURE 5-1

(1) Experience is possible only if unity of consciousness is possible, that is, only if a manifold of representations can be unified in one consciousness.

(2) A manifold of representations can be unified in one consciousness only if those representations refer to an object.

(3) Representations can refer to an object only by being related to each other in a nonarbitrary, rule-governed way.

(4) A manifold of representations can be unified in one consciousness only if those representations are related to each other in a nonarbitrary, rule-governed way [from (2) and (3)].

(5) Representations are apprehended in temporal succession.

(6) If (4) and (5), then unity of consciousness is possible only if representations are synthesized, that is, reproduced in imagination according to a rule.

(7) Unity of consciousness is possible only if representations are reproduced in imagination according to a rule [from (4), (5), and (6)].

(8) Representations can be reproduced in imagination according to a rule only if the categories are objectively valid.

(9) Experience is possible only if the categories are objectively valid [from (1), (7), and (8)].

As we saw, the main reason for the insufficiency of this argument is that the premise listed as step (8) brings in the categories arbitrarily. To remedy this weakness, then, we need to replace that premise with one that will lead to the objective validity of (at least) the categories needed to refute the Humean view of experience, namely, substance and cause. I have already said that Kant seeks to do this from the basic premise of the Analogies, namely, the assertion of the two time-orders. Is there a way, then, to show that the two time-orders are implied by the notions that figure in steps (1)–(7)?

The answer is that the notion of reproducing representations according to a rule does indeed lead to the two time-orders because the order in which representations are apprehended—which is *identical* with the subjective time-order—is not in the relevant sense rule-governed. Of course, if we regard representations merely as episodes in a person's mental history—if we consider them with respect to what Descartes called their "formal reality"—then Kant would say that they do have a rule-governed order, for, like other occurrences, they have causes, in this case both within and external to the self. But in order to know these causes, we must already have information about such objective facts as the perceiver's position and movements relative to the objects of perception, the perceiver's perceptual mechanisms and capacities, and so on. However, in the context of trying to show that the objective validity of the categories of substance and cause is implied by the possibility of mere consciousness of a manifold of representations in time, we cannot assume that we already have any information about such objective facts. Rather, we must confine ourselves to representations regarded as having a certain cognitive content or as referring to their objects; we must consider them only with respect to what Descartes called their "objective reality." The point is then that when representations are regarded in this way, their order is not rule-governed: sometimes, for example, one has representations of the front of a house before having representations of the back of a house; sometimes one has representations of the back of a house before having representations of the front of a house; sometimes one has representations of the front or back of a house not followed or preceded by representations of any other part of the house. This can also be put by saying that the objects of these representations—that is, the front, sides, and back of the house—do not objectively have the temporal order of the way they are apprehended. Furthermore, this latter temporal order (the subjective time-order or order of apprehension), when it is considered by itself, in isolation from the objective facts that explain it, is not rule-governed. Accordingly, it seems that in the place of (8), we may introduce the following premise:

(8') Representations can be reproduced in imagination according to a rule only if the temporal order in which they are reproduced is different from the temporal order in which they are apprehended.

Notice that, strictly speaking, the only time-order that is implied by reproduction according to a rule is the reproduced order, which is also the objective time-order. By contrast, the order of apprehension, which is identical with the subjective time-order, is simply given; it is, so to speak, just "there." As we shall see in chapter 9 on Kant's "Refutation of Idealism," however, this does not mean that the subjective time-order is *known* solely by being given.

It might be argued against (8') that in the Second Analogy Kant emphasizes that sometimes, for example, when viewing a ship moving downstream, the order of apprehension is (even must be) the same as the objective order. But this point does not go against (8'). The claim made by its "only if" clause is that if we consider all of our representations collectively, or *überhaupt*, they possess an order different from the order of apprehension. This is compatible with saying that for some subsets of our representations, the order of apprehension is the same as the objective order. Furthermore, "is different from" in (8') could be replaced by "can be different from" without affecting the argument's validity or soundness.

5.4 The Central Argument of the Transcendental Analytic: First Reconstruction

At this point, I can give a preliminary version of what I call the Central Argument of the Transcendental Analytic—an argument that starts with the Transcendental Deduction and ends with the Analogies of Experience and is intended to establish the objective validity of the categories of substance and cause. The preliminary version includes steps (1) through (7) of the second version of the Deduction (given above), step (8'), and two further steps:

> (9') Representations can have a temporal order other than the order in which they are apprehended only if the categories of substance and cause have objective validity.
>
> (10) Experience is possible only if the categories of substance and cause have objective validity [from (1), (7), (8'), and (9')].

This is only a preliminary version because the introduction of the categories of substance and cause in step (9') is still arbitrary: more argumentation is required to show how the two time-orders lead to the objective validity of these categories. In supplying this additional argumentation, I shall draw on Strawson's interpretation of this part of Kant's argument, much as I drew earlier on Wolff's interpretation of the Deduction.

The first move in expanding the argument is to replace (9') with

> (9") Representations can have a temporal order other than the order in which they are apprehended only if there is a way to determine temporal relations between representations other than the order in which they are apprehended.

This premise rests on the thought that representations, being the epistemological vehicles for all our thought and knowledge, cannot be said to have a time-order of which we could have no knowledge; there can be no content in assigning to *representations* any order other than the one in which they are apprehended unless there is some way to determine or establish what that other order is. We can fancy if we like that there are things of which we have absolutely no knowledge and that those things stand in certain time-relations of which we are wholly ignorant, but we cannot apply this fancy to our own representations.

It might be thought that there is a simple way to determine temporal relations between representations other than the order of apprehension: we can relate or "compare" the representations to time itself; we can think of time as a kind of container of representations and judge where in the container each representation belongs. However, this possibility is blocked by a premise that Kant asserts in several places:

> (10') Time itself cannot be perceived.[7]

As he also puts it, "Now since absolute time is not an object of perception, this determination of position cannot be derived from the relation of appearances to it" (A 200/B 245), and "absolute time is not an object of perception with which appearances could be confronted" (A 215/B 262). This is part of what Strawson means when he says, in the passages quoted in the previous section, that "the pure spatio-temporal framework itself . . . is not a possible object of perception," and Wolff also makes the point:

> Time is not an object, or an objectively existing un-thing. It is not a hollow container, or a clothesline strung across eternity. Therefore if we seek to set a representation in objective time, we cannot do it by attaching it to a pre-existing point of time.[8]

But if time itself cannot be perceived, then, as the passages just quoted bring out, we cannot determine temporal relations between representations by reference to time itself. How, then, can we do so? The only answer available, it would seem, is that we can do it only by relating representations to perceptible objects that are stable and enduring—that can, so to speak, serve as perceptual "stand-ins" for time itself. As Strawson puts it:

> But there is only one way in which perceived things . . . can supply a system of temporal relations independent of the subject's perceptions of them—viz. by *lasting* and being *re*-encounterable in temporally different experiences.[9]

Accordingly, we may enter, as the next premise of the argument, this statement:

(11) If time itself is not perceived, then there is a way to determine temporal relations between representations other than the order in which they are apprehended only if some experiences are conceptualized as being of enduring objects, by reference to which temporal relations can be determined.[10]

This premise turns on the point that if time is not itself an object of perception, then we can establish no time-order at all among any items, other than the order in which we apprehend representations, unless there are perceptible items that are at least conceived as being stable and enduring objects.[11] For only by reference to such objects—only, so to speak, against the background of such objects—can any time-relations be determined if time itself is not perceived, and thus not available to serve as such a "background." But from (1), (7), (8'), (9''), (10'), and (11), there follows this:

(12) Experience is possible only if some experiences are conceptualized as being of enduring objects.[12]

In other words, for experience to be possible, we must take some of our representations as being of objects that exist independently of our perceptions of them; some of our experiences must be conceptualized as being of objects that outlast and stand in different time-relations than the experiences themselves. But this is to say that for experience to be possible, the category of *substance*—in the sense of the term "substance" on which it just means "a thing," "a body," or "a material object"—must be applicable to it. As Strawson puts it:

> To say that objective time-determination [and even experience, by the argument from (1), (7), (8'), (9''), (10'), and (11)] is possible is to say that we can assign to

objects and happenings relations of co-existence and succession and that we can, where necessary, distinguish these relations from the temporal relations of our perceptions, though, of course, we assign them fundamentally on the strength of our perceptions. For this to be possible we must see objects as belonging to, and events as occurring in, an identical, enduring spatial framework. For this in turn to be possible, we must have empirically applicable criteria of persistence and identity, embodied in concepts under which we bring objects of non-persistent perceptions. If we choose to call such concepts "concepts of substances", then we must have and apply concepts of substances.[13]

The other key category needed to refute the Humean view of experience, as we have seen, is the category of causality. In the Second Analogy, Kant offers an argument for the objective validity of this category that turns on an epistemological point that we noted earlier; namely, that since our representations are successive whether we are observing an enduring object like a house or an event like a ship moving downstream, we cannot tell, just from the fact that our representations occur successively, that we are observing an event rather than an enduring object. Kant tries to show that the only way we can determine that we are observing an event is by knowing that that event has some cause, and thus that every event whose occurrence we can know by observation has a cause. Strawson, however, analyzes and then rejects what he takes to be Kant's own argument and substitutes for it what he thinks is a better argument. In chapter 7, I shall argue that although Strawson is right to reject the argument that he attributes to Kant, a different analysis of Kant's argument, by Paul Guyer, is both more authentically Kantian than Strawson's version and immune to his objections. Here, however, I want to explain how Strawson finishes reconstructing the central argument of the Analytic by setting out his version of the argument for the category of causality.

According to Strawson, the best argument that can be made for this category is essentially a continuation of the argument I have been setting out. He characterizes his approach this way:

> [T]he natural procedure [is] to take the conclusion of the first Analogy as the premise of any further argument; to inquire, that is, what further conditions must be satisfied if objective permanence is to be represented in changing perceptions.[14]

Then he restates the conclusion of the First Analogy this way:

> So far we have established the necessity of persistent and re-identifiable objects locatable in a common spatial (or quasi-spatial) framework. We must have such concepts and apply them to objects of perception if we are to make use of the crucial notion of simultaneous existence of objects not simultaneously perceived—a notion which is crucial because without it we can make no use of the distinction between objective and subjective time-determinations.[15]

Now, what are the conditions of our having and applying concepts of persistent objects? They are, as Strawson already indicates in the passage just quoted, that we be able to reencounter and reidentify an object that we now perceive as the same one that we perceived at another time. If we could not recognize an object that we perceived at one time as being the same object that we perceived at another time, then we could not conceptualize our experience as being of stable objects by reference to which we could determine temporal relations between anything in our experience. Thus, we may enter the next premise of the argument:

(13) Some experiences can be conceptualized as being of enduring objects only if some experiences are conceptualized as being of objects that can be reencountered and reidentified.

The requirement that objects be reencounterable and reidentifiable has a further implication, which leads to the vindication of the category of causality. An object that undergoes changes can of course be reencountered and reidentified — but only if it has not changed *too much*:

Objects may change; but they must not, so to speak, change out of all recognition. If they did, we could not know that they had; for we could not recognize *them* as having changed. Objects may retain, or alter, their positions relative to each other; but not in such a way that it is impossible for us to tell which have retained and which have altered their relative positions. Tentatively, then, we may suppose that while perceptions of the world may reveal *some* objective changes which we can characterize as inexplicable, quite unpredictable or utterly random, they can do so only against a background of persistences and alterations which we recognize as explicable, predictable, and regular. . . . These limitations must somehow be reflected in the character of our concepts themselves. That is to say, our concepts of objects, and the criteria of re-identification which they embody, must allow for changes in the objective world subject to the limitation that change must be consistent with the possibility of applying those concepts and criteria in experience.[16]

The next premise of the argument, then, is this:

(14) Some experiences can be conceptualized as being of objects that can be re-encountered and re-identified only if some experiences are conceptualized as being of objects whose changes have a significant amount of order and regularity.

But the requirement that changes in objects be, at least to a significant extent, orderly and regular, is tantamount to the requirement that those changes be, at least to a significant extent, governed by causal laws. As Strawson says:

How is this requirement to be satisfied? The answer seems to lie in the fact that our concepts of objects are linked with sets of conditional expectations about the things which we perceive as falling under them. For every kind of object, we can draw up lists of ways in which we shall expect it not to change unless . . . lists of ways in which we shall expect it to change if . . . and lists of ways in which we shall expect it to change unless. . . . The point is that . . . concepts of *objects* are always and necessarily compendia of causal law or law-likeness, carry implications of power or dependence. Powers, as Locke remarked—and under "powers" he included passive liabilities, and dispositions generally—make up a great part of our concepts of any persisting and re-identifiable items. And without some such concepts as these, no experience of an objective world is possible.[17]

Accordingly, we may now conclude from (12), (13), and (14):

(15) Experience is possible only if some experiences are conceptualized as being of objects whose changes have a significant amount of order and regularity.

5.5 Some Conclusions and Their Status

The argument that we have constructed shows that the categories of substance and cause can be legitimately applied to experience, for if we now supply the premise

(16) Experience is possible

then we can conclude from (12) and (16):

(17) Some experiences are conceptualized as being of enduring objects.

This, as we have said, is tantamount to saying that the category of *substance* is applicable to experience. Furthermore, we can conclude from (15) and (16):

(18) Some experiences are conceptualized as being of objects whose changes have a significant amount of order and regularity.

But this, as we have said, is tantamount to saying that the category of *causality* is applicable to experience.

As worded, (17) and (18) might seem disappointingly weak, for they do not say that we *must* conceive our experiences in the ways described. But the force of the argument is better seen by looking back at step (12), that "experience is possible only if some experiences are conceptualized as being of enduring objects," and at step (15), that "experience is possible only if some experiences are conceptualized as being of objects whose changes have a significant amount of order and regularity." These statements mean that in order for as little as consciousness of a manifold of successive representations to be possible, some experiences have to be conceptualized as being of enduring objects and some as being of objects whose changes have a significant amount of order and regularity. Thus, we may say that Kant has shown that we *must* conceive some of our experiences as being of enduring objects and some of our experiences as being of objects whose changes have a significant amount of order and regularity, where the "must" indicates that conceiving them in these ways is a necessary condition of something that is unquestionably true, namely, that we have experience in the narrow sense of consciousness of a manifold of successive representations. Furthermore, we may now also say that Kant has shown the categories of substance and cause to be objectively valid. For, as we first noted at the outset of Chapter 3, to say that a category is objectively valid is to say that a principle associated with the category has a special status: it is synthetic *a priori*, or it is unobviously analytic, or its truth is a necessary condition of having a kind of experience that we unquestionably have. Now, what the argument shows is that the truth of (17) and (18)—principles associated with the categories of substance and cause, respectively—is a necessary condition of having the kind of experience that we unquestionably have, namely, consciousness of a manifold of successive representations.

On the other hand, I do not believe that the argument shows that (17) and (18) have either of the two other statuses that would render the categories of substance and cause "objectively valid" in Kant's sense of that term, namely, the status of being synthetic *a priori*, or at least unobviously analytic. For the argument could show that (17) and (18) have this status only if all of its premises were themselves synthetic *a priori*, or at least unobviously analytic. To see why this condition is not satisfied, and also as a way of reviewing a lengthy and complex argument, let us summarize the entire argument (I have symbolized each step, so that the reader can more easily verify the validity of the argument, using the rules of elementary logic):

(1) Experience is possible only if unity of consciousness is possible, that is, only if a manifold of representations can be unified in one consciousness (E ⊃ U).

(2) A manifold of representations can be unified in one consciousness only if those representations refer to an object (U ⊃ O).

(3) Representations can refer to an object only by being related to each other in a nonarbitrary, rule-governed way (O ⊃ R).

(4) A manifold of representations can be unified in one consciousness only if those representations are related to each other in a nonarbitrary, rule-governed way [from (2) and (3)] (U ⊃ R).

(5) Representations are apprehended in temporal succession (T).

(6) If (4) and (5), then unity of consciousness is possible only if representations are synthesized, that is, reproduced in imagination according to a rule [(U ⊃ R) . T] ⊃ (U ⊃ L).

(7) Unity of consciousness is possible only if representations are reproduced in imagination according to a rule [from (4), (5), and (6)] (U ⊃ L).

(8') Representations can be reproduced in imagination according to a rule only if the temporal order in which they are reproduced is different from the temporal order in which they are apprehended (L ⊃ D).

(9") Representations can have a temporal order different from the order in which they are apprehended only if there is a way to determine temporal relations between representations other than the order in which they are apprehended (D ⊃ W).

(10') Time itself is not perceived (~P).

(11) If time itself is not perceived, then there is a way to determine temporal relations between representations other than the order in which they are apprehended only if some experiences are conceptualized as being of enduring objects, by reference to which temporal relations can be determined [~P ⊃ (W ⊃ S)].

(12) Experience is possible only if some experiences are conceptualized as being of enduring objects [from (1), (7), (8'), (9"), (10'), and (11)] (E ⊃ S).

(13) Some experiences can be conceptualized as being of enduring ob-

jects only if some experiences are conceptualized as being of objects that can be reencountered and reidentified (S ⊃ N).

(14)   Some experiences can be conceptualized as being of objects that can be reencountered and reidentified only if some experiences are conceptualized as being of objects whose changes have a significant amount of order and regularity (N ⊃ M).

(15)   Experience is possible only if some experiences are conceptualized as being of objects whose changes have a significant amount of order and regularity [from (12)-(14)] (E ⊃ M).

(16)   Experience is possible (E).

(17)   Some experiences are conceptualized as being of enduring objects [from (12) and (16)] (S).

(18)   Some experiences are conceptualized as being of objects whose changes have a significant amount of order and regularity [from (15) and (16)] (M).

The premises of the argument are (1), (2), (3), (5), (6), (8′), (9″), (10′), (11), (13), (14), and (16) since the other steps are each derived from earlier lines in the argument. Now, it seems to me that one of these premises is quite clearly neither synthetic *a priori* nor analytic, namely, (8′), for it turns on the point that the order of apprehension is not rule-governed, and this is an empirical finding: only experience can show us that the order in which we obtain representations is not rule-governed. I must therefore conclude that the argument does not show that (17) and (18) are either synthetic *a priori* or unobviously analytic truths.

I do not think, however, that this result significantly weakens Kant's achievement. As I have said, the argument shows that we must conceive our experience as being of enduring objects whose changes have a significant amount of order and regularity, in the sense that otherwise we could not have the kind of experience we unquestionably have. To see better why this is an important achievement, suppose that we were to replace step (16) with the premise

(16′)   Experience occurs

where this means that consciousness of a manifold of successive representations actually occurs. Unlike (16), (16′) can hardly be an *a priori* truth, whether analytic or synthetic. Rather, (16′) is a very basic, unquestionable empirical truth. So, if we substitute (16′) for (16) in the argument, then it is even clearer that the argument cannot show that (17) and (18) are *a priori* truths. But the argument does show that the truth of (17) and (18) is a necessary condition of our having the kind of experience we unquestionably have. This is a powerful result, and it shows that by the time Kant has developed the argument of the Analytic, the issue of the synthetic *a priori*, to which he initially tried to reduce his basic agenda, has lost much of its importance, thereby strengthening the case for holding that Kant's position does not depend on the legitimacy of the synthetic *a priori*, or even on the unobviously analytic status of his ultimate conclusions.

It might be countered, however, that failure to show that (17) and (18) are synthetic *a priori* or unobviously analytic negatively affects weak Transcendental

Idealism, for a crucial thesis of weak TI is that "we must think of some of the things we perceive as being distinct from ourselves, and of every event we perceive as having a cause." But it now turns out that the force of the "must" in this thesis is conditional because Kant has established only that *if* we have the kind of experience we unquestionably do, *then* we must conceptualize our experience in certain ways. He has not shown that we must conceptualize it in these ways, period. Again, however, I do not think that this result significantly weakens Kant's achievement. For it is beyond question that human experience is a rich manifold of successive representations whose order varies in all manner of ways, and Kant's argument shows that as long as our experience is of this kind, we cannot but conceive it as being of enduring objects whose changes exhibit significant order and regularity.

Nevertheless, it must be admitted that (17) and (18) are in some respects significantly weaker than the conclusions that Kant himself tried to establish. For the notion of substance that Kant seeks to justify in the First Analogy is one on which substance is absolutely permanent and on which its quantity remains ever the same, and the conclusion that Kant tries to establish in the Second Analogy is that *every* observable event must have a cause. Strawson does not believe that such strong conditions can be shown to be necessary conditions of experience. As he puts it:

> They do not represent, in our equipment of concepts, absolutely indispensable elements in terms of which we must see the world if we are to see an objective world at all. They represent, rather, a heightening, an elevation, a pressing to the limit of those truly indispensable but altogether looser conditions which I have argued for.[18]

In the following two chapters, I shall examine how Kant attempts to establish the stronger conclusions of the Analogies. I shall argue in chapter 6 that although the First Analogy is a deep argument, it does not succeed in establishing a conclusion about substance stronger than the one already arrived at. But in chapter 7 I shall try to show that the argument of the Second Analogy can be developed to yield Kant's stronger conclusion about causality, as well as that it can be integrated into the central argument of the Analytic, thereby arriving at a final reconstruction of that argument. If you are especially interested in Kant's attempt to prove the principle of causality and in how his proof can be seen as a further extension of the Central Argument of the Analytic, then you may want read chapter 7 before reading chapter 6. Before discussing either of the Analogies in more depth, however, I shall devote the last section of the present chapter to the second-edition version of the Transcendental Deduction.

5.6 The B-Deduction

Kant's notion of the two time-orders is an extremely powerful idea, for once it is established that representations must have a time-order other than the order in which they are apprehended, the path is laid for the justification of the categories of substance and cause. In the second edition of the *Critique*, Kant completely rewrote the argument that establishes the two time-orders, namely, the Transcendental Deduction. The reconstruction of the deduction that I have given is based mainly on the A-Deduction. We should inquire, therefore, whether the B-Deduction provides an independent case for the introduction of the two time-orders. This is the purpose of the present section.

5.6.1 Analysis and Critique of the B-Deduction

One way in which the B-Deduction differs from the A-Deduction is in its treatment of the unity of consciousness. The A-Deduction starts from the idea that in order for consciousness of a manifold of successive representations (= experience) to be possible, all the representations must be contained in one enduring consciousness. By contrast, the B-Deduction starts from an idea that, although it is mentioned in the text of the A-Deduction, seems not to play a key role in the latter's argument. This is the idea that for consciousness of a manifold of successive representations to be possible, the subject must be able to *ascribe them all to himself* or *herself*, that is, that the representations must all be *self-ascribable*. This point comes out in the way Kant now formulates the principle of the unity of consciousness:

> It must be possible for the 'I think' to accompany all my representations; for otherwise something would be represented in me which could not be thought at all, and that is equivalent to saying that the representation would be impossible, or at least would be nothing to me. (B 131–132)

> All *my* representations in any given intuition must be subject to that condition under which alone I can ascribe them to my identical self as *my* representations, and so can comprehend them as synthetically combined in one apperception through the general expression, '*I think*'. (B 138)

Kant's language here is difficult, but he seems to be saying that unity of consciousness requires an element of self-consciousness, in other words, that it requires not only that all the representations in a manifold be contained in or given to *one* consciousness but also that this consciousness be at least potentially *aware* of its own identity. Kant brings this out by saying that I must be able to *ascribe* my representations to myself—to think of them as mine or as belonging to myself. Indeed, this point can also be found in the A-Deduction:

> It is only because I ascribe all perceptions to one consciousness (original apperception) that I can say of all perceptions that I am conscious of them. (A 122)

Here Kant's language goes so far as to suggest that I must actually ascribe my representations to myself in order to be conscious of them, though the other passages just cited suggest that consciousness of a manifold requires only the *possibility* of self-consciousness.

Is there any argument that can show that consciousness of a manifold requires some form of self-consciousness? The only such argument I can provide turns on the relation between self-consciousness and memory. Suppose that I am conscious of a manifold of successive representations, like the strokes of the bell in Campbell's example.[19] This, as we saw, requires that each successive stroke be contained in one consciousness that retains its identity throughout the succession. Our present question is this: does it also require that this consciousness be (even potentially) *aware* of its own identity throughout the succession? The argument for answering that it does goes as follows. Awareness of a succession of items *as* a succession, as we saw, requires memory. If I forget the first stroke before hearing the second one, then I cannot be aware of the second *as* the successor of the first, or as following it in time. But now, is it not true that I can remember the first stroke only if I am aware that it was I who heard it? If I were unaware that it was I who heard it, how could I remember it? To put the matter differently, it seems that statement (i) below is a conceptual truth, and that statement (ii) below is a contradiction:

(i) If I remember hearing stroke 1, then I am aware that it was I who heard stroke 1.

(ii) I remember hearing stroke 1, but I am unaware that it was I who heard stroke 1.

If this is right, then we can give the following argument:

(a) I can hear stroke 2 as the successor of stroke 1 only if I remember hearing stroke 1.

(b) I remember hearing stroke 1 only if I am aware that it was I who heard stroke 1.

∴ (c) I can hear stroke 2 as the successor of stroke 1 only if I am aware that it was I who heard stroke 1.

If this argument is sound, then it seems to show that consciousness of a manifold of successive representations requires that the subject be able to ascribe all the representations to himself or herself. Indeed, the argument seems to link consciousness of a manifold not merely with potential self-consciousness but also with actual self-consciousness: I must not only be capable of being aware that it was I who heard stroke 1 but also I must actually *be* aware of this fact. But taking only the weaker of these two claims, let us set down, as the first premise of Kant's B-Deduction, the following:

(1) Consciousness of a manifold of successive representations (= experience) is possible for me only if I can ascribe all the representations in the manifold to myself.

If we examine the text of the B-Deduction to see how the rest of Kant's argument goes, we find that he advances four more premises and a conclusion, distributed within the first five numbered sections of his text:[20]

(2) I can ascribe all the representations in a manifold to myself only if I synthesize or combine them. [B 131–139 (sects. 16–17)]

(3) Representations can be combined only by the understanding. [B 129–130 (sect. 15)]

(4) The understanding combines representations by making *objective* judgments. [B 141–142 (sect. 19)]

(5) In all objective judgments representations are combined by means of the categories. [B 143 (sect. 20)]

(6) Therefore, I can be conscious of a manifold of representations only if they are combined in accordance with the categories. [B 143 (sect. 20)]

Let us examine each step in turn.

Premise (2) says that the possibility of ascribing representations to myself depends on my synthesizing them. Here, as in the A-Deduction, Kant implies that unity of consciousness presupposes a synthesis of the manifold, but in the B-Deduction Kant does not repeat his explanation of synthesis. So this is one of the places where what Kant says is opaque unless one reads the text of the B-Deduction against the background of the A-Deduction. Having analyzed the A-Deduction, we know that by synthesis Kant means a rule-governed reproduction of representations. Furthermore, we can recall the main difficulty with this notion: it was not evident why unity of consciousness requires a *rule-governed* synthesis, except in the weak sense that the reproduced representations must be recognized as being replicas of the originals. To justify the rule-governedness requirement in a stronger sense, we had to appeal both to the principle that unity of consciousness requires that the representations to be unified refer to an object and to Kant's analysis of reference to an object as a rule-governed relation among representations. The rule-governedness requirement led in turn to the introduction of the objective time-order because the subjective time-order or order of apprehension is not rule-governed in the relevant sense. The question now before us is whether the unity of consciousness, understood in the stronger sense featured in the B-Deduction (where it requires at least potential self-consciousness) can provide an alternative, independent rationale for introducing the objective time-order.

In dealing with this question, it is helpful to look at how Kant expresses himself when he says that unity of consciousness presupposes synthesis. As we have seen, he makes the point, which Hume had made before him, that consciousness of oneself cannot be based on any particular representation(s) of inner sense because they are always in flux (A 107). He then goes on to ask what consciousness of self *is* based on, and he answers that it is based on consciousness of the *act* of synthesizing representations:

> This unity of consciousness would be impossible if the mind in knowledge of the manifold could not become conscious of the identity of function whereby it synthetically combines it in one knowledge. ... The mind could never think its identity in the manifoldness of its representations ... if it did not have before its eyes the identity of its act, whereby it subordinates all synthesis of apprehension ... to a transcendental condition, thereby rendering possible their interconnection according to *a priori* rules. (A 108)

> This thoroughgoing identity of the apperception of a manifold which is given in intuition contains a synthesis of representations, and is possible only through the consciousness of this synthesis. For the empirical consciousness, which accompanies different representations, is in itself diverse and without relation to the subject. That relation comes about, not simply through my accompanying each rep-

resentation with consciousness, but only in so far as I *conjoin* one representation with another, and am conscious of the synthesis of them. Only in so far, therefore, as I can unite a manifold of given representations in *one consciousness*, is it possible for me to represent to myself the *identity of the consciousness in* [i.e. throughout] these *representations*. (B 133)

In both of these passages—one from the A-Deduction and one from the B-Deduction—Kant is evidently arguing that since consciousness of self cannot be based on the awareness of particular representations, which are fleeting and changing, it must therefore be based on awareness of the unitary *act* of combining representations according to a rule. This is to make self-consciousness depend on awareness of one's own mental activity—a difficult position to maintain because it seems untrue that we are aware of the activity Kant calls "synthesis." It seems just not to be the case that when we apprehend a succession of items, we are aware of any act of reproducing past representations, like the act of reproducing past strokes of a bell or the act of reproducing the previous part of a musical phrase. This comes out from reflecting on a passage from Wolff that I have already had occasion to quote:

> If I look at a tree, then forget it and look at another, then forget it also and look at a third, and so on, I can not in any meaningful sense be said to have seen the forest. What I must do, therefore, as I proceed from one moment to the next, is to reproduce the representation which has just been apprehended, carrying it along in memory while I apprehend the next. In looking at a forest, I must say to myself, "There is a birch; and there is an elm, plus the birch which I remember, etc." The result of this repeated recollecting—or synthesis of reproduction in imagination, as Kant calls it—is the apprehension in one consciousness of a variety of representations which were originally disjoint. By carrying them forward, the mind has made it possible to think of them as a unity.[21]

In a footnote to this passage, Wolff admits that "needless to say, this is a rather flatfooted description. But then, the mind works with such rapidity and deftness that any attempt to spell out its activities must seem ponderous by comparison."[22] If this is supposed to mean that we are actually aware of the activity of synthesis even though it happens so fast that we barely notice it, then it seems very dubious. One may want to say that "either we are conscious of synthesis or we are not. If we are not—as seems to be the case—then what is the status of the theory of synthesis?" To this question, there is a hard-line answer and a soft-line answer. The hard-line answer, suggested by P. F. Strawson, is that the theory of synthesis should be rejected as belonging to "the imaginary subject of transcendental psychology."[23] Of course, rejecting the theory of synthesis would undermine the first-edition version of the Transcendental Deduction. The soft-line answer, which I favor, is that the theory of synthesis is a rational reconstruction of what must take place, perhaps indeed at a subconscious level, when we are aware of a succession *as* a succession: somehow the earlier input or information must be reproduced in the mind for present use; otherwise we could not be aware that what is now present to consciousness belongs to a succession. Strawson himself seems to admit as much, for he goes on to concede that although the claims made by the theory of synthesis "belong neither to empirical (including physiological) psychology nor to an analytical philosophy of mind," still *"some of them may have near or remote analogues in both."*[24]

Suppose that we drop the dubious claim that consciousness of self depends on awareness of the mental activity of synthesis. Then, does anything that Kant says in the passages where he links the two survive? Well, there is the negative, Humean point that to be conscious of oneself is not to be aware of any particular inner representation(s). Then there is Kant's question: what then is consciousness of self based on? His answer is contained in the previously quoted claim that

> unity of consciousness would be impossible if the mind in knowledge of the manifold could not become conscious of the identity of function whereby it synthetically combines it in one knowledge. . . . The mind could never think its identity in the manifoldness of its representations . . . if it did not have before its eyes the identity of its act, whereby it subordinates all synthesis of apprehension . . . to a transcendental condition, thereby rendering possible their interconnection according to *a priori* rules. (A 108)

Our question is, assuming that all Kant's references to *acts* of combining the manifold in this and similar passages are dropped, is there some truth left in what he is saying? Here we may turn for help to none other than Strawson:

> It seems that we may have to look for the explanation of the possibility of self-ascription of experiences in the nature of the *outcome* of the synthesizing activities rather than in any special awareness of those activities themselves or of the powers exercised in performing them. Perhaps the very connectedness of experiences, under concepts of the objective, which synthesis is held to *produce*, is itself the condition—or the fundamental condition—under which alone self-ascription is possible.[25]

Strawson here suggests that instead of focusing on the activity of synthesis, we focus only on what Kant says is the outcome of this activity.[26] This outcome, as we know, is a time-order of representations that must be distinct from the order of apprehension or, as Kant puts it, the "interconnection [of representations] according to *a priori* rules." Thus the question becomes: is there any way, given the materials Kant gives us, to establish a connection between self-consciousness and a time-order of representations distinct from the order of apprehension without bringing in the view that we are conscious of acts of synthesis? I shall return to this key question in the next section. The rest of the present section is devoted to commenting on the remaining steps in Kant's own presentation of the B-Deduction.

Premise (3), that "representations can be combined only by the understanding," is the one that comes first in Kant's own text:

> All combination—be we conscious of it or not, be it a combination of the manifold of intuition, empirical or non-empirical, or of various concepts—is an act of the understanding. To this act the general title 'synthesis' may be assigned. . . . (B 130)

Kant's justification for this premise stems from his faculty psychology, according to which mere sense perception is purely passive and only the understanding is active:

> The combination (*conjunctio*) of a manifold in general can never come to us through the senses. . . . For it is an act of spontaneity of the faculty of representation; and . . . this faculty, to distinguish it from sensibility, must be entitled the understanding. . . . (B 129–130)

It is difficult to see how, in an argument that is supposed to establish that experience is possible only if it possesses structural features in virtue of which certain pure concepts apply to it, a premise of this kind helps to advance matters. Experience, understood as consciousness of a manifold of successive representations, requires synthesis: this we already know from our study of the A-Deduction. But whether this synthesis is carried out by a faculty called "understanding" or is seen as part of the perceptual process seems to matter little. Given the way the next premise, (4), is worded ("The understanding combines representations by making objective judgments"), (3) is needed from a purely formal point of view to complete the argument, but its dispensability is evident from the fact that the argument could be simplified by replacing (3) with

> (3′) representations can be combined only by making objective judgments

and deleting premise (4).

Let us turn to premise (4) [or alternatively, (3′)]. If one considers the B-Deduction, as Kant presumably intends, totally apart from what he will say later in the Analogies, as well as from what he says in the A-Deduction, then premise (4) abruptly introduces into the argument a notion of objectivity for which he has not prepared the ground. He characterizes this notion in the following two passages:

> I find that a judgment is nothing but the manner in which given modes of knowledge are brought to the objective unity of apperception. This is what is intended by the copula 'is'. It is employed to distinguish the objective unity of given representations from the subjective. (B 141–142)

> To say 'The body is heavy' is not merely to state that two representations have always been conjoined in my perception, however often that perception be repeated; what we are asserting is that they are combined *in the object*, no matter what the state of the subject may be. (B 142)

These passages point to a salient feature of objectivity: the objective is that which obtains regardless of the relations between one's perceptions. This point is brilliantly developed later in the Analogies, where the time relations between our perceptions are contrasted with the time relations between the objects that they are taken to be perceptions of. But the introduction of objectivity here in the B-Deduction seems quite unwarranted. Kant simply asserts that a judgment combines representations in an objective manner, that is, in a way that implies that the relations and qualities of the things represented are independent of the relations and qualities of the representations. But this appears to be a definitional fiat: Kant is simply defining judgment in such a way that a combination of representations counts as a judgment only when it is not merely a report of the subject's mental state.

It is noteworthy that in his *Prolegomena to Any Future Metaphysics,* a work designed to present in simplified form the same system of thought as the *Critique,* Kant himself makes a distinction that directly contravenes this narrowing of the meaning of "judgment." This is the distinction between "judgments of experience" (*Erfahrungsurtheile*) and "judgments of perception" (*Wahrnehmungsurtheile*).[27] Judgments of experience pertain to the objective realm and require the application of the categories. But Kant says that judgments of perception state "merely a connexion of perceptions in my mental state, without reference to an object,"[28] adding that such judgments "refer merely to feeling, which everybody knows to be merely subjective."[29] He gives, as examples of such judgments, "the room is warm, sugar sweet, and wormwood bitter," and he says that

> each of these sentences only expresses a relation of two sensations to the same subject, to myself, and that only in the present state of perception; consequently they are not valid of the object. Such judgments are of perception. Judgments of experience are of quite a different nature.[30]

To bring out the subjective character of such judgments, contemporary philosophers would commonly express them as "the room feels warm to me, sugar tastes sweet to me, and wormwood tastes bitter to me," or as "the room *seems* warm to me, sugar *seems* sweet to me, and wormwood *seems* bitter to me," rather than using the verb "is": they would take to heart Kant's statement that "[objectivity] is what is intended by the copula 'is,'" and so avoid the word "is" in favor of a word like "seems" or "appears." But this is merely a linguistic point. The essential point is that in the *Prolegomena,* Kant recognizes that not all judgments have to pertain to the objective world and that, on the contrary, we can perfectly well make judgments that report only our own present mental state. In section 19 of the B-Deduction, on the other hand, he seeks to restrict the meaning of "judgment" in such a way that only what he calls in the *Prolegomena* "judgments of experience" count as genuine judgments, whereas what he there calls "judgments of perception" do not count as judgments at all. But as Jonathan Bennett points out, "this restriction on the meaning of 'judgment' is arbitrary and illegitimate: Kant gives no reason for denying what he clearly admits in the *Prolegomena,* namely that there can be judgments of perception as well as of experience."[31]

In light of this arbitrary restriction on the meaning of "judgment," it seems that premise (4) [or (3′)] is unwarranted, so that strictly speaking we could reject the entire argument without considering premise (5), that "in all objective judgments representations are combined by means of the categories." Nevertheless, let us note that, as Kant himself indicates (B 143), premise (5) rests on the Metaphysical Deduction of the categories from the forms of judgment. Therefore, it inherits the weaknesses of that argument, notably that the table of judgments can hardly be said to contain all and only the most basic forms of judgment. But the chief point to remember about the Metaphysical Deduction is that it can at best show only what categories we in fact use; it cannot show that any of those categories are objectively valid. Hence, even if premise (5) were fully acceptable, this could not salvage the argument, given the weakness we have identified in its crucial premise (4) [or (3′)].

5.6.2 A Reconstruction of the B-Deduction

I have defended the first premise of the B-Deduction but argued that the rest of the argument is vitiated by the arbitrariness of premise (4). This gives rise to the question: can a more plausible argument for the legitimacy of the categories be built upon premise (1), using Kantian materials and insights? More narrowly, since the two time-orders lead to the vindication of the crucial categories of substance and cause, is there a plausible Kantian argument from premise (1) to the two time-orders? In this subsection, I shall attempt to construct such an argument. At the end of the subsection, I shall review the entire argument and symbolize each of its steps.

Our opening premise, then, is this:

(1) Consciousness of a manifold of successive representations (= experience) is possible for me only if I can ascribe all the representations in the manifold to myself.

Now it seems obvious that

(2) I can ascribe representations to myself only if I have a concept of myself.

The basic idea here is that one cannot ascribe states or properties of any kind to X unless one has some concept of X. If one has no idea what X is, one cannot ascribe anything to it. Admittedly, we sometimes use locutions that suggest the contrary, as when someone says, "I have no idea what this thing is, but I can see that it is square." But even in such a case, the person has some concept of what the thing is—if only that it is a physical object of some sort, that it is solid, or that it is something with a shape.

Here, however, it might be thought that the principle "no property ascription to X without some concept of X" is not obviously true in the special case where X is oneself. For Strawson has argued that "no criteria of personal identity [are] invoked in immediate self-ascription of current or recalled experiences," and this might be taken to show that no concept of oneself is needed either.[32] Strawson supports his claim as follows:

When a man (a subject of experience) ascribes a current or directly remembered state of consciousness to himself, no use whatever of any criteria of personal identity is required to justify his use of the pronoun "I" to refer to the subject of that experience. It would make no sense to think or say: *This* inner experience is occurring, but is it occurring to *me?* (This feeling is anger, but is it I who am feeling it?) Again, it would make no sense to think or say: I distinctly remember *that* inner experience occurring, but did it occur to me? (I remember that terrible feeling of loss; but was it I who felt it?) There is nothing that one can thus encounter or recall in the field of inner experience such that there can be any question of one's applying criteria of subject-identity to determine whether the encountered or recalled experience belongs to oneself—or to someone else.[33]

In the same vein, T. E. Wilkerson writes:

Suppose that I have a pain. There are many questions that I can sensibly ask. The sensation may be faint and unfamiliar, and I am not sure how I should classify it. I may not be quite sure whether it is a toothache or earache. It may be so faint that I cannot decide whether or not it has completely subsided. But, Kant would say, there is one thing I can never doubt: I can never wonder who is having the sensation. I can try to work out whether I am suffering from toothache or earache, but I cannot try to work out who is suffering. If I am in pain, I know who is in pain. . . . If I see something or hurt myself or feel depressed, I know who is doing the seeing, who is hurt, who is depressed, without ever having to work it out. When I am self-conscious, I am not doing two things, namely picking out my self and then discovering the right experiences to attach to my self. I am merely doing one much simpler thing, namely identifying my experiences as mine.[34]

I think that Strawson and Wilkerson are right, but I do not think that what they say constitutes an objection to premise (2). For that premise does not say that in order to ascribe a present or remembered experience to myself, I have to apply a criterion of personal identity so as to pick myself out from other things and then check whether the experience belongs to the item picked out. The premise makes only the different and weaker claim that in order to ascribe a present or remembered experience to myself, I have to have some concept of myself—some understanding of the distinction between self and not-self. From the fact that "no criteria of personal identity [are] invoked in immediate self-ascription of current or recalled experiences," it does *not* follow that no concept of oneself is needed either. Even what Strawson calls "criterionless self-ascription" requires that I have a concept of myself; otherwise I could not know to what or whom I was ascribing experiences in a criterionless way.

The next premise is

(3) I can have a concept of myself only if something in my experience answers to that concept.

This premise rests on the doctrine that Kant expresses in his dictum that "thoughts without content are empty, intuitions without concepts are blind" (A 51/B 75), specifically in the dictum's first clause. This doctrine means that for any concept C that can be used to select or to describe something, there must be something that we could encounter in our experience that would answer to it; it must have what contemporary philosophers call a "criterion of application." Strawson calls this doctrine Kant's "Principle of Significance," and he points out that there are dozens of places in the *Critique* where Kant asserts it.[35] Here are a few of them:

Concepts are altogether impossible, and can have no meaning, if no object is given for them, or at least for the elements of which they are composed. (A 139/ B 178)

We demand in every concept . . . the possibility of giving it an object to which it may be applied. In the absence of such an object, it has no meaning and is completely lacking in content. . . . Now the object cannot be given to a concept otherwise than in intuition. . . . Therefore all concepts, and with them all principles, even such as are possible *a priori*, relate to empirical intuitions, that is, to the data for a possible experience. (A 239/B 298)

> We therefore demand that a bare concept be *made sensible*, that is, that an object be presented to it in intuition. Otherwise the concept would, as we say, be without *sense*, that is, without meaning. (A 240/B 299)

As we have seen, Kant's insistence that concepts have empirical criteria of application extends even to the categories:

> What has chiefly to be noted is this, that to such a something [i.e., something that cannot be given to us in sensible intuition] . . . not a single one of all the categories could be applied. We could not, for instance, apply to it the concept of substance, meaning something which can exist as subject and never as mere predicate. For save in so far as empirical intuition provides the instance to which to apply it, I do not know whether there can be anything that corresponds to such a form of thought. (B 149)

> All categories . . . allow only of empirical employment, and have no meaning whatsoever when not applied to objects of possible experience, that is, to the world of sense. (A 696/B 724)

These passages and others like them show that premise (3) is rooted in one of Kant's most deeply held views. The view is also one of his most plausible and one that many contemporary philosophers accept. So to the extent that a version of the Transcendental Deduction can be built upon it, such an argument has a good claim to be Kantian, and commends itself to the attention of contemporary philosophers as well.

The argument's next premise is this:

(4) No particular item(s) of experience answer(s) to the concept of my-self.

This premise is identical with the point, made by Hume and accepted by Kant, that we cannot encounter our own self in experience. As we have seen, Hume famously says that

> when I enter most intimately into what I call *myself*, I always stumble on some particular perception or other, of heat or cold, light or shade, love or hatred, pain or pleasure. I never can catch *myself* at any time without a perception, and can never observe anything but the perception.[36]

As we have also seen, Kant likewise writes that

> consciousness of self according to the determinations of our state in inner perception is merely empirical, and always changing. No fixed and abiding self can present itself in this flux of inner appearances. (A 107)

Kant agrees with Hume, then, that no particular item or group of items that one can find by introspection answers to the concept of oneself since inner experience presents no item or group of items that remains the same throughout one's conscious life.

Here one might object, however, that even if Hume and Kant are right in saying that we cannot encounter the self in introspection, this is not sufficient to establish premise (4). For, the objection would go, Hume and Kant here completely overlook the possibility that *one's own body*, which is an object of ordinary sense perception, answers to the concept of self. This suggestion raises complex and controversial issues about the nature of persons and personal identity, but there can be little doubt that Kant would have rejected it because he stands squarely in the tradition of philosophers who regard the self as the subject of thoughts, feelings, and memories that do not necessarily have to go with one and the same body. John Locke supported this tradition by asking us to imagine a case of body-switch: suppose that a prince and a cobbler both go to sleep one night and that in the following morning a person wakes up with the cobbler's body but all the thoughts, memories, and feelings of the prince, and another person wakes up with the prince's body but all the thoughts, feelings, and memories of the cobbler.[37] Which person, Locke asks, is identical with the prince, and which with the cobbler? His answer is that the person with the prince's thoughts and memories and the cobbler's body is the prince, and the person with the cobbler's thoughts and memories and the prince's body is the cobbler. Although Locke's position has been disputed, it is plausible in its own terms and there can be little doubt that Kant would agree with it. I shall therefore assume that it is correct and continue with the argument on that basis.

The next premise is this:

(5) If no particular item(s) of experience answer(s) to the concept of myself, then the only thing in my experience that can answer to the concept of myself is a temporal order among my representations.

This premise attempts to distill the element of truth in Kant's claim, discussed in the previous subsection, that consciousness of self must be based on consciousness of the unitary act of synthesizing a manifold of representations. As we saw, Kant thinks that in light of the fact that "no fixed and abiding self can present itself in [the] flux of inner appearances," it follows that "unity of consciousness would be impossible if the mind in knowledge of the manifold could not become conscious of the identity of function whereby it synthetically combines it in one knowledge," or in other words, that "the mind could never think its identity in the manifoldness of its representations . . . if it did not have before its eyes the identity of its act" of synthesis. (A 107–108) The objection to this claim was that we are not aware of the mental activity of synthesis. I asked whether, if we concede this objection, this means that there is no truth at all in Kant's claim that consciousness of self depends on consciousness of the activity of synthesis. Here I turned for help to Strawson's suggestion that although self-consciousness is not based on an awareness of the activity of synthesis, it may be based on what Kant takes to be the *outcome* of that activity, namely, a certain order among representations. If Strawson's suggestion is correct, then there is a link between self-consciousness and order among one's representations, and this link does not depend on awareness of the activity of synthesis whereby that order is produced, but only on awareness of that order. Furthermore, this link allows us to deduce, from (4) and (5),

(6) The only thing in my experience that can answer to the concept of myself is a temporal order among my representations.

To see more clearly how the argument as so far developed works, we may look at it this way: premises (1)–(4) present a problem, whereas premises (5) and (6) offer a solution. Premises (1) and (2) together tell us that experience, that is, consciousness of a successive manifold, is possible only if the subject has a self-concept. Premise (3)—that "I can have a concept of myself only if something in my experience answers to that concept"—reminds us that such a concept must, like any concept, have something in experience that answers to it, some criterion of application. Premise (4) compels us to admit that in the case of the concept of a subject of experiences—of the self, or the "I"—this criterion of application cannot be any specific item of experience or group of items of experience. This then raises the question: what in experience does answer to this concept, or what is its criterion of application? This question must have an answer, on pain of violating Kant's fundamental principle that "thoughts without content are empty"—that all concepts must have something answering to them in experience. The answer to the question is offered by steps (5) and (6), namely, that since what answers to the concept of oneself is not any particular item or group of items of experience, it can only be a certain temporal order among items of experience.

The next premise is the analytic truth:

(7) If the only thing in my experience that can answer to the concept of myself is a temporal order among my representations, then something in my experience answers to the concept of myself only if a temporal order among my representations answers to the concept of myself.

The argument then continues with this premise:

(8) A temporal order among my representations can answer to the concept of myself only if at least some of my representations have another temporal order as well.

The rationale for this important premise turns on the principle that something X cannot answer to a descriptive concept if X exhausts the entire field of possible experience. For the corresponding concept would then apply to everything in experience; that is, it would exclude nothing, and so it would be a perfectly vacuous or empty concept, a pseudo-concept that could not be used to describe anything in anyone's experience. Differently put, if anything and everything in experience would answer to a concept C, then the concept C is a perfectly vacuous one that cannot be used to describe, characterize, or attribute a property to anything. Now, it is simply a tautology to say that representations exhaust the field of possible experience, for Kantian representations include all things as we experience them. It follows that if representations have only one temporal order, then that order qualifies the whole field of experience: nothing that we can experience can have any other temporal order. How then can such an order among representations possibly answer to any descriptive concept C? It cannot. Rather, a temporal order among representations can answer to a descriptive or nonvacuous concept only if there is another, contrasting order among representations. Representations ordered in one way can then answer to the concept C, and representations ordered in a contrasting way would answer to the concept non-C.

The next premise is this:

(9) One temporal order among my representations is the order in which they are apprehended.

In other words, one order among items of experience is simply the order in which they are experienced—the subjective time-order of the Analogies of Experience. It is implicit in the argument that this order is precisely what answers to the concept of a subject of experiences, for this order constitutes, in Strawson's phrase, "one subjective experiential route through an objective world." Indeed, Strawson himself virtually says that the subjective time-order is what answers to one's self-concept:

> That experience should be experience of a unified objective world at least makes room for the idea of *one* subjective or experiential route through the world, traced by *one* series of experiences which together yield *one* unified experience of the world—a potential autobiography. We have here, as it were, the basic ground for the possibility of an empirical use for the concept of the subject of such an autobiography, the concept of self.[38]

The reference to an "objective world" that contrasts with any single experiential route through that world is not gratuitous: it is justified, for it follows from premises (8) and (9) that:

(10) A temporal order among my representations can answer to the concept of myself only if some of my representations have a temporal order different from the order in which they are apprehended.

The reason that step (10) follows from premises (8) and (9) is that premise (8) means that a temporal order among my representations can answer to the concept of myself only if it is not the only temporal order that representations possess, but premise (9) says that one temporal order that representations possess is their order of apprehension; it follows, then, that no temporal order among my representations could answer to the concept of myself if their order of apprehension were the *only* temporal order they possessed. To put it a bit more formally, step (10) follows from premises (8) and (9) with the help of the analytic truth:

(9a) If a temporal order among my representations can answer to the concept of myself only if at least some of my representations have another temporal order as well, and one temporal order among my representations is the order in which they are apprehended, then a temporal order among my representations can answer to the concept of myself only if some of my representations have a temporal order different from the order in which they are apprehended.

But it is evident that the time-order introduced in (10) is precisely the objective time-order of the Analogies of Experience. The point of the qualification "some" in (10) is to allow for subjective items of experience like dreams and hallucinations, which have no time-order other than the order in which they are experienced.

From this point on, the argument continues in almost exactly the same way as the last ten steps of the reconstruction of the Central Argument of the Analytic given in the previous chapter. To make this plain, I shall now review the argument as developed so far and then add the final ten steps. So far, the argument has gone as follows:

(1) Consciousness of a manifold of successive representations (= experience) is possible for me only if I can ascribe all the representations in the manifold to myself (E ⊃ A).

(2) I can ascribe representations to myself only if I have a concept of myself (A ⊃ C).

(3) I can have a concept of myself only if something in my experience answers to that concept (C ⊃ S).

(4) No particular item(s) of experience answer(s) to the concept of myself (N).

(5) If no particular item(s) of experience answer(s) to the concept of myself, then the only thing in my experience that can answer to the concept of myself is a temporal order among my representations (N ⊃ O).

(6) The only thing in my experience that can answer to the concept of myself is a temporal order among my representations [from (4) and (5)] (O).

(7) If the only thing in my experience that can answer to the concept of myself is a temporal order among my representations, then something in my experience answers to the concept of myself only if a temporal order among my representations answers to the concept of myself [O ⊃ (S ⊃ T)].

(8) A temporal order among my representations can answer to the concept of myself only if at least some of my representations have another temporal order as well (T ⊃ W).

(9) One temporal order among my representations is the order in which they are apprehended (R).

(9a) If a temporal order among my representations can answer to the concept of myself only if at least some of my representations have another temporal order as well, and one temporal order among my representations is the order in which they are apprehended, then a temporal order among my representations can answer to the concept of myself only if some of my representations have a temporal order different from the order in which they are apprehended {[(T ⊃ W) . R] ⊃ (T ⊃ D)}.

(10) A temporal order among my representations can answer to the concept of myself only if some of my representations have a temporal order different from the order in which they are apprehended [from (8), (9), and (9a)] (T ⊃ D).

The final ten steps, renumbered to dovetail with the ones above and with italics to indicate the few places where they differ slightly from the corresponding steps in the previous reconstruction, are as follows:

(11) Representations can have a temporal order different from the order in which they are apprehended only if there is a way to determine temporal relations between representations other than the order in which they are apprehended (D ⊃ Y).

(12) Time itself is not perceived (~P).

(13) If time itself is not perceived, then there is a way to determine temporal relations between representations other than the order in which they are apprehended only if some experiences are conceptualized as being of enduring objects, by reference to which temporal relations can be determined [~P ⊃ (Y ⊃ B)].

(14) Experience is possible *for me* only if some experiences are conceptualized as being of enduring objects [from (1), (2), (3), (6), (7), (10), (11), (12), and (13)] (E ⊃ B).

(15) Some experiences can be conceptualized as being of enduring objects only if some experiences are conceptualized as being of objects that can be reencountered and reidentified (B ⊃ I).

(16) Some experiences can be conceptualized as being of objects that can be reencountered and reidentified only if some experiences are conceptualized as being of objects whose changes have a significant amount of order and regularity (I ⊃ U).

(17) Experience is possible *for me* only if some experiences are conceptualized as being of objects whose changes have a significant amount of order and regularity [from (14)–(16)] (E ⊃ U).

(18) Experience is possible *for me* (E).

(19) Some experiences are conceptualized as being of enduring objects [from (14) and (18)] (B).

(20) Some experiences are conceptualized as being of objects whose changes have a significant amount of order and regularity [from 17) and (18)] (U).

Here, then, is an alternative reconstruction of the central argument of the Analytic, based on the opening premise of the B-Deduction and on a number of fundamental Kantian ideas. Like the reconstruction based on the A-Deduction discussed earlier, it is a powerful attempt to refute the Humean view of experience. Indeed, in one respect, it may well be superior to the earlier reconstruction: none of its premises appear to be empirical truths; all of them appear to be *a priori*. At least one of them, namely (12)—the premise that time itself is not perceived—is arguably even synthetic *a priori*, though I shall not try to answer the difficult question of whether this premise really is synthetic or merely analytic. But if the premises are all *a priori*, then the conclusions are *a priori*, and Kant has established the objective validity of the categories of substance and cause in a sense that closely approximates and may even vindicate his official view that their associated principles are synthetic *a priori*.[39]

The First Analogy

Substance

6.1 The Permanence Thesis

Kant calls the principle to be proved in the First Analogy the "Principle of the Permanence of Substance." In A, he states it this way: "All appearances contain the permanent (substance) as the object itself, and the transitory as its mere determination, that is, as a way in which the object exists" (A 182).[1] In B, Kant words the principle differently: "in all change of appearance substance is permanent; its quantum in nature is neither increased nor diminished" (B 224). As the wording of these principles suggests and as Kant's ensuing discussion confirms, the principle in B is the stronger one: the first clause of the B-principle, when its meaning is spelled out, entails the A-principle as a whole, but the A-principle does not entail the second clause of the B-principle (regarding the quantum or quantity of substance). More simply put, the B-principle entails the A-principle, but not vice versa. So I shall analyze Kant's arguments as attempts to prove the principle as stated in B. However, I shall initially focus exclusively on the principle's first clause, the claim that "in all change of appearance substance is permanent"—a claim which, as just indicated, means in context the same thing as the A-principle taken as a whole.

An initial difficulty in understanding Kant's position is that just two paragraphs after stating the principle to be proved, he says that "certainly, the proposition, that substance is permanent, is tautological" (A 184/B 227). But if, as this remark implies, the principle is an obvious tautology, that is, is true by definition, then just as obviously it does not need to be proved: so why does Kant go on to offer a proof of it? The answer comes in the very next sentence, where Kant says that in order to justify "applying the category of substance to appearance"—in order to justify using the term "substance" as he has defined it—"we ought first to have *proved* that in all appearances *there is* something permanent" (A 184/B 227; my emphasis). So, Kant clearly thinks that the permanence of what he calls "substance" must be proved by argument and not merely stipulated by definition; he thinks, to put it more simply, that he needs to prove that *there is* such a thing as substance as he has defined it.

Kant gives two versions of the proof of the principle of the permanence of substance, one in A and the other in B. The language of both is terse and quite opaque, and some of it is best understood in the light of points that Kant has already made more fully in other places. I shall focus on the proof in B, supplementing it with points made more explicitly in A as appropriate. For purposes of analysis, I shall divide the proof into segments.

Segment 1

All appearances are in time; and in it alone, as substratum (as permanent form of inner intuition), can either coexistence or succession be represented. Thus the time in which all change of appearances has to be thought, remains and does not change. For it is that in which, and as determinations of which, succession and coexistence can alone be represented. (B 224–225)

The opening clause that "all appearances are in time" pertains to the objective time-order in which all things as we must perceive them ("appearances") exist; it ought to remind us that our representations are of things that are conceived as having different time relations than our representations. But as Kant's twice-repeated references to coexistence and succession indicate, there are only two time-relations in which any two things, X and Y, can stand: they may coexist (exist at the same time), or they may exist in succession (i.e., X begins to exist before Y or Y begins to exist before X). The corresponding passage in A is even more explicit on this point: "simultaneity and succession [are] the only relations in time" (A 182/B 226).

Kant's additional point that time "remains and does not change" has been criticized by some philosophers as being unclear or even false. Thus Edward Caird wrote:

It may be objected that to say that "time itself does not change" is like saying that passing away does not itself pass away. So far the endurance of time and the permanence of the changing might even seem to mean only that the moments of time never cease to pass away, and the changing never ceases to change. A perpetual flux would therefore sufficiently "represent" all the permanence that is in time.[2]

In defense of Kant, however, Henry Allison rightly says that

Caird's contention . . . is true enough, but it is largely irrelevant as a criticism of Kant. The essential point is that the constant flux occurs in a single time. The claim that time is unchangeable or permanent is really equivalent to the claim that it retains its identity as one and the same time (temporal framework) throughout all changes. The most that Kant can be charged with here is a lack of clarity, though it is difficult to imagine what else he could have meant by this claim.[3]

In other words, Kant here puts forward, as a premise of his argument, what we may call the "unity of time." A good definition of this notion is given by James Van Cleve:

I take the unity of time to consist in this: all events belong to one connected
temporal order, which means that any two events are such that either one begins
before the other or they are simultaneous.[4]

The full meaning of Kant's claim that our representations have an objective time-
order, then, is that they are of things that coexist or exist in succession in a single
time; thus to say that we know of an objective time-order is to say that we know
of things existing simultaneously or successively in a single time. So we can summarize the first step of Kant's proof like this:

(1) We know that our representations are of things that coexist and exist
successively in a single, unitary time.

But what are the necessary conditions of such knowledge? Kant's answer
comes in the next segment of his proof:

Segment 2
Now time itself cannot be perceived. Consequently there must be found in the
objects of perception, that is, in the appearances, the substratum which represents
time in general; and all change or coexistence must, in being apprehended,
be perceived in this substratum, and through relation of the appearances to it.
(B 225)

Here Kant first reminds us of his key point that time itself cannot be perceived.
This means that we cannot know that things exist in certain relations of coexistence or succession to each other by ascertaining that they stand in certain perceivable relations to time itself. For that would require that time itself, or moments in
time, be perceivable because one can perceive a relation between X and Y only if
X and Y are both perceivable. It follows ("Consequently"), Kant goes on to say,
that time itself must have some kind of perceptual stand-in, perceptual equivalent,
or perceptual analogue (which he calls "the substratum which represents time in
general"). As Allison puts it:

The unperceivability of time makes it necessary to presuppose some perceptually
accessible model for time itself as a condition of the possibility of determining
temporal relations of appearances.[5]

We can summarize this part of Kant's argument as follows:

(2) Time itself cannot be perceived.
(3) If time itself cannot be perceived, then we cannot know that our
representations are of things that coexist and exist successively in a
single, unitary time unless there is a permanent, perceptually accessible stand-in for time.
(4) There is a permanent, perceptually accessible stand-in for time [from
(1)–(3)].

Some philosophers find Kant's claim that determining time-relations requires
a perceptual stand-in for time unclear or even unintelligible, but I do not see
why.[6] Notice first of all that we cannot in general determine that things coexist or
that they are successive by simple observation, for at any single time one perceives

at best only very few of the things that coexist *in the objective time-order;* their coexistence has to be established solely on the basis of the always successive and incomplete order of one's own representations—that is, on the basis of the subjective time-order. Furthermore, one successively perceives at best only very few of the things that exist in succession in the objective time-order, and this not because one perceives them simultaneously instead but rather because one ever perceives only very few of them at all. Perhaps this is why in segment 1 above Kant speaks of "the time in which all change of appearances has to be *thought* [my emphasis]": the objective time-order has to be reconstructed in thought since at any one time most of the things belonging to it are unperceived. But if in general things are not known to coexist or to exist successively in (the single) objective time by simple observation, then how is this knowledge possible? The only way, it seems, is by knowing how the things are related to time itself—what their respective positions or dates are in the single, absolute time that Kant first discusses in the Transcendental Aesthetic (though he does not there distinguish it explicitly from the subjective time-order introduced in the Analogies). But time itself is not even a possible object of perception: points or moments in time cannot be individuated by perception or by any empirical procedure. Therefore, the only way we can determine relations of coexistence and succession in time is by using a perceptual stand-in or perceptual equivalent for time, by reference to which we can determine things' positions (dates) in time.

Now, it happens that there are in fact many things by reference to which we can establish time-relations. For example, a well-functioning clock operates in a regular manner, so we can determine that any two things that existed while its needles were in the same position existed at the same time, and any two things that existed while its needles were in different positions existed at different times. Here someone may object that if we can tell that something exists "while"—that is, *at the same time as*—a needle is in a certain position on a clock, then we can tell that two things exist at the same time by direct comparison, without using a clock. But again, this overlooks the fact that things that exist at the same time *in the objective time-order* are not all perceived at the same time, so their coexistence cannot in general be known by direct perception.

Of course, the example of the clock is a simplification: we do not really determine time-relations by reference to one well-functioning clock, or any number of them. Rather, time-relations (as well as the well-functioning of clocks) are ultimately determined by such things as the rising and setting of the sun, the progression of seasons, and the movements of planets and stars. Our ultimate "clocks" are not man-made. Note, then, that time-relations are not determined by reference to enduring things *simpliciter* but by reference to certain changes in those enduring things.[7] If a perceptual stand-in for time never changed, we could not determine time-relations by reference to it. Indeed, since 1967 the second, as a unit of time, has been defined by reference to the vibrations of the cesium atom.

Kant's claim that relations in the objective time-order can be determined only by reference to (processes in) enduring things that he calls "substance(s)," then, is neither unintelligible nor implausible. But this is certainly not to say that Kant's position is in all respects clear or free of ambiguity. On the contrary, one ambiguity that should be mentioned before going further concerns the number of substances that Kant believes there are. Throughout much of the First Analogy, Kant uses the term "substance" as a mass noun; that is, he uses it as if it stood for a single stuff, perhaps, as some passages suggest, for matter. But, especially in the latter portion of the Analogy, he talks of "substances" in the plural, thus using "substance" as a count noun, that is, as if it could stand for any one of many individual substances (A 188–189/B 231). Strictly speaking, it would seem that for time to have a perceptual stand-in, by reference to which relations of simultaneity and succession can be determined, only one substance is needed, so the "single stuff" interpretation would fit Kant's purposes. Yet Kant does use the plural "substances," so I shall simply carry this ambiguity along in what follows.

Whether Kant thinks that there are one or many substances, his claim about the permanence of substance/substances is stronger than my discussion up to now may have suggested. For Kant claims that the enduring thing(s) by reference to which time relations can be determined must be *absolutely* permanent, that is, that it (they) can neither come into being nor cease to exist. He does not allow that the enduring thing(s) might be only relatively permanent, or exist for a certain period of time and then cease to exist; rather, he insists that it (they) must be everlasting, or as this is now frequently called, "sempiternal."[8] In what follows, I shall call this view Kant's "permanence thesis." According to this thesis, there is at least one sempiternal entity—one entity that never came into existence and can never go out of existence.

One might think that Kant means to make his permanence thesis true by definition because of his remark that "certainly the proposition, that substance is permanent, is tautological" (A184/B 227). But as we saw, he immediately goes on to say that in order to justify using the term "substance" as he has defined it, we must *prove* that "in all appearances *there is* something permanent." So, to reiterate in strengthened form the point made at the outset, Kant clearly thinks that the absolute permanence or sempiternity of the thing(s) he wishes to call "substance(s)" must be proved and not stipulated by definition; he thinks that one must prove that *there is (are)* substance(s) as he has defined it (them).

How, then, does Kant try to prove the permanence thesis? Many philosophers have accused Kant of fallacy here: they have argued that even if it is granted that he has shown the need for relatively permanent things for time-determinations, he has not shown the need for anything sempiternal.[9] He has been accused, for instance, of arguing from the premise that something permanent must underlie any alteration in a thing (e.g., the same wax must exist both before and after it is melted) to the conclusion that some single permanent thing must underlie multiple alterations collectively.[10] It has also been suggested that so long as our stand-ins for time have an overlapping existence in time—with one beginning to exist before its predecessor ceases to exist—we have all the permanence we need to determine time-relations.[11]

In fact, however, Kant's reasoning here is not so obviously mistaken as these objections suggest. His reason for claiming that something absolutely permanent must exist is that otherwise the unity of time would be lost. To see why he thinks this is so, remember that the permanent thing(s) in question is supposed to serve as a perceptual equivalent for time itself. Now suppose this perceptual stand-in for time ceases to exist. Then time itself, or at least time itself insofar as we can have any experience of it, would also cease to exist. (Of course, this consequence needs to be understood somewhat differently, depending on whether there is supposed to be only one substance or many. If there is only one, then according to Kant its ceasing to exist would result in the end of time itself. If there are many, then it would seem that all except one could cease to exist without such a result.) Or suppose that the permanent thing(s) ceases to exist (it/they was only relatively permanent), and another (others) begins to exist. Then there would be more than one time. It does not help to postulate "overlapping" existence in time here because that assumes that we already have a single time within which the things can be said to temporally overlap, which is precisely the point in question. As Kant puts it:

> If some . . . substances could come into being and others cease to be, the one condition of the empirical unity of time would be removed. The appearances would then relate to two different times, and existence would flow in two parallel streams—which is absurd. (A 188/B 231–232)

The points just made can be incorporated into our summary of Kant's argument, as follows:

(5) If the permanent, perceptually accessible stand-in for time is only relatively permanent, then time as we experience it is not unitary.
(6) Time as we experience it is unitary [from (1), above].
(7) The permanent, perceptually accessible stand-in for time is not only relatively permanent; rather, it is absolutely permanent [Kant's "permanence thesis"—from (5) and (6)].

6.2 The Permanence-of-Substance Thesis

Suppose we grant that Kant has made a plausible case for his permanence thesis. This leaves us with the question: what is Kant's view concerning the nature of the permanent thing(s) required by the unity of time or concerning what this (these) thing(s) is (are)? If we go only on the basis of the proof as so far developed, then calling the permanent thing(s) "substance" (or "substratum") does not itself answer this question, for so far the only meaning given to that term in the argument is "permanent stand-in for time." But what is this stand-in? Is it the earth? The sun? The universe as a whole? Something else? Kant's answer comes in the next segment of his proof:

Segment 3
But the substratum of all that is real, that is, of all that belongs to existence, is *substance*; and all that belongs to existence can be thought only as a determination of substance. Consequently the permanent, in relation to which alone all time-relations of appearances can be determined, is substance in the [field of] appearance, that is, the real in appearance, and as substrate of all change remains ever the same. (B 225)

It might seem as if Kant is here merely making a definitional move: having proclaimed that "substance is permanent" is tautologous, or true by definition, he now applies the label "substance" to the permanent established by the preceding segment of the argument, in accordance with this definition. But this, of course, would in no way increase our knowledge of what substance is supposed to be; it would only amount to saying that "substance is permanent and the permanent is substance." In fact, however, Kant is doing something very different. In the first sentence of this passage, he is introducing into the argument, by means of the phrase "substratum of all that is real, that is, of all that belongs to existence," as well as by the word *"substance,"* the traditional notion of substance that we discussed in chapter 3, in connection with the Metaphysical Deduction. This is the notion of substance as that which bears all properties but is not itself borne by anything. As we saw, Kant himself offers this traditional, Aristotelian definition of substance when he refers to "substance, meaning something which can exist as subject but never as predicate" (B 149; cf. A 147/B 186, A 288/B 289). In the segment just quoted, Kant is saying that "the substratum which represents time in general"—the perceptual stand-in for time that he introduced in the preceding sentence of the proof (in segment 2)—is none other than this bearer of properties. He is saying that the permanent whose existence has been established by appealing to time-determination and unity of time is identical with that to which everything else belongs as a mere property or "determination." This is a bit clearer from the wording of the principle of the First Analogy in A: "All appearances contain the permanent (substance) as the object itself, and the transitory as its mere determination, that is, as a way in which the object exists" (A182). This implies that whatever changes in any way—whatever is at all "transitory"—is only a "determination" (property) of substance, which itself must therefore be not at all transitory but absolutely permanent instead. In the segment just quoted, the phrase "substrate of all change" carries the same implication.

It is apparent, then, that in the First Analogy Kant means to defend more than the permanence thesis. He has another main thesis as well—one that is logically distinct from the permanence thesis, though Kant's language makes it exceedingly difficult to disentangle the two. This is that the thing(s) that bears properties but is not borne by anything else is the absolutely permanent thing(s) required by the unity of time. I propose to call this the "permanence-of-substance thesis."

To bring out the significance of this thesis, let us adopt a strategy invented by Jonathan Bennett.[12] Let us call substance defined in the traditional way "substance₁"; in other words, let us define a substance₁ as something that bears properties but cannot itself be borne by anything (for short, I shall refer to a substance₁ simply as "a property-bearer"). And let us call substance as Kant ultimately defines it in the First Analogy "substance₂"; in other words, let us define a substance₂ simply as a sempiternal entity. Then the permanence-of-substance thesis means that every substance₁ is also a substance₂. This is by no means a trivial thesis because the notions of substance₁ and substance₂ seem to be entirely different, for it certainly seems as if, contrary to the permanence-of-substance thesis, a thing could be a bearer of properties yet come into being or go out of existence. An ordinary object like an apple, for example, seems to be a bearer of properties: it has the properties of roundness, redness, and sweetness, and it is not itself in the same way had by anything, yet it has a beginning of existence and an end of existence. And even if we think of a bearer of properties in the way advocated by the traditional "substance theory" expounded in chapter 3—that is, as something distinct from all its properties taken collectively—there seems to be no obvious reason why it could not come into being or pass out of being.

Of course, the use of the term "substance" to stand for both substance₁ and substance₂ might seduce one into thinking that whatever is a "substance" in one sense is also a "substance" in the other sense. In particular, it might lead one to think that whatever is a substance₁ (a property-bearer) is a substance₂ (a sempiternal or everlasting thing). For the traditional definition entails that

(1) all property-bearers are substances,

whereas Kant's definition of "substance" in the First Analogy entails that

(2) all substances are sempiternal,

from which it seems to follow that

(3) all property-bearers are sempiternal.

So it might seem that once Kant has argued that substance as a stand-in for time must be sempiternal, he has also shown that substance as a bearer of properties is sempiternal, that is, that the permanence-of-substance thesis, (3), is true. Of course, however, (3) does not really follow because the argument commits a fallacy of equivocation: in (1), "substances" means "substances₁," whereas in (2), "substances" means "substances₂."

It might be thought, then, that Kant was simply misled by his own language—or that his permanence-of-substance thesis results merely from a play on the term "substance." But this would be an unfair interpretation of Kant, for the First Analogy contains an argument that is evidently intended to support the permanence-of-substance thesis. To grasp this argument, we need first to understand the analysis of *change* that Kant offers in the First Analogy. Kant distinguishes between two kinds of change, *Wechsel* and *Veränderung*, which I will call "existence change" and "alteration," respectively.[13] Roughly speaking, an existence change occurs when something begins to exist or ceases to exist, and an alteration occurs when a thing's qualities or properties alter. But the distinction is more subtle and difficult to make clearly than this rough characterization suggests. For when a thing undergoes an alteration, when, for example, it goes from being blue to being red, its blueness does cease to exist and its redness does begin to exist, so that what may have seemed to be only an alteration turns out to be an existence change as well. To clarify the distinction, we need to define the notion of an alteration more carefully. We can say that an alteration occurs when something ceases to exist and something else begins to exist yet something distinct from either of these items must exist throughout this change. For example, suppose that a piece of wood goes from being straight to being bent. We could say that some straight wood exists at time 1 and some bent wood exists at time 2. But that would not be an accurate analysis of the fact that a piece of wood altered from being straight to being bent. For that fact is not just a matter of straight wood existing at time 1 and bent wood existing at time 2; rather, it consists in something that exists at least from time 1 to time 2, namely, some wood, changing from one state to another. The first state, "straightness," ceases to exist, and the second, "bentness," begins to exist; the wood persists throughout this change. Or suppose, as in Descartes' famous example, that a piece of wax taken fresh from a beehive is melted. Again, this is not just a matter of some unmelted wax existing at time 1 and some melted wax existing at time 2. Rather, something that exists at least throughout the melting process, namely, some wax, got transformed from one state to another: the "unmelted state" ceases to exist, the "melted state" begins to exist, and the wax persists throughout this change. Kant himself gives a helpful account of what is involved in alteration:

> The correct understanding of the concept of *alteration* is . . . grounded upon [recognition of] this permanence. Coming to be and ceasing to be are not alterations of that which comes to be or ceases to be. Alteration is a way of existing which follows upon another way of existing of the same object. All that alters *persists*, and only its *state changes*. Since this change thus concerns only the determinations, which can cease to be or begin to be, we can say, using what may seem a somewhat paradoxical expression, that only the permanent (substance) is altered, and that the transitory suffers no alteration but only a *change*, inasmuch as certain determinations cease to be and others begin to be. (A 187/B 230–231)

It is instructive, when reading this passage, to substitute "existence changes" for "changes."

In light of the distinction between an existence change and an alteration, we can restate Kant's permanence thesis as follows: there must be at least one entity that can undergo alteration but not existence change. This entity can be transformed, perhaps in countless different ways, but it can never come into being or pass out of being. This thesis, for Kant, is what ultimately follows from the unity of time.

Kant's analysis of change also suggests the argument for the permanence-of-substance thesis to which I have alluded—an argument that I believe Kant had in mind, though he does not spell it out. The argument can be seen as a response to the following challenge, already suggested above: "There are countless things in the world that are property-bearers but came into existence and will cease to exist. In fact, most if not all of the objects we encounter—the ordinary 'furniture of the world,' kings, cabbages and ships—fit this description. Hence Kant is simply wrong to think that all substances$_1$ are substances$_2$." In the rest of this chapter, I shall present and evaluate this argument.[14] I shall first explain the argument informally and then present it in numbered steps.

6.3 An Argument for the Permanence-of-Substance Thesis

We have seen that when a piece of wood goes from being straight to being bent, something, namely, the wood, must persist. There is an existence change, to be sure: some straight wood stops existing and some bent wood begins to exist. But this existence change is merely an alteration in something that existed throughout the change: the piece of wood. Now suppose that we *reapply* this idea to the wood itself, as follows. Let the wood be burned down to a pile of ashes. Again, there is an existence change: some wood ceases to exist and some ashes and smoke begin to exist. But, Kant would say, this existence change is *also* merely an alteration in something that existed throughout the change, namely, an underlying matter, substance, or stuff that altered from one state (the "wooden" state) to another state (the "smoky-ashy" state). Thus he writes:

> A philosopher, on being asked how much smoke weighs, made reply: "Subtract from the weight of the wood burnt the weight of the ashes left over, and you have the weight of the smoke". He thus presupposed as undeniable that even in fire the matter (substance) does not vanish, but suffers only an alteration of form. (A 185/B 228)

You might object, however, that this move to substance is premature, for even the smoky-ashy stuff could undergo an existence change that is merely an alteration. Suppose, for example, that the ashes are dispersed by the wind and that the smoke particles are diffused into the atmosphere: are we forced to say that the smoky-ashy stuff has ceased to exist, yet no other thing had to persist, so that we have an existence change that is not merely an alteration in something? No, for we can say instead that (a portion of) the atmosphere has gone from being clear to being slightly ashy and slightly smoky—has become polluted. It seems that, in principle, there is nothing to stop us from treating even further existence changes as being also alterations in something that lasted throughout those change, for example, from saying that the atmosphere itself might vanish but that this would be only an alteration of some cosmic dust. However, suppose we ascribe to Kant the premise that this cannot be done infinitely many times, that is, that at some point we will reach a last possible alteration. This premise is not implausible: it seems reasonable to suppose that, in cases like the one described, at some point in our search for items to serve as subjects of alterations we will simply run out of candidates and reach a final subject of alteration, which Kant calls "substance," "substratum," and sometimes "matter." It then seems to follow, as Kant puts it:

> All existence and all change in time have thus to be viewed as simply a mode of the existence of that which remains and persists . . . everything . . . which changes or can change belongs only to the way in which substance or substances exist, and therefore to their determinations. (A 183–184/B 227)

This consequence would imply that every existence change in the natural world is ultimately just an alteration in what must be taken to be one or more sempiternal substances, which is presumably why Kant claims to have proved the ancient principles *Gigni de nihilo nihil, in nihilum nil posse reverti* ("nothing comes out of nothing, and nothing reverts into nothing") (A186/B 229).

If we ask what the sempiternal substance is, the answer that naturally suggests itself, and that Kant implies in the passage about the burning wood, is that substance is matter—the material stuff of which all things are ultimately composed. Perhaps it is this idea that explains the very last segment in Kant's proof of the principle of the First Analogy, where he argues that the quantity of substance cannot change:

Segment 4
And as [substance] is thus unchangeable in existence, its quantity in nature is neither increased nor diminished. (B 225)

Kant has often been accused of trying here to give an *a priori* proof of Newton's principle of the conservation of matter. But he need not be seen as doing that because it does seem that we cannot think of pure matter as increasing in quantity or decreasing in quantity without going through an existence change. As David Hume put it:

> Suppose any mass of matter . . . to be plac'd before us; 'tis plain we must attribute a perfect identity to this mass, provided all the parts continue uninterruptedly and invariably the same, whatever motion or change of place we may observe in the whole or in any of the parts. But supposing some very *small* or *inconsiderable* part to be added to the mass, or subtracted from it . . . this absolutely destroys the identity of the whole, strictly speaking. . . .[15]

The point here does not turn on the view philosophers call "mereological essentialism"—the view that nothing can lose or acquire new parts without losing its identity. Rather, it turns on the point that a mere hunk or quantity of *matter*, unlike, say, a tree or a ship, cannot lose or acquire parts without losing its identity.[16]

Before more formally presenting the reasoning that leads to the identification of substance with matter, I should pause to consider a possible objection. If substance is matter, then it may seem that it cannot possibly serve as a perceptual stand-in for time. This objection has been pressed by James Van Cleve:

> Kant himself rejects time as the [stand-in; Van Cleve's term is "backdrop"] on the ground that it is not perceivable, but his own best candidate for substance is not perceivable either. We do not perceive the matter that undergoes transformation from wood to ashes or from caterpillar to butterfly; we only conceive it.[17]

It seems to me that Kant could reply as follows. To perceive wood or ashes or a caterpillar or a butterfly *is* to perceive matter, for it is to perceive matter in some of the forms or configurations that it can take on. Van Cleve's objection is similar to the classical empiricist objection to the substance theory, that substance is unperceivable. If substance is taken to be something distinct from all of its properties taken collectively, then as we saw in chapter 3, it is indeed an unperceivable "something-I-know not what." Now, substance is indeed something distinct from all of its *determinate* properties, such as any *specific* size, shape, or weight. But it need not be distinct from all of its *determinable* properties, such as that of having some shape or other, some size or other, some weight or other. Descartes thought of material substance in this way, for he identified it with extension or three-dimensionality—that is, three-dimensional shape and size—but not with any particular size or shape. In his famous example of the melting wax, he thinks of extension (= substance) as that which can take on various shapes and sizes, not as consisting of any particular shape and size. But if we think of substance on this model, then it seems that we can talk of perceiving substance. We perceive shape *by* perceiving a particular shape and we perceive size *by* perceiving a particular size; just as we see color by seeing, say, red or blue.[18] It is open to Kant to conceive of matter in a similar way, that is, as being identical with some determinable property that science takes as fundamental, such as mass. Then he can say that we perceive matter by perceiving it *in its various transformations.*

Let us now reconstruct in a step-by-step manner the argument that I have attributed to Kant. As before, I shall explain each premise of the argument and then summarize the whole argument so that its validity can be more easily checked. Its opening premise is this:

> (1) If S is a progressive series of existence changes, then every existence change in S is merely an alteration.

To explain the term "a progressive series of existence changes," let me give what I take to be an untendentious example: it is the kind of series that occurs when a piece of painted, straight wood is stripped (so that painted, straight wood ceases to exist and unpainted, straight wood begins to exist), then the wood is bent (so that unpainted, straight wood ceases to exist and unpainted, bent wood begins to exist). The salient features of such a series are (a) that each existence change in the series is merely an alteration and (b) that each subsequent change in the series is an alteration in something more "basic" than the subject of the previous change. Thus, the change from painted, straight wood to unpainted, straight wood is merely an alteration in the straight wood, and the change from straight wood to bent wood is merely an alteration in the wood. Furthermore, the subject of the later change, wood, is something more basic than the subject of the previous change, straight wood. I shall not attempt to give a definition of the notion of "basicness" invoked here, nor indeed to give a more exact definition of a progressive series of existence changes, but I think it is the notion that was operative in Kant's mind and that it is intuitively clear enough from my example for the purpose at hand. Notice that what I have called the salient features of such a series mean that premise (1) is true by definition—it is an analytic truth. Notice also that although (1) means that a series of progressive existence changes could not terminate in an existence change that was not also an alteration in something, (1) leaves open the possibility that such a series might be infinite and so might never terminate at all.

The second premise is this:

> (2) If every existence change in S is merely an alteration, then either S is an infinite series of alterations or S is a finite series of alterations terminating in an existence change that is merely an alteration.

This premise is, I take it, an obvious analytic truth.

The next premise is this:

> (3) If S is a progressive series of existence changes, then S is not an infinite series of alterations.

This premise rules out the above-mentioned possibility of an infinite series of progressive existence changes. Thus, suppose that the wood in my example is burned and that a pile of ashes and a cloud of smoke begin to exist in its place. Then it might be suggested that this existence change is yet another member of a progressive series of existence changes, inasmuch as it is merely an alteration in something more basic than the wood, namely matter. I will argue below that this suggestion should be resisted, but suppose we accept it for the sake of the illustration. Then the claim made by (3) is that the progressive process: painted, straight wood—unpainted, straight wood; straight wood—bent wood; wood—ashes and smoke, could not go on infinitely. This is not to say that it couldn't revert to an earlier stage, for example, that the unpainted wood might not be repainted or that the bent wood might not be straightened or even that some special chemical process might not conceivably turn ashes and smoke back into wood. But those changes would not constitute a *progressive* series of existence changes, as I am here using the term, for as I have said, in such a series the subject of each change must be something more "basic" than the subject of the previous change. But this condition does not hold in a "reversion" case: the wood that replaces the ashes and smoke is not something more basic than the matter that has altered "back" from the smoky-ashy state to the wooden state; the straight wood that replaces the bent wood is not something more basic than the wood that has altered "back" from the bent state to the straight state; and the painted wood that replaces the stripped wood is not something more basic than the straight wood that has altered "back" from the unpainted state to the painted state. According to (3), then, a genuinely progressive series of existence changes must have an end. I do not claim that this premise is unassailable, but I think it is plausible in itself (even if we allow, as we must, that some other kinds of series can be infinite) and plausibly attributed to Kant.

The next step is a proposition that follows from (1), (2), and (3), namely:

(4) If S is a progressive series of existence changes, then S is a finite series of alterations terminating in an existence change that is merely an alteration.

This is a significant result: it means that a progressive series of existence changes not only must terminate but also must terminate in an alteration of something— that it cannot terminate in something ceasing to exist, period, with nothing "left over."

The next premise is this:

(5) Every existence change that ever occurs is either a member of a progressive series of existence changes or an alteration that is not a member of a progressive series of existence changes.[19]

To grasp this premise, consider again the existence changes mentioned in connection with my examples. In the case used to explain the notion of a progressive series of existence changes, the painted piece of straight wood ceased to exist and an unpainted piece of straight wood began to exist; then the straight wood ceased to exist and the bent wood began to exist. In the case where the process reverted to an earlier stage, the bent wood was restraightened, and then the straight wood was repainted. What (5) says is that every existence change that ever occurs is like one of these two cases. Thus, in the case of the progressive series, if, for example, the bent wood is burned and replaced by smoke and ashes, *this is just a continuation of the progressive series*: it is just the alteration of something—presumably matter—from a wooden state to a smoky-ashy state.

The next premise is that:

> (6) If (4) and (5) are both true, then every substance$_1$ is the subject of the terminal alteration in a progressive series of existence changes.

The thought behind this premise is that the only thing that can count as a substance$_1$—that is, as a bearer of properties that cannot itself be borne by anything else—is the last subject of change in a progressive series of existence changes. This is so because all the earlier subjects of change, having been merely transient states of something more basic that underwent an alteration, turn out to be properties of, or adjectival upon, this last subject of change.[20] Thus, the painted, straight wood was only a temporary state of the straight wood; the straight wood was only a temporary state of the wood; and the wood was only a temporary state of matter. So the painted, straight wood and the unpainted, straight wood are not themselves substances$_1$; rather they are only the painted and unpainted states, respectively, of the straight wood. Likewise, the straight wood and the bent wood are not themselves substances$_1$; rather they are only the straight and bent states of the wood. However, since wood can be burned, even the wood is not itself a substance$_1$; rather both it and the ashes and smoke into which it turns are just the wooden state and smoky-ashy states, respectively, of something more basic, presumably matter, which alone qualifies as a bearer of properties that cannot itself be borne by anything else and, thus, as a substance$_1$.

The reason that (5) is included in the antecedent of (6) is that the simpler premise

> (6a) If (4) is true, then every substance$_1$ is the subject of the terminal alteration in a progressive series of existence changes

would be false. For suppose that, contrary to (5), some existence changes were neither members of a progressive series of existence changes nor alterations that were not members of a progressive series of existence changes. Then those existence changes would not have to be merely alterations. Yet the subjects of those existence changes could certainly be substances$_1$. The truth or falsity of (4) would have no bearing on whether they were merely alterations or existence changes that were not alterations since (4) pertains only to progressive series of existence changes. So even if (4) were true, there could be substances$_1$ that were not subjects of the terminal alterations in a progressive series of existence changes, thus making the antecedent of (6a) true and its consequent false. Suppose, for example (and contrary to fact), that the series *straight wood–bent wood* were not a progressive series. Then the straight wood would not be adjectival on wood or on anything else; it would qualify as a substance$_1$ that was not the subject of any alteration in a progressive series of existence changes, and which underwent an existence change that was not merely an alteration but rather a cessation of existence *tout court*.

The next premise is this:

(7) If (4) is true, then every subject of the terminal alteration of a progressive series of existence changes is a substance$_2$.

This is so because, according to (4), the termination of a progressive series of existence changes is always an existence change that is merely an alteration of something. But that thing cannot undergo an existence change because there is nothing else left for that existence change to be an alteration of. So the thing in question can never cease to exist and must accordingly be a sempiternal thing— that is, a substance$_2$.

The remaining steps of the argument are merely conclusions from the foregoing ones. For the sake of clarity, I shall now review those steps and then finish the argument.

(1) If S is a progressive series of existence changes, then every existence change in S is merely an alteration $(P \supset A)$.

(2) If every existence change in S is merely an alteration, then either S is an infinite series of alterations or S is a finite series of alterations terminating in an existence change that is merely an alteration $[A \supset (I \lor F)]$.

(3) If S is a progressive series of existence changes, then S is not an infinite series of alterations $(P \supset \sim I)$.

(4) If S is a progressive series of existence changes, then S is a finite series of alterations terminating in an existence change that is merely an alteration [from (1), (2), and (3)] $(P \supset F)$.

(5) Every existence change that ever occurs is either a member of a progressive series of existence changes or an alteration that is not a member of a progressive series of existence changes (E).

(6) If (4) and (5) are both true, then every substance$_1$ is the subject of the terminal alteration in a progressive series of existence changes $\{[(P \supset F) \cdot E] \supset T\}$.

(7) If (4) is true, then every subject of the terminal alteration of a progressive series of existence changes is a substance$_2$ $[(P \supset F) \supset S]$.

The argument can now be completed as follows. From (4), (5), and (6), this follows:

(8) Every substance$_1$ is the subject of the terminal alteration of a progressive series of existence changes (T).

But this follows from (4) and (7):

(9) Every subject of the terminal alteration of a progressive series of existence changes is a substance$_2$ (S).

Finally, since (8) has the form "all S is M" and (9) has the form "all M is P," this follows from (8) and (9):

(10) Every substance$_1$ is a substance$_2$.

If this argument succeeds, then Kant can at last show that every property-bearer that cannot itself be borne by anything is sempiternal. Accordingly, the countless things in the world that we commonly take to be property-bearers but that come into existence and cease to exist—the ordinary "furniture of the world"—are not really property-bearers or substances$_1$. Instead, they are just transitory "determinations" of one or more everlasting substances.

But does the argument succeed? Although it turns on deep ideas about the nature of change and permanence, I do not think that it succeeds, for at least two reasons. First, even if it shows that no substance$_1$ can cease to exist, it does not show that no substance$_1$ can *begin* to exist ex nihilo. But a substance$_2$ is supposed to exist throughout all time and thus cannot have a beginning of existence anymore than an end of existence. So at best the argument shows only part of what must be shown in order to prove that every substance$_1$ is a substance$_2$.

There is a passage near the end of the First Analogy that might be thought to show that a substance$_1$ cannot just spring into existence out of nothing:

> If we assume that something absolutely begins to be, we must have a point of time in which it was not. But to what are we to attach this point, if not to what already exists? For a preceding empty time is not an object of perception. But if we connect the coming to be with things which previously existed, and which persist in existence up to the moment of this coming to be, this latter must simply be a determination of what is permanent in that which precedes it. Similarly also with ceasing to be; it presupposes the empirical representation of a time in which an appearance no longer exists. (A 188/B 231)

This passage does provide support for the permanence thesis's claim that there must be at least one thing—namely, our perceptual stand-in for time—that never came into existence and never will go out of existence. For the passage shows that it is not the case that such a stand-in might have come into being at the beginning of time or go out of existence at the end of time because it makes no sense to talk of the beginning of anything unless there was a preceding time during which it did not exist, or of the end of anything unless there is a succeeding time during which it no longer exists. But if the thing in question is itself our perceptual stand-in for time, then there cannot be a time before or after it. So the stand-in must be everlasting or sempiternal. However, this does not prove that the stand-in must be substance$_1$, matter, or any other particular kind of entity. For the passage leaves open the possibility that anything to which we can reasonably attribute a permanent existence, perhaps some galactic system or even the universe as a whole, could serve as the stand-in. So the passage does not support the permanence-of-substance thesis since it does not show that it is substance(s)$_1$ that must serve as the stand-in and thus be sempiternal.

But the argument that I have attributed to Kant contains a second and more fundamental difficulty. Premise (5)—that every existence change that ever occurs is either a member of a progressive series of existence changes or merely an alteration that is not a member of such a series—is merely a stipulation that there is no good reason to accept and good reason to reject. The premise is motivated, presumably, by reflection on the nature of many of the existence changes that we know about empirically. Such reflection shows that often such changes are also alterations, so we can fairly easily accept the idea that the disappearance of one thing and the appearance of another is only a transformation (alteration) of something else, of some more basic stuff, as it were. But it does not follow that we must treat *every* existence change that ever occurs as a member of a progressive series of existence changes or merely an alteration that happens not to be a member of such a series. For example, we are not compelled to treat the burning of a piece of wood as being merely an alteration of matter from a wooden state to an ashy-smoky state: we can treat it as the destruction of a substance$_1$—of a property-bearer (the piece of wood) that is not itself borne by or adjectival upon anything else. This is not to say that we *could not* view this change as merely an alteration in matter, but only that we do not have to do so. For regarding this change as merely an alteration of matter, as opposed to the cessation of a substance$_1$'s existence, is not a necessary condition of the unity of time, which requires only that something we can reasonably count as unitary serve as a stand-in for time. Furthermore, there are strong reasons—if only practical ones—for not treating such a change as a mere alteration. If, instead of thinking and saying, "Thing X has ceased to exist," we always had to think or say, "Thing Y has altered from being in state X to being in state Z," then both our language and our thought would become needlessly complicated.[21]

Even if it be conceded contra Kant that the burning of a piece of wood is the cessation of existence of a substance$_1$, however, it is natural to insist that in the burning process something—matter, energy, or whatnot—is conserved. The claim that the burning of the wood is not merely an alteration of this stuff may seem like a relatively superficial linguistic point that obscures the more fundamental truth that, as Bennett puts it, "the stuff of the objective world is neither originated nor annihilated." Bennett also notes that "most of us incline to this view, but Kant thinks he can *prove* it."[22] It is therefore important to recognize that if the argument we have examined is unsound, then Kant seems not to have any proof of the view in question, for the view is equivalent to the claim that there is such a thing as substance$_2$. But it seems that Kant's only way of showing that there is (are) any substance(s)$_2$ is the argument that any substance$_1$ is a substance$_2$, and this is the very argument that we have just criticized. Thus, the view in question may be a natural one for humans to take and may even be true, but Kant's First Analogy does not *prove* that it is true.

As a last resort for establishing that there must be at least one substance$_2$, it might be claimed that the total annihilation of any parcel of matter is simply inconceivable. But why should this be so? It seems that I can perfectly well conceive, for example, that the unsightly boulder in my backyard should one day simply vanish from its place, with no compensating parcel of matter beginning to occupy any other place.[23] But this seems tantamount to conceiving the total annihilation of a parcel of matter. The only possible ground I can think of for denying that this is conceivable would be the Kantian one that the annihilation of a parcel of matter would destroy the unity of time. But as I indicated earlier, even if we grant Kant's view that the possibility of time-determination in a unitary time requires a permanent stand-in for time, the door is left open for anything that we can reasonably count as unitary to serve as this stand-in. The stand-in might, for instance, be the planetary system or, more plausibly, the known physical universe as a whole. All the things within the universe that we normally count as property-bearers, including things whose existence changes are not merely alterations in anything else, might at some time have begun to exist or cease to exist without destroying the unity of time, provided only that they had an overlapping existence in the time represented by the system as a whole. This does not conflict with the point made earlier, that overlapping stand-ins for time cannot preserve the unity of time because, if the system as a whole is the stand-in for time, then its component elements can certainly be temporary things whose careers overlap within the unitary time represented by the system as a whole. By the same token, even if we suppose that "matter" is our stand-in for time, all the parcels of matter within the universe might at some time have begun to exist or cease to exist without destroying the unity of time, provided only that they had an overlapping existence in the time for which matter in general serves as a stand-in. I conclude that Kant's attempt to show that his view that the possibility of time-determination in a unitary time requires a permanent stand-in for time entails the existence of a sempiternal substance(s) is unsuccessful. In other words, he does not succeed in showing that the permanence thesis entails the permanence-of-substance thesis.

The Second Analogy

Causality

7.1 Kant's Strategy

Virtually everyone accepts what philosophers call the "causal principle"—the principle that every event has a cause. We assume that even when we do not know what the cause of a given event or type of event is, still it must have *some* cause. The idea of an event that has no cause, of something happening without any cause that explains why it happened, strikes us as somehow irrational or absurd. In *A Treatise of Human Nature*, however, David Hume famously argued that the causal principle is not self-evident and cannot be proved.[1] Kant's argument in the Second Analogy is widely seen as his "answer to Hume" regarding the status of this principle. It will be both convenient and instructive, therefore, to discuss the argument in relation to Hume's view that the causal principle cannot be demonstrated.

Although Kant disagrees with Hume about the status of the causal principle, it is important to note at the outset some points of agreement between them. First, Kant agrees with Hume that the causal principle is not true simply in virtue of conceptual relationships or meanings of words—that it is not, in the terminology introduced by Kant himself, an analytic proposition but rather a synthetic one.[2] Second, Kant does not think any more than Hume does that the causal principle can be demonstrated by manipulating general concepts like existence, beginning of existence, event, cause, and so on. Rather, Kant tries to show that the principle can be proved by a transcendental argument. This, as we have seen, is an argument that tries to show that the truth of a certain principle (in this case the causal principle) is a necessary condition of experience. So Kant's argument for the causal principle will try to show that unless that principle were true, we could not have the sort of experience that we do. To understand how such an argument works, it is crucial, as we have also seen, to understand exactly how the term "experience" is being used in the argument. In the Transcendental Deduction, I have argued, the term must mean "consciousness" if the argument is to constitute a refutation of the Humean view of experience. But in the Second Analogy, where the results of the Transcendental Deduction are assumed to be established, the term has a richer meaning. As Kant announces in introducing the Analogies, "experience" now refers to "an empirical knowledge, that is, a knowledge which determines an object through perceptions" (B 218). In the Second Analogy, the kind of knowledge Kant has in mind is even more specific: it is knowledge by perception *that an event has occurred*. Kant, as we shall see, tries to show that unless (an appropriately restricted version of) the causal principle is true, we could never know by perception that any event had occurred.

According to Kant, the fact that the causal principle can be proved only by a transcendental argument has an important consequence—that the principle can be proved to hold only for *observable* events; it cannot be proved to hold for events that we could not possibly experience. This means that there is still another similarity between Hume's and Kant's views of the causal principle, namely, that it cannot be used to show that events which are supposed to occur totally outside the field of our experience, such as the origin of the universe, must have a cause. Thus, even if the principle can be demonstrated, it cannot be used, in the way that rationalist philosophers tried to do, to establish the existence of God or other entities that could not fall within the scope of our experience.

Having mentioned some similarities between Hume and Kant's views of the causal principle, I shall henceforth focus on the differences. First, there is an important difference between the version of the causal principle that Hume says cannot be proved and the version Kant thinks he can establish. The version Hume considers is, in his words, that "whatever has a beginning has also a cause of existence," and in discussing the principle he also says that it would apply to any "modification of existence."[3] Hume's version is thus totally unrestricted: it applies to any beginning of existence or change in what exists; simply put, it says that *every event whatsoever* has a cause. Now, the principle that Kant claims to prove in the Second Analogy is this: "Everything that happens, that is, begins to be, presupposes something on which it follows according to a rule"(A 189). The wording of this principle makes it sound very much like the principle that Hume says cannot be proved. Despite its wording, however, Kant's principle contains the restriction just mentioned: it applies only to *observable events*. In other words, Kant thinks that he can prove that every event that we could ever observe must have a cause, but not that every event, period, must have a cause. However, Hume's arguments imply that not even Kant's restricted version of the causal principle can be proved; so the chief difference between Hume and Kant is that Hume holds that no version at all of the causal principle can be demonstrated, whereas Kant argues that a version restricted to observable events can be demonstrated. By showing that a version of the causal principle restricted to observable events can be demonstrated, while maintaining that a totally unrestricted version applying beyond the bounds of any human experience cannot be known to be true, Kant saw himself as defending the foundations of Newtonian physics, without lapsing into the rationalist metaphysics that he rejected no less than Hume did. Finally, Kant's "transcendental" way of arguing for the causal principle implies another difference between his position and Hume's, which is well stated by William H. Brenner:

Hume thought that the principle of causality was a generalization from our experience of events. But if Kant's argument is sound, then all perception of events, and consequently all generalization from experience, *presupposes* the principle of causality. Kant's answer to Hume . . . is that the principle of causality is *presupposed* by the perception of events, not *derived from* it.[4]

For Kant to give an argument for (even his restricted version of) the causal principle that can "answer" Hume, that argument must start from premises that Hume himself would accept. Now, as Lewis White Beck has shown in an article that effectively analyzes Kant's strategy for answering Hume, Kant's argument in the Second Analogy does indeed start from a point that is common ground between Hume and Kant.[5] This is that any knowledge we have of causal relationships must be based on induction: we know that A-events cause B-events only because, in all cases that we have observed, A-events have been followed by B-events—because A-events and B-events have been constantly conjoined in our experience. As Beck says:

> [Kant] is in complete agreement with Hume that our knowledge of causal connections between specific events is a posteriori not a priori, synthetic not analytic, inductive not logical, probable not certain. His methods for finding the cause of B are exactly those which Hume prescribed, and the chances of success in this venture, as estimated by Kant and Hume, are very much the same. Kant's first answer to Hume, then, is to agree with him, and to disagree with the rationalists who thought that logical insight into causal connections was possible.[6]

As Beck points out, however, the ability to infer that A-events cause B-events from observing that A-events have been regularly followed by B-events presupposes something, namely, that we can perceptually identify or discriminate events, that is, tell by observation that an event is occurring. If we could not do this, then we could not establish the *premise* of the inference—that *events* of a certain kind have been regularly followed by *events* of a certain other kind.

Now, Kant's key insight in the Second Analogy is that there is an epistemological problem about how we are able to perceptually identify or discriminate events. Specifically, there is a problem about how we are able to distinguish events from enduring states of affairs, for whether we are perceiving an event or an enduring state of affairs, our perceptions occur successively or serially in time. Kant illustrates this point with the examples of perceiving a ship moving downstream versus perceiving a house. The ship's movement from an upstream position to one further downstream is an event. On the other hand, the existence of the various parts of the house—its front, sides, back, foundation, roof, and so on—is an enduring state of affairs. But in both cases, our perceptions occur successively or serially in time. In the case of the ship, we see it first upstream and then downstream. In the case of the house, we see first one side and then another side or first the foundation and then the roof or first the roof and then the foundation. This shows that we cannot tell, merely from the fact that our perceptions occur serially or successively, that we are perceiving an event rather than an enduring state of affairs. In other words, observation alone provides no criterion by which we can distinguish between the two. How, then, can we tell whether we are perceiving an event or an enduring state of affairs? To quote Beck:ʼ "[Hume] never discussed this problem; no one before Kant even saw that it was a problem."[7] Kant's thesis in the Second Analogy is that this problem can be solved in only one way—namely, if we grant that every observable event has a cause, or as Kant puts it, that "everything that happens, that is, begins to be, presupposes something on which it follows according to a rule." In other words, Kant contends that we can distinguish between events and enduring states of affairs, and so identify events, only if the causal principle is true of those events.[8]

Beck gives a succinct summary of Kant's strategy, involving three propositions:

> H. From observing repeated pairs of similar events, we infer inductively that events like the first members of the pairs are causes of events like the second.
>
> P. Events can be distinguished from enduring states of affairs, even though our perceptions of both are successive or serial.
>
> K. "Everything that happens, that is, begins to be, presupposes something on which it follows by rule."[9]

Proposition H is common ground between Hume and Kant: thus it is a premise that Hume himself accepts and is in no way question-begging.[10] Proposition K is Kant's statement of the causal principle that Hume says cannot be demonstrated. Clearly H implies P: we cannot establish correlations between events unless we can distinguish events from enduring states of affairs. The task of the Second Analogy is to show that P in turn implies K. If this can be shown, it will follow that H implies K, and thus that the causal principle can be demonstrated from a premise that Hume himself accepts.[11]

In what follows, I shall consider two possible arguments for getting from P to K. The first is quite strongly suggested by the text of the Second Analogy and has often been thought to be Kant's authentic argument. However, as Peter Strawson shows in *Bounds of Sense*, it is a fallacious argument.[12] The second argument is also suggested by Kant's text and seems more promising.

7.2 The Irreversibility Argument

The first argument, which I shall call the "irreversibility" argument, is suggested by what Kant says when he compares his examples of the house and the ship. In the case of the house, the series of perceptions obtained by the observer may be said to be *reversible*. This is because, depending on the circumstances and on the way the observer chooses to view the house, the observer can see first the front of the house and then the back of the house or first the back and then the front; likewise, the observer can see first the left side and then the right side or first the right side and then the left side, and first the basement and then the roof or first the roof and then the basement. In other words, in whatever order the observer's perceptions occur, they could have occurred in the opposite or reverse order instead. Kant puts the point this way:

In the . . . example of a house my perceptions could begin with the apprehension of the roof and end with the basement, or could begin from below and end above; and I could similarly apprehend the manifold of empirical intuition either from right to left or left to right. In the series of these perceptions there was thus no determinate order specifying at what point I must begin in order to connect the manifold empirically. (A 192–193/B 237–238)

In the case of the ship moving downstream, on the other hand, the series of perceptions may be said to be *irreversible*. Assuming that the ship is moving downstream, one's perceptions can occur in only one order: first one sees the ship upstream and then one sees it downstream; one cannot see it first downstream and then upstream. One's perceptions cannot occur in any order other than the one that corresponds to the ship's successive positions in the stream:

But, as I also note, in an appearance which contains a happening (the preceding state of the perception we may entitle A, and the succeeding B) B can be apprehended only as following upon A; the perception of A cannot follow upon B but only precede it. For instance, I see a ship move down stream. My perception of its lower position follows upon the perception of its position higher up in the stream, and it is impossible that in the apprehension of this appearance the ship should first be perceived lower down in the stream and afterwards higher up. The order in which the perceptions succeed one another in apprehension is in this instance determined, and to this order apprehension is bound down. (A 192/B 237)

At the end of the same paragraph, Kant concludes that "in the perception of an event there is always a rule that makes the order in which the perceptions (in the apprehension of this appearance) follow upon one another a *necessary* order" (A 193/B 238).

It is chiefly from these passages that the irreversibility argument is drawn. Strawson in effect divides the argument into two stages. In the first stage, Kant is seen as pointing to a criterion whereby our perceptions of an event can be distinguished from those of an enduring state of affairs, despite the fact that the perceptions of both are successive or serial. This criterion is the reversibility or irreversibility of the series of perceptions. Thus the criterion for a series of perceptions being perceptions of an enduring state of affairs is *reversiblity*: the series could have been obtained in the reverse order from that in which it actually occurred, as in the case of the house. And the criterion by which a series of perceptions is apprehended as of (or taken to be of) an event is *irreversibility*: the series could not have been obtained in the reverse order from that in which it actually occurred, as in the case of the ship. In other words, the perceptions are of an enduring state of affairs if and only if they are reversible, whereas the perceptions are of an event if and only if they are irreversible.[13] In the second stage of the argument, Kant is interpreted as arguing from the irreversibility of the perceptions of an event to the truth of the causal principle: since our perceptions of events are irreversible, those events must be subsumed under causal laws.

To evaluate this well-known yet puzzling argument, we need to state it in a somewhat more formal way. From stage 1 of the argument, in which the reversibility/irreversibility criterion is put forward, we can extract the following premise:

(1) Necessarily, if S perceives an event A-B, then S's perceptions occur in the order A, B.

Here "an event A-B" means an event or change whose first stage is A and whose second stage is B; in Kant's example of the moving ship, A would designate the ship's being upstream and B would designate the ship's being downstream. So (1) says that if S perceives an event, such as the ship's movement from an upstream to a downstream position, then S's perceptions of the stages of the event must occur in the same temporal order as the stages of the event: they are "irreversible." I have placed the term (modal operator) "necessarily" in front of the statement, so that it applies to the if-then relation expressed by the statement as a whole (or "governs" the statement as a whole), in order to bring out a claim made by Strawson that seems correct. This is that (1) is a conceptual or analytic truth. Strawson bases this claim on the two more basic claims, which also seem correct: (a) it is a conceptual truth about sense perception that our perceptions of an object are caused by that very object, and (b) it is a conceptual truth about causation that an effect cannot precede its cause but must occur either at the same time as or after its cause.[14] He notes that, provided one stipulation is made, (1) follows from these two conceptual truths and so is itself a conceptual truth. The stipulation is that there must not be any difference in the causal conditions of the two perceptions that makes the perception of A occur after the perception of B, for otherwise one can think of cases where the earlier stage of an event is perceived after the later stage. For example, one could see the ship in its upstream position after seeing it in its downstream position if the light from its upstream position were delayed by being reflected back and forth several times between mirrors; or one might *hear* a whistle blast that the ship emitted upstream after *seeing* the ship downstream simply because sound travels slower than light. (Notice that in such cases the conceptual truth that an effect cannot precede its cause is not violated because both perceptions still occur after their own causes.) Strawson points out that such cases can be circumvented by stipulating that the perceptions of A and B must be equally direct and in the same sensory mode or by stipulating that there can be no difference in the causal conditions of the perceptions that makes the perception of A occur after the perception of B. Provided such a stipulation is understood, Strawson seems right to maintain that (1) is an analytic or conceptual truth.

The second stage of the irreversibility argument moves from (1) to the conclusion that the causal principle is true. In terms of the formulation being constructed here, this is to say that it moves from (1) to the conclusion:

(C) Necessarily, if A occurs, then B occurs.

Here the point of the modal term "necessarily" is just to say that the transition from A to B is governed by whatever type of "necessity" characterizes causation or, as Kant puts it, that B follows upon A "according to a rule." Of course, if Hume's view that causation is nothing more than regularity is correct, then the "necessity" or "rule" in question reduces to a contingent but exceptionless regularity. But for the moment, I shall talk, in a heuristic fashion, in terms of causal necessity; a bit later we shall see that the points I am about to make carry over even when we think of causality purely in terms of regularity or Hume's "constant conjunction."

It is obvious that (C) does not logically follow from (1) alone; another premise is needed. The premise can only be this:

(2) *If* necessarily, if S perceives an event A-B, then S's perceptions occur in the order A, B, *then* necessarily, if A occurs, then B occurs.

Now, if the argument from (1) and (2) to (C) is really Kant's argument, then Strawson is certainly right to say that Kant has committed "a *non-sequitur* of numbing grossness."[15] The problem is not that the argument as I have formulated it is logically invalid, for its form is as follows:

(1) Necessarily (P ⊃ Q)
(2) [Necessarily (P ⊃ Q)] ⊃ necessarily (R ⊃ S)

∴ (C) Necessarily (R ⊃ S)

This is a perfectly valid (modal) *modus ponens.* The "numbing non-sequitur" occurs, rather, within the second premise, in the transition from its complex antecedent to its consequent. For the antecedent says that if we perceive an event, then our perceptions (of the stages of the event) must occur in the same order as the stages of the event. But the consequent says that the stages of the event must occur in a specific order. In other words, the premise as a whole says that just because one's perceptions of (the stages of) an event must occur in the same order as the stages of that event, or just because the order of our perceptions of (the stages of) an event must correspond to the order of the stages of that event, therefore the stages of the event themselves must occur in a certain order. This is fallacious, for it involves, as Strawson shows, a double equivocation on the notion of necessity. First, the *sense* of necessity is not the same in the antecedent as in the consequent. In the antecedent, necessity refers to conceptual or analytic necessity, as I explained earlier, whereas in the consequent, it refers to causal necessity (however that kind of necessity is understood). Second, the *application* of the notion of necessity is not the same in the antecedent as in the consequent. In the antecedent, what is asserted to be necessary is the correspondence between the temporal order of the stages of an event and the temporal order of our perceptions of those stages, whereas in the consequent the notion of necessity is applied to the relation between the stages of an event themselves. Strawson aptly sums up the situation this way: "It is a very curious contortion indeed whereby a conceptual necessity based on the fact of a change is equated with the causal necessity of that very change."[16]

The fallacy can be brought out, as I said above, even if we think of causality purely in terms of regular succession rather than causal necessity. To assert that an event A-B has a cause is then to assert that there is a kind of event E such that events of kind E are regularly followed by events of the kind to which event A-B belongs. Keeping this in mind, we see that what premise (2) asserts is that if our perceptions of the sequence A-B must occur in the order A, B, then there is a kind of event E such that all events of that kind are followed by events of the kind to which A-B belongs. In other words, it asserts this:

> If, necessarily, when S perceives an event A-B, then S's perceptions occur in the order A,B, then there is a kind of event E such that all E-events are followed by events of the kind to which A-B belongs.

But this is fallacious: from the fact that our perceptions of a sequence A-B must occur in the same order as the members of that sequence, one cannot conclude that there is a kind of event E such that sequences like A-B invariably follow upon events of kind E. To see this more clearly, suppose that the event A-B is a random event. Then S's perceptions of it must still occur in the order A, B, but it is false that there is a kind of event E such that events of that kind are always followed by events of the kind to which A-B belongs.

I have dwelt on the irreversibility argument at some length because it is quite commonly thought to reflect Kant's own thinking in the Second Analogy. Since it is a fallacious argument, however, and since Kant's Second Analogy lends itself to more than one interpretation, it is natural to wonder whether Kant has a better argument for the causal principle. Kant scholars have offered many different reconstructions of his reasoning, which have in turn been criticized by other scholars. I shall not survey this extensive and ongoing debate. Rather, I shall present one reading of Kant's argument, by Paul Guyer in *Kant and the Claims of Knowledge*, which seems more faithful to Kant's text, as well as more promising than others.[17] Referring to Guyer's analysis in her introduction to an English translation of the *Critique of Pure Reason*, Patricia Kitcher writes that "although [the argument of the Second Analogy] has been a very difficult argument to interpret, many current scholars believe that Paul Guyer has recently produced a definitive analysis."[18] Guyer's discussion is complex and richly ramified; I shall focus on the core of his interpretation.

7.3 Guyer's Interpretation of the Second Analogy

The question that Kant is raising in the Second Analogy could be put this way: how can I know by observation that an event E is occurring? If we think of an event, as Kant does, as a transition from a state A to a state B, then this question can also be put as follows: how can I know by observation that a state A is followed by a state B in time? Now, Kant's key point, that one's perceptions are successive or serial regardless of whether one is perceiving an event or an enduring state of affairs, means that I cannot know that A is followed by B in time just by knowing that my perception of A is followed by my perception of B because perceptions of coexisting states of an enduring object would also occur successively, as occurs when one views the different sides of a house. According to the irreversibility argument, the way in which I am supposed to be able to tell that A is followed by B in time is by knowing that my perceptions of A and B are irreversible, that is, could not have occurred in the order B, A rather than A, B. However, as Guyer rightly notes, I *cannot* really tell that A is followed by B in time by knowing that my perceptions of A and B are irreversible, for I can know that they are irreversible only if I *already* know that A and B are occurring in the order A, B.[19] This point is obvious in itself, but a Kantian reason can be given for it: that the irreversibility of A and B consists in the *impossibility* that they might have occurred in the opposite order from that in which they actually occurred or (which is the same thing) in the *necessity* that they occurred in the order they actually occurred in; it is a *modal* fact about them. However, as Guyer says:

> But . . . such a modal fact about the sequence of perceptions is *not* given to consciousness by apprehension alone. This is . . . a consequence of Kant's . . . fundamental assumption that experience "to be sure tells us what is, but not that it must necessarily be so and not otherwise" (A 1). No necessities of any kind, whether in the objective realm or even in the subjective arena of representations themselves, are ever given by uninterpreted apprehension.[20]

In any case, the point that I can know that A and B are irreversible only if I *already* know that A and B are occurring in the order A, B seems to me to be Guyer's key insight.[21] First, it goes directly against the "irreversibility" reading of Kant's argument by showing that reversibility/irreversibility could not really be the criterion we use for determining perceptually whether we are observing an event or an enduring state of affairs. But second, and even more important, Guyer's point seems to be just what Kant needs to make his argument work. For if I cannot know that I am perceiving that A is followed by B either by knowing that my perceptions of A and B are successive or by knowing that they are irreversible, then how can I know this? I cannot know it by knowing that A precedes B by reference to absolute time since time itself cannot be perceived (A 200/B 245). I cannot know it by knowing that my perceptions are of successive states of things-in-themselves because things-in-themselves (things as they are apart from the ways in which we must perceive and conceptualize them) are unknowable. So, it would seem that the only way I can know by observation that a transition from a state A to a state B is occurring is by knowing that state B follows state A according to a rule, that is, that the event constituted by the transition from A to B has some cause. Note also that the irreversibility of my perceptions of A and B is a *consequence* of the fact that B follows A according to a rule, rather than a criterion for deciding whether A was followed by B in time.

It may be useful to summarize this reasoning in a problem-solution format, as follows:

Problem:
How can I *know* by observation that an event E is occurring, that is, that a state A is followed by a state B in the objective time-order (where E = the transition from A to B, the coming-to-be of B after A)?

- Not by knowing that my perception of A is followed by my perception of B because perceptions of coexisting states of an enduring thing can also occur in succession (e.g., the house)
- Not by knowing that my perceptions of A and B are irreversible (as in the ship case) because I can know that these perceptions are irreversible only if I *already* know that A and B are occurring in the order A, B

- Not by knowing that A precedes B by reference to absolute time because time itself cannot be perceived
- Not by knowing that my perceptions are of successive states of things-in-themselves since things-in-themselves are unknowable

Solution:
So, the only way I can know by observation that an event E is occurring, that is, that a state A is followed by a state B in the objective time-order, is by knowing that state B follows state A according to a rule, that is, that event E has a cause.

To convey better the power of Guyer's interpretation, let me also quote two passages: first the passage from Kant that seems best to support it, and then a fairly long passage from Guyer that contains the core of his interpretation. The passage from Kant is this:

> Let us suppose that there is nothing antecedent to an event, upon which it must follow according to a rule. All succession of perception would then be only in the apprehension, that is, would be merely subjective, and would never enable us to determine objectively which perceptions are those that really precede and which are those that follow. We should then have only a play of representations, relating to no object. . . . I could not then assert that the two states follow upon one another in the field of appearance [by "field of appearance," Kant here means the objects perceived, such as the moving ship or the house], but only that one apprehension follows upon the other. . . .
>
> If, then, we experience that something happens, we in so doing always presuppose that something precedes it, on which it follows according to a rule. Otherwise I should not say of the object that it follows. For mere succession in my apprehension, if there be no rule determining the succession in relation to something that precedes, does not justify me in assuming any succession in the object. I render my subjective synthesis of apprehension objective only by reference to a rule in accordance with which the appearances [again, "appearances" here means the objects or events perceived], in their succession, that is, as they happen, are determined by the preceding state. The experience of an event (i.e. of anything as *happening*) is . . . possible only on this assumption. (A 194–195/B 239–240)

The passage from Guyer begins this way:

> the present problem is only that of distinguishing between an event occurring among represented states of affairs from the event of a change in representations [i.e., perceptions] themselves.

Guyer is here recognizing that we *always* have the latter ("a change in representations themselves"), even when we are *not* perceiving an event. (If such a change occurred only when we are perceiving an event, there would be no problem.) So how do we distinguish between cases in which we have *only* the change in representations and cases in which we have an event? We cannot do so on the basis of irreversibility, for, as Guyer continues (in a passage from which we have already had occasion to quote):

> [T]he significance of the irreversibility of a sequence of representations . . . is only that such a fact would be a *consequence* of the occurrence of an event in what is being perceived, which *could* be used as a *symptom* of the occurrence of an event

if it were directly given to consciousness. But . . . such a modal fact about the sequence of perceptions is *not* given to consciousness by apprehension alone. This is . . . a consequence of Kant's . . . fundamental assumption that experience "to be sure tells us what is, but not that it must necessarily be so and not otherwise" (A 1). No necessities of any kind, whether in the objective realm or even in the subjective arena of representations themselves, are ever given by uninterpreted apprehension.

Thus, Guyer concludes:

> So Kant's idea is that no alternative remains but that the occurrence of an event be inferred by *adding* to the omnipresent succession of mere representations a *rule* from which it can be inferred that in the circumstances at hand *one state of affairs* could *only* succeed the other, and *therefore* also that one *representation* could only succeed the other. . . . Only from a rule which says that one of the represented states *must* succeed the other can it be inferred that it *does* succeed the other. For . . . though their succession *could* be inferred from the *necessary* sequence or irreversibility of the representations of them if such irreversibility *were* [directly given to consciousness]—since the irreversibility of their representations would be a genuine consequence of the represented states of affairs—the necessity of the sequence of representations is . . . *not* directly given to consciousness. So nothing remains but to invoke a rule from which it follows that one objective state can only succeed and not coexist with the other, from which it *also* follows . . . that the *representation* of the one state not only does but also only could succeed the representation of the other. . . . And a rule which dictates that in a given situation one state of affairs must succeed another is just what Kant means by a causal law. Thus, judgments that events occur are possible only if the states of affairs which comprise them are linked by causal laws.[22]

The argument that Guyer has found in Kant's text may be summarized this way:

(1) We cannot know by observation that an event—that is, a transition from a state A to a state B—is occurring by knowing that the perceptions of A and B occur in the order A, B; by knowing that the perceptions of A and B are irreversible; by knowing that A precedes B by reference to absolute time; or by knowing that these perceptions are of successive states of things-in-themselves.[23]

(2) If (1), then the only way we can know by perception that an event—that is, a transition from a state A to a state B—is occurring is by knowing that B follows A according to a rule, that is, that the event has a cause.

(3) If the only way we can know by perception that an event—that is, a transition from a state A to a state B—is occurring is by knowing that B follows A according to a rule, that is, that the event has a cause, then any event such that we can know of its occurrence by perception must have a cause.

∴ (4) Any event such that we can know of its occurrence by perception must have a cause.

Before concluding this section, I want to offer a brief clarification of the notion of A's following B according to a rule, as it relates to Guyer's interpretation of Kant's argument. What does it mean to say that B follows A according to a rule, given that A is the first stage of an event and B is the second stage of that event?

For example, suppose that A = the existence of an intact egg and that B = the existence of a broken egg: then what does it mean to say that B follows A "according to a rule"? There are two things that it does not mean: it does not mean that A is the cause of B (obviously, the intactness of an egg does not cause its brokenness), nor does it mean that whenever A exists, B exists. Rather, it must mean this:

> *Rule 1:* Whenever A exists and C occurs (where C is, e.g., dropping an intact egg), B follows A.

For another example, a bit closer to Kant's own example, suppose that A = the presence of a sailboat north of Alcatraz and B = the presence of a sailboat south of Alcatraz. Then, again, it is obvious that A does not cause B, nor is it the case that whenever a sailboat is north of Alcatraz, it winds up south of Alcatraz. Rather, to say that B follows A according to a rule must mean this:

> *Rule 2:* Whenever A obtains and C occurs (where C is, e.g., a northerly wind's picking up), B follows A.

Finally, consider another example close to one given by Kant (A 203/B 248): Suppose that A = the existence of a plumped pillow and B = the existence of a pillow with a hollow in it. Then the plumped state of the pillow does not cause its subsequent hollow state, nor do plumped pillows always become hollow. So the statement that B follows A according to a rule must mean this:

> *Rule 3:* Whenever A exists and C occurs (where C is, e.g., the placing of a bowling ball on the pillow), B follows.

As Guyer points out, this last example shows that Kant's Second Analogy is perfectly compatible with cases where the cause and its effect are simultaneous because, although the plumped state of the pillow precedes its hollow state, the placing of the bowling ball and the hollowing of the pillow are simultaneous.[24] To return to the main point: Kant's thesis is that in all such cases, we could not know by observation that A is followed by B, as opposed to A's co-existing with B, unless the transition from A to B were governed by a rule like Rules 1–3.

7.4 A Second Reconstruction of the Central Argument of the Analytic

Guyer's version of the argument of Kant's Second Analogy can be integrated into the reconstruction of the overall argument of Kant's Analytic that I developed in sections 5.4 and 5.5. It will be recalled that the first eight steps, which make use of the insights in Wolff's reconstruction of the Transcendental Deduction, are as follows:

> (1) Experience is possible only if unity of consciousness is possible, that is, only if a manifold of representations can be unified in one consciousness ($E \supset U$).
>
> (2) A manifold of representations can be unified in one consciousness only if those representations refer to an object ($U \supset O$).

(3) Representations can refer to an object only by being related to each other in a nonarbitrary, rule-governed way (O ⊃ R).

(4) A manifold of representations can be unified in one consciousness only if those representations are related to each other in a nonarbitrary, rule-governed way [from (2) and (3)] (U ⊃ R).

(5) Representations are apprehended in temporal succession (T).

(6) If (4) and (5), then unity of consciousness is possible only if representations are synthesized, that is, reproduced in imagination according to a rule [(U ⊃ R) · T] ⊃ (U ⊃ L).

(7) Unity of consciousness is possible only if representations are reproduced in imagination according to a rule [from (4), (5), and (6)] (U ⊃ L).

(8′) Representations can be reproduced in imagination according to a rule only if the temporal order in which they are reproduced is different from the temporal order in which they are apprehended (L ⊃ D).

The next five steps, which are inspired by Strawson's treatment of Kant's "Analytic of Principles," are as follows:

(9″) Representations can have a temporal order different from the order in which they are apprehended only if there is a way to determine temporal relations between representations other than the order in which they are apprehended (D ⊃ W).

(10′) Time itself is not perceived (~P).

(11) If time itself is not perceived, then there is a way to determine temporal relations between representations other than the order in which they are apprehended only if some experiences are conceptualized as being enduring objects, by reference to which temporal relations can be determined [~P ⊃ (W ⊃ S)].

(12) Experience is possible only if some experiences are conceptualized as being of enduring objects [from (1), (7), (8′), (9″), (10′), and (11)] (E ⊃ S).

(13) Some experiences can be conceptualized as being of enduring objects only if some experiences are conceptualized as being of objects that can be reencountered and reidentified (S ⊃ N).

To integrate Guyer's interpretation of the Second Analogy into this argument, we need only note that the problem he begins with—how can I know by observation that I am perceiving an event?—can also be put as a problem about the identification of (enduring) *objects*, for the problem is at bottom that of *distinguishing* between perception of an object and perception of an event since our perceptions occur serially or successively in both cases. In other words, what Guyer calls "the omnipresent succession of mere representations" cuts both ways, raising the question of how we can know by perception that we are perceiving *either* an event *or* an enduring object. With this point in mind, the argument can be continued as follows:

(14) Some experiences can be conceptualized as being of objects that can be reencountered and reidentified only if experiences that are conceptualized as being of objects that can be reencountered and reidentified can be distinguished from experiences of events (N ⊃ H).

(15) Experiences that are conceptualized as being of objects that can be reencountered and reidentified can be distinguished from experiences of events only if we can know by observation whether we are perceiving an object or an event (H ⊃ K).

(16) We cannot know by observation whether we are perceiving an object or an event by our perceptions' being successive, irreversible, of things-in-themselves, or by reference to absolute time (∼V).

(17) If (16), then we can know by observation whether we are perceiving an event or an object only if every event such that we can know by observation that it is occurring has some cause [∼V ⊃ (K ⊃ C)].

(18) We can know by observation whether we are perceiving an event or an object only if every event such that we can know by observation that it is occurring has some cause [from (16) and (17)] (K ⊃ C).

(19) Experience is possible only if every event such that we can know by observation that it is occurring has some cause [from (12), (13), (14), (15), and (18)] (E ⊃ C).

(20) Experience is possible (E).

(21) Some experiences are conceptualized as being of enduring objects [from (12) and (20)] (S).

(22) Every event such that we can know by observation that it is occurring has some cause [(19) and (20)] (C).

It seems reasonable to hold, then, that by incorporating Guyer's analysis of the Second Analogy, the central argument of the Analytic can be developed to yield a proof of Kant's own version of the causal principle.

It is also possible to build a version of the central argument that incorporates Guyer's analysis of the Second Analogy on the reconstruction of the B-Deduction given in section 5.6.2. The argument would then run as follows (I now state the argument in terms of ascribing representations to a nonspecific person, rather than ascribing them to myself, to better bring out its generality):

(1) Consciousness of a manifold of successive representations (= experience) is possible only if one can ascribe all the representations in the manifold to oneself (E ⊃ A).

(2) One can ascribe representations to oneself only if one has a concept of oneself (A ⊃ C).

(3) One can have a concept of oneself only if something in one's experience answers to that concept (C ⊃ S).

(4) No particular item(s) of experience answer(s) to the concept of oneself (N).

(5) If no particular item(s) of experience answer(s) to the concept of

oneself, then the only thing in one's experience that can answer to the concept of oneself is a temporal order among one's representations (N ⊃ O).

(6) The only thing in one's experience that can answer to the concept of oneself is a temporal order among one's representations [from (4) and (5)] (O).

(7) If the only thing in one's experience that can answer to the concept of oneself is a temporal order among one's representations, then something in one's experience answers to the concept of oneself only if a temporal order among one's representations answers to the concept of oneself [O ⊃ (S ⊃ T)].

(8) A temporal order among one's representations can answer to the concept of oneself only if at least some of one's representations have another temporal order as well (T ⊃ W).

(9) One temporal order among one's representations is the order in which they are apprehended (R).

(10) If a temporal order among one's representations can answer to the concept of oneself only if at least some of one's representations have another temporal order as well, and one temporal order among one's representations is the order in which they are apprehended, then a temporal order among one's representations can answer to the concept of oneself only if some of one's representations have a temporal order different from the order in which they are apprehended {[(T ⊃ W) · R] ⊃ (T ⊃ D)}.

(11) A temporal order among one's representations can answer to the concept of oneself only if some of one's representations have a temporal order different from the order in which they are apprehended [from (8), (9), and (10)] (T ⊃ D).

(12) Representations can have a temporal order different from the order in which they are apprehended only if there is a way to determine temporal relations between representations other than the order in which they are apprehended (D ⊃ Y).

(13) Time itself is not perceived (~P).

(14) If time itself is not perceived, then there is a way to determine temporal relations between representations other than the order in which they are apprehended only if some experiences are conceptualized as being of enduring objects, by reference to which temporal relations can be determined [~P ⊃ (Y ⊃ B)].

(15) Experience is possible only if some experiences are conceptualized as being of enduring objects [from (1), (2), (3), (6), (7), (11), (12), (13), and (14)] (E ⊃ B).

(16) Some experiences can be conceptualized as being of enduring objects only if some experiences are conceptualized as being of objects that can be reencountered and reidentified (B ⊃ N).

(17) Some experiences can be conceptualized as being of objects that

can be reencountered and reidentified only if experiences that are conceptualized as being of objects that can be reencountered and reidentified can be distinguished from experiences of events (N ⊃ H).

(18) Experiences that are conceptualized as being of objects that can be reencountered and reidentified can be distinguished from experiences of events only if one can know by observation whether one is perceiving an object or an event (H ⊃ K).

(19) One cannot know by observation whether one is perceiving an object or an event by one's perceptions' being successive, irreversible, of things-in-themselves, or by reference to absolute time (~V).

(20) If (19), then one can know by observation whether one is perceiving an event or an object only if every event such that one can know by observation that it is occurring has some cause [~V ⊃ (K ⊃ C)].

(21) One can know by observation whether one is perceiving an event or an object only if every event such that one can know by observation that it is occurring has some cause [from (19) and (20)] (K ⊃ C).

(22) Experience is possible only if every event such that one can know by observation that it is occurring has some cause [from (15), (16), (17), (18), and (21)] (E ⊃ C).

(23) Experience is possible. (E).

(24) Some experiences are conceptualized as being of enduring objects [from (15) and (23)] (B).

(25) Every event such that one can know by observation that it is occurring has some cause [(22) and (23)] (C).

At the end of chapter 5 I observed that the premises of the B-Deduction all appear to be *a priori* and that at least one of them, namely, the premise that time itself is not perceived, may even be synthetic (though I did not insist that it is synthetic). I think that this observation also applies to the version of the central argument of the Analytic that I have just presented. If this is correct, then it follows that (25) is an *a priori* proposition, so Kant's view that his version of the causal principle is an *a priori* truth (and perhaps even his view that it is synthetic *a priori*) is vindicated.

The Third Analogy

Interaction

8.1 The Principle of the Third Analogy

Kant calls the Third Analogy the "Principle of Coexistence, in accordance with the Law of Reciprocity or Community." He formulates this principle in a number of different ways, but the clearest and most concise formulation is the one that he offers as the conclusion of its proof in B:

> Thus the coexistence of substances in space cannot be known in experience save on the assumption of their reciprocal interaction. (B 258)

On the face of it, this simply says that we can know that two substances exist simultaneously in space only if we also know that they causally interact, that is, that each of them causally affects the other. In other words, Kant seems to be saying that knowing that two substances causally interact is a *necessary condition* of knowing that they coexist in space. He seems to be putting forward the following Principle of Interaction (PI):

> PI: If a person S knows at time t that substances x and y coexist in space,
> then S knows that x and y causally interact at t.

Such a simple interpretation will not do, however, for it would make the principle obviously false. For suppose that at a certain time t, S simultaneously perceives two substances x and y—perceives them, so to speak, in a single perceptual episode. Then S could obviously know that they coexist at time t, without knowing that they causally interact at t. This case is, of course, a counterexample to PI since it is one where PI's antecedent is true but its consequent is false.

But PI is vulnerable to another objection as well. Kenneth Lucey has shown that we can imagine cases where S knows that two substances coexist at t but S also knows that they do *not* causally interact at t. Lucey gives the following example.[1] Suppose that at two remote locations in the universe, two new stars, A and B, burst into existence. The distance between A and B is 100 million light years.

S, who is an astronomer on earth, is located midway between the two stars. At time t, which happens to be 50 million years after the birth of A and B, S has two telescopes aimed in opposite directions. The telescopes are designed in such a way that S is able to perceive A and B simultaneously. Then S knows that A and B coexist at time t, but S also knows that they do not causally interact at time t. For S's knowledge of modern physics informs S that nothing can travel faster than the speed of light, including gravitational attraction (which was probably Kant's favorite example of mutual interaction between bodies). So S knows that it will be another 50 million years before A can have a gravitational (or any other kind of) effect on B and vice versa before B can have any effect on A. So we have a case in which S knows at a time t that two substances x and y coexist and also knows that x and y do *not* causally interact at t. This case provides another counter-example to PI because if S knows that x and y do not causally interact at t then x and y do not causally interact at t, since "S knows that *p*" entails that *p*. But, for this same reason, if x and y do not causally interact at t, then S does not know that x and y causally interact at t. So this is another case where the antecedent of PI is true and its consequent is false.

Of course, Kant could not have anticipated this example since he lived before Einstein and presumably believed, in accordance with the physics of his day, that gravitational attraction is instantaneous. But even the first counterexample given above, which makes no appeal to modern science, shows that we can avoid attributing to Kant an obviously false doctrine only if we qualify PI in some appropriate way. To do that, we need to interpret Kant's principle in light of its textual context. That context makes it clear that what Kant has in mind is not knowledge that things coexist that is based on perceiving them at the same time. Rather, what he has in mind is knowledge that things coexist that is based on a series of successive perceptions of those things, during no part of which the things are perceived simultaneously. As Paul Guyer puts it in his excellent analysis of the Third Analogy:

> The task of the third analogy is to explain how we can be justified in judging that states of affairs coexist, on the basis of our necessarily successive perceptions of them.[2]

Throughout the Third Analogy, Kant himself talks of coexisting substances rather than coexisting "states of affairs." But in this context, Guyer talks interchangeably of coexisting states of affairs and coexisting "objects," and he uses "objects" to mean the same as Kant's "substances"; so it is no distortion of Guyer's meaning to say that according to him the task of the Third Analogy is to explain how we can know that substances coexist on the basis of our necessarily successive perceptions of them. Given what Guyer calls "the omnipresent succession of mere representations," how can we ever know that these successive representations are of nonsuccessive, simultaneously existing substances?[3] The only possible explanation of such knowledge, Kant will argue, is that we know that those substances causally interact. As Guyer says:

> Kant agues . . . that cognitive subjects like us, who cannot simply read off temporal relations of represented objects from the temporal relations of our representa-

tions of them—because, once again, all representations as such are successive—can only confirm judgments that represented objects *coexist* on the basis of knowledge that they *interact*. . . . Since the perception of . . . objects [in different positions in space], even if they coexist, can only be successive, the belief that they coexist can be grounded only by the assumption that they interact. Belief in interaction is epistemically necessary "in order that the succession which is always in the perceptions as apprehensions will not be ascribed to the objects, rather that these can be represented as existing simultaneously." (A 214/B 261)[4]

Accordingly, it would seem that Kant's Principle of Interaction can be accurately stated this way:

PI′: If S knows that substances x and y coexist at t on the basis of a series
of successive perceptions of x and y, during no part of which x and
y are perceived simultaneously, then S knows that x and y causally
interact at t.

This principle is not obviously false, but it, too, is vulnerable to Lucey's objection from modern physics, for we can easily modify Lucey's example in such a way that S knows that stars A and B coexist on the basis of successive perceptions. We need only suppose that the two telescopes are not designed to allow for viewing A and B simultaneously, so that S has to swivel her head back and forth or walk back and forth between the two telescopes in order to see A and B. These movements of S's could take place millions of light years before A and B begin to interact. So this seems to be a case where a person, S, could know that two substances x and y coexist at t on the basis of a series of successive perceptions of those things, during no part of which the things are perceived simultaneously, and yet know that they do not causally interact at t—which provides a counterexample to PI′, by the same reasoning as before.

I see no way, then, to avoid the conclusion that Kant's Principle of Interaction could be true only if the now-outdated physics that Kant knew were correct. Of course, this may well reduce its interest for us. Nevertheless, I propose to examine the argument Kant gives for the principle by exploring the following question: would Kant's argument be sound even if gravity or some other mode of causal interaction *were* instantaneous? In other words, if modern physics did not imply the falsity of Kant's principle, would Kant's argument prove that his principle is true?

Before considering Kant's argument, I want to make four preliminary observations. The first is merely that in his various statements of the Third Analogy's principle, Kant omits the qualification that the coexisting substances in question are known to coexist by successive perceptions of them. For the sake of brevity, I shall sometimes also omit this qualification, but it should always be understood.

Second, there is a question about what Kant means by "substance" in the Third Analogy. For as H. J. Paton points out, if by this term Kant means the same thing as in the *First* Analogy, that is, a thing that exists throughout all time, then (assuming only that we know that there are substances) it automatically follows that we can know that they eternally coexist whether or not we know that they causally interact, so the argument of the Third Analogy must be unsound. Paton rightly says that if all substances are permanent, it immediately follows that all substances coexist always, both in every moment of time, and in every part of time, and in all time taken as a whole. When we know that any substance exists, we know that it coexists with all other substances. . . .[5]

It seems, then, that in the Third Analogy Kant must be using the term "substance" in a different way than in the First Analogy. The most natural interpretation is that the term now refers to enduring material bodies like the earth or the moon, to use his own examples (B 257)—things that, according to the doctrine of the First Analogy, are actually not substances but rather are adjectival on substance(s). However, as W. H. Walsh points out, this still falls far short of telling us exactly what things count as substances: would Mt. Everest qualify?[6] The Eiffel Tower? A grain of sand? Kant does not say.

Third, note that Kant seems to be making an extremely sweeping claim: he seems to be saying that every substance that can be known to coexist in space with other substances (on the basis of successive perceptions of them) must causally interact with every one of those other substances. Thus, *if* the Eiffel Tower and the grains of sand on a beach in Normandy count as substances and are known to coexist on the basis of successive perceptions, then the Eiffel Tower causally interacts with every grain of sand on a beach in Normandy, and if the grains of sand on that beach are substances that are known to coexist on the basis of successive perceptions, then every grain of sand on a beach in Normandy interacts with every other grain of sand on that beach. Even if we could find some nonarbitrary way to limit what things count as substances, the claim that all the ones that are known to coexist on the basis of successive perceptions of them must (be known to) mutually interact may seem wildly extravagant. But perhaps this impression of extravagance can be mitigated by noting that causality in the relevant sense is evidently a transitive relation: if A's being in state s causes B to be in state s' and B's being in state s' causes C to be in state s", then A's being in state s causes C to be in state s". (The qualification "in the relevant sense" is needed here because it is obviously not the case that if A causes *any* change in B and B causes *any* change in C, then A causes a change in C: the rain may cause my car to rust and my car may cause a dent in someone's bumper, but it does not follow that the rain caused the dent.) Thus, the causal action of one substance on another, and therefore also the causal interaction between two substances, need not be direct; it can occur through the intermediation of other substances. In light of this point, the claim that every grain of sand on a beach interacts (in some way) with every other grain of sand on that beach, and ultimately even with all other substances in the world, may seem less extravagant and even theoretically plausible from the point of view of a complete science.

In any case, for at least two different reasons, it seems necessary to read Kant as making the highly general claim that every substance that can be known to coexist in space with other substances (on the basis of successive perceptions of them) must causally interact with every one of those other substances—a textual reason and a philosophical one. The textual reason is that the language he uses in stating the principle, both in A and in B, evidently implies such a claim:

All substances, so far as they coexist, stand in thoroughgoing community, that is, in mutual interaction. (A 211)

All substances, in so far as they can be perceived to coexist in space, are in thoroughgoing reciprocity. (B 256)

These formulations evidently imply not just that (a) each substance mutually interacts with some other coexisting substance but also that (b) each substance mutually interacts with every other coexisting substance. The philosophical reason for interpreting Kant as holding (b) rather than only (a) is that if he held only (a), then it is doubtful that he would need the Third Analogy at all; for the Second Analogy virtually establishes (a), at least on one very plausible assumption. This assumption is that every substance (assuming it changes at all) undergoes at least some changes that are not caused by its own previous states. According to the Second Analogy, these changes must have some cause, and so this cause must be the state of some other substance. Thus, every substance undergoes some changes caused by another substance. But this comes very close to showing that every substance mutually interacts with another substance. For, as Arthur Melnick has pointed out, if a substance A causes a change in a substance B at time t, then it is normally the case that B causes a change in A at time t.[7] For example, suppose that billiard ball A strikes billiard ball B, causing B to roll. Then B's resistance, upon being struck, causes A's direction or speed of movement to change; so A and B stand, to use Kant's language, in mutual interaction or reciprocity. Or suppose that a stream of water causes a fire to be put out; then the fire causes the water to be heated. Someone might here object that this point may hold normally or for the most part but that one can at least conceive of a case where A causes a change in B without B thereby causing any change in A. This may be true, but the point holds so generally that the significance of the Third Analogy would be greatly reduced if it were meant to establish only (a).

Fourth, note that the Third Analogy is not needed for the purpose of overthrowing the Humean view of experience: Kant's view that experience is of objective items that are connected by causal laws does not require that each of those items that is known to coexist with other items on the basis of successive perceptions of them causally interact with every such item. Furthermore, nowhere does Kant show how the principle of interaction follows, as in the case of substance (at least in the sense of enduring physical objects) or causality, from the two time orders that flow from the Transcendental Deduction. As Robert Wolff says:

In the Second Analogy, Kant begins by presupposing the distinction between objective and subjective succession, but . . . he eventually carries the argument so deep that he provides the materials for a proof of that presupposition . . . Kant, however, suggests [no] way of grounding the Third Analogy in like manner, on the Deduction.[8]

To put it differently, Kant nowhere indicates how the argument of the Third Analogy might be integrated into what I have called the Central Argument of the Analytic.

In light of the last three preliminary observations, it is perhaps not surprising that the Third Analogy has received less attention from recent commentators than the other two. Furthermore, some commentators find Kant's proof so defective that they do not even discuss it; thus Jonathan Bennett quotes the principle of the Analogy and then says:

> Kant is here making the interesting and rather Spinozist claim that we could not know that two things coexisted in the same universe unless they had causal commerce (= community) with one another. His attempt to prove this, however, is a failure which is not even incidentally valuable except for a few flickers of light which it throws on the second Analogy.[9]

T. E. Wilkerson offers an even more negative assessment:

> The Third Analogy has a very shadowy existence. In part it reproduces material from the Second Analogy, and in part it makes nonsense of it.[10]

It would be inappropriate, in a work of this kind, to accept that the proof of the Third Analogy is a failure simply on the authority of these commentators, so let us examine it for ourselves.

8.2 The Proof of the Third Analogy

I shall focus on the proof in B. As before, I shall first explain each premise and then review the whole argument. It begins this way:

> *Segment 1*
> Things are coexistent when in empirical intuition the perceptions of them can follow upon one another reciprocally, which, as has been shown in the proof of the second principle [i.e., the Second Analogy], cannot occur in the succession of appearances. Thus I can direct my attention first to the moon and then to the earth, or, conversely, first to the earth and then to the moon; and because the perceptions of these objects can follow each other reciprocally, I say that they are coexistent. (B 256–257)

Here Kant reasserts a point that he made in the Second Analogy, namely, that we perceive coexisting things just in case the series of perceptions that we have is reversible—a point that he now makes by saying that "the perceptions of these objects can follow each other reciprocally." For example, since the earth and the moon exist at the same time, I may perceive first the moon and then the earth, but I could instead have perceived first the earth and then the moon. Conversely, since I may perceive first the moon and then the earth, but I could instead have perceived first the earth and then the moon, it must be true that the earth and the moon exist at the same time. This reversibility, or "order-indifference," as we have seen, cannot obtain when I perceive successive states of affairs such as the upstream and downstream positions of a ship. On the strength of the above passage and against the background of the Second Analogy, then, we can put the first step of Kant's proof this way:

(1) One knows that a series of successive perceptions is of coexisting
    things if and only if one knows that the series of perceptions could
    have occurred in the reverse order from the one in which it actually
    occurred.

In the previous chapter, we saw that we cannot use the reversibility or irreversibility of our perceptions as the *criterion* for determining whether we are perceiving an enduring state of affairs or an event since we can know that our perceptions
are reversible or irreversible only if we already know whether we are perceiving an
enduring state of affairs or an event. But likewise, we cannot use the reversibility or
irreversibility of our perceptions as the *criterion* for determining whether we perceive coexisting things or successively existing things since we can know whether
our perceptions are reversible or irreversible only if we *already* know whether we
are perceiving coexisting things or successively existing things. The fundamental
reason that reversibility/irreversibility of our perceptions cannot play this crite-
rional role, as we saw in discussing the Second Analogy, is that such reversibility
or irreversibility is a modal fact: it pertains to the possibility or impossibility of
having had the perceptions in the reverse order. However, as Guyer reminds us
in his discussion of the Third Analogy, "as always, we are simply given successive
representations, and we are *given* nothing about their *modality*."[11]

Kant tends to obscure this point in the Third Analogy by his talk of perceptions that "can follow upon one another reciprocally." This may suggest that a
series of perceptions can be *actually reversed*, in which case it would of course be
rever*sible*. But no series of perceptions can ever be actually reversed because a
perception that has already occurred is over and done with and can never reoccur.
At best, a perception that is *exactly like* an earlier one can occur, but that would
not provide any evidence that one was perceiving coexisting things since the same
thing could occur if one were perceiving similar things that existed successively.[12]

Properly put, then, Kant's question is this: how do we know that we are perceiving coexisting things, given that reversibility cannot be the criterion? It is
strictly analogous to the question of the Second Analogy about how we can know
that we perceive an objective succession, given that irreversibility cannot be the
criterion. It will not do to answer that we can know that we are perceiving coexisting things by direct inspection of momentary arrays of representations since the
question pertains to the objective time-order, and things that exist simultaneously
in that order need not be and typically are not simultaneously perceived, if only
because they are spatially removed from each other. (This is why the restriction of
the principle Kant seeks to prove to things that are known to coexist by successive
perceptions of them is not arbitrary.) Perhaps this is Kant's point when he says, in
the version of the proof that he gives in A, that if coexisting substances did not
interact, then it would follow that

> their *coexistence* would not be an object of a possible perception and . . . the exis-
> tence of the one could not lead by any path of empirical synthesis to the existence
> of another. For if we bear in mind that they would be separated by a completely
> empty space, the perception which advances from one to another in time would

indeed, by means of a succeeding perception, determine the existence of the latter, but would not be able to distinguish whether it follows objectively upon the first or is not rather coexistent with it. (A 212/B 259)

Kant's proof in B continues as follows:

Segment 2
Now coexistence is the existence of the manifold in one and the same time. But time itself cannot be perceived, and we are not, therefore, in a position to gather, simply from things being set in the same time, that their perceptions can follow each other reciprocally. The synthesis of imagination in apprehension would only reveal that the one perception is in the subject when the other is not there, and *vice versa*, but not that the objects are coexistent, that is, that if one exists the other exists at the same time, and that it is only because they thus coexist that the perceptions are able to follow one another reciprocally. (B 257)

Some of what Kant says here, notably the point that empty time cannot be perceived, is by now very familiar. As we have seen, when this point is understood to mean that there is no way to identify positions or "dates" in time by reference to time itself, it is both true and important. Kant now implies that if we could tell that things coexisted just by reference to time itself, then we could also tell that our perceptions were reversible just by reference to time itself. This is true enough since when things are coexistent the perceptions of them are reversible. But one may wonder why the issue of reversibility or irreversibility would matter at all if coexistence could be determined by reference to time itself: that two things coexist could then be determined just by comparing their position to time itself, thus bypassing the issue of reversibility or irreversibility. Of course, this would not go against the claim that we perceive coexisting things if and only if our perceptions are reversible—that coexistence of objects and reversibility of our perceptions of those objects go, so to speak, hand in hand. Still, Kant's emphasis on reversibility in this proof seems somewhat misleading, and he may even be trading on the term "reciprocity" to suggest that objects whose perceptions can "follow each other reciprocally" must stand in "reciprocal" causal relations to each other.[13] Be that as it may, it seems that if we want to reconstruct Kant's argument in a way that is faithful to what he says, we must formulate the steps he takes in segment 2 as follows:

(2) Time itself cannot be perceived.
(3) If time itself cannot be perceived, then one cannot know that two things coexist by perceiving their relation to time itself.
(4) If one cannot know that two things coexist by perceiving their relation to time itself, then one cannot know that a series of perceptions could have occurred in the reverse order from the one in which it actually occurred by reference to time itself.
(5) One cannot know that a series of perceptions could have occurred in the reverse order from the one in which it actually occurred by reference to time itself [from (2), (3), and (4)].

Kant's proof continues as follows:

Segment 3

Consequently, in the case of things which coexist externally to one another, a pure concept of the reciprocal sequence of their determinations is required, if we are to be able to say that the reciprocal sequence of the perceptions is grounded in the object, and so to represent the coexistence as objective. But the relation of substances in which one contains determinations the ground of which is contained in the other is the relation of influence; and when each substance reciprocally contains the ground of the determinations of the other, the relation is that of community or reciprocity. Thus the coexistence of substances in space cannot be known in experience save on the assumption of their reciprocal interaction. (B 258)

Kant seems to be moving very quickly here, for he seems to be concluding, just from the point that the reversibility of a series of perceptions of objects cannot be determined by reference to time itself, that therefore it can be determined only by grounding it in mutual causal interaction of the objects. In other words, his complete argument seems to be this:

(1) One knows that a series of successive perceptions is of coexisting things if and only if one knows that the series of perceptions could have occurred in the reverse order from the one in which it actually occurred ($K \equiv 0$).

(2) Time itself cannot be perceived ($\sim P$).

(3) If time itself cannot be perceived, then one cannot know that two things coexist by perceiving their relation to time itself ($\sim P \supset T$).

(4) If one cannot know that two things coexist by perceiving their relation to time itself, then one cannot know that a series of perceptions could have occurred in the reverse order from the one in which it actually occurred by reference to time itself ($\sim T \supset \sim R$).

(5) One cannot know that a series of perceptions could have occurred in the reverse order from the one in which it actually occurred by reference to time itself [from (2), (3), and (4)] ($\sim R$).

(6) If one cannot know that a series of perceptions could have occurred in the reverse order from the one in which it actually occurred by reference to time itself, then one can know that a series of perceptions could have occurred in the reverse order from the one in which it actually occurred only if one knows that the perceptions are of things that mutually affect each other [$\sim R \supset (O \supset C)$].

(7) One can know that a series of perceptions could have occurred in the reverse order from the one in which it actually occurred only if one knows that the perceptions are of things that mutually affect each other [from (5) and (6)] ($O \supset C$).

(8) One knows that a series of successive perceptions is of coexisting things only if one knows that the perceptions are of things that mutually affect each other [from (1) and (7)] ($K \supset C$).

If this is indeed all there is to Kant's argument, then it lends credence to Wolff's comment that "unhappily, Kant lets down after the exertion of analyzing objective succession [in the Second Analogy] and gives us a hasty account of coexistence which adds little or nothing to the remarks in the Second Analogy."[14] For clearly, the key premise of the argument is (6), but Kant has given no support for it. The premise may be true, but if so Kant has left the task of figuring out why it is true entirely to the reader.

8.3 Guyer's Analysis of the Third Analogy

Let us make a fresh start. Can we, drawing on the points Kant has made, construct a more plausible version of the Third Analogy's argument? I think that we can, with the help again of Paul Guyer's *Kant and the Claims of Knowledge*. What follows is loosely based on his dense but rewarding discussion, although my conclusion will be less favorable to Kant than his appears to be.[15]

As we have seen, Guyer locates Kant's problem as that of showing how it is possible for us to know that substances exist at the same time on the basis of successive perceptions of them, and he interprets Kant as arguing that such knowledge is possible only if we know that those substances causally interact. To understand the reasoning that Guyer attributes to Kant, we may put the matter like this. Let A and B be two different substances, let A_r be a perception of A only and B_r a perception of B only, and suppose that A_r is followed in time by B_r. Then Kant's problem in the Third Analogy is this: how can we know, on the basis of A_r and B_r, that A and B both exist throughout a given duration of time D? Several possibilities must be ruled out:

(1) We cannot know that A and B both exist during D by having A_r during D because A_r provides no direct evidence about B.

(2) We cannot know that A and B both exist during D by having B_r during D because B_r provides no direct evidence about A.

(3) We cannot know that A and B both exist during D by knowing that, during D, we could have had either the sequence of perceptions A_r, B_r or the sequence of perceptions B_r, A_r, that is, by knowing that the sequence A_r, B_r is reversible, because we can know this only if we *already* know that A and B both exist during D.

(4) We cannot know that A and B both exist during D by having the sequence of perceptions A_r, B_r during D and the sequence B_r, A_r during some earlier or later duration of time D' (i.e., by knowing that we can have perceptions of A and B in a different order during some other duration D'), or vice versa, because what perceptions we have during D' provides no evidence about what existed during D.

According to Guyer, Kant's key idea is that, in light of the possibilities ruled out by (1)–(4), the only remaining way in which we can know that A and B both exist during D is by virtue of *some causal relationship between A and B*. However,

(5) We cannot know that A and B both exist during D by virtue of the fact that A's being in some state a during D causes B to be in some state b during some other duration D' or that B's being in some state

c during D causes A to be in some state d during some other duration D′ because this fact provides no evidence that A and B both existed during D.

Therefore, it seems that we can know that A and B both exist during D only by knowing that A's being in state a causes B to be in state b during D and B's being in state c causes A to be in state d during D—that is, only by knowing that A and B mutually interact during D.[16]

Here someone might object to the talk of one substance causing another to be in a certain state "during a certain duration," on the ground that causes operate *at* a given time rather than *during* a given duration of time. But this objection would be mistaken because some causes do operate throughout durations of time. Gravity, for example (which provides one of the best illustrations of causal interaction), certainly operates that way: the earth continuously attracts the moon and the moon continually attracts the earth. What are sometimes called "sustaining causes" likewise operate through time: cold continuously causes water to be in a frozen state, a furnace continuously causes a house to be warmed, a bowling ball on a resilient cushion continually causes it to remain hollow, and so on.

In any case, the above reasoning need not be put only in terms of one substance causing another to be in a certain state during a certain duration; it can be reiterated in terms of the notion of a substance causing another to be in a certain state *at* a time t. Putting it in the problem-solution format that we used for the Second Analogy, the reasoning would then go as follows:

Problem:

Let A and B be two different substances, and let A_r be a perception of A only and B_r a perception of B only. Then how can we know, on the basis of A_r and B_r, that A and B both exist at time t_1?

- Not just by having A_r at t because A_r provides no direct evidence about B
- Not just by having B_r at t because B_r provides no direct evidence about A
- Not by knowing that at t, we could have had *either* A_r *or* B_r because we can know this only if we *already* know that A and B both exist at t
- Not by having A_r at t and B_r at a different time t′ or by having B_r at t and A_r at t′ because what perceptions we have at t′ provide no evidence about what existed at t
- Not by virtue of the fact that As being in some state a at t causes B to be in some state b at a different time t′ or that B's being in some state c at t causes A to be in some state s at d because this fact provides no evidence that A and B both existed at t

Solution:

So, the only way we can know that A and B both exist at time t is by knowing that A's being in state a causes B to be in state b at t and B's being in state c causes A to be in state d at t.

Assuming that the nature of Kant's problem and proposed solution are now clear, I can state the reasoning of the Third Analogy as an argument. Recurring first to the somewhat more intuitive formulation in terms of substances causing each other to be in certain states throughout a certain duration D, the argument would go as follows.

(1) We can know, on the basis of successive perceptions of A only and B only, A_r and B_r, that A and B both exist throughout a certain duration of time D only if we can eliminate the possibility that A existed during D but B existed only during a different duration D' and the possibility that B existed during D but A existed only during a different duration D' (K ⊃ E).

(2) We cannot eliminate these two possibilities just by having A_r during D (~A).

(3) We cannot eliminate these two possibilities just by having B_r during D (~B).

(4) We can know that during D, we could have had either the sequence of perceptions A_r, B_r or the sequence of perceptions B_r, A_r, that is, that the sequence A_r, B_r is reversible, only if we *already* know that A and B both exist during D (R ⊃ D).

(5) If (4) is true, then we cannot eliminate these two possibilities by knowing that during D we could have had either the sequence of perceptions A_r, B_r or the sequence of perceptions B_r, A_r [(R ⊃ D) ⊃ ~S].

(6) We cannot eliminate these two possibilities by knowing that during D we could have had either the sequence of perceptions A_r, B_r or the sequence of perceptions B_r, A_r [from (4) and (5)] (~S).

(7) We cannot eliminate these two possibilities by virtue of the fact that A's being in some state a during D causes B to be in some state b during a different duration D' or that B's being in some state c during D causes A to be in state d during D' because this fact provides no evidence that A and B both existed during D (~O).

(8) If (2), (3), (6), and (7) are all true, then we can eliminate the possibility that A existed at t but B existed only during a different duration D' and the possibility that B existed during D but A existed only during D' only if we know that A's being in state a causes B to be in state b during D and B's being in state c causes A to be in state d during D—that is, only if we know that A and B mutually interact during D {[(A · ~B · (~S · ~O)] ⊃ (E ⊃ C)}.

(9) We can eliminate the possibility that A existed during D but B existed only during a different duration D' and the possibility that B existed during D but A existed only during D' only if we know that A's being in state a causes B to be in state b during D and B's being in state c causes A to be in state d during D—that is, only if we know that A and B mutually interact during D [from (2), (3), (6), (7), and (8)] (E ⊃ C).

(10) We can know, on the basis of successive perceptions of A only and B only, A_r and B_r, that A and B both exist throughout a certain duration of time D only if we know that A's being in state a causes B to be in state b during D and B's being in state c causes A to be in state d during D—that is, only if we know that A and B mutually interact during D [from (1) and (9)] (K ⊃ C).

The argument can also be formulated in terms of coexistence at a time rather than over a duration of time, as well as in a style that is typical in current philosophical analysis. The thesis to be proved can be put this way:

(T) If person S can know, based only on the evidence of a perception of x at time t_1 followed by a perception of y at time t_2, or based only on the evidence of a perception of y at time t_1 followed by a perception of x at time t_2, that x and y coexist at time t_1, then S knows that x and y causally interact at t_1 (K ⊃ C).

The argument for (T) goes as follows:

(1) If S can know, based only on the evidence of a perception of x at time t_1 followed by a perception of y at time t_2, or based only on the evidence of a perception of y at time t_1 followed by a perception of x at time t_2, that x and y coexist at time t_1, then S can eliminate (a) the possibility that x exists at t_1 but y exists only at t_2 and (b) the possibility that y exists at t_1 but x exists only at t_2 (K ⊃ E).

(2) S cannot eliminate these two possibilities just by perceiving x but not y at t_1 (~X).

(3) S cannot eliminate these two possibilities just by perceiving y but not x at t_1 (~Y).

(4) S can know that S could have perceived either x or y at t_1 (i.e., that S's perceptions of x and y were "reversible") only if S already knows that x and y coexisted at t_1 (R ⊃ A).

(5) If (4), then S cannot eliminate possibilities (a) and (b) by knowing that S could have perceived either x or y at t_1 [(R ⊃ A) ⊃ ~P].

(6) S cannot eliminate these two possibilities by knowing that S could have perceived either x or y at t_1 [from (4) and (5)] (~P).

(7) S cannot eliminate these possibilities by knowing that x caused y to be in state s at some time other than t_1 or that y caused x to be in some state s′ at some time other than t_1 (~O).

(8) If (2) and (3) and (6) and (7) are all true, then S can eliminate possibilities (a) and (b) only if S knows that x caused y to be in state s at t_1 and that y caused x to be in state s′ at t_1 {[(~X · ~Y . (~P · ~O)] ⊃ (E ⊃ C)}.

(9) S can eliminate possibilities (a) and (b) only if S knows that x caused y to be in state s at t_1 and that y caused x to be in state s′ at t_1 [from (2), (3), (6), (7), and (8)] (E ⊃ C).

(T) If S can know, based only on the evidence of a perception of x at time t_1 followed by a perception of y at time t_2, or based only on the evidence of a perception of y at time t_1 followed by a perception of x at time t_2, that x and y coexist at time t_1, then S knows that x caused y to be in state s at t_1 and that y caused x to be in state s′ at t_1—that is, that x and y causally interact at t_1 [from (1) and (9)] (K ⊃ C).

Although the above reasoning is the most plausible reconstruction of Kant's argument that I can find, it is unfortunately open to serious objections. The main problem stems from the fact that it can at best establish only a necessary condition of knowledge of coexistence. It tells us nothing about what would be sufficient for such knowledge. Yet this is really the problem toward which Kant's Third Analogy points: how, after all, *do* we ever know, on the basis of perceptions that are always successive, that they are of coexisting things? How do we know, when a perception of x is followed in time by a perception of y, that by the time the perception of y occurs, x has not ceased to exist altogether and that y has not just begun to exist? To be told that we can know this only if x and y causally interact is of no help, especially in the absence of any independent reason to think that they do interact.

It would certainly not solve the difficulty to suggest that we can know by perception that x and y *are causally interacting* and that this knowledge is (not only necessary but also) *sufficient* for knowing that x and y coexist. First, if there is a problem about how we can know on the basis of successive perceptions of x and y that they coexist, then surely there is an even greater problem about how we can know on such a basis that they causally interact. How could a perception of x at time t_1 followed by a perception of y at time t_2, or a perception of y at time t_1 followed by a perception of x at time t_2, possibly be sufficient to show that x and y causally interact at time t_1? Even if we could perceive causal relations in the way that we perceive shapes and colors (which Hume powerfully argued that we cannot), the separation of time between the perceptions of x and y would make this impossible. Second, as Ken Lucey has shown, it is not even true that causal interaction between x and y establishes their coexistence. Lucey asks us to consider two objects A and B, namely, a light-sensitive light switch and a light bulb separated in space by a certain distance. Suppose that flipping the switch into the on position causes the light to go on and that the light from the bulb in turn activates the light-sensitive switch mechanism, causing the switch to go off. This appears to be a case of genuine causal interaction. But A's causal effect on B takes time to propagate, and likewise B's causal effect on A takes time to propagate. So the fact that A and B causally interact cannot establish that there is a single time during which they coexist.[17]

To some extent, the difficulty that no sufficient conditions have been offered for knowing that things coexist on the basis of successive perceptions of those things can be mitigated by appealing to the First Analogy. There, as we saw, Kant makes a case for holding that the unity of time requires a perceptual stand-in for time. But on the assumption that there is more than one substance (an assumption without which questions about coexisting substances could, of course, never even arise), and on the assumption that these substances are not all sempiternal (in which case they would, of course, all coexist forever, as Paton pointed out), this stand-in must be composed of substances whose existence overlaps in time. But to say that the existence of x overlaps in time with the existence of y is to say that, during at least part of their histories, x and y coexist. Thus Kant could argue that the mere unity of time guarantees that, in any world of experience where there is a plurality of things, at least some of them must sometimes coexist. He would then have a transcendental argument showing that in order for us to have one kind of experience we unquestionably do have—experience of many things existing in a unitary time—at least some of those things must (be conceived to) coexist. But this is still far from showing that, *in any particular case* in which we have successive perceptions of x and y, x and y are known to coexist. What conditions are sufficient for such knowledge of particular coexistence? Kant does not say.

It might now be said, in Kant's defense, that these difficulties do not refute his argument because the purpose of that argument is precisely *not* to give sufficient conditions for knowledge of coexistence but only to give a necessary condition, and nothing I have said so far shows that the argument fails to establish a necessary condition. Unfortunately, however, we are now in a position to argue that it does fail to establish a necessary condition. For suppose that Kant or someone else did provide a plausible account of what is sufficient for a person to know, by successive perceptions of x and y, that x and y coexist at a time t. Suppose also, as seems very plausible, that this account appealed to principles (such as certain conservation principles or considerations of theoretical simplicity) that did not entail that x and y causally interact at time t. Now, it is a perfectly general point of logic that if P is sufficient for Q, then nothing that is not entailed by P can be necessary for Q. Applying this to the Third Analogy yields the following result: if some conditions C are sufficient for a person S to know that x and y coexist at time t, and those conditions do not entail that S knows that x and y causally interact at t, then knowing that x and y causally interact at t cannot, contrary to Kant's main thesis, be a necessary condition of knowing that x and y coexist at time t. Furthermore, if some such condition is sufficient for knowledge that x and y coexist, then premise (8) of the two arguments above must be false; for then it must be possible to eliminate the possibility that A existed during D but B existed only during a different duration D' and the possibility that B existed during D but A existed only during a different duration D' without knowing that A and B interact during D, and it must likewise be possible to eliminate the possibility that x exists only before y or y exists only before x without knowing that x and y causally interact.

In light of this difficulty, I must conclude that even on the most insightful analysis of the Third Analogy that I know of, Kant does not solve its problem. That problem is that one kind of knowledge that is both pervasive and important—knowledge of the coexistence of things based on non-coexistent, successive perceptions of them—is problematic and even vulnerable to skeptical challenge. Kant addresses the problem by arguing for a necessary condition for this kind of knowledge, but he offers no sufficient conditions for it. Thus, we are still left wondering how we manage to have such knowledge. Furthermore, it seems very likely that any sufficient conditions Kant could propose for such knowledge would show that the necessary condition he argues for is not necessary after all.

Kant's Refutation of Idealism

9.1 Introduction

As we saw in section 4.2, the Humean view of experience implies the thesis that the only way to gain knowledge of physical objects is by a causal inference from our subjective impressions to objects—an inference that Hume himself rejects as worthless. We have now examined Kant's most sustained and complex attempt to refute this thesis, in the Transcendental Deduction and in its sequel, the Analogies of Experience. Later in the *Critique*, however, Kant offers an independent refutation of the thesis, in the brief section called "Refutation of Idealism," sandwiched between the second and third Postulates of Empirical Thought in the second edition. The nominal target of Kant's Refutation of Idealism is not Hume but rather Descartes, who is the main source of the view that our knowledge of the existence of physical objects must be based on a causal argument from our own subjective conscious states. Kant fastens on Descartes' influential claim that the only empirical statements that are immune to all skeptical doubt are those describing one's own states of consciousness, such as, paradigmatically, the statement "I am thinking."[1] Kant calls this view "problematic idealism," and he describes it as "the theory which declares the existence of objects in space outside us to be . . . doubtful and indemonstrable" (B 274).[2] In a long footnote expanding on his Refutation of Idealism in the Preface to the second edition, he famously declares:

> It still remains a scandal to philosophy and to human reason in general that the existence of things outside us (from which we derive the whole material of knowledge, even for our inner sense) must be accepted merely on *faith*, and that if anyone thinks good to doubt their existence, we are unable to counter his doubts by any satisfactory proof. (B xl, n. *a*)

As against this "scandalous" opinion, Kant proclaims that he will give "a proof that even our inner experience, which for Descartes is indubitable, is possible only on the assumption of outer experience" (B 275). In other words, Kant proposes to stand "problematic idealism" on its head by contending that we could not have the kind of knowledge that Descartes took to be totally unproblematic—knowledge of our own subjective conscious states—unless we had the kind of knowledge he took to be highly problematic: knowledge of physical objects. This contention stands behind the parenthetical remark in the passage just quoted, to the effect that we derive even knowledge of our own inner states from knowledge of things outside us.

9.2 The Refutation of Idealism in the *Critique*

Kant formulates the thesis that he claims to prove in the Refutation of Idealism as follows:

> The mere, but empirically determined, consciousness of my own existence proves the existence of objects in space outside me.

Here is his proof of this thesis:

> I am conscious of my own existence as determined in time. All determination of time presupposes something *permanent* in perception. This permanent, however, cannot be something in me, since it is only through this permanent that my existence in time can itself be determined. Thus perception of this permanent is possible only through a *thing* outside me and not through mere *representation* of a thing outside me; and consequently the determination of my existence in time is possible only through the existence of actual things which I perceive outside me. Now consciousness [of my existence] in time is necessarily bound up with consciousness of the [condition of the] possibility of this time-determination; and it is therefore necessarily bound up with the existence of things outside me, as the condition of the time-determination. [Thus], the consciousness of my existence is at the same time an immediate consciousness of the existence of other things outside me. (B 275–276; the interpolations in square brackets are in Kemp Smith's translation)

In the footnote on the Refutation of Idealism in the second-edition Preface, Kant says that the third sentence of this proof should be replaced as follows:

> But this permanent cannot be an intuition in me. For all grounds of determination of my existence which are to be met with in me are representations; and as representations themselves require a permanent distinct from them, in relation to which their change, and so my existence in the time in which they change, may be determined. (B xl n. *a*)

In light of Kant's view that "no fixed and abiding self can present itself in [the] flux of inner appearances" (A 107), the opening premise that "I am conscious of my own existence as determined in time" calls for some explanation. I shall take it to mean, as suggested by Kant's own revision in the footnote just quoted, that *I am aware that I have representations or experiences that occur in temporal succession*, for these experiences are the sole "grounds of determination of my existence"; it is precisely and only by being aware of them, as they succeed each other in temporal order, that I can be said to be aware of my own existence and its continuation in time. This way of understanding Kant's premise is confirmed in the first of three "notes" that he appends to the proof:

> Certainly, the representation 'I am' . . . immediately includes in itself the existence of a subject; but it does not include any *knowledge* of that subject, and therefore also no empirical knowledge, that is no experience of it. For this we require . . . intuition, and in this case inner intuition, in respect of which, that is, of time, the subject must be determined. (B 277)

In line with this proposed interpretation of Kant's opening premise, we can construct his proof this way:

(1) I am conscious of my own existence in time; that is, I am aware that I have experiences that occur in a specific temporal order (E).

(2) I can be aware of having experiences that occur in a specific temporal order only if I perceive something permanent by reference to which I can determine their temporal order (E ⊃ P).

(3) No conscious state of my own can serve as this permanent frame of reference (~C).

(4) Time itself cannot serve as this permanent frame of reference (~T).

(5) If (2), (3), and (4) are true, then I can be aware of having experiences that occur in a specific temporal order only if I perceive persisting objects in space outside me by reference to which I can determine the temporal order of my experiences.

$$\{[(E \supset P) \cdot (\sim C \cdot \sim T)] \supset (E \supset O)\}.$$

∴ (6) I perceive persisting objects in space outside me by reference to which I can determine the temporal order of my experiences (E ⊃ O).

Kant does not state premise (4), but we have seen that it is a premise he accepts (on the grounds that time itself cannot be perceived), and it seems necessary to include it in order to rule out the possibility that it rejects.

Regarding this argument, one eminent Kant scholar writes: "That this celebrated argument establishes something of real importance is not in doubt."[3] It can be shown, however, that the argument falls short of establishing its conclusion. The main difficulty lies with premise (2), which Kant expresses as "all determination of time presupposes something *permanent* in perception." The temporal order of experiences mentioned in this premise is not a time-order distinct from the order in which we have the experiences; it is not the objective time-order of the Analogies of Experience. Rather, it is just the order in which we have the experiences themselves; it is the subjective time-order of the Analogies. But, then, why should one need anything permanent in order to know what this order is? As Paul Guyer puts it:

> It remains unclear why anything more than mere *acquaintance* with representations which in fact succeed one another in otherwise uninterpreted experience, or anything other than the mere *occurrence* of such representations, should be necessary for one to *judge* that there has been such a succession.[4]

Our key question still remains: *Why* is the successiveness of consciousness insufficient for its own recognition, and why should spatial, let alone independent objects be necessary for this purpose?[5]

Despite this incisive objection, Guyer himself thinks that Kant's refutation of idealism ultimately succeeds; indeed, he believes that ultimately it is "[Kant's] only successful strategy for achieving a transcendental theory of experience."[6] To show this, however, Guyer argues that one must go beyond the text of the Refutation of Idealism in the *Critique* and extract Kant's argument from his later writings, especially certain *Reflexions* contained in the *Handschriftliche Nachlass* that forms part of the complete German edition of Kant's writings. In the next section, I present and defend the argument that Guyer extracts from these Kantian texts.

9.3 The Refutation of Idealism: An Improved Version

One of Kant's later *Reflexions*, entitled *Wieder den Idealism*, contains the following passage:

> Since the imagination (and its product) is itself only an object of inner sense, the empirical consciousness (*apprehensio*) of this condition can contain only succession. But this itself cannot be represented except by means of something which endures, with which that which is successive is simultaneous. This enduring thing, with which that which is successive is simultaneous . . . cannot in turn be a representation of the mere imagination but must be a representation of sense, for otherwise that which lasts would not be in the sensibility at all.[7]

Guyer explains the basic idea of this passage as follows:

> The starting point of this argument is clearly that the mere occurrence of a succession of representations is not sufficient for the representation or recognition *of* this succession. But Kant's further claim that such recognition can be grounded "only on something which endures, with which that which is successive is simultaneous" can only mean that successive representations in one's own experience can be judged to be successive only if they are judged to be severally simultaneous with the severally successive states of some enduring object.[8]

To understand the argument, look at it this way. Each of us has what might be called an "experiential history"; we have a series of subjective experiences or conscious states that stretch back in time over the hours, days, months, and years. Now ask yourself: what enables you, *right now*, to set all or most of your past experiences in their proper time order, thereby giving you knowledge of your own past? After all, the only thing you have to go on right now is your *present* memory of the experiences, which have come and gone. To quote Guyer, this "manifold of successive appearances is not in fact before [your mind] at the moment of its recollection in the way in which a dozen eggs can be before [your] eyes."[9] Furthermore, the experiences did not come adorned with little clocks, like the ones in the corner of a television sportscast, which would enable you to date or order them.[10] What then enables you to know the order in which they occurred? Kant's answer, according to Guyer, is that you correlate the remembered experiences with successive states of an enduring reality that exists independently of the experiences—you take them to be "severally simultaneous with the severally successive states of some enduring object." Suppose that you did not correlate any of your past experiences with the successive states of some enduring reality. Then, given that the experiences have come and gone, and did not come with time markers, how could you possibly set them in their proper time-order?

There is a possible misunderstanding that may obscure the force of this argument. It may seem that the argument assumes that knowledge of one's own past *experiences* rests on memory but that, by contrast, one has some kind of direct access, unmediated by memory, to past *objective* states of affairs. But since any knowledge of the past, whether it be of one's own subjective experiences or of objective past states of affairs, must of course rest on memory, the argument may seem to be based on a false assumption. But this is not the case. Rather, the argument's core idea is that one class of memories, namely, memories of the order of one's subjective experiences, rests on another class of memories, namely, memories of the order of successive states of an enduring reality. This idea should not be confused with saying that any knowledge of time-orders based on memory depends on some other knowledge of time-orders also based on memory. Such a view would obviously lead to an infinite regress, and it would entail that no knowledge of time-orders based on memory would ever be possible for us.[11] Rather, the idea is that knowledge by memory of the time-order *of one's subjective experiences* depends on knowledge by memory of the time-order of states of an enduring reality. The reason for this dependence is that subjective experiences are fleeting and transitory and do not come with time markers, whereas, by contrast, the enduring reality is relatively permanent. This is not to say that it does not change but only that its changes are sufficiently regular that it can serve as a "clock" by which we can "date" our successive experiences. To recur to the language used in analyzing the First Analogy, it can serve as a perceptual stand-in for time.

Here is a schematic way of putting the basic argument. Suppose that you have had two successive experiences, E_1 that occurred at time t_1, and E_2 that occurred at the later time t_2. Kant takes it as a datum, or basic premise, that at a still later time, t_3, you can know that you had E_1 before E_2. But he points out that one can certainly ask for an explanation of how you know this, for at t_3 both E_1 and E_2 have come and gone, so that you cannot tell by perception alone whether they occurred in the order E_1, E_2 or in the order E_2, E_1. In other words, your present state at t_3—call it E_3—does not in itself contain E_1 or E_2 but only the memory of E_1 and of E_2. But this memory, itself a momentary state, could represent these states as having occurred in either order. What, then, prevents you from now thinking that they occurred in the order E_2, E_1 rather than E_1, E_2? Only, according to Kant (as Guyer interprets him), that you correlate E_1 with an objective state of affairs S_1 that occurred before another objective state of affairs S_2; only, as I shall argue later, that you take E_1 to have been caused by an objective state of affairs that occurred before the objective state of affairs that caused E_2. If you did not in this way "anchor" your past experiences in objective states of affairs having determinate time relations, then you could not determine the order of your own conscious states.

Guyer believes that for the argument to work, it need not even be the case that E_1 and E_2 are both past experiences; it could instead be that E_2 is a present experience and only E_1 is past, for in determining the order of E_1 and E_2, one has only the present experience to go on. One does not have both E_1 and E_2 since at least one of these has come and gone. So, at the moment that I have E_2, I can consider E_1 *either* as having preceded E_2 or as being simultaneous with E_2; my faculty of imagination, as Kant calls it, can "place" them in either order. So, how can I determine that E_2 is present and E_1 is remembered, rather than that E_1 and E_2 are both present? Only, argues Guyer's Kant, by correlating E_1 with an objective state of affairs that occurred earlier than the objective state of affairs that caused E_2.

Guyer gives an example. Suppose that I *now* have a representation whose content includes both a chair and a desk. Then how can I tell whether this representation is

(a) my *now* seeming to see both a chair and a desk (or, in language current in contemporary epistemology, my now being "appeared to" both "chairishly" and "deskishly")

or

(b) my *now* seeming to see a chair and *now* remembering *previously* seeming to see a desk (my now being appeared to chairishly and now remembering previously having been appeared to deskishly)?[12]

There are at least two ways in which I cannot know whether (a) is the case or (b) is the case:

(1) I cannot know this just in virtue of the fact that my representations actually occurred in the sequence, "something other than a desk or chair—desk + chair" (the case where I now seem to see both a desk and a chair) or, alternatively, that they actually occurred in the sequence "desk only—desk + chair" (the case where I now seem to see a chair but only remember seeming to see a desk), because whichever sequence they actually occurred in, all I have to go on *now* is my *present* representation of "desk + chair."

(2) I cannot know this because representations come with time markers, like the clocks in the corner of a TV sportscast.

Guyer also thinks, however:

(3) Contra Hume, I cannot know whether (a) or (b) is the case because memories must have less "vivacity" than sense impressions.

As Guyer says, "unlike Hume, [Kant] never suggests that there is any phenomenological feature such as degree of vivacity which could automatically mark one appearance as . . . a present impression and another as a mere memory."[13] According to Guyer's Kant, then, I can know whether (a) or (b) is the case only by knowing whether (a′) my present representation is simultaneous with the actual presence of both a desk and a chair

or

(b′) my present representation is simultaneous with the actual presence of a desk and a chair but subsequent to the actual presence of a desk, with which my remembered representation was simultaneous.

In other words, I can know whether (a) or (b) is the case only by knowing such an objective fact as that a desk and a chair are both in the room now [as in (a′)], or that a chair was brought into the room only after the desk had already been there for some time [as in (b′)].

I suggest, however, that Guyer's attempt to extend Kant's argument to cases in which the experiences to be ordered include present sense perceptions only serves to detract from its plausibility.[14] For as Kenneth Lucey asks: "Does this argument really depend on my somehow not being able to distinguish my current appearances from my apparent memories? If so, that seems ABSURD."[15] There may be some cases, perhaps ones involving vivid flashbacks, which are in this way delusional. But it would compromise the generality of Kant's argument to make it turn on such unusual cases. Furthermore, although it may be true, as Guyer says, that Kant nowhere says that there is a phenomenological difference between current sense perceptions and memories, as far as I know he does not *deny* that there is (virtually always) such a difference. So I shall formulate the argument solely in terms of cases in which the experiences to be ordered in time are all past ones:

(1) I can correctly determine the order in time of my own subjective experiences (C).
(2) When I remember two or more past experiences, my recollection of those experiences does not itself reveal the order in which they occurred (~M).
(3) If (2), then I cannot correctly determine the order in time of my own subjective experiences just by recollecting those experiences (~M ⊃ ~R).
(4) I cannot correctly determine the order in time of my own subjective experiences just by recollecting those experiences (~R) [from (2) and (3)].
(5) If I cannot correctly determine the order in time of my own subjective experiences just by recollecting those experiences, then I can correctly determine the order in time of my own subjective experiences only if I know that some of my experiences are caused by successive objective states of affairs that I perceive [~R ⊃ (C ⊃ K)].
(6) I can correctly determine the order in time of my own subjective experiences only if I know that some of my experiences are caused by successive objective states of affairs that I perceive [from (4) and (5)] (C ⊃ K).

(7) I know that some of my experiences are caused by successive objective states of affairs that I perceive [from (1) and (6)] (K).

Here one can object that nothing I have said so far justifies the expression "caused by" in steps (5)–(7) and that this expression should be replaced by "correlated with." The reader is free to read the argument with "correlated with" in place of "caused by" for the time being. I shall defend the use of "caused by" below, in discussing premise (5). But let me first discuss premise (2) since it is the other key premise of the argument and it, too, might be called into question.

Guyer supports premise (2) by observing that any determination of the order of my past experiences must rest on my present mental state, which does not itself contain either of the past experiences. He traces this observation to a sentence in the first-edition Transcendental Deduction, where Kant, just after reminding us of the temporality of all consciousness, says this:

> Every intuition contains in itself a manifold which can be represented as a manifold only in so far as the mind distinguishes the time in the sequence of one impression upon another; for each representation, *in so far as it is contained in a single moment*, can never be anything but absolute unity. (A 99)

Guyer explains this passage and its implications partly as follows:

> Kant's premise that all representations are fleeting and transitory means that *in fact* no more than one representation is ever present to us; the manifold of successive representations is not in fact before one's mind at the moment of its recollection in the way in which a dozen eggs can be before one's eyes. And what all this means is that for us to have any knowledge of even a subjective succession of representation—a manifold even apart from any objective significance it may have—*some form of interpretation* by (extralogical) rules or concepts must be placed on our present representation in order to allow it to represent such a multiplicity. Without such an interpretation the present representation is simply a *new* representation without any connection to a temporally extended—or "gradual"—act of representing, or a succession of representations. Yet representation of such a succession is surely the minimal condition of any empirical determination of the self and its history in time.[16]

Although Guyer's language is powerful, one might still object that, at least sometimes, one knows by simple recollection, without any "interpretation," much less any appeal to objective considerations, that one experience has preceded or succeeded another in time. Jonathan Bennett, in an illuminating discussion of an argument that he calls Kant's "ordering argument," but which seems to be virtually identical with Guyer's construal of the Refutation of Idealism, mentions three types of cases in which this seems to be true:

> (a) If Y occurred so soon after X that one can recall a specious present containing both, then one can simply recall that X preceded Y. If this were not so, one could not simply recall hearing someone say 'damn' rather than 'mad'. (b) From this it follows that one can simply recall that X preceded Y if one can recall a continuous sequence of happenings starting with X and ending with Y. . . . (c) One may simply recall that X preceded Y by recalling a time when one experienced Y while recalling X.[17]

As Bennett immediately goes on to note, however:

> These counter-examples to Kant's thesis cover only a small fragment of all the temporal orderings we wish to establish. If I am asked 'Did you clean your shoes before or after you went for a walk?', I may be able—in the manner of (a)—to recall the moment when I straightened my back from shoe-cleaning, put the brush down and strode off into the street; or (b) to relive the detail of my day from the shoe-cleaning episode through to the walk two hours later; or (c) to recall thinking, while on my walk, that it had been a mistake to clean my shoes before going out in the mud. But it is far more likely that my answer will have to be based on my recollection that I cleaned my shoes while the sun rose and walked as it was setting, or that I heard the one o'clock news while cleaning my shoes and arranged to go for a walk at three o'clock, or something else equally dependent for its relevance on the truth of . . . statements about the objective realm. It would be—to put it mildly—a queer personal history which could be ordered solely in the manner of (a), (b) and (c).[18]

This passage supports both premise (2) and premise (5) of the argument. For on the one hand it shows that, except in rare cases, we do not order our past experiences solely on the basis of recollecting them, thus supporting premise (2), or rather this slightly qualified version of it:

> (2′) When I remember two or more past experiences, my recollection of those experiences usually does not itself reveal the order in which they occurred.

But on the other hand, the passage shows that instead we usually order our past experiences by appealing to the objective realm, thus supporting premise (5), or at least this slightly qualified version of it:

> (5′) If I cannot usually determine correctly the order in time of my own subjective experiences just by recollecting those experiences, then I can usually correctly determine the order in time of my own subjective experiences only if I know that some of my experiences are caused by successive objective states of affairs that I perceive.

Of course, as the alert reader will have noticed, the passage would better illustrate the point that ordering one's subjective experiences usually depends on correlating them with the objective realm if Bennett had spoken in (a)–(c) of *experiences as of* straightening my back, *experiences as of* cleaning my shoes, and so on, rather than already referring in (a)–(c) to the objective realm. But it is easy enough to read him in that manner, and when we do so, he seems quite right to draw the conclusion that "the ordering argument [brings] out one . . . way in which the appeal to objectivity is necessarily involved in our talk about our own inner states."[19]

In light of Bennett's discussion, it seems that the objection that one sometimes knows that one experience has preceded or succeeded another in time by simple recollection shows only that the argument should be amended along the following lines (the logical form of the argument is the same as that of the previous version, so I shall dispense with the symbolization):

(1′) I can usually correctly determine the order in time of my own subjective experiences.

(2′) When I remember two or more past experiences, my recollection of those experiences usually does not itself reveal the order in which they occurred.

(3′) If (2′), then I cannot usually determine correctly the order in time of my own subjective experiences just by recollecting those experiences.

(4′) I cannot usually determine correctly the order in time of my own subjective experiences just by recollecting those experiences [from (2′) and (3′)].

(5′) If I cannot usually determine correctly the order in time of my own subjective experiences just by recollecting those experiences, then I can usually correctly determine the order in time of my own subjective experiences only if I know that some of my experiences are caused by successive objective states of affairs that I perceive.

(6′) I can usually correctly determine the order in time of my own subjective experiences only if I know that some of my experiences are caused by successive objective states of affairs that I perceive [from (4′) and (5′)].

(7′) I know that some of my experiences are caused by successive objective states of affairs that I perceive [from (1′) and (6′)].

The word "usually" in premise (1′), unlike the "usually" in premise (2′), is not motivated by Bennett's points, but adding "usually" to premise (1) seems both harmless and appropriate.

Before addressing premise (5′) more directly, it is worth mentioning that Bennett finds evidence that Kant may have accepted something like the "ordering argument" in the *Critique of Pure Reason* itself, rather than, as Guyer suggests, only in Kant's later *Nachlass*.[20] Bennett finds this evidence not in the Refutation of Idealism but in the Second Analogy. He cites several passages:

> In this case, therefore, we must derive the *subjective succession* of apprehension from the *objective succession* of appearances. Otherwise the order of apprehension is entirely undetermined. . . . (A 193/B 238)

> Imagination . . . determines inner sense in respect of the time-relation [but can connect] two states in two ways, so that either the one or the other precedes in time. (B 233)

> [If] the relation between two states [is to be determined it] must be so thought that it is thereby determined as necessary which of them must be placed before, and which after. (B 234)

> In the imagination this sequence is not in any way determined in its order, as to what must precede and what must follow, and the series of sequent representations can indifferently be taken either in backward or in forward order. (A 201/B 246)

Since these passages come from the Second Analogy, they might be read as only making the point that we cannot know whether our perceptions are reversible or irreversible unless we already know truths about the objective world, and Bennett himself admits that such a reading is quite possibly right. But their wording (especially that of the first passage) does suggest that Kant may have had something like the ordering argument in the back of his mind even in the *Critique*.

Let us now turn our attention to premise (5′). It will be useful to start by examining an objection raised by T. H. Irwin in a review of Guyer's *Kant and the Claims to Knowledge*:

> Guyer's argument seems to face objections that have often been raised against Kantian arguments. Guyer gives plausible examples . . . to show that we sometimes form beliefs about the order of our representations (for example, the appearance of a chair and the appearance of a table) by appeal to our beliefs about an objective succession (for example, that I was in the room from 9:00 a.m. until 9:30, that the chair was carried in at 9:10 and the table at 9:20). But it does not follow that recognition of subjective succession must rest on beliefs about objects. Guyer needs to show that we could *never* trace subjective sequences unless we *sometimes* took ourselves to be tracing objective sequences. But I do not see how he shows this.[21]

The requirement that Kant show that "we could *never* trace subjective sequences unless we *sometimes* took ourselves to be tracing objective sequences" is too demanding: he need only show that we could not trace some of the subjective sequences that we do in fact unquestionably trace unless we sometimes took ourselves to be tracing objective sequences. But Irwin says nothing to establish that Kant does not succeed in showing this, for he suggests no alternative to the claim that to trace certain subjective sequences, such as those not covered by Bennett's options (a), (b), and (c), I must know that the experiences included in them are caused by successive objective states of affairs that I perceive. So I think that Irwin's objection may be safely laid aside.

A more pertinent possible objection to premise (5′) is that the reference to objective states of affairs *that I perceive* is unjustified. Kant evidently thinks, of course, that his Refutation of Idealism does prove that we perceive physical things: in the *Critique* he claims to have shown that "the determination of my existence in time is possible only through the existence of actual things which I perceive outside me" (B 275–276), and there is no reason to think that he means to weaken this conclusion in his other presentations of the argument. But what is the justification for the requirement that the things be perceived? I suggest that it is simply that we could not possibly correlate remembered experiences with successive states of an enduring reality if, when those states occurred, they were unperceived or unperceivable. One cannot correlate A's with B's if B's are unperceived—if B's do not enter into our experience.

A more powerful-looking objection to premise (5′) is that its introduction of causation is unwarranted and gratuitous. For, it might be said, Kant is only entitled to hold that to trace certain subjective sequences, one must *correlate* their members with successive states of enduring objects; there is no justification for the further claim that these objects must *cause* the experiences. Thus, it might be said, the premise ought to be formulated as saying only this.

α   β

A   B

FIGURE 9–1

(5″) If I cannot usually determine correctly the order in time of my own subjective experiences just by recollecting those experiences, then I can usually correctly determine the order in time of my own subjective experiences only if I know that some of my experiences are correlated with successive objective states of affairs that I perceive (that are, as Guyer puts it, "severally simultaneous with the severally successive states of some enduring object[s]").

But although (5″) would still lead to Kant's main desired conclusion—that I perceptually know the existence of objective states of affairs—Guyer makes a point that supports the stronger (5′):

> Kant's present argument that the epistemological conditions for determinate judgment of even subjective sequences of representations require the correlation of the latter with successive states of enduring objects entails that those objects are objects *acting on* the self . . . enduring objects are conceived as agents of the empirical succession of self-consciousness. . . .[22]

Guyer's point is that the thought that successive experiences correlate with successive states of enduring objects already includes the thought that they are caused by those objects. He does not explain why this is so, but I suggest the reason must be this: the subjective order is known to be what it is *only* on the grounds that it could not have been different than it is, but this is to say that it is causally determined by the successive states of the enduring objects. To see this point more clearly, suppose I judge that a past experience α occurred before β by correlating those experiences with successive objective states A, B, as illustrated in figure 9–1. But suppose I also allow that this correlation is just a coincidence, so that β might just as well have occurred with A and α with B, as illustrated in figure 9–2. Then how can the knowledge that A occurred before B support my judgment that α occurred before β? It cannot. If α might just as well have occurred with B and β

β   α

A   B

FIGURE 9–2

with A as α with A and β with B, then my knowledge that A occurred before B gives me no reason to think that α occurred before β. For my knowledge that A occurred before B to support the judgment that α preceded β, I must postulate that A caused α and B caused β, as illustrated in figure 9–3. As these figures illustrate, the dependence of the knowledge of α's and β's time-order on A's and B's time-order can rest only on the ground that α was caused by A and β was caused by B; had it been only a coincidence that α occurred with A and β with B, then knowledge of A's and B's temporal order could not make possible the knowledge of α's and β's temporal order.

As Guyer further argues, this point also shows that the enduring objects that cause experiences cannot possibly be identified with the empirical self. Given Kant's view that "no fixed and abiding self can present itself in [the] flux of inner appearances" (A 107), the empirical self can be nothing but the entire subjective sequence of experiences. So to say that the empirical self causes the experiences would be to say that the experiences are parts of their own cause—that they are both effects and component parts of the empirical self—which is absurd. Thus Guyer can say:

> It is precisely because enduring objects are conceived of as agents of the empirical succession of self-consciousness . . . that they must also be conceived of as numerically distinct from the self. . . . The states of the self are judged to have a unique order just insofar as they are judged to be caused by the successive states of enduring objects. It is because they must stand in a causal relation to the empirical self . . . that the objects which function in subjective time-determination must indeed be external to or independent of the self, objects conceived of as ontologically distinct from the self.[23]

From the consequence that the objects that function in subjective time determination must be independent of the self, we may draw the further conclusion that they must be spatially outside the self. To establish this final conclusion, we can invoke a point that we have already seen several times, namely, that to conceive the things we perceive as being distinct from the self and its states is to conceive them as being spatially outside the self. As Guyer puts it:

> The argument . . . emphasizes that enduring objects play their role in subjective time-determination just by being regarded as agents of change in the empirical self which are numerically distinct from the latter, and Kant would have inferred the further conclusion that such objects must be represented spatially simply by adding the further premise that space is the form of intuition by which we represent things other than ourselves and our states. . . . That spatiality is our form for

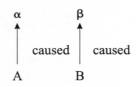

FIGURE 9–3

representing that which is ontologically independent of ourselves seems to have been a premise to which Kant had long subscribed. . . . [According to Kant] if I must think of myself as standing in relation to something which is ontologically distinct from my empirical self and my representations, then I must represent this thing—or more precisely the fact of its independence from me—by representing it as separated from me in space.[24]

Before concluding this section, I want to consider briefly a question regarding the conclusion of the argument—that "I know that some of my experiences are caused by successive objective states of affairs that I perceive." The question is this: how "enduring" or "permanent" must the objective states of affairs referred to in this conclusion be? Kant's talk of "permanence" and Guyer's talk of "enduring objects" suggests that they must be constituted by continuously existing physical objects or bodies. But, as James Van Cleve pertinently asks, why would not "a series of objective flashes with no continuant lighthouse" serve the purpose?[25] I think this challenge shows the limitations of Kant's argument. The argument shows at best that something with a lasting existence—something that continues to exist and that maintains its identity in a way that contrasts with and cannot be ascribed to our fleeting and transitory experiences—must exist if we are to be able to order our subjective experiences in time. It also shows that this lasting reality is perceived by us and is causally responsible for our experiences. But beyond that, it shows nothing about the nature of this reality; it operates at too abstract a level for that. A series of objective flashes of light, for all the argument can show, might conceivably possess enough unity and stability to qualify as the enduring reality in question. Of course, if the flashes of light were as evanescent as our subjective experiences, then they could not provide enough structure to serve as a frame of reference for ordering our past experiences. Likewise, if they occurred very infrequently or at intervals that varied in a random way, then it is difficult to see how they could fulfill this function. But beyond the general and admittedly vague requirement that the perceived objective states of affairs possess a certain degree of unity and stability, Kant's argument cannot show what they must be like. Only a variety of considerations not implicated in the argument—considerations of an empirical and scientific nature—can reveal in any detail the nature of the perceived objective reality by reference to which we can order our past experiences.

9.4 The Refutation of Idealism and Transcendental Idealism

There remains an important question about Kant's Refutation of Idealism: how does it relate to his Transcendental Idealism? In light of the approach to Transcendental Idealism that I have taken, this breaks down into two questions: (1) how does Kant's Refutation relate to the strong version of Transcendental Idealism (strong TI), according to which reality consists of nonspatial and nontemporal things-in-themselves, and space and time are built-in features of humans who know only the appearances that exist in space and time? (2) How does it relate to the weak version of Transcendental Idealism (weak TI), according to which we humans must conceive experience as being of objects causally interacting in space and time, and we cannot intelligibly suppose that things might be different from the ways in which we must conceive them? In light of (what I have argued to be) the unattractiveness of strong TI and the plausibility of weak TI, question (2) is much more interesting than question (1), but let me nevertheless begin with some brief remarks about question (1).

According to strong TI, things-in-themselves are not in space. It immediately follows, then, that the Refutation of Idealism is not intended to prove the existence of things-in-themselves since it is supposed to prove the existence of objects in space. But aside from this obvious consequence, it is not easy to see how the Refutation of Idealism fits together with strong TI, for the Refutation purports to prove the existence of "objects in space outside me," but what sense does this phrase make if space itself is really in me? If space is really "in us," then would not proving that there are things in space prove that those very things are in us rather than outside us? And would not proving that there are things outside us prove that those things are not in space? Once again, we are here up against the paradoxes of strong TI.

This is not to say that Kant has no tools at his disposal to try to soften these paradoxes. Thus, for example, in the Aesthetic he says that whereas space is indeed "transcendentally ideal," it is nonetheless "empirically real." So, he might say that although the Refutation of Idealism does not prove that there are things-in-themselves, it does prove that there are empirically real objects. He might also say that "space is in us" must not be taken literally to mean, absurdly, that space is itself spatially inside us. The challenge, however, is to explain, in an understandable and nonmetaphorical way, and not by just repeating Kant's terminology without explaining what it means, what Kant's formulations do mean. When I try to do this, I find myself forced to resort to the language of weak TI—to say, for example, that space is "in us" means only that we humans cannot conceive of perceived or perceivable objects distinct from ourselves and our own mental states except as being in space, and that Kant's "empirically real" objects are just the ones we must *conceive* as being distinct from ourselves and therefore also as being outside us in space. I can find no other understandable and nonmetaphorical way of interpreting such claims as that space is "in us" yet the things in space are outside us. But this interpretation amounts to abandoning strong TI in favor of weak TI, and so takes us directly to question (2), about how the Refutation relates to *weak* TI, to which I now turn.

Let us approach question (2) by asking a closely related one: is Kant's Refutation of Idealism supposed to prove that *there really are* objects distinct from and independent of oneself or that *we must conceive* objects *as* being distinct from and independent of oneself? Guyer, whose analysis of Kant's argument I have largely followed, is less than clear on this point. In the next-to-last passage quoted in the previous section, he says:

> The objects which function in subjective time-determination must indeed be external to or independent of the self, objects conceived of as ontologically distinct from the self.

But, of course, it is one thing to say that the objects "must indeed *be* external to or independent of the self" and another to say that they must be "*conceived of as* ontologically distinct from the self." The same ambiguity is present in the following passage:

> Objects distinct from the empirical self . . . are necessary because their *causal* role in determining the sequence of representations of them . . . can be fulfilled *only* by objects distinct from the self. It is the epistemological function of objects conceived to be distinct from the self but capable of acting on it . . . that makes such objects indispensable for subjective time-determination.[26]

Here, again, one is struck by Guyer's shift from "objects *distinct* from the self" to "objects *conceived to be distinct* from the self." On the whole, however, it seems that Guyer favors the "conceived as" distinct/independent reading, for in summarizing what he takes to be Kant's achievement in the Refutation of Idealism, he says such things as the following:

> On [Kant's] argument these objects *must be regarded as* ontologically independent of these representations and the empirical self . . . because they are enduring but also agents of change which *must be conceived of as* independent of the self upon which they act [my emphasis]. . . .[27]

> Kant has argued that we can make determinate judgments about the temporal course of our own subjective states only if *we interpret such states as* representations of our law-governed interactions with a realm of enduring physical objects distinct from our representations and our empirical selves [my emphasis].[28]

But putting aside the question of what Guyer takes Kant's achievement to be, let us ask: what does Kant's argument really show? Clearly, if the argument is formulated as I have proposed, then it leads validly to this conclusion:

> (7') I know that some of my experiences are caused by successive objective states of affairs that I perceive.

But from this conclusion it follows, not just that I must *conceive* some of my experiences as being caused by successive objective states of affairs that I perceive, but also that some of my experiences *really are* caused by successive objective states of affairs that I perceive. From one point of view, this is a welcome result, for it shows that anyone who grants that she knows the order of her own past experiences is logically committed to the existence of physical objects. Since many external-world skeptics would presumably grant that they can know at least the time-order of their own past experiences, this provides a powerful response to them. But from another point of view, the result is disturbing, for it seems to establish a more robust form of realism than is warranted by (even my "weak" interpretation of) Kant's Transcendental Idealism. If Kant's conclusion were formulated within the framework of weak TI, it would have to read this way:

> (7") I must conceive some of my experiences as being caused by successive objective states of affairs that I perceive.

The difficulty here should not be exaggerated. There is certainly no incompatibility or inconsistency between (7') and (7"). What is odd is only that all of Kant's previous arguments could establish only conclusions in the vein of (7"), whereas suddenly, in the Refutation of Idealism, he seems to argue for a conclusion that breaks out of the self-imposed limits set by his Transcendental Idealism (even on the "weak" reading of it).

I will conclude this chapter by sketching two responses to this difficulty. One response, which you may well have anticipated in light of earlier discussions in this book, is that the difference between (7′) and (7″) does not matter. For according to weak TI, we cannot intelligibly suppose that things might be different from the ways we must conceive them; so establishing (7″) is neither more nor less significant than establishing (7′).

But Kant could give a further response—one that stems from the fact that it is quite possible to be a skeptic even about knowledge of the order of one's own past experiences. Bertrand Russell once suggested that he might have been born only five minutes ago, with a whole set of false memories. In a somewhat similar vein, we can suppose that the real order of our past experiences might be completely different from the order that we now assign to them—that the latter might be a thoroughly scrambled version of the former. To accommodate this kind of skepticism, the *opening* premise of Kant's Refutation of Idealism would have to be reformulated. It could no longer say that

(1′) I can usually correctly determine the order in time of my own subjective experiences

where this means that I can usually *know* this order. Rather, it would have to say that

(1″) I usually *seem* to be able correctly to determine the order in time of my own subjective experiences.

Furthermore, the rest of the argument would have to be reworked to conform to this revised premise, as follows:

(2″) When I remember two or more past experiences, my recollection of those experiences usually does not itself reveal the order in which they seem to me to have occurred.

(3″) If (2″), then I cannot usually determine the order in which in my own subjective experiences seem to me to have occurred just by recollecting those experiences.

(4″) I cannot usually determine the order in which my own subjective experiences seem to have occurred just by recollecting those experiences [from (2″) and (3″)].

(5″) If I cannot usually determine the order in which my own subjective experiences seem to have occurred just by recollecting those experiences, then I can usually seem to be able correctly to determine the order in time of my own subjective experiences only if I conceive some of my experiences as being caused by successive objective states of affairs that I perceive.

(6″) I can usually seem to be able correctly to determine the order in time of my own subjective experiences only if I conceive some of my experiences as being caused by perceived states of affairs that I perceive and that occur in determinate temporal relations [from (4″) and (5″)].

(7″) I conceive some of my experiences as being caused by successive objective states of affairs that I perceive [from (1″) and (6″)].

As worded, the conclusion of this argument may seem disappointing, for it fails to say that I *must* so conceive my experiences. But the force of the argument is better seen by looking back at its previous step, (6″). For (6″) means that in order to be able to do as little as to seem usually to be able correctly to determine the order in time of my own subjective experiences, I have to conceive some of my experiences as being caused by successive objective states of affairs that I perceive. Thus, it is quite legitimate to say that Kant has shown that I *must* conceive some of my experiences in this way, where the "must" indicates that my so conceiving them is a necessary condition of my being able to do something that I unquestionably can do. Kant's Refutation of Idealism, then, seems to succeed in showing that even if one is skeptical about knowledge of the order of one's own past experiences, as long as it is granted that one at least seems to be able to assign a determinate order to them, one must conceive of them as experiences of an objective world.

Appendix

The Schematism

Between the Transcendental Deduction and the long chapter on the "System of all Principles of Pure Understanding" into which Kant packs the Axioms of Intuition, Anticipations of Perception, Analogies of Experience, Postulates of Empirical Thought, and Refutation of Idealism, he inserts a chapter entitled "The Schematism of the Pure Concepts of the Understanding." I briefly described the schematism in section 3.3.1 but did not discuss it in detail, mainly because (a) the material that is relevant to the central argument of the analytic is limited and presented to better effect in portions of the *Critique* that come both before and after the schematism (notably the Aesthetic and the Analogies), and (b) the schematism intertwines this material with other themes not strictly relevant to the central argument. So discussing the schematism at an earlier stage would have both interrupted the flow of an already complex line of argument and prevented us from appealing to certain ideas in terms of which the schematism itself is best understood. In addition, the schematism is an especially obscure and difficult chapter, where Kant's language is at its most cryptic and figurative. It is also highly controversial; some commentators regard it as a useless artifact of Kant's architectonic, although others think it addresses a fundamental issue.[1]

In the schematism, Kant raises and tries to solve a problem concerning the application of the categories. To see what this problem is, let us start by asking a question about concepts in general. The question is this: what justifies us in applying a given concept to particular instances, for example, the concept 'dog' to dogs or the concept 'plate' to plates? Plainly what justifies us in so doing can only be the existence of some special relationship between a concept and its instances. So the more basic question is: what is the relationship between a concept and the instances to which it is applied? One traditional answer to this basic question, often attributed to John Locke, is that the relation is pictorial: the concept pictures each of its various instances. On this view, the concept must be treated as a (mental) picture or image of its instances. However, to depict each of its many different instances, this image must not be too specific. The concept of a (nondisfigured) man, for example, may depict its instances as having two legs and feet, two arms and hands, two eyes and two ears, and so on. But it cannot depict him as having red hair, green eyes, and freckles because then it would not depict a blond, blue-eyed, and fair-skinned man or a black man or an Asian man. So the image associated with the term "man" must have a certain kind of generality; it must be generic or (to point in the direction of Kant's term, "schema") schematic. Accordingly, Locke calls it a *general idea* or, sometimes, an *abstract idea*.

This view, however, was trenchantly criticized by Locke's successor in the line of British empiricists, George Berkeley. In a famous passage in the Introduction to his *Treatise Concerning the Principles of Human Knowledge*, Berkeley quotes the following passage from Locke:

> *Abstract ideas* are not so obvious or easy to children or the yet unexercised mind as particular ones. If they seem so to grown men, it is only because by constant and familiar use they are made so. For when we nicely reflect upon them, we shall find that general ideas are fictions and contrivances of the mind, that carry difficulty with them, and do not so easily offer themselves, as we are apt to imagine. For example, does it not require some pains and skill to form the general idea of a triangle (which is yet none of the most abstract comprehensive and difficult) for it must be neither oblique nor rectangle, neither equilateral, equicrural, nor scalenon, but *all and none* of these at once. In effect, it is something imperfect that cannot exist, an idea wherein some parts of several different and *inconsistent* ideas are put together.[2]

Berkeley then retorts:

> If any man has the faculty of framing in his mind such an idea of a triangle as is here described, it is vain to pretend to dispute him out of it, nor would I go about it. All I desire is, that the reader would fully and certainly inform himself whether he has such an idea or no. And this, methinks, can be no hard task for any one to perform. What more easy than for any one to look a little into his own thoughts, and there try whether he has, or can attain to have, an idea that shall correspond with the description that is here given of the general idea of a triangle, which is, *neither oblique, nor rectangle, equilateral, equicrural, not scalenon, but all and none of these at once?*[3]

Berkeley's argument is this: if a concept is an image of its instances, then the concept of a triangle must be an image of a triangle that is at once oblique and not oblique, right-angled and not right-angled, equilateral and not equilateral, equicrural and not equicrural, scalene and not scalene, and so on, for only so could this single concept represent all these different kinds of triangle. But there cannot be such an image, containing incompatible elements. So a concept cannot be an image of its instances.

It is not necessary for us to determine here whether Berkeley's criticism is fair to Locke, or even correct in its own terms. But we should take note of Berkeley's own proposed answer to the question of how a concept relates to its instances since it helps to set the stage for Kant's answer. Berkeley does not reject the view that the relation is a pictorial one; in fact he embraces it even more definitely than Locke. But Berkeley claims that a single, absolutely determinate "idea" can serve the function of representing many different instances. Thus, for example, the idea of an equilateral triangle can serve to represent right triangles, scalene triangles, equicrural triangles, and so on. Berkeley argues for this claim by saying that when a geometer demonstrates truths about triangles, for example, that their three angles equal 180 degrees, the geometer can ignore the question of whether the figure by reference to which the demonstration is carried out is right-angled, scalene, equicrural, and so forth. The idea of the equilateral triangle can serve as a "sign" for any other triangle because many (though, of course, not all) truths that apply to it also apply to all other triangles.[4]

Berkeley's successor in the line of British empiricists, Hume, takes us still closer to Kant. Hume approves of Berkeley's view that an absolutely determinate idea can acquire a general significance, but he adds the point that the general term that calls such an idea to mind also serves to revive in our minds, or stimulates our minds to produce, other resembling but equally determinate ideas answering to the same term. Thus, if the term "triangle" calls to my mind an equilateral triangle, it also stimulates my mind to form ideas of all manner of other triangles. In a recent book on Hume, Don Garrett gives a lucid summary of Hume's view:

> Hume rejects Locke's theory of abstract ideas, in favor of a theory according to which "all general ideas are nothing but particular ones, annexed to a certain term, which gives them a more extensive signification." Upon noticing a certain resemblance among objects, Hume claims, we apply a single term to them all, notwithstanding their differences. This term is directly associated with the determinate idea of a particular instance. That determinate idea nevertheless achieves a general *signification*—and hence *serves as* an abstract idea—because the term also revives the "custom" or disposition to call up ideas of other particular instances. I will call this appropriate set of ideas of particular instances associated with a general term its "revival set." We are especially disposed to call up ideas of counterexamples (if we can find them) to claims that employ the term whenever we encounter such claims in the course of reasoning. Thus, for example, noticing a certain resemblance among a number of shapes, one calls them all "triangles." A particular occurrence of this term brings to mind the idea of a particular triangle, say an equilateral triangle, and *revives the custom* of calling up other ideas of triangles (the revival set) as needed. And if someone claims that all triangles have three sides of equal length, then although one's idea of an equilateral triangle does not itself happen to provide a counterexample, one will quickly find an idea of, say, a right triangle coming to mind, and one will therefore be able to reject the original claim.[5]

Kant was aware of the difficulty that Berkeley had raised for Locke's view of abstract ideas. Echoing Berkeley, Kant writes:

> No image could ever be adequate to the concept of a triangle in general. It would never attain that universality of the concept which renders it valid of all triangles, whether right-angled, obtuse-angled, or acute-angled; it would always be limited to only part of this sphere. (A 141/B 180)

Yet as did Berkeley and Hume, Kant seeks to retain the view that an empirical concept like that of a dog, or even a mathematical one like the concept of a triangle, cannot be defined except by reference to an image or picture. Thus in the same paragraph as the previous passage, he writes:

> The concept 'dog' signifies a rule according to which my imagination can delineate the figure of a four-footed animal in a general manner, without limitation to any single determinate figure such as experience, or any possible image that I can represent *in concreto*, actually presents. (A 141/B 180)

How does this view differ from Locke's? The most important difference is the reference to a *rule*: for Kant the concept is not an image but rather a rule for generating an image or images. In this respect Kant's view resembles Hume's view because the latter implies that a concept would have to be a tendency or disposition of the mind (when suitably affected) to produce an image or images. A rule that the imagination follows in generating images is very much like a disposition or tendency of the mind to generate images. What is less clear is whether Kant agrees with Berkeley and Hume that the images generated must be entirely determinate, or whether he retains Locke's view that they are to a certain extent indeterminate, or "general." It would be nice to be able to say that for Kant the images generated by the imagination in accordance with a rule must be absolutely determinate since this would make Kant's view immune to Berkeley's criticism and very similar to Hume's view. But the language of the above passage suggests that for Kant the image has a certain generality, making it more akin to a Lockean abstract idea.

Be that as it may, Kant has his own special term for the kind of rule just described—"schema":

> This representation of a universal procedure of imagination in providing an image for a concept, I call the schema of this concept. (A 140/B 179–180)

Jonathan Bennett says that, "the nasty phrase 'representation of a universal procedure' just means 'rule'"; I think this is right.[6] In the same vein, Henry Allison interprets Kant's last-cited remark as meaning that the schemata of mathematical and empirical concepts are "rules for the construction of images."[7]

How, then, does a schema differ from a concept? In the case of empirical concepts and even certain mathematical ones such as those of geometry, there is no difference. Kant's own example of the concept 'dog' bears this out since he characterizes that concept as "a rule according to which my imagination can delineate the figure of a four-footed animal in a general manner," which is exactly what the schema of the concept 'dog' would have to be, given that a schema is "a universal procedure of imagination in providing an image for a concept" and that this just means "a rule of imagination in providing an image for a concept." What Kant says about the thought of a "number" in general (presumably, the general concept of a number), although his language is very difficult, likewise suggests that in this case concept and schema are identical: "this thought is . . . the representation of a method whereby a multiplicity, for instance a thousand, may be represented in an image in conformity with a certain concept, rather than the image itself" (A 140/B 179).

It is crucial to notice that for Kant the schema is the only thing that preserves a pictorial relationship, if only in an attenuated sense, between a concept and its instances. Given that a concept is, as Kant insists, not itself an image, then if it were not at least a rule for the generation of an image or images, there would be no basis at all for saying that the relation between a concept and its instances is pictorial. Therefore, absent some other way to characterize the relation between a concept and its instances, Kant would have no answer at all to the basic question of what is the relationship between a concept and the instances to which it is applied. By the same token, he would have no answer to the question we began with, of what justifies us in applying a given concept to instances since what can so justify us can only be the existence of some special relationship between a concept and its instances.

This key point, however, raises a fundamental problem regarding the categories or pure concepts. Unlike the empirical concept of a dog or the geometrical concept of a triangle, a pure concept like substance or cause or necessity is not a rule for the generation of any image. As Kant puts it, "the schema of a *pure* concept of the understanding can never be brought into any image whatsoever" (A 142/B 181). His language here does not do justice to the seriousness of the problem he faces. The problem is that in the case of the pure concepts, it seems that there is nothing that could count as their schemata. For example, there seems to be nothing at all that is picturable in a causal relationship or a substance (as distinct from its properties) or a modality since none of these can be perceived or "intuited" in Kant's sense. As Lauchlan Chipman says,

> There is nothing something must look like if it is to look like a cause or a possibility. . . . One can call something a dog because of what it looks like—it presents a doggish appearance—but one cannot call something a cause because it presents a cause-ish appearance![8]

But if the pure concepts have no schemata—if they cannot be "schematized"—then Kant has no account at all of how these all-important concepts relate to their instances. By the same token, he would have no account of what justifies applying these concepts to a manifold of intuitions.

To avoid this consequence, Kant maintains that appearances to the contrary notwithstanding, there is something that qualifies as schemata for pure concepts. But this something cannot, as in the case of empirical and geometrical concepts, be identical with the concept, for it cannot be a rule for the generation of any images. Instead, it must be a "third thing," distinct from, yet appropriately related to, both the pure concepts and the intuitions to which they are applied.

Before considering what this third thing is, let us look at how Kant himself states the problem we have just described. He does so in highly figurative language that has been much criticized but that should be more understandable in light of the above discussion. Kant begins by asserting that in order for a concept to be applicable to intuition, it must have something in common with it. Concept and intuition must be, as he puts it, "homogeneous." For instance, when I apply the concept circular to a plate, the same roundness that is thought in the concept can be exhibited in the intuition; so there is no special problem about the application of the concept. In the case of a pure concept, on the other hand, there is a problem, for the pure concept has no sensible content whatever: it is utterly heterogeneous from intuition. This raises the question "How, then, is the *subsump-tion* of intuitions under pure concepts, the *application* of a category to appearances, possible?" (A 138/B 177).

The answer, Kant says, is obvious: "Obviously, there must be some third thing, which is homogeneous on the one hand with the category, and on the other hand with the appearance, and which thus makes the application of the former to the latter possible" (A 138/B 177). This third thing must be "homogeneous" with the pure category in being *intellectual*. And it must be "homogeneous" with appearances in being *sensible*. So it must have both an intellectual and a sensible aspect; only thus can it bridge the gap between understanding and sensibility. We must, then, find something that is in one respect like a category and in one respect like appearances. This something will be called the transcendental schema. What is this something?

Kant's answer is that each schema of a category is what he calls a "determination of time," for time is "homogeneous" with both pure concepts and appearances. It is "homogeneous" with appearances in that all appearances are in time, as the form of inner sense. As we first learned in the Aesthetic and as Kant emphasizes throughout much of the Analytic, all of our sensible representations occur in time. Kant's reason for saying that time is homogeneous with pure concepts is highly obscure. He says that "a transcendental determination of time is so far homogeneous with the category, which constitutes its unity, in that it is universal and rests upon an *a priori* rule" (A 138/B 177–178). But if we look at the categories in light of what Kant says about them both in the Metaphysical Deduction and in the "Principles" chapter, then we can cut through his difficult language.

Let us consider first the categories of relation since they provide the best illustration of what Kant is trying to say. This is especially true for the category of causality, so let us start with that. We know from the Second Analogy that every event that we could ever observe is supposed to have a cause, which means that the pure concept of causality must be applicable in an untold number of cases. That the concept of causality must be applicable in indefinitely many cases shows the importance of schematism: surely we need some account of the relation between the concept of cause and the intuitions that are its instances if we are to understand how the category applies to the intuitions. But the concept of cause that was extracted from the hypothetical form of judgment in the Metaphysical Deduction is highly abstract. It is just the notion of a ground and its consequent, or of "becauseness." As already mentioned, there is nothing picturable in this notion; it is certainly not an image or, more to the point, even a rule for the production of any images. In virtue of what, then, can it stand in any kind of pictorial relation at all to its instances? Kant's answer is that it can do so by being interpreted in *temporal* terms, specifically, in terms of one kind of state of affairs always being succeeded in time by another. Now, succession in time can certainly be called a "determination of time" or a "time determination," and by extension, so can regular succession in time. But bare succession in time is not itself anything picturable and, by extension, neither is regular succession in time. However, particular states of affairs can enter into relations of succession in time, and *their* succession in time is picturable as is, by extension, their regular succession in time. For as Hume pointed out, the relation consisting of a state of affairs of kind A being always followed in time by a state of affairs of kind B is an *observable* relation. Thus, although the schema of the pure concept of cause can "never itself be brought into any image whatsoever," it can be *exhibited* by states of affairs standing in observable relations of succession. We can also say that these successive states of affairs *conform* to this schema. By contrast, the bare concept of cause—ground-consequence or "becauseness"—cannot be so exhibited: on being asked to spot cases of "becauseness" apart from any temporal relation whatsoever, we simply would not know what to look for. Likewise, on being asked what, apart from any temporal relation, conforms to or can be subsumed under this concept, we would not know what to answer. These observations, I suggest, justify Kant in holding that the pure concept of cause applies to its instances only by virtue of its schema and that this schema can be defined as a determination of time, namely, as "succession of the manifold, in so far as that succession is subject to a rule" (A 144/B 183). They also explain Kant's talk of "homogeneity" in the case of causality: the schema *succession of the manifold according to a rule* is "homogeneous" with intuition because it is a temporal relation and all intuitions occur in time (have time as their "form"), and also because it can be exhibited only in intuition. It is "homogeneous" with the pure category of cause in the sense that it is a reasonable way to interpret in experiential terms the abstract notion of ground-consequence or "becauseness."[9]

Next, let us consider the category of substance. As a *pure* concept extracted from the categorical form of judgment, it is simply the idea of "something which can exist as subject but never as predicate" (B 149). It is something to which properties can be attributed but which cannot itself be attributed to anything else. But again, there is nothing picturable in this notion; it is neither an image nor even a rule for the production of any images. In virtue of what, then, can it stand in any kind of pictorial relation at all to its instances? Kant's answer is, again, that it can do so by being interpreted in *temporal* terms, specifically, as "permanence of the real in time" (A 143/B 188). Now, of course, bare permanence in time is not picturable, for it cannot be perceived or "intuited," if only because time itself cannot be perceived. However, as Kant argues in the First Analogy, a permanent thing can serve as a perceptually accessible stand-in for time. It can thus exhibit "permanence of the real in time," in somewhat the same way as observable states of affairs occurring in regular succession exhibit succession according to a rule. We have seen that it is questionable whether Kant has shown that this permanent must be absolutely permanent; perhaps the stand-in for time is nothing other than a system of relatively permanent things. Nevertheless, if we grant that permanence of the real in time is both (a) something that can be exhibited in experience and (b) a reasonable interpretation of the abstract notion of substance, then Kant seems justified in holding that the pure concept of substance applies to its instances in virtue of its schema and that this schema can be defined as a determination of time, namely, as the at least relatively permanent existence of "real" things. And again, some sense is made of his talk of "homogeneity": the schema *permanence of the real in time* is "homogeneous" with intuition because it is a temporal characteristic that can be exhibited only in intuition, and it is "homogeneous" with the pure category because it is a reasonable way to interpret in experiential terms the abstract notion of something that can be a subject but never a predicate. For if everything in our experience altered as frequently as do "predicates" or properties, then it seems that there would be no basis for regarding anything as a subject of properties rather than as a mere property.

Kant says that the schema of the third category of relation—causal reciprocity—is "the co-existence, according to a rule, of the determinations of the one substance with those of the other" (A 144/B 183). It is clear enough that the category of reciprocity needs some schema because "mutual becauseness" is no more picturable than "becauseness." Furthermore, just as regular succession in time (succession "according to a rule") may well strike us as a reasonable way to interpret "becauseness" in experiential terms, and permanence as a reasonable way to interpret "being something that can be a subject but never a predicate" in experiential terms, so rule-governed coexistence may strike us as a reasonable way to interpret "mutual becauseness" in experiential terms. This way of interpreting "mutual becauseness" seems especially natural if we bear in mind the argument of the Third Analogy, which illustrates the point that some of what Kant says in the schematism chapter is best understood in light of things that he says in later parts of the *Critique*.

The schematism of the categories of quantity and quality is unrelated to the central argument of the Analytic and is even more difficult to grasp than that of the categories of relation, but I shall discuss it briefly. In the case of quantity, Kant offers only one schema corresponding to all three categories (unity, plurality, totality), just as he offers only one principle (the Axioms of Intuition) for all three. He says that this schema is *number*: "the pure schema of magnitude (*quantitatis*), as a concept of the understanding, is *number*, a representation which comprises the successive addition of homogeneous units" (A 142/B 182). This needs to be interpreted in light of what Kant says later about the Axioms of Intuition, and the reader is urged to review the account that I gave in the penultimate paragraph of 3.3.1. The problem, again, is to specify something that is empirically observable, and therefore also at least in a general way picturable, corresponding to the abstract categories of unity, plurality, and totality and to the universal, particular, and singular forms of judgment from which Kant derives them. I suggest that if we think of Kant's invocation of number as a reference to *countability* or *numerability*, then what he is saying makes sense. We cannot distinguish among all the dogs in the world, some of the dogs in the world, and a single dog, unless we can count or enumerate dogs. As for Kant's implication that number, being the schema of a pure concept, must be a determination of time, I have already suggested that this is implausible. However, if we think of number here as signifying countability or numerability, then Kant's view becomes a bit more understandable (albeit rather artificial) since counting is a process that takes place in time.

Under the heading of quality, Kant again offers only one schema corresponding to the three categories (reality, negation, limitation), just as he offers only one principle (the Anticipations of Perception) for all three. He begins by connecting reality and negation (he simply ignores limitation) with time by saying that reality is what "fills time" whereas negation leaves it empty: "The opposition of these two rests upon the distinction of one and the same time as filled and as empty" (A 143/B 182). The rest of what he says needs to be interpreted in light of the Anticipations of Perception. As we have seen, the pivotal notion of the Anticipations is that of the intensive magnitude or degree of all sensations. Kant now connects the categories of reality and negation (again, he ignores limitation) with the intensity of a sensation in the following way: the more intense a sensation is, the more reality it exhibits; the less intense it is, the more its reality approaches to negation, or not-being. This presupposes that there is a possible gradation of any sensation from very intense (Kant mentions no upper bound) "down to its cessation in nothingness (= 0 = *negatio*)" (A 143/B 182). Furthermore, since no single sensation can have two different degrees at the same moment of time, this gradation can actually occur in experience only over a stretch of time. Accordingly, Kant says:

> The schema of a reality, as the quantity of something in so far as it fills time, is just this continuous and uniform production of that reality in time as we successively descend from a sensation which has a certain degree to its vanishing point, or progressively ascend from its negation to some magnitude of it. (A 143/B 183)

What Kant has said here makes sense verbally, but one may wonder whether it adds anything of importance to the doctrine we discussed approvingly in connection with the Anticipations of Perception, namely, that every sensation has a degree or intensive magnitude. One may also wonder whether the categories of reality and negation are not sufficiently "schematized"—given some sort of pictorial interpretation—simply by being connected with the intensity of sensation. But perhaps Kant could reply that since the schema of reality cannot be any particular or determinate degree of intensity, it must be, as the above passage suggests, a *continuum* of degrees of intensity.

In the case of the categories of modality, it is difficult to see why schematism is even needed, whether we look at (a) the forms of judgment that employ those categories or at (b) the principles associated with them (the "Postulates of Empirical Thought"). Regarding (a), recall Kant's point that whether a judgment is problematic, assertoric, or apodictic "contributes nothing to the content of the judgment" (A 74/B 100) but pertains only to the judgment maker's attitude toward the judgment. If this is so, then it does not seem that the notions of possibility/impossibility, existence/nonexistence, and necessity/contingency that Kant extracts from the modalities of judgments, and which up to that point get their meaning solely from those modalities, are concepts that relate to certain instances in any kind of pictorial manner. Rather, they simply pertain to the attitude one holds toward the application of a concept to something, toward the linkage of two or more concepts in a proposition, or toward the linkage of two or more propositions to each other.

Regarding (b), recall that the Postulates of Empirical Thought are really definitions of empirical or real (as opposed to merely logical) possibility, of actuality, and of empirical or real (as opposed to merely logical) necessity. As such, do they employ concepts needing schematization, in the way that, say, the principle of causality employs the concept of cause? Kant thinks so, for he does offer three separate schemata: for the concept invoked by the First Postulate (possibility), he offers "agreement of the synthesis of representations with the conditions of time in general; for the Second (actuality), "existence in some determinate time"; for the Third (necessity), "existence of an object at all times" (A 144–145/B 184). Paul Guyer suggests that the schematization of actuality is unproblematic.[10] This seems right, for if a thing is actual in the sense of the First Postulate—that is, actually perceived or caused by something actually perceived—then it does exist at some time or other and that fact is perceivable and so "picturable" in the sense required by the schematism. On the other hand, as Guyer goes on to argue, the schematization of possibility and of necessity both run into difficulty. For the former arbitrarily singles out time since, according to Kant's own doctrine of possibility in the Postulates, a thing must conform not only to the form of time but also to that of space and to the conditions laid down by all the other categories.[11] The latter, on the other hand, fails to connect with the notion of real or empirical necessity that concerns Kant in the Third Postulate, according to which the necessary is what is governed by causal laws. Instead, the schematization of necessity as existence at all times seems to be derived from the traditional, rationalistic notion of a being whose existence is necessary and therefore eternal.[12] Not only is this notion completely different from that of being governed by causal laws, but also it is a notion that Kant himself holds cannot be proved to apply to anything since it is not a necessary condition of experience. I must agree with Guyer, then, that "Kant seems to have no justification for equating the schema of necessity with existence at all times."[13]

We have seen that the primary rationale for Kant's theory of schematism is to explain what justifies us in applying pure concepts to particular instances: it is that the schema of a pure concept can, in a suitably qualified, attenuated, and indeed "schematic" sense, be said to pictorially represent the concept's instances. This is most clearly true in the case of cause, where states of affairs occurring in regular succession can be said to exhibit or conform to the schema, *succession according to a rule*, despite the fact that bare succession cannot itself be "brought into any image whatever." Kant, however, has another reason for introducing schemata, one that relates to the broader aspects of his Critical Philosophy and which I want to describe very briefly by way of conclusion.

As we have seen, although Kant denies that we can have any knowledge of a nonempirical reality, he does not deny that the existence of such a reality is a legitimate and even inevitable human concern. In particular, he thinks that we must postulate the existence of God and of a free and immortal human soul in order to do justice to our moral convictions. This requires that we be able at least to *think* or *conceive* of God, freedom, and immortality, even if we cannot show that they exist. But if the most fundamental categories in terms of which we must conceptualize anything apply only to objects of possible experience, then how can we even think or speak intelligibly about a nonempirical reality? Kant's solution is to distinguish between the bare, "unschematized" categories and the schematized categories. Although only the schematized categories apply to experience and yield *a priori* knowledge of its structure, the bare, unschematized categories are not entirely without meaning, for by means of them, we can at least think of God and of the free immortal soul. For example, consider once again the category of cause.

As a bare, unschematized form of thought, it is just the idea of ground and consequence. This highly abstract idea cannot be related to experienced instances unless it is interpreted in terms of temporal succession according to a rule—unless
it is "schematized." But even in its bare, unschematized form, it has enough content for us to be able to think by its means of an ultimate ground or ultimate
explanation of all being, that is, of God. Or consider the category of substance. As
an unschematized form of thought, it is just the idea of a subject that cannot be
predicated of anything. This highly abstract idea can be related to experienced
instances only by being interpreted in terms of permanence of something in time.
But Kant maintains that even apart from such an interpretation, it has enough
content so that by its means we can think of an ultimate subject of properties,
such as the soul. Thus, the theory of schematism allows Kant to say that although
we cannot know God, Immortality or Freedom, still we are entitled to postulate
them. If Kant believed that any attempt to use pure concepts outside the field of
experience were wholly meaningless or nonsensical, then he would have to admit
that these postulates are meaningless and nonsensical, which he refuses to do, if
only because he thinks they are necessary conditions of morality. Thus the theory
of schematism is an essential part of the Critical Philosophy as a whole.[14]

Notes

Chapter 1

This chapter should be read along with the Introduction of the *Critique of Pure Reason*. If you are reading the *Critique* for the first time, it is suggested that you also read the Preface to the first edition.

1. The extent to which Hume is a skeptic is a controversial question among Hume scholars. But Kant certainly sees Hume as a skeptic, or at least as a thinker whose position inevitably leads to skepticism.

2. Derk Pereboom insightfully suggests (in correspondence) that fundamentally, *a priori* signifies "*justified* independently of experience." For ease of exposition, I shall nevertheless stick with the more common definition of the *a priori* as pertaining to knowledge (I do assume that knowing that *p* entails being justified in believing that *p*; see note 4 below).

3. Stephan Körner, *Kant* (Hardmondsworth, Eng.: Penguin, 1955), p. 18.

4. The close relationship between the first statement and the second stems from the fact that, as epistemologists generally recognize, justification is a necessary condition for propositional knowledge; that is, "S knows that *p*" entails "S is justified in believing that *p*." Thus, the "close relationship" between the two statements is that the first entails the second.

5. Kant's explanation of why "a body is extended" is *a priori*, in terms of the predicate "extended" being extracted from the subject "body" in accordance with the principle of contradiction, rests on his notion of an analytic proposition, to be explained below. The point to note for now is simply the one about the impossibility of resting the necessity of "a body is extended" on experience.

6. Saul Kripke, *Naming and Necessity* (Cambridge, Mass.: Harvard University Press, 1980), pp. 128–129.

7. The *locus classicus* of Quine's attack on the analytic/synthetic distinction is his "Two Dogmas of Empiricism," in Willard Van Orman Quine, *From a Logical Point of View; 9 Logico-Philosophical Essays* (Cambridge, Mass.: Harvard University Press, 1953), pp. 20–46. One of the many responses to Quine is H. P. Grice and P. F. Strawson, "In

Defense of a Dogma," *The Philosophical Review* 65 (1956): 141–158. For a bibliography that lists many works relevant to this issue, see Paul K. Moser, ed., *A Priori Knowledge* (Oxford: Oxford University Press, 1987), pp. 210–219.

8. The standard example of an analytic statement is "all bachelors are unmarried males." However, since, as the text goes on to indicate, the statement's analyticity is supposed to stem from its being a definition, and since neither male infants nor male nonhumans are bachelors, "all bachelors are unmarried men" would be a better example. However, as Derk Pereboom observes (in correspondence): "Maybe Roman Catholic priests are not bachelors. Perhaps 'bachelor' has the sense of eligibility." I think this is right, and so I have modified the standard example even further.

9. David Hume, *Treatise of Human Nature*, 2nd ed., ed. Lewis A. Selby-Bigge and Peter H. Niditch (Oxford: Oxford University Press, [1748] 1975), p. 82. I have slightly modified the wording of Hume's example; he has "every husband has a wife" instead of "every husband is married."

10. It must be admitted that this passage is not decisive since the propositions Kant cited may be reformulated as subject-predicate ones: "All wholes obtained by adding equals to equals are equal"; "All remainders obtained by subtracting equals from equals are equal."

11. One could also say that analytic judgments provide information about *conceptual* reality, but for simplicity's sake I do not here distinguish between linguistic and conceptual reality. The crucial point is the negative one that analytic judgments provide no information about anything other than meanings of words or relations between concepts.

12. Epistemologists generally accept the principle that "S knows that *p*" entails that *p* is true as an analytic truth turning on the meaning of "knows"—that is, as a conceptual truth about knowledge. According to this "truth-condition" (as it is called) for knowledge, one cannot *know* things that aren't so (e.g., that the earth is flat), though of course this does not mean that one cannot *believe* such things. Statements that seem to violate this principle, for example, "Little Johnny just knows that there is a tiger under his bed," are regarded either as simply false or as employing a nonstandard or deviant sense of the term "knows."

13. It is commonly assumed that David Hume's "relations of ideas" are coextensive with 1's and that his "matters of fact" are coextensive with 4's. For reasons given in my *Hume's Epistemology and Metaphysics: An Introduction* (London: Routledge, 1998), pp. 49–55, I believe that this assumption is mistaken.

14. For a more nuanced treatment of this point, see ibid., pp. 46–48.

15. Ibid., pp. 49–55, I argue that even this weaker form of empiricism must be qualified to avoid a self-refutational problem analogous to the one that vitiates logical positivism.

16. This is not to say that he has nothing to say about such cases, as can be seen from his chapter on "schematism" (discussed in the appendix of this book).

17. For the sake of emphasis, I slightly oversimplify things here. Kant also has at least one other "background" constraint in mind, namely, that the explanation must not appeal to some supernatural claim, such as that God stamps the knowledge of synthetic *a priori* truths on our minds. The essential point, as I go on to say in the text, is that Kant does not require that we have independent evidence for the *explanans*.

18. Kant first raised this question in a famous letter to his pupil, Marcus Herz, in 1772. The key portion of the letter is quoted in Robert Paul Wolff, *Kant's Theory of Mental Activity: A Commentary on the Transcendental Analytic of the Critique of Pure Reason* (Magnolia, Mass.: Peter Smith, [1963] 1990), pp. 22–23.

19. Immanuel Kant, *Prolegomena to any Future Metaphysics*, ed. Beryl Logan (London: Routledge, 1996), p. 33.

20. In an unpublished paper, "A Last Shot at Hume's Reminder," Rolf George ques-

tions whether Kant's "dogmatic slumber" remark really refers to Hume's critique of the causal principle, on the ground that this critique appears only in Hume's *A Treatise of Human Nature*, which Kant could not have read because he could not read English and the *Treatise* had not yet been translated into German. George argues that the remark refers instead to Kant's realization, based on arguments Hume gives in his *Enquiry Concerning Human Understanding*, which Kant had read in German translation, that certain "conservation principles" are untenable. However, as George also points out, Kant was no doubt familiar with Hume's position on the causal principle in the *Treatise* because he had access to a synopsis of it in the German edition of a work by Beattie and because it was a topic of discussion among Kant's English-speaking friends. I therefore do not think that George has refuted the standard view that Kant's remark refers, or at least refers in part, to Hume's critique of the causal principle.

21. As previously indicated, I will later argue that there is reason to doubt that (the constructive part of) Kant's project can really be reduced to proving the possibility of synthetic *a priori* judgments, but the present characterization of a progressive argument is a good enough approximation for now.

Chapter 2

This chapter is intended to be read along with the Preface to the second edition (especially B vii–B xxxi) and the Transcendental Aesthetic of the *Critique*.

1. H. J. Paton, *Kant's Metaphysics of Experience*, vol. 1 (London: George Allen & Unwin [1936] 1970), p. 166. See also p. 143n.

2. Peter F. Strawson, *The Bounds of Sense: An Essay on Kant's* Critique of Pure Reason (London: Routledge, [1966] 1990), p. 38.

3. The analysis that follows is based, in a manner that involves some simplification but, I believe, no distortion, on Stephen F. Barker, "Geometry" (pp. 286–287 and pp. 288–290, especially pp. 288–289) in Paul Edwards, ed., *The Encyclopedia of Philosophy*, vol. 3 (New York; Macmillan, 1967), pp. 285–290.

4. In A there are five arguments, but the third one is an earlier version of the argument that Kant presents in B as the "Transcendental Exposition of the Concept of Space," which I have already discussed under the rubric "Argument from Geometry."

5. Henry E. Allison, *Kant's Transcendental Idealism* (New Haven, Conn.: Yale University Press, 1983), pp. 83, 85. Allison points out that for Kant, space also serves as a means for representing objects as distinct *from each other*.

6. Paul Guyer, *Kant and the Claims of Knowledge* (Cambridge: Cambridge University Press, 1987), p. 346.

7. The Allison-Guyer interpretation is disputed in Daniel Warren, "Kant and the Apriority of Space," *The Philosophical Review* 107, 2 (April 1988): 179–224. See especially pp. 184–187.

8. Immanuel Kant, *Theoretical Philosophy, 1775–1770*, ed. David Walford and Ralph Meerbote (Cambridge: Cambridge University Press, 1992), p. 395.

9. Strawson, *Bounds of Sense*, pp. 58–59.

10. One major recent commentator who attributes the two-world view to Kant is Guyer in *Kant and the Claims of Knowledge*. A classic English-speaking commentator who interprets Kant in this way is Norman Kemp Smith, *A Commentary on Kant's 'Critique of Pure Reason'* (New York: Humanities Press, [1923] 1962).

11. Probably the most influential proponent of attributing the one-world view to Kant is Allison, *Kant's Transcendental Idealism*. For other references and an in-depth discussion

of the issue, see James Van Cleve, *Problems from Kant* (New York: Oxford University Press, 1999), pp. 143–150.

12. Van Cleve, *Problems from Kant*, p. 135.

13. The quote is from Guyer, *Kant and the Claims of Knowledge*, p. 336.

14. The idea of treating Kant's "synthetic *a priori*" propositions as unobvious analytic truths comes from Jonathan Bennett, *Kant's Analytic* (Cambridge: Cambridge University Press, 1966), pp. 41–44.

15. As far as I can tell, it is possible that Strawson himself would accept thesis (3) as being both constitutive of Kant's position and philosophically tenable, though he does not say so. If he would accept (3), then my reading of Kant is even closer to his than my remarks at the end of section 2.4 suggest.

16. Bennett, *Kant's Analytic*, p. 14.

Chapter 3

This chapter is designed to be read along with the introductory sections (A 50/B 74–A 67/ B 91), with Chapter I of Book I of the Transcendental Analytic ("The Clue to the Discovery of all Pure Concepts of the Understanding"), and with the following three subsections of Chapter II of Book II of the Transcendental Analytic: "Axioms of Intuition," "Anticipations of Perception," and "The Postulates of Empirical Thought" (excluding the "Refutation of Idealism" and "General Note on the System of Principles"). You may find it more efficient to read these three subsections along with their corresponding subsections in this chapter (3.3.1, 3.3.2, and 3.3.4, respectively).

1. In *Kant's Analytic* (Cambridge: Cambridge University Press, 1966), Jonathan Bennett rejects the view that any judgment can be both synthetic and *a priori* (p. 10), and he accordingly proposes to treat *all* of the claims that Kant calls synthetic *a priori* as unobvious analytic or conceptual truths (pp. 42–43). However, he also argues, quite persuasively it seems to me, that one of Kant's most basic principles—that all experience is temporal—is not analytic, and he adds that "it is here [i.e., in connection with the temporality of experience] that one feels most sympathy with Kant's belief that there are extremely basic, not-quite-empirical statements which can be known to hold for all humans" (p. 49). Although he adds immediately that "this is not to allow that such statements can be neatly classed as synthetic and a priori," it is difficult to see why they should not be so classified. But then even if there is only one synthetic *a priori* statement (i.e., the temporality thesis), and that statement serves as a premise in Kant's arguments for the objective validity of some of his categories (which it certainly does, as we shall see later), then the principles associated with those categories cannot be merely unobviously analytic. So, we may have to grant Kant's claim that they are synthetic *a priori* after all.

2. Kant's own name for this argument is "The Deduction of the Pure Concepts of the Understanding."

3. As we will see later, there is a case to be made for saying that the pure concept invoked by "all A's are B's" is totality rather than unity, but I ignore this point for the time being.

4. Justus Hartnack, *Kant's Theory of Knowledge*, trans. M. Holmes Hartshorne (Indianapolis: Hackett, [1967] 2001), p. 33. Hartnack offers an exceptionally clear and sympathetic account of the metaphysical deduction (somewhat of a rarity in recent works on Kant, which tend to downplay the metaphysical deduction because of some of its weaknesses, to be discussed later in this chapter), which I shall draw upon substantially in this chapter.

5. Kant's way of expressing the part of this sentence before the semicolon is "the functions of thought in judgment can be brought under four heads, each of which contains three moments" (A 70/B 95).

6. Here you may want to object to the contrast drawn, on the ground that the class of living things could have an infinite number of members (e.g., if there were extraterrestrial life); at least thinking alone cannot show that it does not. Kant could reply that whereas thinking alone allows that the class of living things *could* be finite, it shows that the complement of any class (i.e., with respect to any class C, the class non-C) *must* be infinite, at least on the assumption that the universe is infinite.

7. Hartnack, *Kant's Theory of Knowledge*, p. 34.

8. Ibid., p. 35.

9. Ibid., p. 42.

10. Kenneth Lucey has pointed out to me that Frege had a symbol for assertion, sometimes called the turnstile, which is a vertical line with a horizontal line extending from the middle to the right.

11. Kant's own example of a hypothetical judgment is "if there is perfect justice, then obstinate evil will be punished," and his example of a disjunctive judgment is "the world exists either through blind chance, or through inner necessity, or through an external cause." As Hartnack points out, however, the first example has "the shortcoming that it is virtually (not to say entirely) a tautology" (*Kant's Theory of Knowledge*, p. 41n); the latter also seems to be analytic (at least given that there is a world).

12. The first two illustrations are adapted from ones given by ibid., pp. 36–37.

13. You may ask why the logical structure of a sentence in the past tense ("Kant *was* German" should be represented in a way ("a is G") that uses the present tense. The reason is that the standard system of modern symbolic logic does not discriminate between past, present, and future tenses; so the copula "is" is neutral with regard to tense, or "tenseless." The same is true of the copula in the classical Aristotelian logic that Kant knew, so that the "is" in "all S is P," for example, is understood tenselessly. There now exist also systems of "tense logic," but we need not go into that here.

14. The variables are "x" and "y"; the quantifiers are "there exists" and "for any." As you may know if you have had a course in symbolic logic, the sentence is symbolized as follows: $(\exists x)[Wx \cdot (y)(Wy \supset y = x) \cdot Gx]$.

15. Symbolized as $G(\textrm{l}x)(Wx)$.

16. This argument can be symbolized as

$$(x)\,(Cx \supset Ax)$$
$$\overline{}$$
$$\therefore\ (x)[(\exists y)(Cy \cdot Hxy) \supset (\exists y)(Ay \cdot Hxy)]$$

17. Peter F. Strawson, *The Bounds of Sense: An Essay on Kant's* Critique of Pure Reason (London: Routledge [1966], 1990, p. 15.

18. In *Kant's Analytic* Bennett interprets the Metaphysical Deduction as attempting to prove that all twelve of Kant's categories are "indispensable," in the sense that all of them are necessary conditions of the possibility of experience. But Kant does not claim that the metaphysical deduction by itself shows that *any* of his categories are in this way "indispensable"; that task is left for the Transcendental Deduction and its continuation in the Principles chapter. Bennett also faults Kant for arguing in the Principles chapter only that the three categories of relation (substance, cause, reciprocity) are necessary conditions of experience (p. 95). Although it is true that the central argument of the Analytic addresses only the categories of relation, I try to show in the present chapter that Kant makes a case for the objective validity of his categories of quantity and quality by proving their corre-

sponding principles, the Axioms of Intuition and the Anticipations of Perception. The principles corresponding to the categories of modality, namely, the three Postulates of Empirical Thought, are really only definitions that do not require proofs.

19. As we will see later, this claim needs qualification, for the *Third* Analogy seems not to depend on the Transcendental Deduction.

20. Hartnack, *Kant's Theory of Knowledge*, p. 38.

21. Ibid., p. 39.

22. Henry E. Allison, *Kant's Transcendental Idealism* (New Haven, Conn.: Yale University Press, 1983), p. 350, n. 33.

23. H. J. Paton, *Kant's Metaphysic of Experience*, vol. 2 (New York: Macmillan, [1936] 1970), p. 44, n. 1. Bennett also calls this "a slip" (*Kant's Analytic*, p. 77).

24. Regarding this remark, Hartnack (*Kant's Theory of Knowledge*, p. 39, n. 4) notes that "Richard Falckenberg makes the following comment: 'It is this "neat" remark by Kant which has occasioned Fichte's Triaden and Hegel's dialectical method (*Hilfsbuch zur Geschichte der Philosophie seit Kant*, p. 13)."

25. Paton, *Kant's Metaphysic of Experience*, p. 44, n. 1.

26. Ibid.

27. Robert Paul Wolff, *Kant's Theory of Mental Activity: A Commentary on the Transcendental Analytic of the* Critique of Pure Reason (Magnolia, Mass.: Peter Smith, [1963] 1990), p. 62.

28. Bennett, *Kant's Analytic*, p. 168.

29. Paul Guyer, *Kant and the Claims of Knowledge* (Cambridge: Cambridge University Press, 1987), pp. 190–191.

30. For example, see Wolff, *Kant's Theory of Mental Activity*, p. 228, and Norman Kemp Smith, *A Commentary on Kant's 'Critique of Pure Reason'* (New York: Humanities Press, [1923] 1962), p. 346.

31. This way of resolving the apparent contradiction is suggested by Guyer, *Kant and the Claims of Knowledge*, p. 193.

32. Bennett, *Kant's Analytic*, p. 169. In *Kant's Theory of Knowledge*, Hartnack attempts to defend Kant by saying that he did not mean that "one cannot imagine a line without drawing it in thought," but rather that "one cannot conceive of a line without conceiving it as drawn" (p. 60). But not only is this still disputable, it also conflicts with Kant's saying that "only in this way [i.e., by drawing the line in thought] can the *intuition* [my emphasis] be obtained" (A 163/B 203).

33. Bennett, *Kant's Analytic*, p. 165.

34. For a suggestion to the contrary, see Guyer, *Kant and the Claims of Knowledge*, p. 191.

35. I discuss the Schematism in more detail in the appendix

36. As Bennett *Kant's Analytic*, p. 52, pithily puts it: "[Kant] thinks that arithmetic relates to time as geometry relates to space, so that the a priority of '5 + 7 = 12' is secured by the form of inner sense. This part of Kant's theory is wrong in a thoroughly boring way. I shall ignore it." Guyer, *Kant and the Claims to Knowledge*, p. 173, makes a similar point, albeit in less fiery language: "This assertion [that "*number* itself is essentially temporal"] is certainly difficult to entertain in our post-Fregean epoch, where number is linked to timeless relationships of sets."

37. By placing the Axioms of Intuition after the Transcendental Deduction in the *Critique*, Kant invites us to think of the principle of the axioms as being dependent on the Deduction. But in fact that principle seems not to depend at all on the Deduction, which is why I am discussing it in the present chapter. The same point applies to the Anticipations of Perception and even to the Postulates of Empirical Thought, though the definitions that

make up the Postulates would have little point except against the background of the Deduction and the Analogies.

38. Hartnack, *Kant's Theory of Knowledge*, p. 40.

39. Paul Guyer, *Kant and the Claims of Knowledge*, pp. 198–199.

40. The classic defense of this view is H. P. Grice, "The Causal Theory of Perception," in Robert J. Swartz, ed., *Perceiving, Sensing, and Knowing* (Berkeley: University of California Press, [1961] 1976). I defend the view in Georges Dicker, *Perceptual Knowledge: An Analytical and Historical Study* (Dordrecht: Reidel, 1980), pp. 80–87.

41. I have defended this view in Dicker, *Perceptual Knowledge*, pp. 156–167, especially on pp. 163–164, and also in Georges Dicker, "Berkeley on the Impossibility of Abstracting Primary from Secondary Qualities," *The Southern Journal of Philosophy* 39, 1 (Spring 2001): 23–45, on pp. 31–32.

42. Immanuel Kant, *Opus postumum*, ed. Eckart Förster, trans. Eckart Förster and Michael Rosen (Cambridge: Cambridge University Press, 1993), pp. 106–110, 116–117.

43. Quoted in James Van Cleve, *Problems from Kant* (Oxford: Oxford University Press, 1999), p. 134.

44. Roderick Milton Chisholm, *Perceiving: A Philosophical Study* (Ithaca, N.Y.: Cornell University Press, 1957), p. 149.

45. Guyer, *Kant and the Claims of Knowledge*, p. 201.

46. Why not say that any sensible quality, rather than only "certain sensible qualities," must have intensive magnitude? The reason is that intensive magnitude seems to be a feature only of the so-called secondary qualities, namely, color, sound, taste, smell, and temperature. It does not seem to be a feature of primary qualities, such as size and shape. Indeed, on certain views about the nature of secondary qualities, such as the dispositional view according to which they are merely capacities to cause sensations of color, sound, taste, smell, and temperature, it is not clear that even secondary qualities have intensive magnitude, unless one distinguishes between what I have elsewhere called the "dispositional aspect" and the "manifest aspect" of a secondary quality, in which case intensive magnitude can be ascribed at least to the manifest aspect. On the other hand, it seems right to hold that any *sensation* must have an intensive magnitude because, as Berkeley pointed out, there cannot be a sensation of size or shape lacking any color. For discussion relevant to these observations, see my "Primary and Secondary Qualities: A Proposed Modification of the Lockean Account," *The Southern Journal of Philosophy* 25, 4 (Winter 1977): 457–471, and my "Berkeley on the Impossibility of Abstracting Primary from Secondary Qualities," pp. 23–45.

47. Compare Guyer, *Kant and the Claims of Knowledge*, pp. 197–198.

48. Bennett, *Kant's Analytic*, p. 92.

49. Van Cleve, *Problems from Kant*, p. 105.

50. I discuss the argument from change in some depth in Georges Dicker, *Descartes: An Analytical and Historical Introduction* (Oxford: Oxford University Press, 1993), pp. 50–53, 57–58, and in more depth in Georges Dicker, *Hume's Epistemology and Metaphysics: An Introduction* (London: Routledge, 1998), pp. 15–17, 21–31.

51. Hartnack, *Kant's Theory of Knowledge*, p. 41.

52. "We have . . . no idea of substance, distinct from that of a collection of particular qualities, nor have we any other meaning when we either talk or reason concerning it." David Hume, *A Treatise of Human Nature*, 2nd ed., ed. L. A. Selby-Bigge and P. H. Nidditch (Oxford: Oxford University Press, [1740] 1978), p. 16.

53. John L. Mackie, *Problems from Locke* (Oxford: Oxford University Press, 1976), p. 77.

54. Ibid., pp. 78–79.

55. The discussion of (1)–(4a) is modeled on ibid., p. 79.

56. E. Jonathan Lowe, "Locke," in Robert L. Arrington, ed., A *Companion to the Philosophers* (Oxford: Blackwell, 1999), p. 372.

57. Hartnack, *Kant's Theory of Knowledge*, pp. 41–42.

58. Ibid., p. 41n.

59. Guyer, *Kant and the Claims of Knowledge*, p. 452, n. 17.

60. Allison, *Kant's Transcendental Idealism*, p. 127.

61. Derk Pereboom points out (in correspondence) that Kant's considered view of real possibility may be broader than that of conforming to the formal conditions of experience, for in discussing the Ontological Argument for the existence of God, he raises the question of whether the idea of God is of a really possible entity (A603/B 631). But presumably he is not asking whether God would conform to the formal conditions of experience.

62. David Hume, *An Enquiry Concerning Human Understanding*, 3rd ed., ed. L. A. Selby-Bigge and P. H. Nidditch (Oxford: Oxford University Press, [1748] 1975), pp. 45–46.

63. Hartnack, *Kant's Theory of Knowledge*, p. 86.

64. Wolff, *Kant's Theory of Mental Activity*, p. 298.

65. W. H. Walsh, *Kant's Criticism of Metaphysics* (Edinburgh: Edinburgh University Press, 1975), p. 148.

66. Ibid., p. 152.

Chapter 4

This chapter is designed to be read along with Book I, Chapter II, of the Transcendental Analytic ("The Deduction of the Pure Concepts of the Understanding"), exclusive of the "Deduction as in the Second Edition" (B 151–169), which should be read in conjunction with the next chapter.

1. James Van Cleve, *Problems from Kant* (New York: Oxford University Press, 1999), p. 79.

2. The reconstruction of the Transcendental Deduction that I shall offer is indebted to the work of some recent commentators, notably Robert Paul Wolff, *Kant's Theory of Mental Activity: A Commentary on the Transcendental Analytic of the* Critique of Pure Reason (Magnolia, Mass.: Peter Smith, [1963] 1990). The reconstruction of the continuation of the argument in the Analogies of Experience is indebted to the work of Peter Strawson, *The Bounds of Sense: An Essay on Kant's* Critique of Pure Reason (London: Routledge, [1966] 1990), and of Paul Guyer, *Kant and the Claims to Knowledge* (Cambridge: Cambridge University Press, 1987).

3. As will be seen later, that experience must be *spatial*, and not merely temporal, is really shown in the Analogies of Experience (despite the fact that space is introduced in the Transcendental Aesthetic) because only in the Analogies is it shown that some things must be perceived as being distinct from the self and its states.

4. David Hume, *An Enquiry Concerning Human Understanding*, 3rd ed., ed. L. A. Selby-Bigge and P. H. Nidditch (Oxford: Oxford University Press, 1975), p. 24.

5. In the recent translation of the *Critique* by Paul Guyer and Allen Wood (Cambridge: Cambridge University Press, 1997), "toward which" is used in place of "according to which."

6. As we saw in section 3.3.3, there are at least two concepts of substance, one on which a substance is simply what would ordinarily be called a "thing," and one on which it is an underlying substrate distinct from all of a thing's properties. The concept of substance that Kant favors in his First Analogy (the chief text on substance in the *Critique*) is

evidently a variant of the latter. However, in order to refute the Humean view of experience, Kant need only demonstrate the "objective validity" of the former. The reconstruction of Kant's argument to be proposed here leads to the objective validity of substance only in this modest but crucial sense. Kant's attempt to defend a stronger concept of substance in the First Analogy will, however, be discussed in chapter 6.

7. Some commentators have interpreted the term in still other ways. Strawson, for example, takes it to mean thinking, in the Kantian sense of applying concepts to intuitions (see *Bounds of Sense*, pp. 72ff.). Van Cleve, *Problems from Kant*, pp. 74–76, begins his discussion of the Transcendental Deduction by distinguishing *eight* different senses of "experience."

8. Two such writers are Justus Hartnack, *Kant's Theory of Knowledge*, trans. M. Holmes Hartshorne (Indianapolis: Hackett, [1967] 2001), and Frederick Copleston, *A History of Philosophy*, vol. 6 (New York: Doubleday, 1960). See also Karl Ameriks, "Kant's Transcendental Deduction as a Regressive Argument," in Patricia Kitcher, ed., *Kant's Critique of Pure Reason: Critical Essays* (Lanham, Md.: Rowman & Littlefield, 1998), pp. 85–102.

9. Wolff, *Kant's Theory of Mental Activity*.

10. The principle is introduced at A 107 and is stated at the following places, among others: A 116, A 117n, A 122, A 123, B 132, and B 138.

11. Wolff, *Kant's Theory of Mental Activity*, p. 106. Wolff points out that the quotation from James is from his *Principles of Psychology*, vol. 1, p. 160; that James took the example from Brentano; and that Norman Kemp Smith, in his *A Commentary on Kant's 'Critique of Pure Reason'* (New York: Humanities Press [1923] 1962), quotes it from James.

12. Erich Adickes, *Kants Lehre von der Doppelten Affektion Unseres Ich als Schüssel zu Seiner Erkenntnistheorie* (Tübingen: Mohr, 1929); Hans Vaihinger, *Commentar zu Kant's Kritik der Reinen Vernunft*, 2bde. (Stuttgart: W. Spemann, 1881–1882).

13. Smith, *Commentary on Kant's 'Critique of Pure Reason.'*

14. H. J. Paton, *Kant's Metaphysic of Experience*, 2 vols. (London: George Allen & Unwin, [1936] 1970).

15. For an authoritative and illuminating genetic account of how Kant conceived the overall structure of the argument of the "Transcendental Analytic," see Guyer and Wood's Introduction to the *Critique of Pure Reason*, pp. 60–61.

16. For brevity's sake I shall refer to the A-Deduction throughout the rest of this chapter simply as "the Deduction."

17. David Hume, *A Treatise of Human Nature*, 2nd ed., ed. L. A. Selby-Bigge and P. H. Nidditch (Oxford: Oxford University Press, 1978), pp. 251–253.

18. Ibid., p. 251.

19. Not all philosophers agree with Hume that the self cannot be introspected. For an opposing view, see Roderick Milton Chisholm, "On the Observability of the Self," *Philosophy and Phenomenological Research* 30 (1969): 7–21. Reprinted in Quassim Cassam, ed., *Self-Knowledge* (Oxford: Oxford University Press, 1994), pp. 94–108.

20. Wolff, *Kant's Theory of Mental Activity*, pp. 113–114.

21. Hume (*Treatise*, pp. 635–636) himself attempts to account for the unity of consciousness in terms of association in *Treatise* I IV 6, "Of Personal Identity." But in the Appendix, where he recants the view of the self proposed in that section, he seems to realize that such an account cannot work: "All my hopes vanish, when I come to explain the principles, that unite our successive perceptions in our thought or consciousness."

22. Wolff, *Kant's Theory of Mental Activity*, pp. 108–109.

23. Ibid., p. 115.

24. John Locke, *An Essay Concerning Human Understanding*, ed. Andrew S. Pringle-

Pattison (Oxford: Oxford University Press, [1689] 1924), p. 15. Quoted in Wolff, *Kant's Theory of Mental Activity*, p.110.

25. Wolff, *Kant's Theory of Mental Activity*, p. 116.

26. Ibid.

27. It is interesting that Wolff (ibid., p. 244) himself reverts to this idea in explaining the final version of Kant's argument that incorporates also the argument of the "Analogies of Experience."

28. This objection was raised by Eli Hirsch, in conversation.

29. Van Cleve, *Problems from Kant*, p. 94.

30. Some philosophers may object to my reliance on what can and cannot be *imagined*. But since I am here quite deliberately describing a pertinent thought-experiment, I see no problem with appealing to imaginability/unimaginability.

31. This objection was made by Christopher Plochocki, a student in my Kant seminar at SUNY Brockport in Spring 2003.

32. C. I. Lewis, *Mind and the World Order* (New York: Dover, [1929] 1956), p, 221. Lewis White Beck took up the issue raised by Lewis in the article "Did the Sage of Könisberg Have No Dreams?" in his *Essays on Kant and Hume* (New Haven, Conn.: Yale University Press, 1978), pp. 38–60.

33. Van Cleve, *Problems from Kant*, p. 97.

34. Kant's reference here to "time-relations" will be explained later.

35. This is not to say that we can dispense altogether with resemblance in our notion of representation. For, as Derk Pereboom points out (in correspondence), if the representation of the back of the chair (which gets organized with the other representations mentioned) did not resemble the back of a chair, and none of those other representations resembled what they were of either, then it is doubtful that the result of the organization would be a representation of a chair. But in agreeing that these representations resemble what they are of, we must be careful, if we are to stay with Kant, about what this means. It must not be taken to mean that the representation of, say, the back of a chair resembles something that is what it is independently of the ways we perceive and think of it—that would be the correspondence theory, which Kant rejects. Rather, it must be taken to mean that the representation is qualitatively "back-of-a-chairish," that it consists, as some contemporary philosophers would put it, in being appeared to "chairbackishly."

36. Strawson, *Bounds of Sense*, p. 25.

37. Ibid., p. 50.

38. Charles Arthur Campbell, "Self-Consciousness, Self-Identity and Personal Identity," in Richard T. DeGeorge, ed., *Contemporary and Classical Metaphysics* (New York: Holt, Rinehart & Winston, 1962), p. 226. This article originally appeared as Lecture V in Campbell, *On Selfhood and Godhood* (London: George Allen & Unwin, 1957).

39. Wolff, *Kant's Theory of Mental Activity*, pp. 128–129. In a footnote, Wolff adds: "Needless to say, this is a rather flatfooted description. But then, the mind works with such rapidity and deftness that any attempt to spell out its activities must seem ponderous by comparison."

40. Ibid., p. 129.

41. Ibid., pp. 129–130.

42. Ibid.; compare pp. 116 and 119 with pp. 132, 161, and 278.

43. This point was confirmed in my mind by an essay by Dieter Henrich. In an endnote that praises Wolff's book as "rich in insights and arguments" and "a considerable achievement," Henrich nonetheless writes: "[Wolff] does not show that the unity of consciousness is possible only as the consciousness of synthesis according to a rule, or that the unity of self-consciousness requires such a regulated synthesis. Where this problem ought

to be discussed Wolff gives merely a variant of Kant's analysis of recognition (p. 129), an analysis which . . . cannot bear the burden of proof. Wolff's book thereby overlooks Kant's most crucial problem. . . ." Henrich, *The Unity of Reason: Essays on Kant's Philosophy* (Cambridge, Mass.: Harvard University Press, 1994), p. 236.

44. As mentioned in note 27 above, Wolff himself reverts to the idea that "we connect mental contents by relating them, *qua* representations, to an independent object" much later in his book, while introducing the Analogies of Experience, where he says that Kant completes the argument begun in the Transcendental Deduction. See *Kant's Theory of Mental Activity*, p. 244.

45. This and the preceding two sentences just repeat the key ideas of the first version of the Deduction initially introduced in the previous section as (a), (b), and (c) and then absorbed into the argument as steps (2), (3), and (4).

Chapter 5

Sections 5.1 through 5.5 of this chapter should be read along with the introductory section to the Analogies of Experience (A 176/B 218–A 181/B 224), and the reader should also obtain a preview of the three Analogies by reading the first portion of each of them (B 224–227, 232–239, 257–259). Section 5.6 is designed to be read along with the second-edition version of the Transcendental Deduction (B 151–169).

1. Robert Paul Wolff, *Kant's Theory of Mental Activity: A Commentary on the Transcendental Analytic of the* Critique of Pure Reason (Magnolia, Mass.: Peter Smith, [1963] 1990), p. 243n. In their recent translation of the *Critique* (Cambridge: Cambridge University Press, 1997), Paul Guyer and Allen W. Wood (Cambridge: Cambridge University Press, 1997) translate the clause as follows: "the relation in the existence of the manifold is to be represented in it not as it is juxtaposed in time but as it exists objectively in time."

2. Wolff, *Kant's Theory of Mental Activity*, pp. 243–244.

3. Peter F. Strawson, *The Bounds of Sense: An Essay on Kant's* Critique of Pure Reason (London: Routledge, [1966] 1990), pp. 123–124.

4. One might object that this sentence illicitly changes the subject from "representations" to "perceptions." But this shift is harmless. Typically, what Kant calls "representations" will be sense perceptions of objects; sometimes, they will be thoughts of an object had in the absence of the object. The points being made here hold good whichever of these two ways we think of representations.

5. Strawson, *Bounds of Sense*, p. 128.

6. Ibid.

7. Kant asserts this premise at A 166/B 207, A 177/B 219, A 182/B 225, A 183/B 226, and A 211/B 257.

8. Wolff, *Kant's Theory of Mental Activity*, p. 244.

9. Strawson, *Bounds of Sense*, p. 127.

10. It might be thought that the final clause should be formulated as "some experiences *are* of enduring stable objects by reference to which temporal relations can be determined." But this would be to overlook the point that Kant's argument can only yield conclusions about how we must conceive things, not how things may be in themselves, that is, apart from the ways we must conceive them; so that only the "weak" version of Transcendental Idealism, to the effect that we cannot intelligibly suppose that things are different from the ways we must conceive them, blocks the possible objection that Kant's argument shows only how we must think of things but not how they really are, or what beliefs we must have but not that those beliefs are true.

236 Notes to Page 123

11. Why not say instead "only if there *are* perceptible objects that are stable and enduring"? The answer is that this would be to ignore the point that the objective time-order is the order in which we must *conceive* perceptible objects to exist if we are to have experience. Again, it must be remembered that the argument as a whole is designed only to show, and cannot show more than, how we must conceive things. It is significant that Strawson, in *Bounds of Sense*, despite the realist language in which he explains the steps of Kant's argument, invariably puts its conclusions in language that recognizes this point. For example:

> A course of argument we might have hoped for . . . could be set out as follows. It is impossible to draw the necessary distinctions between (1) the time-relations of the members of a subjective series of perceptions and (2) the time-relations of at least some objects which the perceptions are perceptions of, unless the objects in question are *seen as* [my emphasis] belonging to an enduring framework of relations in which the objects themselves enjoy their temporal relations (of co-existence and succession) with each other independently of the order of our perceptions of them. This enduring framework is spatial. . . . But there is no question of perceiving the necessary framework itself, of perceiving, as it were, pure spatial permanence. So *we must perceive some objects as enduring objects* [my emphasis except on the first occurrence of "objects"], even if our perceptions of them do not endure, must *see them as falling under concepts of persistent objects* [my emphasis], even though objects of non-persistent perceptions. (p. 125)

> But there is, for the subject himself, no access to this wider system of temporal relations except through his own experiences. Those experiences, therefore, or some of them, *must be taken by him to be* [my emphasis] experiences *of* things (other than the experiences themselves) which possess among themselves the temporal relations of this wider system. (pp. 126–127)

> Kant, we may say, has succeeded in establishing a metaphysical conservation-principle of some kind. He has established the principle of the necessary conservation of the world of things in space. This is what *must be conceived as* [my emphasis] absolutely permanent and abiding: the spatio-temporal frame of things at large. It is also perfectly true that this . . . frame is not itself . . . a[n] object of perception and that its abidingness must therefore somehow be empirically represented for us in our actual perception of objects. But all that is required is that we should in principle be able to locate in the enduring framework everything objective we encounter, i.e. to relate everything that *we count as* objective to everything else that *we count as* objective in one system of spatio-temporal relations [my emphasis]. And for this . . . what is necessary . . . is that we should be able to identify places, and hence objects or processes, as the same at different times. Given the limitations of our perceptual experience, this in turn requires that we should *perceive* some objects *as* [emphasis in the original] having a permanence which our perceptions of them do not have. (p. 129)

> To say that objective time-determination is possible is to say that we can assign to objects and happenings relations of co-existence and succession and that we can, where necessary, distinguish these relations from the temporal relations of our perceptions, though, of course, we assign them fundamentally on the strength of our perceptions. For this to be possible we must *see objects as belonging to*, and events *as occurring in*, an identical, enduring spatial framework. (p. 132)

12. For brevity's sake, here and in the rest of the argument, I drop the words "by reference to which time-relations can be determined."

13. Strawson, *Bounds of Sense*, p. 132.

14. Ibid., p. 133.

15. Ibid., p. 143.

16. Ibid., pp. 144–145.

17. Ibid., pp. 145–146.

18. Ibid., p. 146.

19. The example was discussed on page 106.

20. Dieter Henrich, "The Proof-Structure of Kant's Transcendental Deduction," *Review of Metaphysics* 22 (1968–1969): 640–659, has influentially argued that the argument of sections 15–20 of the B-Deduction is only the first stage of a two-stage proof that resumes and ends in section 26. Since such a two-stage proof can succeed only if its first stage succeeds, and since for reasons to be given below I do not think the argument of sections 15–20 does succeed, I shall confine myself to that argument.

21. Wolff, *Kant's Theory of Mental Activity*, p. 128.

22. Ibid., n. 4.

23. Strawson, *Bounds of Sense*, p. 97.

24. Ibid. [Strawson's emphasis].

25. Ibid., p. 96.

26. The same suggestion is made in Derk Pereboom, "Self-understanding in Kant's Transcendental Deduction," *Synthese* 103 (1995): 15.

27. Immanuel Kant, *Prolegomena to Any Future Metaphysics*, in Beryl Logan, ed., *Immanuel Kant's* Prolegomena to Any Future Metaphysics *in Focus* (London: Routledge, 1996), pp. 65–68 (sects. 18–20).

28. Ibid., 67.

29. Ibid., p. 66, n. 1.

30. Ibid., p. 66.

31. Jonathan Bennett, *Kant's Analytic* (Cambridge: Cambridge University Press, 1966), p. 132.

32. Strawson, *Bounds of Sense*, p. 164.

33. Ibid., p. 165.

34. T. E. Wilkerson, *Kant's Critique of Pure Reason: A Commentary for Students*, 2nd ed. (Bristol: Thoemmes, 1998), pp. 50–51.

35. Strawson, *Bounds of Sense*, p. 16 and n.

36. David Hume, *A Treatise of Human Nature*, 2nd ed., ed. L. A. Selby-Bigge and P. H. Nidditch (Oxford: Oxford University Press, [1748] 1978), p. 252.

37. John Locke, *An Essay Concerning Human Understanding*, ed. Andrew S. Pringle-Pattison (Oxford: Oxford University Press, [1689] 1924), p. 340. I have slightly altered the example.

38. Strawson, *Bounds of Sense*, p. 163.

39. This does not imply, absurdly, that those conclusions are both *a priori* and *a posteriori*, or both analytic and synthetic. Rather, it means that the argument based on the A-Deduction establishes only that the conclusions [numbered (17) and (18) in that argument] are *true*, whereas only the argument based on the B-Deduction can show that those conclusions [numbered (19) and (20) in that argument] are both true and *a priori*.

Chapter 6

This chapter is designed to be read along with the First Analogy.

1. I shall henceforth sometimes refer to the first and second editions of the *Critique* simply as "A" and "B," respectively.

2. Edward Caird, *The Critical Philosophy of Kant* (New York: Macmillan, 1889), vol. 1, p. 541. The citation is from Henry E. Allison, *Kant's Transcendental Idealism* (New Haven, Conn.: Yale University Press, 1983), p. 202.

3. Allison, *Kant's Transcendental Idealism*, p. 202.

4. James Van Cleve, *Problems from Kant* (New York: Oxford University Press, 1999), p. 108.

5. Allison, *Kant's Transcendental Idealism*, p. 203.

6. See, for example, Jonathan Bennett, *Kant's Analytic* (Cambridge: Cambridge University Press, 1966), p. 201.

7. Arthur Melnick, *Kant's Analogies of Experience* (Chicago: University of Chicago Press, 1973), pp. 63–64.

8. Dictionary definitions of "sempiternal" seem to mean the same as "eternal," though the etymology of "sempiternal" traces back in part to the Latin *semper* ("always"). I conjecture that commentators like Bennett, Allison, and Van Cleve use "sempiternal" rather than "eternal" in connection with the Third Analogy in order to avoid the religious and theological connotations of "eternal."

9. See, for example, P. F. Strawson, *The Bounds of Sense: An Essay on Kant's* Critique *of Pure Reason* (London: Routledge, [1966] 1990), p. 129.

10. Bennett, *Kant's Analytic*, pp. 199–200.

11. Melnick, *Kant's Analogies of Experience*, pp. 67–68.

12. Bennett, *Kant's Analytic*, p. 182.

13. Here I follow ibid., p. 187, except that Bennett hyphenates "existence change," yielding "existence-change." Norman Kemp Smith, in his translation of the *Critique* (A 197/B 230), translates *Veränderung* as "alteration" and *Wechsel* simply as "change," but I agree with Bennett that Kant's contrast between the two comes out better if *Wechsel* is translated as "existence change." Allison (*Kant's Transcendental Idealism*, p. 204) translates *Wechsel* as "replacement change." Van Cleve (*Problems from Kant*, p. 284, n. 8) sticks with Kemp Smith's "change," trusting the reader to keep Kant's technical meaning in mind.

14. Something very close to the argument I am about to present is at work in Allison's discussion of the First Analogy (*Kant's Transcendental Idealism*, pp. 208–209). The argument was suggested to me by this passage in Allison's book. See also Justus Hartnack, *Kant's Theory of Knowledge*, trans. M. Holmes Hartshorne (Indianapolis: Hackett, [1967] 2001), p. 77.

15. David Hume, *A Treatise of Human Nature*, 2nd ed., ed. L. A. Selby-Bigge and P. H. Nidditch (Oxford: Oxford University Press, [1740] 1978), pp. 255–256. John Locke (*An Essay Concerning Human Understanding*, II, xxvii, 3) had made the same point before Hume: "If two or more atoms be joined together into the same mass . . . the mass, consisting of the same atoms, must be the same mass, or the same body, let the parts be never so differently jumbled: but if one of these atoms be taken away, or one new one added, it is no longer the same mass, or the same body."

16. This is not to say that Hume himself was not a mereological essentialist. He was, for he held that nothing can change at all in any way and retain its identity. But the context of the passage quoted is not one in which Hume is putting forward his own view. Rather, he is contrasting what he thinks most people would say about the identity conditions for a "mass of matter" with what he thinks they would say about the identity conditions for other kinds of things, such as a plants, animals, ships, and houses.

17. Van Cleve, *Problems from Kant*, p. 107.

18. For fuller discussion relevant to this point, see my *Descartes: An Analytical and Historical Introduction* (New York: Oxford University Press, 1993), pp. 215–216.

19. One might wonder why premise (5) is not stated simply as "every existence change

that ever occurs is a member of a progressive series of existence changes." The reason is that every existence change would then be a step on the way toward a final alteration in a thing that could never change again. But then our perceptual stand-in for time could never again change, and so we could no longer determine time relations by reference to it. This was pointed out in a paper by Melissa Birmingham, a student in my Kant seminar at SUNY Brockport in Spring 2003.

20. This is a slight oversimplification. As Van Cleve (*Problems from Kant*, pp. 105, 109) has shown, there are items that are adjectival on other items without being properties of the latter. For example, my fist is adjectival on my hand but is not a property of it; rather it consists in my hand's having the property of being closed. Van Cleve calls such things—things whose existence depends on other things' having a certain property—"modes," and he points out that such things can bear properties but are not substances₁. I would say that when my hand opens so that my fist goes out of existence, there is a progressive existence change, no less than when a piece of wood is bent and the straight wood goes out of existence.

21. The following remarks by Jonathan Bennett incisively capture this line of criticism:

> I have construed Kant's claim that every happening must be an alteration—i.e. that everything which undergoes an existence-change must be a property of other things—as implying that if something to which we had given a substantival status were annihilated, we ought retroactively to deprive it of that status and admit that we should have dealt with it in the adjectival mode all along. This is why Kant finally takes substance₂ as his only acknowledged concept of substance: anything which underwent an existence-change and so failed as a substance₂ would also lose the right to the substantival treatment which is definitive of substance₁.

> This is an extravagant conclusion. In one of the passages where he stresses that *we* divide our world into substances and properties, Kant implies that the only acceptable reason for treating something substantivally is that it is sempiternal:

>> If I leave out permanence (which is existence in all time), nothing remains in the concept of substance save only the logical representation of a subject—a representation which I endeavour to realize by representing to myself something which can exist only as subject but never as predicate. But not only am I ignorant of any conditions under which this logical pre-eminence may belong to anything; I can neither put such a concept to any use, nor draw the least inference from it. For no object is thereby determined for its employment, and consequently we do not know whether it signifies anything whatsoever. [A 243–244/B 300–301]

> This is just wrong. One good reason for treating something substantivally is that it is conceptually efficient to do so. (*Kant's Analytic*, pp. 197–198)

22. Bennett, *Kant's Analytic*, p. 188.

23. Bennett (ibid., p. 189) gives a more complex and very persuasive example, involving the disappearance of a porcelain pig.

Chapter 7

This chapter is designed to be read along with the Second Analogy. It would also be useful to read David Hume, *A Treatise of Human Nature*, Bk. I, Pt. III, sect. III ("Why a cause is always necessary?").

1. David Hume, *A Treatise of Human Nature*, 2nd ed., ed. L. A. Selby-Bigge and P. H. Nidditch (Oxford: Oxford University Press, [1740] 1978), pp. 78–82.

2. Hume would say that the causal principle does not express a mere "relation of ideas."

3. Ibid., p. 79.

4. William H. Brenner, *Elements of Modern Philosophy: Descartes through Kant* (Upper Saddle River, N.J.: Prentice Hall, 1989), p. 128.

5. Lewis White Beck, "Once More unto the Breach: Kant's Answer to Hume, Again." In Lewis White Beck, *Essays on Kant and Hume* (New Haven, Conn.: Yale University Press, 1978), pp. 130–135.

6. Ibid., p. 134.

7. Ibid., p. 135.

8. Paul Guyer, *Kant and the Claims of Knowledge* (Cambridge: Cambridge University Press, 1987), pp. 243–244, gives an especially fine statement of Kant's problem: "Kant clearly explains the problem which can be solved only by the employment of the relation of cause and effect. The problem arises from the following circumstance: 'The apprehension of the manifold of appearance is always successive. The representations of the parts follow one another. Whether they also follow one another in the object is a further point for reflection, which is not contained in the first' (A 189/B 234). That is, any pair or series of distinct *representations*, whether they *represent* states of affairs which coexist but are successively perceived or states of affairs which succeed one another and thus comprise the several states of an actual event or alteration, *themselves* succeed one another. So the fact that the represented *states of affairs* succeed one another in a determinate order—that an alteration or event is taking place in the *objects* of perception and not just in the *subjective* series of representations itself—where there are, of course, *always* changes taking place—cannot be inferred from the successive occurrence of the *representations of* those states of affairs themselves."

9. Beck, "Once More unto the Breach," p. 135. I have slightly modified Beck's wording of H and P.

10. More accurately, H is a proposition that Hume accepts when he puts to one side his skepticism about perception, as he invariably does when discussing causality and induction.

11. Beck, "Once More unto the Breach," p. 135.

12. Peter Strawson, *The Bounds of Sense* (London: Routledge, [1966] 1990), pp. 133–139.

13. Strawson calls reversibility "order-indifference." Thus his way of making the present point is to say that for Kant, "Lack or possession of order-indifference on the part of our perceptions is . . . our criterion . . . of objective succession or co-existence" (ibid., p. 134).

14. Ibid., p. 136. For an influential defense of claim (a), see H. P. Grice, "The Causal Theory of Perception," in Robert J. Swartz, ed., *Perceiving, Sensing, and Knowing* (Berkeley: University of California Press, [1961] 1976), pp. 438–472 (see especially pp. 460–465). Some philosophers have questioned claim (b) and suggested that there could be cases of "backward causation," but I shall not go into this matter.

15. Strawson, *Bounds of Sense*, p. 137.

16. Ibid., p. 138.

17. Guyer, *Kant and the Claims of Knowledge*, chap. 10.

18. Patricia Kitcher, "Introduction," Immanuel Kant, *Critique of Pure Reason*, trans. Werner S. Pluhar (Indianapolis: Hackett, 1996), p. 1, n. 8.

19. Guyer, *Kant and the Claims of Knowledge*, p. 256.

20. Ibid., p. 248.

21. As Guyer notes (ibid., p. 448, n. 17), his point is anticipated in Arthur Melnick, *Kant's Analogies of Experience* (Chicago: University of Chicago Press, 1973): "Bringing in the irreversibility in the apprehension of succession . . . is not the introduction of a criterion in terms of which we determine a succession as objective. We do not ascertain that what we apprehend is successive by ascertaining that our apprehensions are irreversible" (pp. 82–83). Also: "We do not determine that A and B are coexistent by determining that our perceptions of A and B are reversible. I perceive A and then perceive B. If A and B coexist throughout the time of my successive perceptions, then it was possible to have perceived B and then to have perceived A and, in so doing, to have perceived the same state of affairs (the coexistence of A and B through time), but I do not ascertain that A and B coexist by ascertaining that my perceptions might have been in the reverse order. Again, we derive facts about the subjective order of our perceptions (i.e. whether the order is reversible) from the objective connection of appearances that are perceived (whether they coexist). . . . Thus, the knowledge of appearances as coexisting is not grounded on the knowledge of the reversibility in the order of our perceptions. Rather, the reversibility of our perceptions is based on the fact that they are perceptions of appearances that coexist through the time of the perceptions" (pp. 94–95).

22. Guyer, *Kant and the Claims of Knowledge*, pp. 247–249. Regarding this passage, Derk Pereboom writes (in correspondence):

> Guyer claims that the fact that one state is followed by another in the objective time order is not inferred from irreversibility, which seems right, but that on Kant's view it is *inferred* from the subjective succession together with a rule. [But] it seems implausible that anything is actually *inferred* from a rule at all . . . this is too intellectualistic, and moreover . . . nothing in the text supports this claim. The alternative is that our ability to represent objective successions *is explained* by a rule. . . . It does not seem necessary to make the further claim that we represent the rule and then infer objective succession from it.

I think this is right, and my reconstruction of Guyer's version of Kant's argument avoids the suggestion that our knowledge of the objective succession is inferred from the subjective succession together with a rule and allows that it may instead depend on knowledge of these in the sense of being explained by it.

23. The last two options rejected in this premise are not explicitly mentioned by Guyer in the place where he presents his analysis, but they may fairly be taken as implicit.

24. Paul Guyer, "Kant's Second Analogy," in Patricia Kitcher, ed., *Kant's Critique of Pure Reason: Critical Essays* (Lanham, Md.: Rowman & Littlefield, 1998), pp. 129–141. For a detailed, brilliant explanation of this point, see Melnick, *Kant's Analogies of Experience*, pp. 97–102.

Chapter 8

1. Lucey offers this example in correspondence. I have slightly amplified it.

2. Paul Guyer, *Kant and the Claims of Knowledge* (Cambridge: Cambridge University Press, 1987), p. 269.

3. Ibid., p. 248.

4. Ibid., p. 268.

5. H. J. Paton, *Kant's Metaphysic of Experience*, vol. 2 (London: George Allen & Unwin, [1936] 1970), p. 298.

6. W. H. Walsh, *Kant's Criticism of Metaphysics* (Edinburgh: Edinburgh University Press, 1975), p. 143.

7. Arthur Melnick, *Kant's Analogies of Experience* (Chicago: University of Chicago Press, 1973), pp. 102–110. I have simplified Melnick's extremely subtle discussion.

8. Robert Paul Wolff, *Kant's Theory of Mental Activity: A Commentary on the Transcendental Analytic of the* Critique of Pure Reason (Magnolia, Mass.: Peter Smith, [1963] 1990), p. 289.

9. Jonathan Bennett, *Kant's Analytic* (Cambridge: Cambridge University Press, 1966), p. 181.

10. T. E. Wilkerson, *Kant's Critique of Pure Reason: A Commentary for Students*, 2nd ed. (Bristol: Thoemmes, 1998), p. 70.

11. Guyer, *Kant and the Claims of Knowledge*, p. 270.

12. Cf. ibid., p. 271. This point is also made in Bennett, *Kant's Analytic*, p. 221, and in Wolff, *Kant's Theory of Mental Activity*, p. 290. Guyer usefully suggests that misunderstanding Kant's point can be avoided by use of the type/token distinction: whereas no *token* of a perception can occur more than once, so that it cannot reoccur in the reverse order, one token of the same type can occur in the reverse order from another token of that type (p. 271).

13. P. F. Strawson, *The Bounds of Sense: An Essay on Kant's* Critique of Pure Reason (London: Routledge, [1966] 1990), pp. 139–140.

14. Wolff, *Kant's Theory of Mental Activity*, p. 284.

15. Guyer, *Kant and the Claims of Knowledge*, pp. 267–276.

16. Ibid., pp. 270–272, for Guyer's presentation of this reasoning.

17. This example was also suggested by Kenneth Lucey in correspondence.

Chapter 9

This chapter should be read along with the Refutation of Idealism (B 274–B 279) and the final footnote of the Preface to the second edition (B xl–xli).

1. Kant actually says that the "one empirical assertion that [Descartes holds to be] absolutely certain is 'I am'" (B 274). But since Descartes claimed to derive "I am" from "I am thinking," and since Kant characterizes his Refutation of Idealism as the attempt to prove that "our inner experience, which for Descartes is indubitable, is possible only on the assumption of outer experience" (B 275), the issue between him and Descartes is better joined if Kant is seen as trying to show that knowledge of one's own inner experience, epitomized by the knowledge that "I am thinking," rather than knowledge of one's own existence, is directly parasitic on knowledge of external things.

2. The use of the label "problematic idealism" to characterize this Cartesian view is peculiar to Kant. He contrasts "problematic idealism" with "dogmatic idealism," which holds that the existence of objects in space is not merely doubtful but "false and impossible," and which he ascribes to Berkeley (B 274).

3. W. H. Walsh, *Kant's Criticism of Metaphysics* (Edinburgh: Edinburgh University Press, 1975), p. 190.

4. Paul Guyer, *Kant and the Claims of Knowledge* (Cambridge: Cambridge University Press, 1987), pp. 285–286.

5. Ibid., p. 293

6. Ibid., p. 328.

7. Kant, *Wieder den Idealism* (*Reflexion* 6313), quoted ibid., p. 305. The translation is Guyer's.

8. Guyer, *Kant and the Claims of Knowledge*, p. 306.

9. Ibid., p. 302.

10. Ibid., p. 244.

11. I am indebted to James Van Cleve for calling this point to my attention.

12. Guyer, *Kant and the Claims of Knowledge*, pp. 306–307.

13. Ibid., p. 306.

14. Indeed, I find it an odd feature of Guyer's excellent discussion that he initially presents the argument in term of such a scenario.

15. Quoted from correspondence.

16. Guyer, *Kant and the Claims of Knowledge*, p. 303.

17. Jonathan Bennett, *Kant's Analytic* (Cambridge: Cambridge University Press, 1966), p. 228. Bennett numbers the three possibilities as (1), (2), (3); I have substituted (a), (b), (c) to avoid confusion with the numbering of the steps in the argument under discussion.

18. Ibid., pp. 228–229.

19. Ibid., p. 229.

20. Ibid., pp. 224–225, 227–228.

21. T. H. Irwin, "Review of Paul Guyer's *Kant and the Claims of Knowledge*," *The Philosophical Review* 100, 9 (April 1991): 338.

22. Guyer, *Kant and the Claims of Knowledge*, p. 308.

23. Ibid., pp. 308–309.

24. Ibid., p. 311.

25. In correspondence.

26. Guyer, *Kant and the Claims of Knowledge*, p. 310.

27. Ibid., p. 317.

28. Ibid., p. 323.

Appendix

This appendix is designed to be read with Chapter I of Book II of the Transcendental Analytic ("The Schematism of the Pure Concepts of Understanding").

1. The most illuminating sympathetic account of the schematism that I have found is W. H. Walsh, "Schematism," in Robert P. Wolff, ed., *Kant: A Collection of Critical Essays* (Garden City, N.Y.: Doubleday, 1967), pp. 71–87. A highly critical but philosophically instructive treatment is Jonathan Bennett, *Kant's Analytic* (Cambridge: Cambridge University Press, 1966), pp. 141–152. A clear, brief, critical discussion is T. E. Wilkerson, *Kant's Critique of Pure Reason: A Commentary for Students*, 2nd ed. (Bristol: Thoemmes, 1998), pp. 95–98.

2. George Berkeley, *A Treatise Concerning the Principles of a Human Knowledge*, ed. Jonathan Dancy (Oxford: Oxford University Press, [1710] 1998), p. 95 (sect. 13 of Berkeley's "Introduction"). The passage is from Locke's *An Essay Concerning Human Understanding*, bk. IV, chap. 7, sect. 9. The italics are Berkeley's, not Locke's.

3. Ibid.

4. Ibid., pp. 94–96 (sects. 12–15).

5. Don Garrett, *Cognition and Commitment in Hume's Philosophy* (Oxford: Oxford University Press, 1997), p. 24.

6. Bennett, *Kant's Analytic*, p. 141.

7. Henry E. Allison, *Kant's Transcendental Idealism* (New Haven, Conn.: Yale University Press, 1983), p. 180.

8. Lauchlan Chipman, "Kant's Categories and Their Schematism," in Ralph C. S. Walker, ed., *Kant on Pure Reason* (Oxford: Oxford University Press, 1982), p. 104.

9. Here I am largely following Walsh's account in his "Schematism." See especially pp. 81–82.

10. Paul Guyer, *Kant and the Claims of Knowledge* (Cambridge: Cambridge University Press, 1987), p. 174.

11. Ibid.

12. Ibid.

13. Ibid., p. 175.

14. For an excellent elaboration of this point, see Robert Paul Wolff, *Kant's Theory of Mental Activity: A Commentary on the Transcendental Analytic of the* Critique of Pure Reason (Magnolia, Mass.: Peter Smith, [1963] 1990), pp. 214–218.

Bibliography

Adickes, Erich. *Kants Lehre von der Doppelten Affektion Unseres Ich als Schüssel zu Seiner Erkenntnistheorie.* Tübingen: Mohr, 1929.

Allison, Henry E. *Kant's Transcendental Idealism.* New Haven, Conn.: Yale University Press, 1983.

Ameriks, Karl. "Kant's Transcendental Deduction as a Regressive Argument." In Patricia Kitcher, ed., *Kant's* Critique of Pure Reason: *Critical Essays,* pp. 85–102. Lanham, Md.: Rowman & Littlefield, 1998.

Barker, Stephen F. "Geometry." In Paul Edwards, ed., *The Encyclopedia of Philosophy,* vol. 3, pp. 285–290. New York: Macmillan, 1967.

Beck, Lewis White. "Did the Sage of Könisberg Have No Dreams?" In Lewis White Beck, *Essays on Kant and Hume,* pp. 38–60. New Haven, Conn.: Yale University Press, 1978.

———. "Once More unto the Breach: Kant's Answer to Hume, Again." In Lewis White Beck, *Essays on Kant and Hume,* pp. 130–135. New Haven, Conn.: Yale University Press, 1978.

Bennett, Jonathan. *Kant's Analytic.* Cambridge: Cambridge University Press, 1966.

Berkeley, George. *A Treatise Concerning the Principles of Human Knowledge,* ed. Jonathan Dancy. Oxford: Oxford University Press, [1710] 1998.

Brenner, William H. *Elements of Modern Philosophy: Descartes through Kant.* Upper Saddle River, N.J.: Prentice Hall, 1989.

Caird, Edward. *The Critical Philosophy of Kant.* New York: Macmillan, 1889.

Campbell, Charles Arthur. "Self-Consciousness, Self-Identity and Personal Identity." In Richard T. DeGeorge, ed., *Contemporary and Classical Metaphysics,* pp. 224–235. New York: Holt, Rinehart & Winston, 1962. First published as Lecture V in Campbell, *On Selfhood and Godhood.* London: George Allen & Unwin, 1957.

Cassam, Quassim, ed. *Self-Knowledge.* Oxford: Oxford University Press, 1994.

Chipman, Lauchlan. "Kant's Categories and Their Schematism." In Ralph C. S. Walker, ed., *Kant on Pure Reason,* pp. 100–116. Oxford: Oxford University Press, 1982.

Chisholm, Roderick Milton. "On the Observability of the Self." *Philosophy and Phenomenological Research* 30 (1969): 7–21. Reprinted in Quassim Cassam, ed. *Self-Knowledge,* pp. 94–108. Oxford: Oxford University Press, 1994.

————. *Perceiving: A Philosophical Study.* Ithaca, N.Y.: Cornell University Press, 1957.

Copleston, Frederick. *A History of Philosophy*, vol. 6. New York: Doubleday, 1960.

Dicker, Georges. "Berkeley on the Impossibility of Abstracting Primary from Secondary Qualities." *The Southern Journal of Philosophy* 39, 1 (Spring 2001): 23–45.

————. *Descartes: An Analytical and Historical Introduction.* New York: Oxford University Press, 1993.

————. *Hume's Epistemology and Metaphysics: An Introduction.* London: Routledge, 1998.

————. *Perceptual Knowledge: An Analytical and Historical Study.* Dordrecht: Reidel, 1980.

————. "Primary and Secondary Qualities: A Proposed Modification of the Lockean Account." *The Southern Journal of Philosophy* 25, 4 (Winter 1977): 457–471.

Edwards, Paul, ed. *The Encyclopedia of Philosophy*, vol. 3. New York: Macmillan, 1967.

Garrett, Don. *Cognition and Commitment in Hume's Philosophy.* New York: Oxford University Press, 1997.

George, Rolf. "A Last Shot at Hume's Reminder." Unpublished manuscript.

Grice, H. P. "The Causal Theory of Perception." In Robert J. Swartz, ed., *Perceiving, Sensing, and Knowing*, pp. 438–472. Berkeley: University of California Press, [1961] 1976.

Grice, H. P., and P. F. Strawson. "In Defense of a Dogma." *The Philosophical Review* 65 (1956): 141–158.

Guyer, Paul. *Kant and the Claims of Knowledge.* Cambridge: Cambridge University Press, 1987.

————. "Kant's Second Analogy." In Patricia Kitcher, ed., *Kant's Critique of Pure Reason: Critical Essays*, pp. 117–143. Lanham, Md.: Rowman & Littlefield, 1998.

Hartnack, Justus. *Kant's Theory of Knowledge*, trans. M. Holmes Hartshorne. Indianapolis: Hackett, [1967] 2001.

Henrich, Dieter. "The Proof-Structure of Kant's Transcendental Deduction." *Review of Metaphysics* 22 (1968–1969): 640–659.

————. *The Unity of Reason: Essays on Kant's Philosophy.* Cambridge, Mass.: Harvard University Press, 1994.

Hume, David. *An Enquiry Concerning Human Understanding*, 3rd. ed., ed. Lewis A. Selby-Bigge and Peter H. Nidditch. Oxford: Oxford University Press, [1748] 1975.

————. *A Treatise of Human Nature*, 2nd. ed., ed. Lewis A. Selby-Bigge and Peter H. Nidditch. Oxford: Oxford University Press, [1740] 1978.

Irwin, T. H. "Review of Paul Guyer's, *Kant and the Claims of Knowledge.*" *The Philosophical Review* 100, 9 (April 1991): 332–341.

James, William. *Principles of Psychology*, 2 vols. New York: Dover, [1890] 1950.

Kant, Immanuel. *Critique of Pure Reason*, trans. Paul Guyer and Allen W. Wood. Cambridge: Cambridge University Press, 1997.

————. *Critique of Pure Reason*, trans. Norman Kemp Smith. New York: St. Martin, 1965.

————. *Critique of Pure Reason*, trans. Werner S. Pluhar. Indianapolis: Hackett, 1996.

————. *Opus postumum*, ed. Eckart Förster, trans. Eckart Förster and Michael Rosen. Cambridge: Cambridge University Press, 1993.

————. *Prolegomena to Any future Metaphysics.* In *Immanuel Kant's Prolegomena to Any Future Metaphysics in Focus*, ed. Beryl Logan. London: Routledge, 1996.

————. *Theoretical Philosophy, 1775–1770*, ed. David Walford and Ralph Meerbote. Cambridge: Cambridge University Press, 1992.

Kemp Smith, Norman. *A Commentary on Kant's 'Critique of Pure Reason.'* New York: Humanities Press, [1923] 1962.

Kitcher, Patricia. "Introduction" to Immanuel Kant, *Critique of Pure Reason*, trans. Werner S. Pluhar. Indianapolis, Ind.: Hackett, 1996.

Körner, Stephan. *Kant*. Hardmondsworth, Eng.: Penguin, 1955.

Kripke, Saul. *Naming and Necessity*. Cambridge, Mass.: Harvard University Press, 1980.

Lewis, C. I. *Mind and the World Order*. New York: Dover, [1929] 1956.

Locke, John. *An Essay Concerning Human Understanding*, ed. Andrew S. Pringle-Pattison. Oxford: Oxford University Press, [1689] 1924.

Lowe, E. Jonathan. "Locke." In Robert L. Arrington, ed., *A Companion to the Philosophers*, pp. 369–375. Oxford: Blackwell, 1999.

Mackie, John L. *Problems from Locke*. Oxford: Oxford University Press, 1976.

Melnick, Arthur. *Kant's Analogies of Experience*. Chicago: University of Chicago Press, 1973.

Moser, Paul K., ed. A Priori *Knowledge*. Oxford: Oxford University Press, 1987.

Paton, H. J. *Kant's Metaphysic of Experience*, 2 vols. London: George Allen & Unwin, [1936] 1970.

Pereboom, Derk. "Self-understanding in Kant's Transcendental Deduction." *Synthese*, 103 (1995): 1–42.

Quine, Willard Van Orman. *From a Logical Point of View: 9 Logico-Philosophical Essays*. Cambridge, Mass.: Harvard University Press, 1953.

Strawson, Peter F. *The Bounds of Sense: An Essay on Kant's* Critique of Pure Reason. London: Routledge, [1966] 1990.

Swartz, Robert J., ed. *Perceiving, Sensing, and Knowing*. Berkeley: University of California Press, 1976.

Vaihinger, Hans. *Commentar zu Kant's Kritik der Reinen Vernunft*, 2bde. Stuttgart: W. Spemann, 1881–1882.

Van Cleve, James. *Problems from Kant*. New York: Oxford University Press, 1999.

Walker, Ralph C. S., ed. *Kant on Pure Reason*. Oxford: Oxford University Press, 1982.

Walsh, W. H. *Kant's Criticism of Metaphysics*. Edinburgh: Edinburgh University Press, 1975.

———. "Schematism." In Robert P. Wolff, ed., *Kant: A Collection of Critical Essays*, pp. 71–87. Garden City, N.Y.: Doubleday, 1967.

Warren, Daniel. "Kant and the Apriority of Space." *The Philosophical Review* 107, 2 (April 1998): 179–224.

Wilkerson, T. E. *Kant's Critique of Pure Reason: A Commentary for Students*, 2nd ed. Bristol: Thoemmes, 1998.

Wolff, Robert Paul. *Kant's Theory of Mental Activity: A Commentary on the Transcendental Analytic of the* Critique of Pure Reason. Magnolia, Mass.: Peter Smith, [1963] 1990.

———. ed. *Kant: A Collection of Critical Essays*. Garden City, N.Y.: Doubleday, 1967.

Index

Italicized page numbers refer to figures.